Advances in Information Systems and Business Engineering

Edited by
U. Baumöl, Hagen, Germany
J. vom Brocke, Vaduz, Principality of Liechtenstein
R. Jung, St. Gallen, Switzerland

The series presents current research findings based on diverse research methods at the interface between information systems research, computer science, and management science. The publications in this series aim at practical concepts, models, methods, but also theories which address the role of information systems in the innovative design and sustainable development of organizations. Contributions are selected which on the one hand propose innovative approaches how modern information and communication technologies can enable new business models. On the other hand, contributions are eligible which present considerable improvements to existing solutions. The publications are characterized by a holistic approach. They account for the socio-technical nature of work-systems and suggest that the development and implementation of information systems need to consider the multifaceted organizational context driven by people, tasks, and technology.

More information about this series at http://www.springer.com/series/11032

Tomasz Janasz

Paradigm Shift in Urban Mobility

Towards Factor 10 of Automobility

With forewords by Prof. Dr. Uwe Schneidewind, Simon Kettner and Alain Groff

Springer Gabler

Tomasz Janasz
Basel, Switzerland

Dissertation at Schumpeter School of Business and Economics, University of Wuppertal, 2016

OnlinePlus material to this book is available on
http://www.springer.com/978-3-658-20460-0

Advances in Information Systems and Business Engineering
ISBN 978-3-658-20459-4 ISBN 978-3-658-20460-0 (eBook)
https://doi.org/10.1007/978-3-658-20460-0

Library of Congress Control Number: 2017961102

Springer Gabler

Printed on acid-free paper

This Springer Gabler imprint is published by Springer Nature
The registered company is Springer Fachmedien Wiesbaden GmbH
The registered company address is: Abraham-Lincoln-Str. 46, 65189 Wiesbaden, Germany

Foreword

by Professor Dr. Uwe Schneidewind

The global environmental and development issues have induced essential transformational processes in the society. This is a major challenge for science, economy and politics to organize this transformation in a sustainable manner. In that matter, not only production, but also consumption patterns and people's lifestyles need to be adjusted to decrease greenhouse gas emissions to an absolute minimum in the next decades.

In the course of rapid urbanization, urban areas are in the spotlight. They are both the source and the victims of global change. Therefore, the challenges and potentials for sustainability seem to reside also in the cities. In this respect, transportation and mobility are core issues for tackling sustainability in urban areas.

Today's personal mobility relies mainly on the motorized private transport that is based on fossil and non-renewable energy sources such as oil and gas. Latest since the Paris Agreement it has become clear that fossil fuels have no future. Hence, in the recent years an interpretative and normative framework has been developed: the paradigm of sustainable mobility. On the one hand, it refers to decarbonizing cars. A post-fossil mobility must be based on new mobility patterns, improved energy efficiency and renewable energy sources. Electromobility and synthetic fuels play a key role here. It is not enough, however, to simply replace an internal combustion engine with an electric or fuel cell-powered motor. There is a need for a holistic strategy for mobility, if the energy transition is to succeed and the negative externalities of the transportation sector are to decrease in the foreseeable future.

Another and often ignored aspect of sustainable mobility is the massive resource consumption. The current depletion of resources is enormous: the ′ecological rucksack′ of a single car is about 70 tones of input of natural resources and one car requires approximately 140 qm of space in a city. Only through an absolute reduction of the number of automobiles and of the resulting resource and space wastage, there is a chance for a holistic mobility transition in cities.

The digitalization and automation of cars, new forms of mobility and a change of values, especially within the young generation of digital natives, allow for new urban mobility concepts to emerge. The vision of ′Factor 10 of Automobility′ represents such a new concept, in which people's mobility needs are met with only one-tenth of current number of vehicles.

The idea of radically increasing the intensity of car usage, which currently amounts to only 5-10%, seems quite realistic. For some years now, the digitalization strategies of automotive and many IT companies have been aiming at implementing autonomous taxis, which could be used efficiently in urban areas. These Internet-connected 'robot taxis' are dispatched automatically at the push of a button by matching algorithms of ride-hailing apps. The highly capitalized digital business models from the Silicon Valley are already trying to implement such concepts for commercial use and hence to determine the future of urban mobility.

The focus on innovative technologies and digital business models is appealing in many respects. However, the underlying cultural change needs to be kept in mind likewise. It needs to be investigated and answered how these emerging efficiency boosts in mobility can be integrated into the local cultural and socio-political context in consistent manner. The overall aim should be the social wealth and prosperity in the cities, and not yet another business model.

This book focuses on the challenges of a holistic transition towards sustainable mobility and offers a multifaceted analysis of the resulting transformational processes. By drawing on the concept of 'Factor 10', this work dares a look that reaches beyond just incremental improvements. Considering the technological and digital business model upheaval, such a radical change perspective is justified.

The investigation does not only focus on a knowledgeable analysis of the efficiency potentials for car usage, but is also embedded in the existing institutional and social strategies for sustainable mobility. In that regard, multimodality, integrated infrastructure and spatial planning, parking management, mobility management as well as city logistics play a key role. This multidimensional perspective offers an impressive and integrative view, and a convincing framework for the current discussion about the new paradigm and business models for urban mobility.

Professor Dr. Uwe Schneidewind

Wuppertal Institute for Climate,
Environment and Energy,
Germany

Foreword

by Simon Kettner and Alain Groff

Cities suited for cars are characterized by wide roads which need a lot of space. Therefore you have to drive long ways to your job or to the next shopping centre, while crossing a street as a pedestrian becomes a hassle and cyclists live a dangerous life. There are no attractive destinations in walking distance and public transport cannot be operated in an efficient way, due to the low density. A sustainable city on the other hand, is liveable. A lot of attractive activities are close by and it is easy to walk and bike. In short, you get a lot of mobility with a minimum of traffic. In this sustainable city a reasonable amount of cars are still needed, but they drive at low speed and they park mostly underground instead of consuming valuable public space.

It is quite easy to demonstrate the inefficiency of cars: The average car is parked 90 to 95% of the day, 1,5 out of 5 seats are occupied and the land use per person is 10-times bigger than with public transport. These inefficiencies are the main reasons that cars do not suit to sustainable cities. Should we believe that autonomous cars in the future really improve the efficiency of automobility, as the announcements of the automobile industry or from Silicon Valley suggest? Here my first answer is a clear "No". Driverless cars need the same amount of space as normal cars. Furthermore children or handicapped people, who cannot drive a car by themselves today, will be able to use cars instead of bikes or public transport and even empty trips will occur and increase the number of total car trips.

But driverless cars are also a big opportunity for car sharing and ride-sharing schemes. It is much more comfortable to order a driverless car, which will pick you up, wherever your are, with a few clicks on your smartphone, than to make a reservation call far in advance and walk all the way to the next car sharing station. Shared autonomous cars or shuttles, which are used most of the day with a high occupancy, are much more efficient than today's privately owned cars. They can become an attractive part of the future mobility offer in a sustainable city. But it cannot be the only offer: a high share of walking and biking and an attractive and rapid mass transit system will still be needed as well.

It is one of the big upcoming challenges for the traffic and transportation planner, to assure, that autonomous vehicles are used in an efficient way. To achieve this, public authorities must support car- and ridesharing by suitable incentives. On the other hand pricing schemes and traffic regulation measures are needed, which reduce the private ownership and the single use of cars. In order to tackle the main problem of the dense urban areas, a fair charge for occupying valuable public space should play an important role in future mobility pricing schemes.

A car is a nice and practical invention, which used to promise his owner freedom, fun and prestige. But their current way of use, is just too inefficient and cities can only become liveable if smarter mobility patterns take over which reduce the number of required vehicles.

Simon Kettner and Alain Groff

Office of Mobility,
Municipal Construction and Transportation
Department of the Canton Basel-City,
Switzerland

Acknowledgments

First and foremost, I would like to express my special appreciation and thanks to my supervisor Professor Dr. Uwe Schneidewind, who oversaw me as a PhD-student at the Wuppertal Institute for Climate, Environment and Energy, Germany. I would like to thank you for encouraging me as a researcher and for fully supporting my research endeavor throughout the doctoral studies. I have appreciated your comments and suggestions during our countless meetings, one of which took even place during a train ride. Thanks to your brilliant ideas it has been possible not only to revitalize the notion of 'Factor 10' and to apply it to the system of automobility and urban mobility, but also to establish 'Transformative Literacy' as a resilient research framework.

I am very obliged to SAP SE for providing me with the unique opportunity to pursue the PhD degree during my employment as a business consultant. SAP has served as an exceptional thought leadership platform which has helped me to explore state of the art digital technologies, platforms and innovative business models. Moreover, the entitlement of the sabbatical leave has given me the opportunity to successfully finish my thesis. In particular I want to thank Tim Teinzer.

I am also deeply grateful to Mr. Simon Kettner from the Office of Mobility from the administration of the City of Basel, Switzerland. He provided me with the extraordinary opportunity to explore the forward-looking mobility system of the City of Basel in-depth. I am extremely thankful for the access to all mobility experts who have shaped my understanding about the paradigm of sustainable mobility in modern cities. At this point, I also want to express my true recognition to all the mobility experts, politicians, municipal policy makers, mobility lobbyists and entrepreneurs I have had the honor to meet. You have helped me grow as a researcher and substantially influenced the body of knowledge that I present in this thesis.

Special thanks go also to Swiss Forum Electromobility, BRUSA Elektronik AG and Touring Club Suisse (TCS) for awarding me with the Swiss Electric Mobility Award back in 2012. The award helped me in two respects (i) prepare, conduct, transcribe and analyze all expert interviews, of which almost all were onsite meetings, and (ii) develop the innovative idea of 'Smart Ways'. I truly hope that with both results I have commemorated the Swiss electromobility visionary Arno Mathoy in a most appropriate way.

I also want to thank the team of Adroit Research from Brisbane, Australia, in particular Dr. Jenine Beekhuyzen and Dr. Sue Nielsen. You equipped me with 'special weapons and tactics' to effectively conduct qualitative research in the field. Additionally, Sue undertook a thorough and careful English language check of this dissertation. I can only recommend their services to other students.

My time at SAP was made enjoyable in large part due to many colleagues and groups that became a part of my life during the last years. Especially, I am grateful for time spent with Alexander Schmid, my office colleague, friend and a faithful companion in 'PhD-suffering'. Our never-ending discussions have broadened my worldview and helped me understand what team-work is really about. Now, I keep my fingers crossed for your successful completion of your suffering.

Words cannot express how grateful I am to my mother and my father who always believed in and fully supported me during my graduate and postgraduate studies in Germany. Special thanks go of course to my sister, Dominika, for her great contribution to the Smart Ways project. I hope you gained a great deal of professional knowledge out of this endeavor.

I would also like to thank all of my friends from Switzerland, Germany and Poland who admittedly made a good deal of sacrifices on my behalf. You always motivated me to strive towards my goal and I really appreciated every enjoyable moments that we spent together, either skiing, sailing or just hanging around.

At the end, but not least, I would like to express special appreciation to Justyna who once said that together we could manage it. Your support for me was what sustained me thus far. Today, I can say with full confidence: Yes, we can! Thank you.

Basel, 03rd of May, 2016 Tomasz Janasz

Abstract

This dissertation postulates the concept of '*Factor 10 of Automobility*'. The author demonstrates that innovative mobility concepts and services based on the latest technological advancements can lead to a reduction of the total number of automobiles in urban areas by a factor of 10, while maintaining equal mobility levels as today. Furthermore, he develops a comprehensive understanding of technological, economic, societal and political requirements required for overcoming car dependence in modern cities. He applies the research framework of '*Transformative Literacy*'.

First, the study illustrates how the patterns of shared mobility bear a great potential for substantial efficiency gains in the usage of cars. The author develops a new notion of car efficiency and describes possible sharing scenarios for leisure and work traffic in Switzerland. In order to evidence the factor 10 hypothesis the researcher explores the mobility concept of shared autonomous vehicles, while considering its promised advantages as well as possible drawbacks for cities.

Then, the dissertation focuses on establishing the Transformative Literacy for the paradigm shift towards sustainable mobility in urban areas. The aim is to develop an integrative perspective on economic growth as well as social wealth improvements in urban areas which are expected from less car dependence and more sustainability in the urban transport sector. On the one hand, the researcher explores new technology-enabled urban mobility concepts and associated business models that aim at their commercialization. The author develops six prototypes for digital business models for 'Shared Automobility Services', which can be integrated into a highly efficient urban mobility system. On the other hand, he concentrates on required societal and institutional prerequisites for establishing patterns of sustainable mobility, without compromising the aspects of accessibility, traffic security and the urban quality of life. For this purpose he analyzes the ongoing transformation of the transport policy in the City of Basel (Switzerland). The author establishes a set of critical factors for overcoming car dependence in cities and proposes three main strategies for the required paradigm shift: efficiency, sufficiency and the underpinning consistency in mobility.

With this work the researcher establishes a holistic framework for forward-looking mobility experts and practitioners who seek to overcome car dependence and to facilitate a transition towards a sustainable mobility system in their own urban context.

Table of Contents

List of Figures

List of Tables

List of Regular Abbreviations

ABS	antilock braking system
Agglo Basel	Agglomeration Program Basel
ASTRA	Swiss Federal Roads Office
AV	autonomous vehicle
BFS	Bundesamt für Statistik
BLT	Baselland Transport
BVB	Basler Verkehrsbetriebe
B2C	business-to-customer
CEO	chief executive officer
CO	carbon monoxide
COS	costs of service
CSF	critical success factors
CSR	corporate social responsibility
CO_2	carbon dioxide
C2C	customer-to-customer
EV	electric vehicles
GDP	gross domestic product
GHG	greenhouse gas
GWh	energy consumption in gigawatt-hour
GWP100	global warming potential over 100 years
HLS	high-capacity streets (Germ. Hochleistungsstrassen)
HOT	high occupancy toll lanes
HOV	high occupancy vehicle lane
ITS	intelligent transportation systems
KPI	key performance indicators

MaaS	Mobility as a Service
MCC	marginal congestion costs
MIS	Multimodal Information Systems
MoD	mobility on demand
MPB	marginal private benefits
MPC	marginal private costs
MSB	marginal social benefits
MSC	marginal social costs
NIST	National Institute for Standards and Technology
OEM	Original Equipment Manufacturer
PEV	plug-in electric vehicles
PRT	personal rapid transportation
PM10	particulate matter
P2P	peer-to-peer
P&R	park and ride
ROI	return on investment
SAV	shared autonomous vehicles
SBB	Schweizerische Bundesbahnen
TEB	Trinational Euro District Basel
TNW	Tarifverbund Northwestern Switzerland
TRB	Transportation Research Board
TRID	Transportation Research Integrated Database
U-Abo	Umwelt-Abonnement
VMT	vehicle miles travelled
VOT	value of time

List of Abbreviations Related to Digital Technologies

API	application programming interfaces
AR	augmented reality
CAN-bus	controller area network
ECU	electronic control units
GNSS	Global Navigation Satellite System
GPS	Global Positioning System
GSM	Global System for Mobile Communications
HDD	hard drive disks
HUD	head-up display
IaaS	Infrastructure-as-a-Service
ICT	information and communication technology
IoT	Internet of Things
IP	internet protocols
IT	information technology
LIDAR	Light Detection and Ranging
LTE or 4G	Long Term Evolution
M2M	machine-to-machine communication
NAND	'not and' flash memory
NFC	Near Field Communication
NUI	Natural User Interfaces
PaaS	Platform-as-a-Service
RAM	Random-Access Memory
SDD	solid state drives
UMTS or 3G	Universal Mobile Telecommunication System
RFID	radio-frequency identification sensors
SaaS	Software-as-a-Service
V2I	Vehicle-to-Infrastructure
V2V	Vehicle-to-Vehicle
WAP	Wireless Application Protocol

Wi-Fi	wireless local area network
WSN	wireless sensor networks

"Um eine zukunftsfähige Wirtschaft zu schaffen, müssen wir beides parallel angehen: nach neuen Wohlstandsmodellen suchen und bessere technische Lösungen zur Befriedigung unserer maschinenabhängigen Bedürfnissen schaffen."

"In order to create a sustainable economy, we must tackle both aspects in parallel: search for new models of prosperity and provide better technical solutions in order to satisfy our machine-dependent needs." (author's own translation)

Prof. Dr. Friedrich Schmidt-Bleek in
„Wieviel Umwelt braucht der Mensch?
MIPS, das Mass für ökologisches Wirtschaften" (1994, p. 105).[1]

[1] Courtesy of Springer Basel AG.

PREFACE
Introduction to the Dissertation

1 Sustainable Development

1.1 Current State of Affairs

1.1.1 Green Economy

"Our Common Future", also known as the Brundtland Report, published back in 1987 by the United Nations World Commission on Environment and Development (WCED), was the basis to convoke the Earth Summit in 1992. The Summit resulted in the adoption of Agenda 21, the signature of the Rio Declaration and the establishment of the Commission on Sustainable Development. An oft-quoted definition of sustainable development is defined in the report as (World Commission on Environment and Development 1987, p. 45):

> "development that meets the needs of the present without compromising the ability of future generations to meet their own needs."

In the meantime, there seems to be a common agreement regarding the sustainable development goals, which have been identified to be: economic development, social development and environmental protection (United Nations General Assembly 2005). The three pillars are interdependent and cannot exist independently in the long term (Morelli 2013). This has set the foundation for the currently dominant branch of the environmental debate which calls for an absolute decoupling of economic growth from environmental degradation by means of technological efficiency gains (Paech 2012). This has been labeled as the Green Economy concept, a development model which does not focus on economics first and environment later, but instead aims at encouraging an economy oriented toward environmental sustainability, economic profitability and social inclusion (The Levin Institute 2012). Such an approach is believed to open up the prospect of green growth, i.e. a radical technological revolution in the direction of significant ecological efficiency increases (Paech 2012). The Green Economy concept is appealing as it promises to link environmental challenges and concerns with further economic development opportunities. That is why this concept of an ecological industrial revolution has been heavily discussed in the national debates regarding environmental protection, for example during the Rio+20 conference in 2012. However, thus far no absolute decoupling has succeeded on this path in the relevant environmental sectors. It seems that efficiency achievements have been systematically negated by rebound and systemic growth effects (Schneidewind 2013b).

1.1.2 Substantial Change

In fact, what the Brundtland Report along with the famous Report of the Club of Rome (Meadows 1972) actually achieved was the awakening and increasing the public consciousness about ecological limits and that human activities need to take these boundaries into account. The statement by Wilhelm Ostwald, the German Nobel laureate, underpins it in a profound way: "The paradox of modernity: we are going to perform on a finite basis an infinite consumption experiment".[2]

It has been argued that the established sustainability paradigm based on the three aforementioned dimensions, i.e. the society, economy and environment has actually led to the dilution of the ideas of the Brundtland Commission and the Club of Rome. The effect has been that sustainability concerns are indeed increasingly considered in new projects or investments, but only in terms of whether the environmental and societal externalities do not exceed acceptable limits and if so how to manage them. The sustainability concept is accused of focusing on economics first and environment later (van Ierland et al. 2001) and hence, blamed that in this way the basic idea of the Brundtland Commission has been somehow compromised and watered down (Manns 2010; Schmidt-Bleek 2014).

Therefore, growth-critical approaches have emerged, as opposed to Green Economy, which argue that a real technological decoupling cannot succeed and that sustainability-oriented social change is only possible by means of a comprehensive socio-cultural transformation. This would mean that comprehensive institutional reforms are only socially and environmentally feasible, if alternative values and lifestyles have spread to a significant extent throughout society. This approach has been labeled as 'Substantial Change' and encompasses such radical concepts as 'sufficiency', 'subsistence', 'industrial dismantling' and 'de-globalization' (Paech 2012). It also pleads for a bottom-up cultural transition as opposed to an institutional top-down approach, as described in the

---

[2] Author's own translation of the following statement (in German): „Das Paradoxon der Moderne: Wir sind im Begriff, auf einer endlichen Grundlage ein unendliches Konsumexperiment durchzuführen". An alleged citation of Friedrich Wilhelm Ostwald retrieved from an interview with Peter Sloterdijk (see Tschudin, Beck 2013)

next section. It needs to be noted, however, that 'Substantial Change' represents indeed a substantial break with the current scope of the capital-based world economic system in favor of increasing local resilience (Schneidewind 2013b).

1.1.3 Sustainability as a Regulative Idea

An additional approach to sustainability has been taken from the institutional perspective. Schneidewind et al. (1997) have proposed the notion of sustainability as an regulative idea for the design of institutions. According to this perspective a real sustainability transformation is feasible only through a comprehensive institutional change in the economic system (see Figure 1). Schneidewind (2013b) states that the institutional reforms can be approached through three distinct approaches: a consistent internalization of external effects (see Weizsäcker, Desha 2010), via the property rights (see Helfrich 2012) or through an appropriate governance of modern monetary systems (see Binswanger 2009).

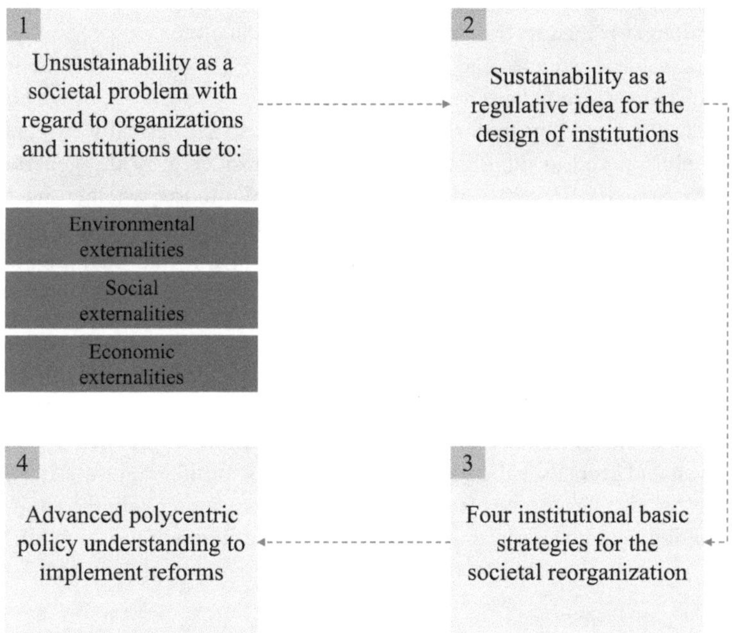

Figure 1: Sustainability as a regulative idea for the design of institutions. (Author's own diagram and translation based on Schneidewind et al. 1997, p. 183).

From this perspective, sustainability goals are to be considered as additional constraints that are regulated and need to be considered when establishing a business strategy. For example, companies from different industries such as utilities and infrastructure businesses have been subject to regulatory and governmental intervention such as pricing on emissions by means of emission permits and carbon taxes. There has been also a whole regulatory framework for financial sustainability and competition in banking or insurance sectors, at least regarding the retail area. In such cases one single regulatory decision can either wipe off or add billions of dollars of profitability (Browne et al. 2016). By complying with such additional regulations companies need to incorporate sustainability aspects into their decision-making processes.

1.2 The Great Transformation

Currently, transformation processes such as exiting from nuclear and fossil-fuel energy and shifting toward renewable energy sources seem to be approached particularly in technical terms. While there seems to be a good understanding of technological options and potential development scenarios, very often there is little understanding of other important aspects and implications. For example, with regard to electromobility the public debate has been often confined to the immaturity of the technology with regard to the limited ranges that electric vehicles can attain. The fact that, for example, in Switzerland the average distance travelled per day per person amounts to 36,7 km, of which as much as 24,4 km is conducted by motorized individual transport (basically by car) seems to be completely ignored in this discussion and not considered by the general public (Bundesamt für Statistik BFS 2012d). Therefore, it is valid to ask whether there is a need for a battery electric vehicle (BEV) to achieve 500-700 km for everyday purposes. Perhaps there are more flexible mobility patterns other than unconditional private car ownership which could reduce the concern about limited range while sustaining the access to flexible mobility.

If sustainability goals are to be pursued and prosperity is to be made available to 9 billion people in 2050, considerations need to go far beyond technological innovations and their quick implementation, diffusion and adoption. In order to guarantee prosperity and wealth within the given and globally valid ecological boundaries, further cultural, social and distributional factors also need to be clearly addressed. Hence, along with the adoption of radical technological innovations, gradual, global reconstruction of the structures of entire economies and societies need to be considered and implemented (Schneidewind 2013b).

A transformation of such a scale has been recently proposed by the German Advisory Council on Global Change (WBGU). It has been designated as the 'Great Transformation' (Schellnhuber et al. 2011). The 'Great Transformation' can be seen as a plea for a comprehensive program of institutional reforms for sustainability (Minsch et al. 1998; Schneidewind et al. 1997). At its core it aims at strengthening the institutional structures of modern societies in terms of their reflection, participation and innovation competencies for a global transition towards sustainability (Schneidewind 2013b).

The German Advisory Council on Global Change clearly indicates that the 'Great Transformation' towards sustainability requires not only technology but also important and sometimes even radical adaptations in production structures, consumption patterns and institutions (Schellnhuber et al. 2011). A good example constitutes the German energy transition where technological, institutional and cultural changes have been taking place simultaneously (Schneidewind 2013b).

Along with these considerations, however, some essential issues arise: how to anchor such a paradigm shift in modern societies, what strategies to implement to avoid any rebound effects and how to anticipate and steer complex transition processes that are being caused in the society. To address these challenges the understanding of sustainability needs to go beyond the 'technocratic' knowledge.

1.3 Transformative Literacy

Socio-technical transition processes constitute a central topic in many disciplines, such as economic growth theories or in social theories, and therefore explained from different perspectives: technological, economic, institutional or cultural. In fact, it is claimed that transformation processes take place today at three levels: one can observe technical (e.g. green growth), institutional (e.g. internalization of externalities) and cultural transformations (e.g. sufficiency strategies) (Paech 2012). These dimensions need to be understood as twofold (Schneidewind 2013b):

1) As independent approaches to explain and promote transformation processes. For example, cultural changes in lifestyles can directly influence people's energy consumption scope and patterns.

2) As interdependent structural arrangements within socio-technical systems. For example, technological structures are embedded in economic structures, which are in turn influenced by institutional structures.

To incorporate these dimensions in political and economic decisions about the 'Great Transformation' towards sustainability, the ability to understand, interpret and shape societal transformation processes is crucial. It requires new forms of holistic knowledge acquisition and knowledge integration within all the above mentioned transformation areas. Schneidewind (2013b) proposes an integrative conceptual framework - Transformative Literacy.

The framework depicts a heuristic approach which aims at providing a structure for acquiring a comprehensive understanding about the complex transformation dynamics regarding a specific domain. As such it constitutes an analysis instrument covering four dimensions: technology, economy, culture and society, and institutions and politics. Accordingly, it aims at eliminating the technology-bias, which has been often experienced in current discussions about important paradigm shifts (such as energy or mobility). Moreover, it helps to derive recommendations and actions to support and promote desirable transition processes.

The author will now introduce Schneidewind's four dimensions of Transformative Literacy in more detail to open up the prospects for an 'integrative knowledge' (Schneidewind 2013a, 2013b).

Technology

The first pillar of the Transformative Literacy is *Technology*. Technological innovations aim at challenging the existing socio-technical regimes. In addition to economic impacts the technological progress can also have cultural and social impacts that could implicate a structural change and system innovation.

Economy

The second pillar of the Transformative Literacy is *Economy*. This dimension aims at an efficient organization of social and corporate-related processes and to mobilize efficiency reserves through new and innovative business concepts and approaches. At the micro level, i.e. the level of enterprises and individual economic actors, it is expressed in the form of more efficient organizational and production methods. Interestingly, in many industries innovative technological developments do not play a supporting role anymore, but rather they enable new business models or business networks, which were not feasible or conceivable before. This results in new business dynamics and possible economic growth and prosperity.

Culture and Society

The third dimension is *Culture and Society*. This pillar aims at dealing with the dynamics and determinants of social change processes. Conducting research in this area helps to develop an understanding for cultural and value systems in the society. Especially, it helps to comprehend the dynamics of cultural change processes induced and catalyzed by developments such as technological innovations or the growing importance of post-material values. This dimension encompasses also the recognition of different stakeholders and their roles in shaping cultural processes.

Institutions and Politics

The fourth dimension is *Institutions and Politics*. Institutions are rules and mechanisms that organize human interactions. An important expression of formal rules are laws. Therefore, the politics holds a key role in shaping the social functions such as mobility and in ensuring the stability of the system regimes. However, in times of increasing globalization, the importance of the legislation by national states (Government) diminishes in favor of a variety of institutional control mechanisms and policies (Governance). This pillar seeks to develop a comprehensive understanding and picture of the institutional background and structures. By doing so it aims at making political and social transition processes more effective.

2 Object of Investigation: Automobility

Such a multidimensional approach, as described above, requires a strong capacity for interdisciplinary work, which in turn may have a significant impact on the capacity for proper knowledge acquisition. Being aware of this challenge and at the same time motivated by this assignment, the author of this dissertation will apply the research framework proposed by Schneidewind for the first time onto a specific field of application. The topic under investigation is the future of automobility. He approaches it within the context of the observable shift in urban mobility towards the paradigm of sustainable mobility and the ongoing digitization of societies and industries.

2.1 Problem Statement

In recent years, ubiquitous digitization has generated business innovation processes which have touched upon almost every single sphere of human life (Uhl et al. 2014b). Recently, one further domain has been affected – the system of automobility, i.e. the usage of automobiles as the dominant form of transportation. Prominent examples of digital business innovations in automobility include Uber Technologies Inc., the game changing company within the taxi sector and Car2Go, the German on-demand mobility service provider.

Automobility refers to the use of cars as the major means of transportation (Urry 2008). Moreover, it is about centering the "society and everyday life around automobiles and their spaces" (Henderson 2006, p. 293). However, it is thought that automobility is characterized by severe cracks in its underlying system design (see Figure 2). Firstly, there is the radical unsustainability of cars which is expressed by their substantial contribution to greenhouse gas (GHG) emissions and to the considerable consumption of space in urban areas by parking lots. Secondly, the inefficiency of cars is reflected by their extreme underutilization: the average car remains parked for 95% of a day (Shoup 2005; Barter 2013) and once it is moved it often carries only one passenger (Center for Sustainable Systems, University of Michigan 2015; Bundesamt für Statistik BFS 2012d).

However, the most striking flaw in automobility is the land consumption in cities. If a car is idle for most of the time it not only costs in the form of depreciation but it also occupies valuable space capacity in cities. A single car takes on average 13,5 square meters of space when it rests and while it is in movement (at 50 km/h) it can consume up to 140 square meters of space (Randelhoff 2014). A direct comparison with other means of transport shows that the automobile is the most space intense mode of mobility (see Figure 3). This has a fundamental implication for the required infrastructure and parking space. For example, land and space have been critical resources as they have been finite and extremely scarce, especially in conurbations. For instance, the need for supplying parking lots for vehicles is an extremely burning issue for municipalities, as parking is what cars do the most of the time (see Figure 2). Parking spaces increase the cost of construction which are passed on to consumers in the form of higher prices on goods and rent. Some cities have as much as one third of their useable land dedicated to parking, and a parking lot can cost up to 3'000-55'000 USD to build (Bureau of Planning and Sustainability 2012). Portland's Bureau of Planning and Sustainability (2012) found that parking can add as much as $500 per month in rental costs to a low-rise apartment building in the city. Generous parking requirements tend to create automobile-oriented transportation systems and land use patterns, with implications such as: increased urban sprawl, reduced design flexibility, reduced efficiency of alternative modes (e.g. walking, ridesharing or public transit) or increased traffic problems (Litman 2006). These are additional indirect costs which are imposed to the municipalities (Litman, Doherty 2009).

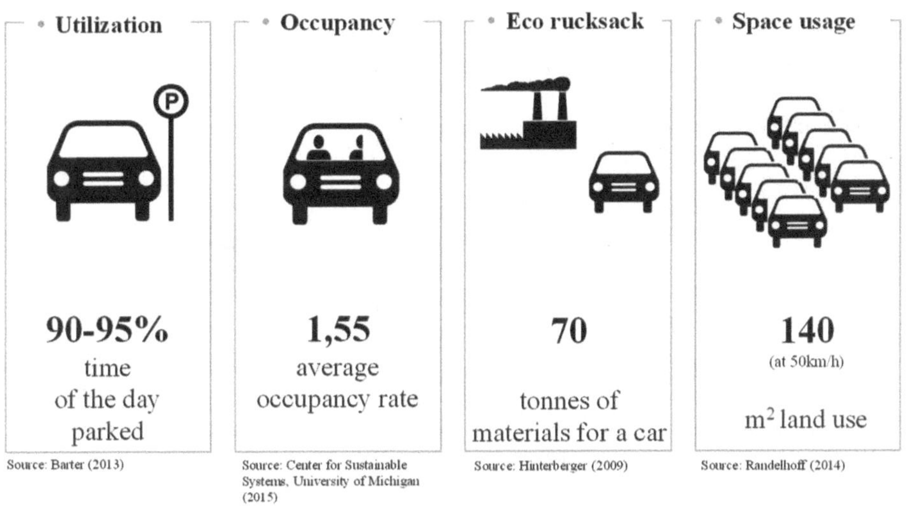

Figure 2: Automobility and current problems. (Diagram by author).

It has been recognized that, from economic, ecological and social perspectives, the mobility paradigm solely based on private car ownership is unsustainable (Marletto 2011).

Newman (2007, p. 22) contends that "cities must plan and build to overcome car dependence" and Henderson (2006, p. 294) argues that the contestation of automobility is "about reclaiming urban spaces from automobiles, limiting their use, and more broadly, changing cultures so that the whole concept of high speed mobility and car ownership is de-emphasized". Therefore, a paradigm shift towards 'sustainable mobility' has been proposed. This paradigm encompasses three main areas: increase in efficiency of car usage, modal shift and reduction of mobility needs (see Figure 4). The author's research aims at drawing special attention to the first area by depicting opportunities for a radical increase in the efficiency of the car. Above all, it takes a closer look at innovative mobility concepts which flourish at the frontier of shared mobility patterns, autonomous vehicles, digital technologies and business model innovations.

Figure 3: Comparison of the space consumption of different transport modes in urban areas.

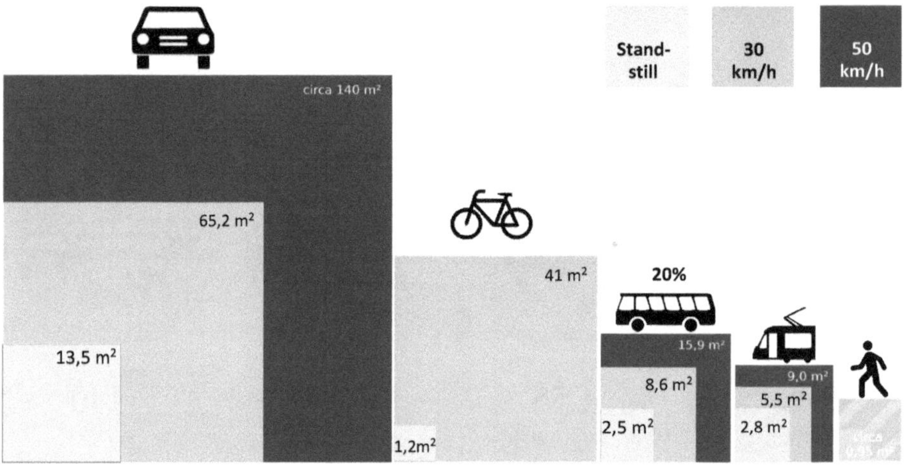

Figure 3: Comparison of the space consumption of different transport modes in urban areas.
(Source: adapted from Randelhoff 2014) .

Fundamental to this research is the author's conviction that the digitization processes have both an innovative and transformative character. What began with the introduction of microprocessors in the seventies of the twentieth century, today is being referred to as the 'Fifth Technological Revolution'. Recent developments in the arena of digital technology set the foundation for ubiquitous computing, big data analytics, social media and internet of things. These innovations signal that the digital era is going into the next

[3] Distributed under a CC BY 3.0 license: https://creativecommons.org/licenses/by/3.0/deed.de.

disruption wave. One important dimension of this disruption is the emergence of new companies - the 'Schumpeterian' companies (Dosi 1982). These early adopter companies do not develop the technology themselves, but they generate added value for the consumers by means of creative applications. The notion of value is important as it denotes that an offering has to satisfy customers' needs (Uhl et al. 2014a). It is thought that pairing innovative technology offerings with corresponding commercialization approaches is a prerequisite for the scaling of groundbreaking technology. Therefore, innovative companies should create, deliver and capture value for the end-users. The recent management literature refers to these value added processes as business models. In order to build purposeful and economically feasible applications, another research field has been coined, that of business model innovation.

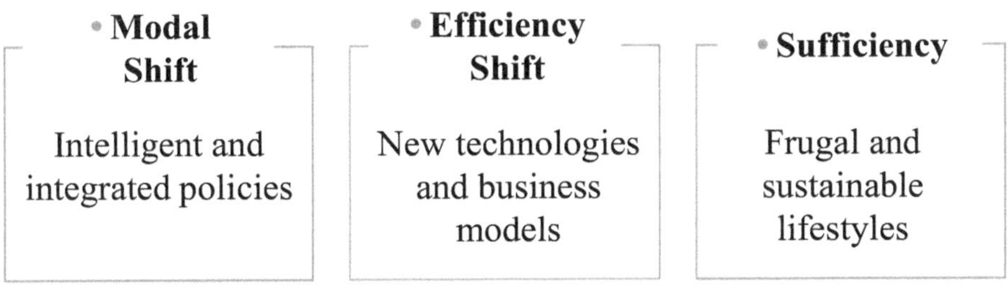

Figure 4: The paradigm of sustainable mobility.
(Diagram by author based on own comprehension of sustainable mobility).

Regarding the arena of automobility there are three distinct fields of business model innovation: digital carsharing, digital ridesharing and shared autonomous automobility. The first two innovation domains are characterized by the emergence of innovative business endeavors such as smexx (innovation in smart car access), Car2Go (innovation in carsharing and mobility-on-demand, i.e. free-floating carsharing), TwoGo® by SAP (innovation in ridesharing) or UBER (a total market disruption in the taxi sector). These cases demonstrate that important adjustments are currently happening to the prevailing automobility paradigm. The third realm of innovation, however, represents the prospect of a total redesign of this paradigm. Hence, the idea of sharing autonomous vehicles has the capacity to change the car ownership paradigm and provide flexible on-demand and door-to-door mobility services also for disabled people and non-drivers, at least in urban mobility systems.

2.2 The Concept of Factor Ten

The concept known as 'Factor Ten' was proposed by Prof. Friedrich Schmidt-Bleek (Robèrt et al. 2002). It refers to the idea of dematerializing economies in such a way that material flows in the industrialized countries should be decreased by factor 10 to reach more sustainable levels of material use. The aim is to increase resource productivity and increase the welfare created from the existing resources (Schmidt-Bleek 2014).

The combination of patterns of shared economy, car digitization and vehicle automation bears a great potential for overcoming the aforementioned inefficiencies in the usage of cars and possibly also for contributing to the dematerialization of the required size of car fleets. Therefore, the author aims at applying the concept of 'Factor 10' to demonstrate the potentials of the innovative application of the disruptive technology for raising the efficiency of car radically. Especially, the author focuses on finding an answer to the question of whether this efficiency boost could lead to a reduction of the total number of automobiles in urban areas by a factor of 10, while maintaining equal mobility levels. The author investigates innovative concepts and business models at the microeconomic level and showcases the possible trajectory for the future of automobility.

2.3 Transformative Literacy for the Paradigm Shift in Urban Mobility

According to the current concerns associated with sustainable development, as described in Chapter 1, not only does the author aim at depicting further economic growth potentials which might result from implementing novel technologies, innovative mobility concepts and new business models, but also the wealth considerations in terms of securing and possibly extending the societal prosperity. In the author's opinion, for the shift towards the paradigm of sustainable mobility to be successful the transition must be able to produce both (i) economic growth and (ii) wealth (see Figure 5).

On the one hand the transition requires new and innovative business models and their developers as motors for the implementation of new mobility concepts. However, not only should they be driven economically, but also try to integrate and follow the principles of sustainability in their business strategy considerations (in terms of 'radical engagement', see Browne et al. 2015). On the other hand, the transition needs to take place in the sociopolitical environment to ensure that the growth resulting from new business models does not compromise societal wealth in terms of e.g. accessibility, traffic security and the urban quality of life.

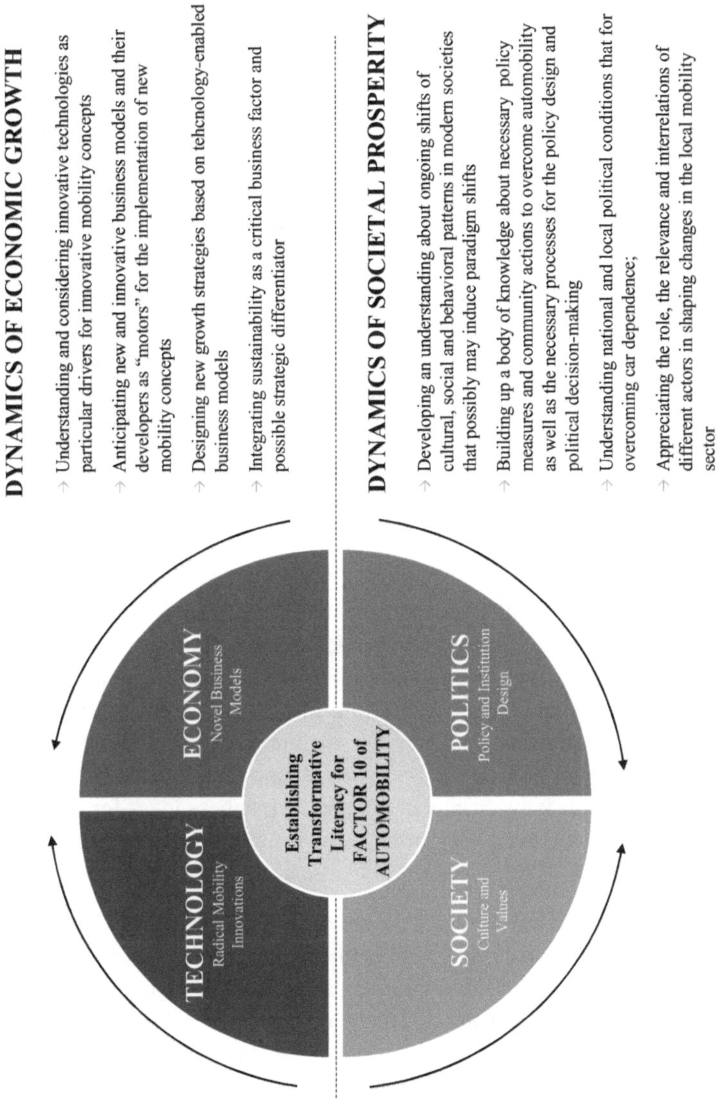

Figure 5: Analysis scheme along the dimensions of the Transformative Literacy. (Diagram by author).

Using the elements of the underlying framework of Transformative Literacy (Schneidewind 2013a) the dissertation is organized into the following parts:

Part I: *Factor 10 of Automobility: Undiscovered Potentials*

To establish a strong backbone for the dissertation the author hypothesizes that the factor 10 of automobility is possible, at least in urban areas, by using two approaches. The first one is the development and testing of a calculation model to determine hypothetical efficiency factors for cars. The calculation model takes into consideration car- and ridesharing as mobility concepts that feature the potential to radically raise the efficiency of cars in modern cities. The author shows possible reduction potentials of the total number of cars for leisure and work traffic in Switzerland. The second approach aims at identifying and synthetizing the findings resulting from the most recent research stream which investigates the application of autonomous vehicles for urban mobility. The main goal is to illustrate how the efficiency mechanisms behind these mobility concepts work and what their limitations are.

Part II: *Digital Technologies and Business Model Innovations for Urban Mobility*

Motivated by previous hypothetical considerations regarding the possible efficiency boosts in car usage in part I, the researcher focuses on the first and second aspect of Transformative Literacy: Technology and Business Models. The author has recognized that with regards to digital technologies and digital business models for new mobility concepts there has been a substantial gap in academic research. Admittedly, current contributions chiefly represent the applied research stream and therefore are rather strongly business-oriented. In this way, fresh and innovative business ideas for the mobility sector can be identified. However, they often show limited academic rigor and methodological discipline.

Therefore, in the first step a thorough desk research is conducted to identify and discuss the latest research in both areas. The goal is to develop a deep understanding of technological innovations. Answers to following questions will be sought: what are the latest technologies in urban mobility and radical advancements in vehicle technologies? What are digital technologies? What are the categories of innovative mobility concepts for sustainable mobility? Which technologies are regarded to have the strongest impact on resource efficiency in urban passenger transport?

In the author's opinion comprehending the knowledge about innovative technologies is a necessary prerequisite for further exploratory research on possible options of embedding these technologies into the prevailing mobility system. With that the author establishes a bridge to the new research field of developing new business models. This part is based on the finding that at times when new technologies emerge one observes a multiplicity of risk-taking actors, so called 'Schumpeterian' companies. They come into existence to pair innovative technology offerings with business models to realize the technologies' full potential. The research questions are: what are the organizational and managerial concepts that make it possible to offer innovative mobility services to the users? What do these models look like? How are they different to traditional approaches? What are the possible business model innovations? Two case studies have been investigated in detail. For that research the author develops and applies a framework for business model exploration. Based on the findings of the desk and exploratory research the author proposes a typology of Digital Business Models for Shared Automobility Services.

Part III: *Overcoming Automobility Dependence: Policy Interventions*

This part assumes that a mere technology-orientation will be insufficient for a comprehensive shift in the existing mobility paradigm. The author is also aware that the policy-design has a crucial role in shaping societal functions and in ensuring the stability of system regimes. Therefore, the purpose of this part is to achieve an appropriate level of familiarity and mastery with the phenomenon of sustainable mobility and the policies that are supporting and promoting this emerging paradigm of urban mobility. This part aims at creating a comprehensive body of knowledge about possible policy interventions for gradually overcoming the auto dependence in the context of urban mobility systems. With that the author intends to give a guidance to urban policy-makers and other involved parties who need to deal with the diversity of policy instruments and approaches for establishing the paradigm of sustainable mobility in their specific urban context. Attention is drawn to policies that constitute rules and mechanisms for urban mobility organization, with a distinction between push, pull and spatial measures. The author also intends to extend the descriptive character of this part and contributes with the introduction to the concept of policy integration and consistency.

Part IV: *Transformative Literacy: Case Study City of Basel*

Irrespective of how effective the innovative technologies are and how advanced the available policies appear to be, the reality of policy practice at local levels is an extremely complex field. Unexpected dynamics may result from changes in basic needs of local societies as well as from cultural shifts on the global scale. Additionally, there are many involved parties which pursue partially contradictory goals. In this part of the dissertation the focus lies in acquiring the knowledge about the dynamics within the sociopolitical environment of modern cities when overcoming structural car dependence and transitioning towards the paradigm of sustainable mobility. For that purpose, the author delivers an in-depth analyzes of the case of the City of Basel, a Swiss progressive canton-city, which has been on the path of reducing its car dependence since the 1970s. The researcher elaborates on critical success factors and barriers that influence the required transition based on extensive expert interviews.

Based on the acquired pool of knowledge, the author presents his own notion of 'Integrated Sustainable Urban Mobility' which incorporates the concepts of efficiency, sufficiency and consistency. With that he intends to establish a holistic framework that should help integrate the paradigm of sustainable mobility into the long-term policy planning of modern cities.

Part V: *Conclusions and Further Research*

In the last part of the dissertation the author summarizes the conducted work and draw the conclusions from all previous research parts. The results are critically reviewed and blind spots of the research as well as important limitations are discussed. Based on these considerations the author derives essential areas and possible topics for further research undertakings. Furthermore, the author makes some suggestions regarding possible research approaches.

The foundation for this research work is a dedicated research design, which was developed by the author at the end of 2013 and accepted by his supervisor in the beginning of 2014.[4]

2.4 Limitations

The author intentionally does not address the widely discussed topic of energy efficiency of automobiles which is expected to be achieved by gradually exchanging the powertrain. There is no doubt that further optimization of cars in this field needs to be pursued. Even more so because the technological transformation seems to be inevitable in the long run in terms of achieving ambitious sustainability goals. These goals relate chiefly to reducing GHG emissions and reaching target values for the sales of vehicles without local emissions. In the European Union, new car fleet average CO_2 emissions for car manufacturers is to be reduced to 95g CO_2/km until the year 2021 (International Council on Clean Transportation 2014). In order to meet these GHG regulations automobile manufacturers will need to increase the shares of full hybrids and plug-in hybrids as well as zero emission vehicles (ZEV) in their car fleets. Walther et al. (2010) have shown that the market penetration with new powertrains will most likely take a long time, even if the technology adoption takes place across many vehicle segments at the same time. Shifting towards the paradigm of sustainable mobility could considerably accelerate

[4] The research design is stored in Appendix 10 and can be accessed via OnlinePLUS.

these diffusion processes. Assuming that the efficiency of cars could be raised by a factor of 10, for instance by means of introducing shared autonomous car fleets and other innovative mobility concepts, it would be indeed of a primary matter whether the remaining 10% of the car fleet would be based on a conventional powertrain (ICE), an electric motor or possibly operated by regenerative hydrogen fuel cell. The considerations behind that is the major uncertainty about possible rebound effects associated with a mobility system featuring a radically smaller number of vehicles. Depending on the configuration of such a mobility system and the level of societal acceptance, the total vehicle miles travelled (VMT) by cars could potentially be increased compared to today, as some experts indicate. In such a case concerns regarding CO_2 and GHG emissions would be valid even stronger than today. Further important consideration is also the aspect of the fleet turnover. The question is to what extent such a radical efficiency shift in car usage would contribute to the fluctuation of vehicles in the fleets. If cars were to be utilized much more intensively than today then the fleet would need to be replaced much more frequently. Hence, the transition towards innovative powertrains could be significantly accelerated. However, the investigation of these important aspects is not the main intention of the author in the work at hand. Hence, it has been excluded from further research. With that in mind, the researcher focuses on the concrete strategies to reduce the overall number of cars on the streets and not on the issue of energy efficiency.

PART I
Factor 10 of Automobility: Undiscovered Potentials

3 Part I: Introduction

In this part the researcher investigates mobility concepts of carsharing and ridesharing. Based on his understanding of efficiency of cars in the urban context he has developed a calculation model which has enabled him to determine hypothetical efficiency factors for cars, and to show possible reduction potentials with regard to the total number of cars. The calculations have been carried out for the case of leisure and work traffic in Switzerland and have been based on real data input. The main goal is to illustrate how the efficiency mechanisms behind these mobility concepts work. Following that the author has concentrated on the introduction of the functionality and the mode of operation of shared autonomous vehicles. He presents the results of several of the most recent simulation cases which show that an organized and area-wide fleet of shared autonomous vehicles can realistically contribute to the goal of reducing the number of cars in cities by the factor of 10.

4 Towards a New Concept of Car Efficiency

4.1 Resource Management

Concept of Ecological Rucksack

A total resource consumption includes both the products that reach end consumers and the resource requirements of those products, termed 'ecological rucksack' - which refers to the fact that every product, service or even energy possesses an intangible 'rucksack of used resources' (Lexikon der Nachhaltigkeit 2014). For example, each ton of hard coal during the combustion process for energy production produces 5 tons of excavation materials and water, and round about 3,3 tons of carbon dioxide emissions. The ecological rucksack of hard coal is therefore almost 8,5 times as heavy as the coal itself (Lexikon der Nachhaltigkeit 2014). In case of a car the ecological rucksack amounts up to 70 tons of materials and resources to produce a single unit that weighs 1,6 tons in average (Hinterberger 2009). The idea of total resource consumption takes into account the use of natural resources and also the environmental impacts of this usage '*from cradle to grave*', in other words over the full life cycle of products and services delivered for consumption. The full life cycle encompasses the entire chain from extraction, production, consumption to disposal and recycling (Bringezu et al. 2014).

Sustainable resource management

Developing such a holistic understanding regarding resource consumption raises the awareness of management and consumers about the real scale of environmental impacts and hence, creates the need for an efficient and sustainable resource management to decrease these impacts. The sustainable resource management approach requires identification of opportunities that lead to the reduction of losses and to optimization of systems across the entire life cycle (Bringezu et al. 2014). This can be accomplished by improving efficiency at each phase of the life cycle or by implementing more radical alterations toward greater efficiency, for instance by establishing other usage patterns or by influencing and changing the preferences of consumers. Such an approach to resource management bears the potential to contribute to a better understanding of how to decouple economic growth from environmental degradation (Bringezu et al. 2014).

Life Cycle Assessment

To measure the total resource consumption across the entire life cycle several approaches have been proposed. The most recognized one is the Ecobalance, also labeled the Life-Cycle Assessment (LCA). It is an analysis technique to assess environmental impacts associated with all the stages of a product's life from raw material extraction through materials processing, production, distribution, product usage or consumption, repair, service and maintenance, and recycling. The goal is to compare the full range of environmental impacts that can be assigned to products, processes and services by assessing and quantifying all inputs and outputs of material flows and analyzing how these material flows impact the environment (U.S. General Services Administration 2016). The analysis compiles an inventory of relevant energy and material inputs and helps interpret the results in order to make a more informed decision (Scientific Applications International Corporation 2006).

Even though, LCA has been codified in an international standard (ISO 14040:2006) there is no single method for conducting LCA. Organizations have the flexibility to implement it in accordance with their intended application and requirements. The author will present two specific methods for measuring material input and land-use intensity: the MIPS and the FIPS.

MIPS and FIPS

In his book "Faktor 10 – das Mass für ökologisches Wirtschaften" (Schmidt-Bleek 1994) Schmidt-Bleek conceptualized two units for measuring the intensity of environmental impact: the MIPS ('material input per unit of service') and the FIPS ('Flächenintensität per Serviceeinheit'). Both concepts are not absolute measures. They relate to the service performance which is provided by a specific product, process or service. The more the product is used, the lower the environmental impact (Wittig, Niekisch 2014). However, it needs to be stated that these approaches have been regarded as 'reductionist approaches'. While they intend to assess the complete use and consumption of resources throughout the life cycle, they do not provide a thorough impact assessment considering all environmental aspects. This limitation is justified by the fundamental impossibility of investigating and quantifying all possible effects on ecological systems (Nickel 2013).

The MIPS concept can be used to measure eco-efficiency of a product or service. The calculation takes into account materials required to produce a unit of product or a service (Schmidt-Bleek 1994). The total material input (MI) is divided by the number of service units (S) provided by the product or service. The whole life-cycle of a product or service can be measured by calculating the MIPS values. This allows comparisons of resource consumption of different solutions to produce the same service (Ritthoff et al. 2002).

The MIPS concept is based on the idea that goods are mostly used for services since the consumers do not have any benefits out of raw materials. They demand services such as communication, information, heating, housing or mobility and not the raw materials needed for their provision. Thus, the main essence is the relation to the benefits generated by that product or service unit. These benefits can be also referred to as the 'value proposition' (Osterwalder, Pigneur 2010). The notion of value is important for this work and will be elaborated on in more detail later in this dissertation.

The FIPS is defined as an area-based environmental indicator that expresses the land-use intensity per service unit (Schmidt-Bleek 1994, p. 174). It is based on the consideration that if an area or a property is occupied for any purpose or activity, it is simultaneously excluded from the usage for any other purpose or activity (Schmidt-Bleek 1994).

There are several critical reasons to highlight the importance of the efficiency of land and space usage. The population growth, ongoing urbanization, as well as changes in diets and consumption behaviors have implications for global land use dynamics. Global land use and soil management play a central role in determining people's food, material and energy supply. This may have considerable implications for the long-lasting resource security of humanity (Bringezu et al. 2014).

Another important aspect is the land consumption and degradation which is associated with the supply of biofuels. According to Bringezu et al. (2009) it would be feasible to save around 500-600 m^2 of land per person in Germany with just one demand-side measure: reducing the total fuel consumption of cars by 26-30% (i.e. emission mitigation for automobiles to 130 g CO_2/km) and phasing out first generation of biofuels.

In the context of the ongoing urbanization and the associated increase in demand for mobility services in cities it seems to be appropriate to include the issue of land and space consumption into the overall discussion about the shift towards the paradigm of sustainable urban mobility.

4.2 Extending the Understanding of Car Efficiency

In order to develop an understanding of car efficiency for the purpose of this work the author will deploy Schmidt-Bleek's definition of MIPS (Schmidt-Bleek 1994, p. 132)[5]:

> "The measure of the intensity of the ecological damage is the material intensity per unit of service over the entire product life cycle, in other words the use of materials from the cradle to cradle per unit of service or function - the MIPS."

Today, the productivity measurement of cars is based on the relation of the total material input for assembling one unit of car to the total passenger-kilometers. The author seeks to develop his own definition of car productivity, however. In his opinion it should be based on the value proposed by cars. The reason for that is that the author takes a value-oriented perspective. He assumes that users of automobiles are not demanding passenger-kilometers but rather the service that is being provided by car usage. The service requested by consumers is the mobility, or to be more specific a journey/trip from A to B. Hence, consumers are demanding car-journeys rather than passenger-kilometers. It needs to be emphasized that a car-journey in itself is usually not a purpose for consumers. The purpose is the fulfillment of some other higher-order needs. Therefore, the car-

[5] Author's own translation of the following quotation (in German): "Das Mass für Umweltbelastungintensität ist die das ganze Produktleben umspannende Material-Intensität Pro Serviceeinheit, also der Metrialverbrauch von der Wiege bis zur Wiege pro Einheit Dienstleistung oder Funktion – die MIPS." Schmidt-Bleek 1994, p. 132.

journey should be seen as a service for the consumers to help them fulfill their other demands. Hence, car-journey can be regarded as a mobility from A to B which is derived from other higher-order needs of consumers (Berger et al. 2014).

In the course of the text the author refers to a car as a 'black-box'. Thereby he disregards the actual material input, i.e. the ecological rucksack, which is needed to create it. The author seeks to emphasize that the car is a commodity or utility that provides value to the users in the form of mobility services. A service unit of the car is defined as a car-trip. This approach to describing the productivity of a car is especially interesting for urban areas, since the trips tend to be shorter and more frequent when compared to long-distance trips between the cities.

With that in mind the author will apply the concept of MIPS to develop the definition of car efficiency. The author aims at showing how many service units a car is able to deliver, for example, during a day. He will refer to it as 'car input per service unit' (CIPS). In other words, with CIPS the author will be able to compare the intensity of car usage based on the provided number of car-trips. For example, if a car delivers 2 trips per day then the CIPS rate will amount to 0,5 (1/2). Whereas, if it provides 10 trips then the CIPS will go down to 0,1 (1/10). Consequently, the less the CIPS, the more productive the car is.

Furthermore, the CIPS concept should consider efficiency in a holistic way. This means that the efficiency of a car needs to be extended by the total capacity available in a car. Therefore, the CIPS should actually indicate that the productivity of a car is dependent on both:

- the intensity of the car usage in the form of performed car-trips per day and
- the intensity of its seat utilization, i.e. its occupancy rate.

This would result in the following notion of the car productivity:

Total number of cars / Total car-journeys provided

For example, the CIPS for a private car which provides 2 trips per day (e.g. home-work and work-home) with an average occupancy rate of 1 would amount to: 1 / (2*1) = 0,5. Whereas, the CIPS for a taxi which performs on average 20 journeys a day and has an average occupancy rate of 2 would result in: 1 / (20*2) = 0,025.

4.3 Redefining the Notion of Car Efficiency

The common metrics for measuring the performance of transport services for people is that of passenger-kilometers. Even though it specifies the traffic volume performed by cars it does not indicate how efficient the usage of a car unit has been. It states the overall mobility performed by people, but entirely disregards the efficiency of the chosen transport mode. Thus, the metric of passenger-kilometer does not indicate how efficiently the car was utilized. For example, the measurement instruments within the car measure only the total mileage of the car. The productivity in terms of the total number of trips and journeys provided during a year are not considered.

The following definition of resource productivity was provided by Schmidt-Bleek (1994, p. 140):

> "The totality of available units of services divided by the total consumption of material for the product that provides the service […]. In other words, the resource productivity of a product is the inverse of its MIPS, measured in units per kilogram". (Based on author's own translation)

Therefore, the productivity notion of a car can be defined as the inverse of CIPS. I.e. it would be the result of the multiplication of the number of possible car-trips per time frame (e.g. per day) multiplied by the number of available seats in the vehicle. The unit of measurement would be actual/possible car-journeys per specific time frame. This implies that the possible car efficiency is dependent on:

- the number of possible car trips a day,
- the capacity of the car (number of seats).

Consequently, there would be two possible ways to raise the efficiency of car usage:

- increase the number of car trips per car, i.e. make the car drive more,
- increase the number of car journeys per car, i.e. increase the occupancy rate of car trips in order to utilize the available space.

It is argued that driving a car at least 10'000-15'000 km per year justifies the economic feasibility of a private car ownership (Litman 2000). For example, in Switzerland an average person conducts 10'831 km per year by means of a motorized individual vehicle (Bundesamt für Statistik BFS 2012d). This would economically justify a private car ownership. However, from this perspective the private car owner entirely disregards the alternative profits that would be possible if the car was highly productive, for example, four times that much, i.e. 40'000-60'000 km. In these terms a car should be regarded purely as an investment good. Therefore, the aim of every car owner, or more specifically 'car investor', should be the achievement of a maximal yield on that investment because if the car remains idle then it causes only costs in the form of, for example, depreciation. Hence, car owners should be given the possibility to utilize their cars in a more productive way. This would contribute to a much higher utilization of available cars and possibly to the reduction of the overall number of the cars.

5 Concepts for Shifting the Efficiency of Car Usage

It is being claimed that the today's mobility system is car-dependent but there also seems to be an observable shift towards 'sustainable mobility' (Banister 2008). This new paradigm has three main strategies (Berger et al. 2014): efficiency shift, modal shift and the reduction of mobility needs. From the author's perspective the most interesting arena of innovation is that of 'efficiency shift'. It aims at optimizing both: the aspect of energy inefficiencies (for example, by means of electromobility or fuel cell) and the inefficiencies in usage of cars. The author focuses particularly on overcoming the latter.

Based on the efficiency definition derived in the last chapter, there are two strategies for increasing the efficiency of car usage: more trips per car and more journeys per car. There are two central mobility concepts that have been developed for implementing these car productivity strategies:

- carsharing: timely synchronized usage of cars,
- ridesharing: increase of the occupancy factor of cars.

Carsharing is a type of car rental designed to be convenient for people who want to rent cars for short periods of times. Whereas ridesharing is a form of ad hoc, informal carpooling between friends, acquaintance or strangers in order to utilize the available space within the cars. In this dissertation these concepts are referred as 'Shared Automobility Services' explained below.

5.1 Carsharing: What is it?

Carsharing is a type of a car rental mobility scheme where cars are rented for short periods of time, often by the hour or more recently also by the minute. Carsharing is defined as the organized, shared use of vehicles by a larger number of people (Pieper et al. 2013). The main idea behind carsharing services is that the individuals receive the benefits of a private car without the need to be concerned about the costs and responsibilities associated with the actual ownership. A carsharing scheme is attractive to customers who make only occasional use of a vehicle, as well as those who need occasional access to a vehicle of a different type than they usually use. In practice, the primary target groups of the carsharing service include (Liu et al. 2014):

- customers who have difficulties affording a variety of high variable costs, such as insurance, parking, or gasoline that are associated with the private car ownership,
- customers who occasionally need a different type of car for unusual purposes, such as a SUV for off-road excursions or a van for transporting larger goods,

- customers who mostly use public transportation for daily work but once in a while will need a car for personal activities such as grocery shopping,
- customers who are frequent travelers and need cars in major cities and airports around the world,
- customers who desire a greener life style, for example, due to strong sustainability awareness.

Typically, the carsharing service providers offer so called turnkey solutions, whereby drivers do not need to care for insurance, gasoline, maintenance, or parking in chosen urban areas. They are charged for the time the vehicles are used, for the distance covered, or a combination of both (Cohen, Kietzmann 2014). Usually, the carsharing schemes are bound to stations, i.e. the customer needs to return the car to its base location, which has always been one of the major drawbacks of carsharing programs. To date, the majority of car-sharing programs feature a roundtrip vehicle rental model (Spieser et al. 2014). In these systems, vehicles must be returned to the same station they were rented from. For example, American Zipcar's current rental service, is based on this approach. In the meantime some carsharing organizations, for example German Car2Go or Swiss Catch-a-Car, offer also one-way trips without the need to return the car to the original location. This carsharing scheme is called free-floating carsharing and seems to be the next generation of carsharing in urban areas. For example, in Germany the total number of customers in this segment increased by 51%, from 437'000 in 2013 to 660'000 in 2014 (bcs 2015b).

Carsharing programs that operate as short-term vehicle rentals (for example ZipCar in US or Mobility in Switzerland) have quickly expanded and have become one of the most important branches within the sharing sector (Tils et al. 2015). For example in the US the number of users have been doubling every 1-2 years over the past decade (Fagnant, Kockelman 2014). There were over 1 million people registered in over 150 carsharing organizations in Germany in January 2015 (bcs 2015b). The number of vehicles used in carsharing programs has increased more than fourteen times since the establishment of the first pilots in Germany back in 1997 (Tils et al. 2015). However, it needs to be noted that the user numbers must be treated with caution as they refer to registrations. On the one hand it might be that the same users are registered in several carsharing organizations to gain access to the variety of services. On the other hand not every registered person constitutes also an active user of the carsharing service. It is rather difficult to determine the exact number of actual users since carsharing organizations tend to provide only the data about the registrations on their online platforms rather than the concrete usage statistics.

5.2 Ridesharing: What is it?

As opposed to carsharing where the car itself is the subject to the service offering, ridesharing aims at offering and utilizing the available space within the cars. The space refers to the seats which are freely available in cars that carry less people than it is actually possible. Therefore, ridesharing is associated with vehicle drivers allowing other passengers to ride in the same vehicle from the same or similar departure point to the same or similar destination (Cohen, Kietzmann 2014; Chan, Shaheen 2012). Ridesharing is often organized and offered by the drivers in exchange for compensation. However, traditional ridesharing is defined as non-profit. Therefore, the majority of ridesharing programs are not associated with drivers seeking to gain profits. The goal is rather to contribute to the cost relief of the vehicle owner, while contributing to reduced traffic congestion and pollution at the same time (Cohen, Kietzmann 2014; Chan, Shaheen 2012). In this respect ridesharing is also referred to as a cost sharing service.

On the one side ridesharing aims at reducing each traveler's variable travel costs such as fuel costs, tolls, and the stress of driving by having more people using one single vehicle. On the other side it is also thought that ridesharing is an environmentally friendly and sustainable mode of transportation. Sharing journeys reduces carbon emissions, traffic congestion on the roads, and the need for parking spaces. Therefore, authorities tend to encourage ridesharing, for example during periods of high pollution or high fuel prices (Chan, Shaheen 2012).

Interestingly, ridesharing is not a novel mobility concept at all. The first ridesharing programs emerged already during the World War II. Back then the Office of Civil Defense of USA had supported ridesharing in order to save rubber for military purposes (Columbia Law Review 1942). Similarly, the 1973-74 period of the Oil Embargo in the USA was a time of great interest in ridesharing. Authorities encouraged these initiatives in order to reduce the civil consumption of oil. After that it was hoped that ridesharing will take off as an additional mode of transportation in the USA. However, low oil prices and strong economic growth throughout 1980's and into the 1990's did not bring about the expected development (MIT "Real-Time" Rideshare Research 2009). While early versions of matching services relied on word-of-mouth, governmental campaigns or bulletin boards in companies, the recent advancements in digital technologies have considerably enabled an intelligent approach to support modern ride-matching schemes.

6 Efficiency Potentials of Automobility

6.1 Calculation Model for Efficiency Potentials

6.1.1 Fundamental Terminology

The concept of activities, routes and stages allows a detailed description of everyday mobility. This enables to understand the precise sequence of travel purposes and also the changes in transport modes on routes throughout the day (Bundesamt für Statistik BFS 2012d, p. 39). The most important terms and definitions are listed in Table 1.

Table 1: The most important terms and their definitions.
(Source: Bundesamt für Statistik BFS 2012d, p. 39)

Term	Definition
Stage	The stage is the smallest unit in this concept. A stage has a minimum length of 25 m and is defined by the use of a particular mode of transport. If the mode is changed, a new stage begins.
Route	A route consists of one or more stages, i.e. one or more modes of transport used in succession. A route is defined by the travel purpose, which may vary depending on the type of activity at the destination (such as shopping). Once the final destination is reached, the route ends. A new route begins if the purpose changes or if one travels back home.
Trip and round trips	A trip is a sequence of routes which begins at home and ends at home. A trip may thus consist of at least two routes (back and forth) or of multiple routes, if one combines multiple purposes. With respect to the car usage for a trip one applies also the notion of round trips, i.e. the starting point and the destination must be the same (e.g. at home).

A calculation model is proposed to estimate the potential reduction of the overall number of automobiles in a city. It is not the intention of the author to apply the common traffic performance indicator of 'vehicle kilometers' but, according to the objectives of this doctoral thesis, rather the number of cars in the city. Thereby account must be taken of the following variables[6]:

[6] The list of variables has been identified based on an expert interview coded at *20141027_BS22*, see Appendix 8 (access via OnlinePLUS).

- transport sectors,
- average duration of activity,
- average household size,
- average occupancy level of a vehicle in a transport sector,
- average duration of a tour for the transport sectors and
- possible maximum life-cycle of vehicles in a traffic sector.

6.1.2 Carsharing: Calculation for timely synchronized rides

Step 1: Determination of the number of possible tours per vehicle, day, and transport sector

It is assumed that once the intention has been undertaken to pursue an activity (e.g. for the purpose of leisure), the car is being booked for the entire duration of this activity. For this calculation model a combination of different routes is excluded for the time being (e.g., leisure and shopping). Thus the tour will consist only of two car trips: back and forth, i.e. a round trip.

To calculate the number of possible round trips per vehicle, an average duration of a trip must be determined by transport sector. This will result in the potential number of round trips per day, vehicle and transport sector.

Step 2: Determination of the number of journeys carried out in the examined transport sector per household and day

The Swiss Sample Census for Mobility (Bundesamt für Statistik BFS 2012d) provides the data of how many trips per person, day, and transport purpose are undertaken by means of motorized individual transport. In this way one can determine how many trips can be made in a specific transport sector per day per person.

To determine the magnitude of possible trips per household in a specific transport sector the previously determined number of trips per person needs to be multiplied by an average household size. This calculation step will result in an estimated number of trips in the examined transport sector per household. If the result is then divided by the average vehicle occupancy level, the number of trips per household per day in the specific transport sector can be determined.

Step 3: Determination of the efficiency quotient

If the possible time windows are put in relation to the number of calculated trips activities per household, a quotient results which indicates the potential increase in efficiency of a car in the investigated transport sector.

6.1.3 Ridesharing: Calculation for higher occupancy level of a car

The method of calculation of the efficiency ratio for the mobility concept of ridesharing can be represented in a simple way by the following relation:

- the maximum number of persons that can be transported per vehicle (the denominator),
- the present occupancy level according to a specific transport purpose (the counter).

By combining them, i.e. denominator/counter, an efficiency factor results which could be potentially improved by increasing the occupancy level of vehicles.

6.2 Hypothetical Efficiency Calculations for Car- and Ridesharing

To highlight certain efficiency potentials in mathematical terms the author proposes to approach the calculation by focusing on transport sectors. The main reason for this is that for the calculation a specific data base can be utilized, for example, from the Swiss Sample Census for Mobility which provides reliable data (Bundesamt für Statistik BFS 2012d). Thus, this approach can be based on real data even if the calculation has a purely hypothetical character. Switzerland will serve as a good insofar as the country has on the one hand a very stringent constraint in the form of its limited area, and it also has to deal with a high volume of motorized traffic on the other hand. The country is also proactively seeking for solutions which would allow both to achieve sustainability in urban as well as rural mobility.

In 2010, on average nearly 37 kilometers daily were conducted domestically by every inhabitant of Switzerland (Bundesamt für Statistik BFS 2012d). Leisure traffic is by far the dominant transport purpose of the Swiss. It amounts to approx. 40% of the average daily distance (s. Figure 6). Driving to work is the second important purpose. Together, they make nearly 65% of the daily distance conducted by the average Swiss. Moreover, about two-thirds of the daily distances are covered by car, a quarter is accounted for public transport (rail, postbus, bus, tram) and a bit less than a tenth by slow transport modes (walking and cycling).

It has been recognized in Switzerland that effort must be undertaken to make work and leisure traffic environmentally oriented in the future to meet the requirements of a sustainable society, which Switzerland aims to become (Müller 2012, p. 20). Therefore, considering the prevailing high dependence on automobility in daily traffic as well as the negative effects on the environment and society, a high priority has been placed on reducing the dominance of cars in the cities and urban areas in Switzerland.

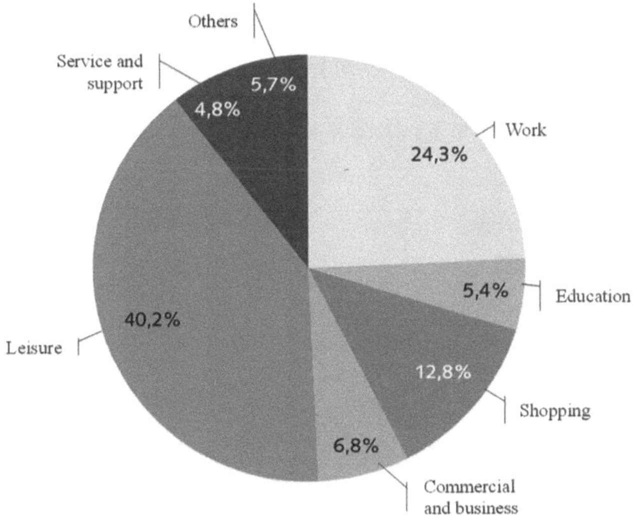

Figure 6: Transport purposes in percentage of the daily distance.
(Source: Bundesamt für Statistik BFS 2012d, p. 8 based on author's own translation).

For this reason the author of this work aims at depicting the potentials of shared automobility services for possible efficiency increases in the car usage which would lead to overcoming the car-dependence in the Swiss agglomerations and cities. The author will focus on Swiss leisure and work traffic. He seeks to answer the following question:

> What are the hypothetical potentials for efficiency shifts in the car usage for leisure and work traffic in Switzerland based on the concepts of shared automobility services?

6.2.1 Leisure Traffic in Switzerland

Leisure traffic is mostly done by car (see Figure 7) and takes place chiefly in urban areas (see Figure 8). From the perspective of trip 'routinization' it is evident that 62,5% of the Swiss habitually drive their leisure routes (Ohnmacht et al. 2008). Also, it has been observed that the Swiss leisure traffic is relatively evenly distributed throughout the day as compared to other transport purposes (see Figure 9). Due to these circumstances, the author suggests that a synchronous arranging of car trips, i.e. carsharing, for leisure traffic is quite conceivable and realistic. For this reason, he will explain possible efficiency potentials of carsharing for leisure traffic in Switzerland.

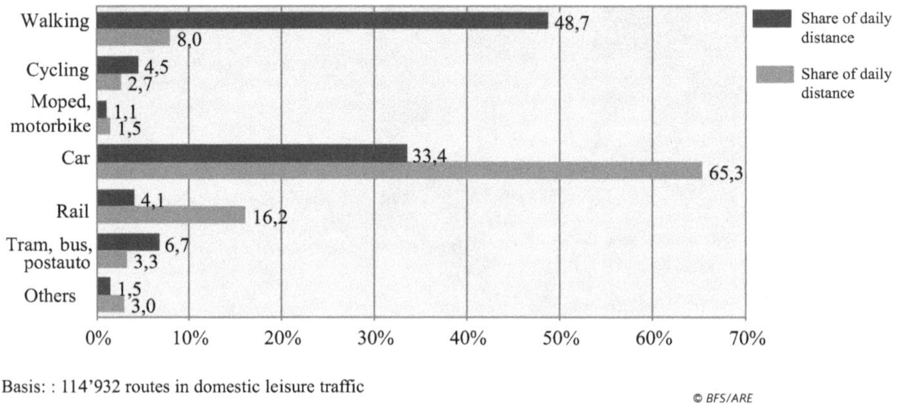

Figure 7: Choice of transport in leisure traffic.
(Source: Bundesamt für Statistik BFS 2012d, p. 63 based on author's own translation).

In the sector of leisure traffic it should be also possible to let other people share the ride in one's car if they are going in the same direction and at the same time (ridesharing). The author will include the potential of ridesharing for the calculation to showcase the possible efficiency increases, even though the Swiss-wide average occupancy level for leisure traffic is relatively high – on average two persons per car.

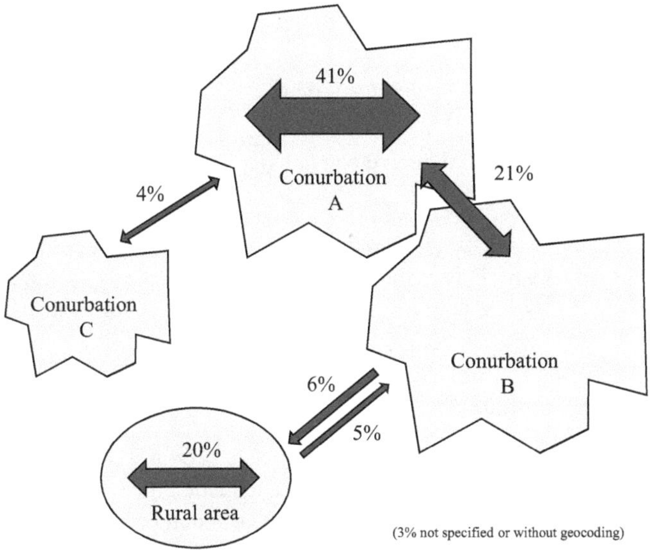

Figure 8: Spatial distribution of leisure traffic within and between (contiguous) urban areas and rural areas (Source: Author's own diagram based on Ohnmacht et al. 2008).

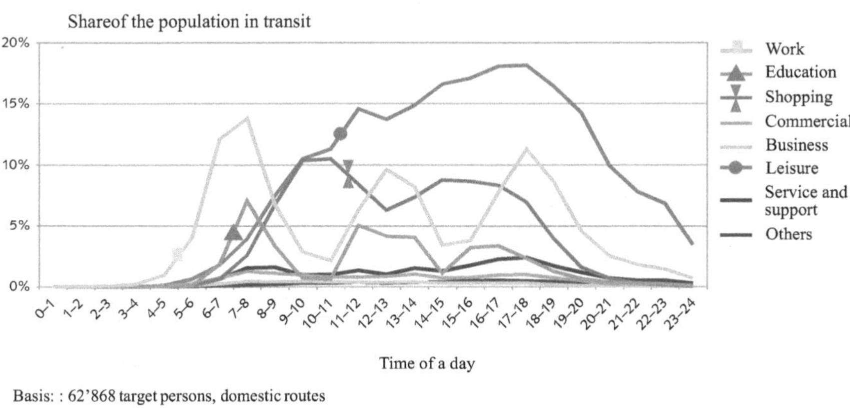

Figure 9: Traffic throughout the day according to travel purposes.
(Source: Bundesamt für Statistik BFS 2012d, p. 44 based on author's own translation).

6.2.1.1 Carsharing: Efficiency Potentials

Step 1: Determination of the number of possible journeys per car, day and transport sector

For the estimation of the efficiency potential an average activity duration in the leisure sector can be estimated as follows:

- it is assumed that a recreational activity takes approximately 1,5 hours,
- a round trip takes about 1 hour. This assumption is based on the daily average trip duration for leisure in Switzerland of 34 minutes (Bundesamt für Statistik BFS 2012c),
- an additional time buffer of approximately 0,5 hour is assumed is assumed to allow for a lead and a follow-up time.

On average this results in the assumed journey duration for leisure activities in Switzerland of up to 3 hours. Furthermore, an assumption regarding a realistic time window for leisure activities during the day is made. For the purpose of the calculation at hand this period may be up to 15 hours (e.g. from 7 a.m. to 10 p.m.). This is the assumed time period that a shared vehicle can be utilized.

Assuming the activity duration of 3 hours, a total of 5 time sequences results, in which a vehicle could be used by different households for their leisure trips. Hence, every car can provide up to 5 mobility service units (round tours) per day for leisure traffic.

Step 2: Determination of the car round tours carried out per household and day in Switzerland in leisure traffic

- Determining the number of leisure activities in Switzerland per household per day

First, the number of leisure trips per person and day must be determined. According to the Swiss Sample Census for Mobility 2010 (Bundesamt für Statistik BFS 2012a) the daily number of trips for leisure activities is 1,3 routes per person. According to the assumption that no other travel purposes are combined, then the number of leisure routes determines at the same time the number of tours. This means that if a route is taken with leisure purpose, then after the activity a return route back home must take place. For this reason, the author assumes that in Switzerland 1,3 round trips are conducted per person and day with the aim of reaching a leisure activity.

Following that, the number of leisure activities in Switzerland per household per day must be determined. The following calculation method applies:

Number of activities per person and day * Average household size

The average household size in Switzerland was 2,3 persons in 2010 (Eurostat 2015). Hence, the average household in Switzerland conducts 3 leisure activities per day (calculation: 1,3 x 2,3 = 2,99 ≈ 3).

- Determining the number of car tours (round trips) in leisure traffic per household per day

Not all trips are made by car. Therefore, it has to be determined how many car round trips are performed on average in the Swiss leisure traffic. According to Ohnmacht et al. (2008) the route-based modal-split for leisure traffic for the car as the main mode of transport amounts to 46% in Switzerland. That means that on average 1,38 leisure trips are conducted daily by car in Switzerland (calculation: 3 * 46%).

Taking into account the average occupancy level of cars in leisure traffic being at 1,99 ≈ 2 persons per car (Bundesamt für Statistik BFS 2012b), then the average number of car trips for leisure activities per household and day can be calculated:

Number of trips per household / Medium car occupancy level

Hence, the average number of car trips for leisure per household and day is 0,69 (calculation: 1,38 / 2 = 0,69). In other words, Swiss households conduct approximately 21 car trips for leisure activities per month, which seems to be a realistic value.

Step 3: Calculation of the efficiency ratio in leisure traffic

The following calculation method is applied:

Number of time slots for trips / Number of car trips per household

Calculation: 5 / 0,69 = 7,25

The rounded efficiency factor amounts to 7,25.

6.2.1.2 Ridesharing: Efficiency Potentials

Assuming that households create also carpools for the same purposes and similar destinations, which nowadays is made possible through intelligent and dynamic ridesharing offers for urban mobility (e.g. MatchRider, Flinc, TwoGo by SAP), a much higher efficiency ratio can be achieved. Therefore, the author assumes that in the same time slot of car usage a higher occupancy could be attained by enabling intelligent matching services for the same or similar routes.

Hence, if the occupancy level of a car changes, then the number of car tours in leisure traffic per household and day will change accordingly. Table 2 shows some exemplary calculations of possible efficiency factors for the average occupancy rates of 3 and 4 persons per car.

Table 2: List of indicators and their values for the synchronized use of vehicles (carsharing) and higher occupancy rates (ridesharing).

Indicators	Values
Number of possible tours per day, car and transport sector (in tours or in this case, round trips)	5
Number of leisure trips per person per day (in routes)	1,3
Average household size in Switzerland (in persons)	2,3
Number of leisure activities per household per day	3
Car as main mode of transport for leisure in Switzerland	46%
Number of leisure trips per household by car (in tours)	1,38
Average occupancy rate of a car in leisure traffic (in persons)	2 / 3 / 4
Number of car tours in leisure traffic per household and day (depending on the occupancy rate)	0,69 / 0,46 / 0,345
Efficiency factor for the car occupancy level of 2	5 / 0,69 ≈ 7,25
Efficiency factor for the car occupancy level of 3	5 / 0,46 ≈ 11
Efficiency factor for the car occupancy level of 4	5 / 0,345 ≈ 14,5

6.2.1.3 CIPS: Calculation with Real Data

For the calculation of the CIPS (Car Input per Service) for leisure traffic in Switzerland the author will use the official statistical data from Switzerland, the Swiss Sample Census for Mobility (Mobilitätszensus) for the year 2010 (Bundesamt für Statistik BFS 2012d; Bundesamt für Statistik 2007).

Mobility Demand

In 2010 there were 3'505'616 households in Switzerland (Bundesamt für Statistik BFS 2013a). Considering that every Swiss household demands on average 1,38 car journeys (i.e. mobility service) to reach leisure activities per day, the demand amounts up to

4’837’750 car journeys (tours or round trips) per day. The average occupancy rate of cars for leisure activities in Switzerland is 2 persons per car. Hence, there is a total demand for 2’418’875 car tours per day in order to reach a destination for conducting leisure activities.

Mobility Supply

As much as 49% of the Swiss households possess one car and 30% of them at least two. Hence, there are at least 3’821’121 cars that are available every day for Swiss households. The following calculation applies:

(3’505’616 * 49%) * 1 + (3’505’616 * 30%) * 2 = 1’717’751 + 2’103’370 = 3’821’121

This estimated number corresponds with the general Swiss statistics which show that in 2010 there were 4'075'825 private cars registered in Switzerland (Bundesamt für Statistik BFS 2015). However, here the author considers only cars which are in the possession of Swiss households. Therefore, the number is lower.

Efficiency Factor

As shown above, every car could be used at least 5 times a day for car trips to reach leisure activities. Hypothetically, the total supply of potential car trips to leisure activities amounts up to as much as 19’105’605 per day. However, Swiss households use their cars only for 2’418’875 trips every day in the investigated traffic sector. Hence, theoretically the Swiss demand could be covered by only as little as 483’775 cars.

2’418’875 / 5 = 483’775

Therefore, the hypothetical efficiency factor is 7,9. This factor results from the following calculation:

Number of currently available cars / Number of required cars

3’821’121 / 483’775 = 7,89

Car Input per Service Unit (CIPS)

Using the CIPS concept the following relation applies for the current leisure traffic in Switzerland:

Number of cars available / Number of car journeys in demand

3’821’121 / 4’837’750 = 0,79

In contrast, the CIPS of a privately-owned car of an average Swiss household for leisure traffic amounts theoretically 0,1. This result is based on the following calculation:

Car unit / Possible car journeys per car unit

1 / (5 possible trips * 2 occupancy rate) = 0,1

Therefore, the calculated efficiency factor is 7,9, which results from the following calculation scheme:

0,79 / 0,1 = 7,9

This result corresponds approximately with the estimates provided above based on another calculation approach which indicated an efficiency factor of 7,25. Table 3 lists the calculated efficiency factors for hypothetically higher occupancy rates.

Table 3: List of indicators and their calculated values for CIPS.

Indicators	Calculation	Efficiency Factor
Calculated efficiency factor (occupancy rate of 2)	0,79 / 0,1	7,9
Calculated efficiency factor (occupancy rate of 3)	0,79 / 0,066	12
Calculated efficiency factor (occupancy rate of 4)	0,79 / 0,05	16

The extrapolation of the calculation indicates that the efficiency factor of 10 could be achieved by increasing the occupancy rate to approximately 2,5 persons per car trip, while fully harvesting the potentials from the previously proposed sequenced carsharing scheme.

6.2.2 Work Traffic in Switzerland

In addition, also the work traffic will be considered. Similar to the leisure traffic it takes place mostly on the road (see Figure 10) and influences significantly the congestion level in Switzerland. Between 2008 and 2012, the amount of congestion time on the highways has doubled. Between 2000 and 2012 the number of commuters increased by additional 230'000 people. Moreover, around 85% to 90% of all congestion hours occur in urban areas (Adler et al. 2014, 2014). In more than 90% of the travel stages the occupancy level in work traffic is only one person per car (Bundesamt für Statistik BFS 2012d, p. 49). The routinization of the routes in the work traffic, in the sense of using the same routes regularly, is significantly higher than in leisure traffic. It is not surprising that work traffic features 88,5% of regularly driven commutes (Ohnmacht et al. 2008).

The daily routine in the work traffic has a significantly different structure as compared to the other types of traffic. Figure 9 shows that there are three peaks during the day: in the morning, during lunch and in the evening.

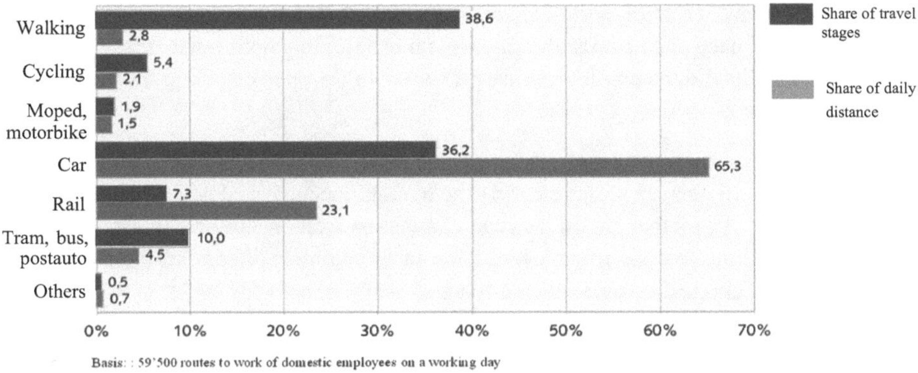

Figure 10: Choice of transport for work traffic.
(Source: Bundesamt für Statistik BFS 2012d, p. 63 based on author's own translation).

Therefore, the structure of work traffic favors ridesharing as a mobility concept for the reduction of the car traffic. In such a ridesharing mobility scheme all commuters would continue to travel by car to work, however, the occupancy level would increase. This would lead to the decrease in number of cars which are on the roads during the aforementioned peaks.

As opposed to ridesharing as a mobility concept to increase the efficiency of cars in the work traffic carsharing seems to be rather inappropriate. Work traffic takes place chiefly during traffic peaks and aims at transporting people from home to their place of work in the morning, and back home in the evening, which makes the redistribution of cars to the next commuter for his commute rather difficult. Unless, it is assumed that there is also the possibility to share cars for other travel purposes between the morning and afternoon peak. The car would need to be available again in the afternoon for the trip back home. This is a viable option which, however, would require a considerable effort to synchronize the demand side with the supply side with these time constraints.

The author considers the ridesharing concept for this calculation purpose as he is only interested in in overcoming the traffic peaks associated with work travel.

6.2.2.1 Ridesharing: Efficiency Potentials

If commuters create shared rides for the same or similar commute destination, a higher car efficiency ratio can be achieved. It is assumed that a higher occupancy level can be achieved by means of intelligently matching similar commuters. Drivers and commuters can meet at one place and arrange the ride. In a more flexible option the arrangement is made dynamically and the commuters are picked up or dropped off along the way to the final destination.

In other words, ridesharing as mobility concept aims at exploiting the inefficiency of the available but unutilized seats in the car. If the average occupancy level of cars change, then the number of cars that are on the road changes as well. Therefore, ridesharing can positively contribute to a significant reduction in the number of cars on the roads and thus help reduce congestion and parking issues.

What needs to be noted is that the number of passenger-kilometers traveled does not change as commuters still use the car as a mode of transport. However, what changes definitely are vehicle miles traveled (VMT) since there are less cars on the roads.

In Switzerland, the current occupancy level of cars is 1 in 90% of the journeys to work, and the average is 1,12 (Bundesamt für Statistik BFS 2013d). If assumed that cars have an average capacity of 5, then a potential efficiency factor of 4,5 can be hypothetically achieved (s. Table 4).

Table 4: The efficiency factor for carpooling in work traffic.

Indicators	Value	Efficiency Factor
Average occupancy level of a car in leisure traffic (in persons)	1,12	n.a.
Efficiency factor for a car with a capacity of 5	5 / 1,12	4,5

However, the premise is that such a matching system is in place which facilitates an intelligent mapping of commuters in real time and automatically organizes the rides. Such an area-wide ridesharing system for work travel is conceivable and also possible to implement. Especially in agglomerations which usually feature a high number of workplaces and commuters with convergent destinations (Bundesamt für Statistik BFS 2013d) such a system would be feasible without any further ado. Nowadays, a dynamic and intelligent ridesharing system which allows total flexibility and security in carpooling can be achieved by means of innovative digital technologies. There are also other concepts, which could lead to the establishment and acceptance of ridesharing for work travel. These include: Park & Ride Facilities, High Occupancy Vehicle Lanes (HOV), Mobility Pricing, etc. These concepts are presented in detail in the course of this work (see chapter 14.3).

6.2.2.2 CIPS: Calculation with Real Data

Mobility Demand

In Switzerland, a total of 3'666'864 workers was recorded as commuters in 2011. Slightly more than half of them (53%) chose the car as the main mode of transport to commute (Bundesamt für Statistik BFS 2013d). Hence, there were approximately 1'943'437 commuters in Switzerland in 2011 that traveled by car. Assuming that commuters' round trip is only the way to work and then straight back home, a total demand for 3'886'874 car journeys (a trip back and a trip forth) every day would result.

1‘943‘437 * 2 = 3‘886‘874

Mobility Supply

Taking the current occupancy level for car commutes in Switzerland of 1,12 into account (Bundesamt für Statistik BFS 2012d, p. 50), it can be stated that 1'735'212 cars are on their way to work and back home every day.

1‘943‘437 / 1,12 = 1‘735‘212

Car Input per Service Unit

Using the CIPS concept following relation applies for work traffic:

Total number of cars for commutes / Total car journeys required

If the total number of cars for commutes is 1‘735‘212 and the total demand for car journeys to work and back home is 3‘886‘874, then the current CIPS in Switzerland for commutes amounts to:

1‘735‘212 / 3‘886‘874 = 0,45 CIPS.

If assumed that an average car features 5 available seats and that every car conducts 2 commuting trips every day (home-work and work-home), then the maximal possible CIPS for commutes would amount to:

1 / (5 * 2) = 0,1 CIPS.

Therefore, the calculated efficiency potential which could be achieved by means of implementing an intelligent ridesharing system is:

Current CIPS / Max. CIPS

0,45 / 0,1 = 4,5

Calculation for the required number of cars

Having the previous calculation in mind a hypothetical number of cars needed to cover every day commutes in Switzerland could be reduced from 1‘735‘212 today to exactly 385’602.

1‘735‘212 / 4,5 = 385’602

Table 5 depicts the list of indicators, their values and the calculated efficiency factor based on the proposed CIPS measurement concept.

Table 5: List of indicators and their calculated values for CIPS.

Indicators	**Values**
Number of commuters in Switzerland	3‘666‘864
Percentage of commuters using cars as their main mode of transport	53%
Number of commuters using cars	1‘943‘437
Number of passenger car-journeys in demand	3’886’874
Occupancy rate for work traffic	1,12
Number of cars used for commutes today	1‘735‘212
Current CIPS	0,45
Max. CIPS for cars with capacity of 5	0,1
Calculated possible efficiency factor	4,5
Hypothetical number of cars with ridesharing option	385’602

6.3 Conclusions

Following the proposed calculation methods one can determine the required conditions for achieving the efficiency factor of 10 of automobility. For leisure and work traffic in Switzerland the following conclusions can be drawn (see Table 6):

(1) Cars need to be utilized much more frequently than today. Based on the average data there could be a maximum of 5 time windows per day for conducting trips to leisure activities. This bears an efficiency potential between 7,25 - 7,9.
(2) In order to exacerbate the efficiency rate to the desired factor order of 10 the required occupancy rate of the car trips in the leisure traffic sector would need to be between 2,5 - 2,75 persons per car, as opposed to today's 2.
(3) Both concepts could lead to the overall reduction of the required fleet of cars for leisure traffic from 3'821'121 to 382'112.
(4) The structure of the work traffic favors the mobility concept of ridesharing. If all commutes by car were shared by more commuters the efficiency rate could reach the level of 4,5.
(5) This would reduce the number of cars used for commutes today 1'735'212 to approximately 385'602.

The findings indicate that the cars need to be utilized much more productively than they are today. This has two main implications regarding the intensity of the car usage:

- Cars will need to be shared in a timely synchronized way to allow more parties to use them much more frequently,
- Freely available seats in the cars will need to be utilized at higher rates. Otherwise, they cause additional costs. In consequence, travelers will need to accept to share rides with others.

Hence, in order to harvest substantial efficiency potentials in the automobility sector both a sophisticated carsharing approach and intelligent ridesharing schemes will need to be established. These efficiency potentials could be further amplified if additional strategies for modal shift and mobility sufficiency are implemented and accepted by the society (see chapter 19.2.2).

Table 6: Summary of the conducted calculations and possible efficiency factors.

Indicators	Leisure traffic	Work traffic
Number of cars today	3'821'121	1'735'212
Number of car journey required today	4'837'750	3'886'874
Occupancy rate today	2	1,12
CIPS today	0,79	0,45
Required occupancy rate	2,5-2,75	5
Possible CIPS	0,07-0,08	0,1
Possible efficiency factor	10	4,5
Number of cars in the future	382'112	385'602

The interesting finding that has resulted from the conducted calculations is the possible size of the car fleet that could be achieved if the efficiency strategies were implemented. Both results indicate the total number of required cars to be roughly 385'000 units. This raises an interesting question of what is the lower bound of the required number of cars that under specific conditions could be entirely shared and instantly requested by the users to provide the required mobility levels. Obviously, such a system would need to be fully flexible and highly convenient. Hence, it would require that a car can easily be relocated between the users to provide mobility services on-demand, i.e. without previous preparations, reservations or the need to pick it up. Such a flexibility could be only provided by a mobility system which works in a fully autonomous way, i.e. without human drivers. This is the topic which is outlined in more detail in the next chapter.

6.4 Limitations

There are several limitations to the calculations conducted in the chapters above. These need to be expressed and shorty discussed here.

- The scenarios that have been drawn relate only to the sector of leisure and work traffic. In reality there is a plethora of other traffic sectors (business trips, shopping traffic, service traffic, etc.),
- The assumption that there is only one round trip is limited. In reality transportation destinations can be combined (e.g. leisure and shopping). Therefore, a car can be used flexibly for other purposes during a car-trip,

- The Factor 10-scenario assumes that the demand for a specific purpose can be equally distributed over a day (e.g. between 7 and 22 o'clock). In reality households can flexibly decide when to depart for a car-journey,
- Furthermore, there are sector-specific distributions per day that would need to be taken into consideration (commuters travel chiefly in following time periods e.g. 7-8 and 16-18),
- It is also being assumed that people would have no attachments to their cars. Hence, a car would need to be regarded as a commodity with no emotions and symbolism attached,
- A further assumption is that there exists a possibility to synchronize the mobility needs of households and that there is an intelligent possibility for households to match the same or similar car-trips to share a car. Consequently, Factor 10-scenario assumes that there is a state of perfect information and that this information is available,
- Eventually, the scenario assumes that there is a computation system in place that can flawlessly manage all available data in an intelligent way and in real-time.

7 On the Way to Factor 10 of Automobility

The previously discussed concepts of carsharing and ridesharing allow individuals to subscribe to shared fleets whose vehicles they reserve, access and use only if they require the automobility services, i.e. on demand. Such as taxis or car rental services they have proven popular in many urban areas since they provide access to cars without the need to necessarily owning them. Both mobility concepts, carsharing and ridesharing, are not new at all. However, recently they have taken full advantage of digital technologies and their applications such as: smartphones, instant Internet access or dedicated app-based services. Hence, since the late 1990s the shared automobility services have evolved significantly to become much more convenient for the users (Cohen, Kietzmann 2014). This has added to the plurality and sophistication of these services and considerably contributed to their popularity around the world. This phenomenon is the result of the convergence of digital technologies and shared mobility concepts.

Even though these advanced shared automobility services have become more and more convenient for the end users, they possess two main drawbacks. Firstly, they still require an abundance of parking space within city areas where the cars need to be stored before they are used by other users (e.g. carsharing stations). Secondly and most importantly, the vehicles still require human control of the wheel. However, considering most recent advancements and developments in the arena of autonomous vehicles and self-driving, new technological trajectories have opened up for mobility systems of the future. The author refers to it as the convergence of shared automobility services and autonomous vehicles.

7.1 Shared Autonomous Vehicles: What is it?

Technological innovation and intelligent vehicle technologies have found their way into modern day vehicles. They are being implemented under the concept of driver assistance. Driver assistance systems aim at supporting drivers with activities, such as automatic reverse parallel parking, adaptive cruise control with lane-keep assist or autonomous driving based on a vision camera (Baber et al. 2005).

The more advanced concept is the fully self-driving car which enables the vehicle to drive independently along the road (Vlacic et al. 2001). In this respect advanced robotics is thought to considerably foster safety of driving by handing over the control over the wheel to a machine (Thrun 2010). The recent estimates set the horizon for the adoption of such a technology between 2020 and 2030 (Nissan Motor Company 2013; Krisher 2013).

Finally, the most advanced paradigm is the concept of cooperative autonomous driving based on a fleet of shared autonomous vehicles (SAV). This paradigm enables a plethora of autonomous vehicles to coexist on the roads, autonomously drive in cooperation with each other and provide on-demand mobility services (Baber et al. 2005; Fagnant, Kockelman 2015b). It is a prospect of an additional transportation mode which currently emerges at the frontier of driverless cars and on-demand mobility. Actors such as American Google or Uber, and European CityMobil2 aim at implementing early pilot projects, within this field of innovation (Markoff 2014).

The SAV paradigm has following characteristics (International Transport Forum 2015):

1) Each shared self-driving car drives without human intervention, i.e. fully autonomously.
2) It carries at least one passenger to his or her final destination point.
3) Intermediate stops are possible, i.e. stops between origin and destination, to board additional passengers.
4) After disembarking passengers the SAV is relocated to the next passenger that requests an on-demand mobility services.

It is thought that the further development and deployment of this emerging technology for personal mobility purposes bears enormous benefits for the society (Thrun 2010). On the one hand fully autonomous vehicles promise safer and more comfortable personal transportation based on cars at lower insurance costs and better fuel-efficiency (Marks 2012). On the other hand they are expected to contribute to the resolution of the congestion issue in urban areas and to enhance the productivity of cars (Kornhauser 2013). These benefits could be achieved by enabling entirely new mobility concepts based on the hybridization of mobility services such as: carsharing, ridesharing and taxi services (Thrun 2010). Along with an efficient public transportation system and increased slow modes of transportation, SAV could become an important building block of a sustainable mobility system for urban areas in not that distant future. Such a system would aim at improving transportation security, radically shifting resource efficiencies (both cars and space) and substantially reducing gas emissions (Sweeting, Winfield 2012).

7.2 Efficiency Potentials

7.2.1 Literature

The recent literature indicates that there is an increasing interest in the research area of mobility systems that are partially or solely based on autonomous vehicles. In recent years several publications and reports have been published that aim at disclosing the potentials of such transportation systems. Interestingly, many of these investigations indicate that intelligent mobility services based on the combination of shared mobility patterns and autonomous vehicles could lead to a considerable adjustment of our mobility system in many aspects, one of which is the number of cars on the streets. These simulations show a clear tendency that under specific circumstances and conditions over 90% of privately owned cars could be successfully removed from streets in urban areas and agglomerations. This leads to some important implications with respect to the possibilities to considerably raise the utilization rate of currently underused cars and the reduction of the overconsumption of the space for parking purposes. In the Table 7 below a list of most relevant publications on mobility systems based on SAV have been depicted. It needs to be stated that the list is not the result of a structured literature review. The topic of the combination of shared mobility patterns and autonomous vehicles has just emerged. Therefore, the author created the list based on his interest in the topic and suggestions from experts with whom he conducted interviews during his research.

Table 7: List of most recent publications and simulations assessing possible impacts of SAV on the mobility system.

Authors and Year	Title	Modelling Framework	Assessed Mobility Concept
Bischoff, Maciejewski 2016	Autonomous taxicabs in Berlin–a spatiotemporal analysis of service performance.	Open source transport simulation MATSim and Dynamic Vehicle Routing Problem (DVRP) extension	Autonomous taxi system
Burns et al. 2013	Transforming personal mobility.	Approximate analytical model and an additional simulation model	Carsharing only
Boesch et al. 2016	Required autonomous vehicle fleet sizes to serve different levels of demand.	MATSim, an activity-based multi-agent transport simulation framework	Autonomous taxi system
Fagnant 2015	Dynamic ride-sharing and Fleet Sizing for a System of Shared Autonomous Vehicles in Austin, Texas.	Agent-based simulation framework	Carsharing Dynamic Ridesharing
Fagnant, Kockelman 2014	The travel and environmental implications of shared autonomous vehicles, using agent-based model scenarios.	Discrete trip-vehicle allocation model	Carsharing only

Authors and Year	Title	Modelling Framework	Assessed Mobility Concept
International Transport Forum 2015	Urban Mobility System Upgrade. How shared self-driving cars could change city traffic.	Agent-based model that simulates the daily operation of a shared mobility system	Carsharing Dynamic Ridesharing
Kornhauser 2013	Personal Rapid Transit. A Transportation Plan for New Jersey.	Discrete trip allocation model	Ridesharing only
Rigole 2014	Study of a Shared Autonomous Vehicles Based Mobility Solution in Stockholm.	Dynamic simulation model for allocation of SAV to passenger trips	Carsharing Ridesharing
Santi et al. 2014	Quantifying the benefits of vehicle pooling with shareability networks.	Shareability Networks	Ridesharing only Taxi system No automation
Spieser et al. 2014	Toward a Systematic Approach to the Design and Evaluation of Automated Mobility-on-Demand Systems - A Case Study in Singapore.	Analytical guidelines for sizing Automated Mobility-on-Demand (AMoD) systems based on transportation data	Carsharing only

The results of these different studies that assess transport systems based on SAV can be put in relation to each other and discussed in more detail. The author will outline below some of the most important implications that are related to his own work, which is the expected reduction of the number of cars on the streets.

7.2.2 Shared Mobility Concepts and Autonomous Vehicles

Autonomous Vehicles and Carsharing

It is being widely recognized that the complementary trends of sharing vehicles may lead to on-demand services that are provided by dedicated mobility service providers and away from the paradigm of owning cars (Fagnant, Kockelman 2015b). Therefore, all studies assume that autonomous vehicles will be shared, in one form or the other, and self-driving cars are usually referred to as SAV. Shared usage of vehicles means that trips are synchronized in a timely fashion, hence, leading to a much higher utilization and frequency of car usage. In other words, a fleet of SAVs can enable a highly efficient carsharing scheme, serving many trips during the day and considerably reducing the number of vehicles. The actual size of the fleet of SAVs depends on the trip demand, the assignment scheme of cars and the quality of the service provided to the customers, i.e. waiting and travel time (Rigole 2014a).

Autonomous Vehicles and Ridesharing

Further efficiency gains are expected by the incorporation of the concept of dynamic ridesharing into the mobility system based on SAVs. Preferably, a transportation solution which enables sharing of autonomous vehicles, as described above, also provides an efficient and effortless real-time ridesharing service. A mobility system which intelligently combines the mobility concepts of carsharing and ridesharing would bring the technology of autonomous vehicles to its full potential. Integrating ridesharing can contribute to a further decrease of the required fleet size and an increase in the total number of trips served by a single car (Rigole 2014). So far, only a few studies have included ridesharing into their simulations. This is due to the fact that the theoretical problem underlying dynamic ridesharing is a subcase of the classical pick-up and delivery optimization problem (i.e. travelling salesman problem). This makes it difficult to implement for large-scale applications, such as cities with thousands of possible nodes and tens of thousands of users (Fagnant, Kockelman 2015b). Hence, authors reduce the ridesharing concept to most frequent scenarios (e.g. same origin and destination) and then apply them into the algorithm of the simulation.

7.2.3 Case Studies

In the following section the author will outline 10 case studies that aim at showcasing the main potentials and limitations of mobility systems based on fleets of SAV (see Table 8)[7]. Please note that carsharing is the mobility concept by default. The most important distinction between these cases is whether they also allow for dynamic ridesharing as an additional mobility option. This will be noted in every case study.

Table 8: List of all cases of SAV-based mobility systems and the expected impacts on the current mobility system.

Cases	Mobility Concepts	Reduction Potential (% of the current fleet)	Impact on Service Quality (waiting time, max. or avg.)	Impact on Service Quality (extra travel time, max. or on avg.)	Impact on the distance travelled (% extra VMT)
Model city in US	Only Carsharing	approx. 10%	< 1 minute	0	+10,7%

[7] References to the sources of the case studies are given in the course of the presentation.

Cases	**Mobility Concepts**	**Reduction Potential (% of the current fleet)**	**Impact on Service Quality (waiting time, max. or avg.)**	**Impact on Service Quality (extra travel time, max. or on avg.)**	**Impact on the distance travelled (% extra VMT)**
Singapore	Only Carsharing	33%	5,5 minutes	not specified	not specified
Ann Arbor, Michigan	Carsharing only	15%	< 1 minute	0	~ +10% (additional empty miles)
Babcock Ranch, Florida	Carsharing only	20%	< 1 minute	0	+5% (additional empty miles)
Manhattan, New York	Carsharing only	70%	< 1 minute	0	+11% (additional empty miles)
Lisbon, Portugal	Only Carsharing	22,8%	ca. 3,5 minutes	-13% (on average)	+89,4%
Lisbon, Portugal	With Ridesharing	10,4%	ca. 4 minutes	-37,9% (on average)	+6,4%
Austin, Texas	Only Carsharing	8,5%	ca. 2 minutes	0	+8,68%
Austin, Texas	With Ridesharing	9,5%	ca. 1,5 minute	max. +40%	+1,52%
Stockholm	Only Carsharing	8,6%	max. 15 minutes	0	+71,6%
Stockholm	With Ridesharing	4,9%	max. 10 minutes	max. +30% (+27% on average)	-24%
New Jersey	Ridesharing only	45%	5 minutes	not specified	not specified
Zürich	Only Carsharing	10%	max. 10 minutes (less than 5 min. in 95%)	not specified	not specified
Berlin	Only Carsharing	10%	ca. 2,5 minutes	not specified	+10%

Case of a Model City

Fagnant and Kockelman (2014) based their calculations on a hypothetical city which is constituted by a ten-mile by ten-mile square area. The authors assume a synthesized mobility demand based on national travel statistics in the US to simulate the travel and environmental implications of SAVs. The study considers implementation of autonomous vehicles in a carsharing mobility scheme only. The results indicate that a system of SAVs could reduce the number of self-owned personal vehicles by 90%. However, the results also indicate that the system will contribute additional 11% to the overall travel distance. This is due to the need to relocate the vehicles to reach the 'next in line' traveler. Nonetheless, the study concludes there might be benefits related to gas emissions as older and more polluting vehicles could be replaced with technologically advanced and cleaner ones more quickly.

Case of Singapore

Spieser et al. (2014) designed a mobility-on-demand system based on shared-vehicles. The study aims at determining the appropriate size of the fleet to replace all modes of personal transportation in the city of Singapore with a daily trip demand amounting to as much as 5,6 million trips. The results imply that the fleet size could be reduced to a minimum of 92'693 shared vehicles, however, in an unrealistic scenario of unacceptably high waiting times. Assuming the service quality below 15 minutes at all times of the day, the required number of self-driving cars would amount to 300'000 vehicles. To put these numbers into perspective, in 2011 there were 779'890 passenger vehicles operating on Singaporean roads. Hence, the mobility demand of the entire population of Singapore could be realistically met with less than 33% of the total passenger vehicles currently in operation implying. In such a setting each SAV would serve 20 trips per day.

Case of Ann Arbor

Burns et al. (2013) investigated a shared, autonomous and centrally dispatched fleet of autonomous vehicles in three different environments: mid-sized American city (Ann Arbor, Michigan), low-density suburban area (Babcock Ranch, Florida) and densely-populated urban development (Manhattan, New York). In the case of Ann Arbor the simulation focused on 120'000 vehicles travelling less than 70 miles a day within the urban area and serving as much as 528'000 trips per day. The authors find that an automated carsharing scheme could provide instant access to car trips in less than 1 minute waiting time, however, with a fleet of only 15% of the vehicles currently needed to cover this demand. However, they also find out that the overall travel would increase due to the need for repositioning vehicles.

Case of Babcock Ranch

The calculations for Babcock Ranch, which is a 100% solar powered US city currently under development, indicate that approximately 3'500 SAV could serve a population that is predicted to reach 50'000 people with a demand for 115'000 trips per day (2,3 trips per person and day) (Burns et al. 2013). The service quality would be well under one minute and the utilization rate of the fleet would amount to 70% in the peak hours and on average only slightly less throughout the entire day. Assuming that each of the predicted 17'870 households (Lubbes 2006) would possess only one car the reduction factor would reach 80%.

Case of Manhattan

In Manhattan there is a daily demand for ca. 410'000 internal trips with 'yellow' taxicabs. The high density of customers and vehicles in Manhattan is a fundamental prerequisite for a centrally coordinated system of SAV. Such a system could serve customers with high quality of service (waiting and travel time). A SAV-fleet of 9'000 taxis that can be hailed on-demand with a smartphone could replace all of the trips covered today by over 13'000 human-controlled taxis with an average waiting times of 0,6 minutes which in fact would be much lower than today. This would be 70% of the currently operating fleet size of yellow taxicabs on Manhattan.

Case of Lisbon

The International Transport Forum (2015) examined the changes that could result from the large-scale implementation of a shared fleet of autonomous vehicles in a mid-sized European city. The study explored two different mobility concepts for self-driving vehicles: carsharing and ridesharing. The report explicitly investigated several scenarios for the case of Lisbon, Portugal. The main difference between these scenarios was the configuration of both mobility concepts and the existence of a high-capacity public transportation system. The best-case scenario, a fully-fledged SAV-system with ridesharing option and high-capacity public transport, would make 9 out of 10 cars obsolete (10,4% of the baseline) in Lisbon. The worst-case scenario, i.e. without ridesharing and without high-capacity public transportation would remove 8 out of 10 cars (22,8% of the baseline). Interestingly, these calculations also show an increase in the number of car-kilometers travelled. The scenario with ridesharing resulted in +6% of the total distance because the SAV-mobility system in this scenario would also aim at replacing bus services. In the case with carsharing as an only mobility concept and without high-capacity public transportation, the SAV system would generate additional +86% to the travel distance. This is due to trips associated with relocating and servicing. As regards to the service quality, both scenarios (best and worst) assumed a maximum of 5 minutes waiting time. Interestingly, the total daily travel time required to deliver all trips would be reduced by 30% respectively 18%. However, in peak hours travel time increases by an average of 8% respectively 2%.

Case of Austin

Another example of implementing dynamic ridesharing into the SAV-mobility concept is presented by Fagnant, Kockelman (2015b). Their work seeks to extend their existing SAV mobility framework which was meant for autonomous vehicles with carsharing option only (see section 0: Case of a Model City) and to understand the potentials of dynamic ridesharing for US urban areas. The case study applied is Austin (Texas) with the underlying base-case scenario for mobility demand amounting to roughly 56'500 person trips per day. The simulation of a SAV-based mobility system with an incorporated ridesharing scheme indicates a possible fleet size reduction to the level of 9,5% of the current state. In such a scenario 11% of trips would be shared (6'150). Again, this result is based on the assumptions regarding the service quality, i.e. the users need to accept longer travel times. The basic scenario assumed a maximum delay in travel time of 20%. Relaxing this constraint to 30% respectively 40% would further reduce the fleet size to 8,9% respectively 8,5% of the current fleet, however, at the cost of higher ridesharing rates, 16% respectively 20% of all trips.

The authors recommend that a replacement rate for conventional vehicles in this type of context should be around 1-to-10. Furthermore, findings indicate that ridesharing appears also to be a critical concept for avoiding additional congestion problems that are expected to be caused by automated mobility systems. Generally speaking, if travelers accept to share their trips with others the excess in additional distance traveled can be alleviated.

Case of Stockholm

The geographical border for the study conducted by Rigole (2014) was Stockholm metropolitan area. Stockholm is characterized by a dense traffic structure and therefore is suitable for the implementation of a SAV-based mobility solution. Similarly to other studies the author examined a variety of performance indicators require for SAV fleet to serve the need for personal transportation in Stockholm. The calculations included the size of the required fleet, the distance traveled, the number of required parking spaces and the portion of rides that will be shared by riders. The simulation is based on the actual demand model, but encompasses only one specific traffic segment: work traffic (home-to-work and reverse). The demand in Stockholm for this segment amounts to 271'868 trips per day. Rigole runs several scenarios with two different optimization goals: (i) minimizing empty distance travelled by SAVs and (ii) minimizing parking time of SAVs. Similarly to other studies, the results indicate that in order to provide environmental benefits and lower congestion, the SAV-based personal mobility system requires travelers to accept ridesharing and lower service quality. Accepting waiting time for a pick-up at the level of maximum 10 minutes and the delay in travel time at the level of maximum 30%, both the fleet size and the total distance travelled by vehicles can be considerably reduced. The former could be cut to the level of as little as 5,4% of today's number of vehicles. The latter could be throttled to the level of 89% of the baseline distance travelled. In conclusion, ridesharing offers a further reduction in the size of the fleet and the total distance, but at the cost of decreasing the quality of service for the passengers, i.e. increased travel time and variable waiting times. Hence, the author concludes that ridesharing is beneficial for reducing congestion and parking impacts which are associated with the current car traffic in Stockholm.

Case of Zürich

Boesch et al. (2016) investigated the greater Zürich region, Switzerland. The simulation design accounts for fleets of SAV which aim at serving a predefined demand levels. This paper finds that, if passengers are willing to accept waiting times of up to 10 minutes, a reduction of up to 90% of the amount of vehicles is possible. This is achieved without active fleet management in the form of vehicle redistribution which could bring further gains.

An important characteristic of this study is that the calculation has been based on highly detailed and realistic travel demand which, according to authors, overcomes the simplifications of previous studies in this arena. The simulation provides different scenarios by combining different levels of demand for car trips in greater Zürich with different possible levels of supply, i.e. the size of the fleet of SAV. The main finding is that the minimal fleet of SAV is dependent on the level of demand. This means that for a given service quality of the fleet (e.g. 95% of all requests need to be served in less than 5 minutes), the relationship between the mobility demand and the required fleet size is non-linear. Furthermore, this ratio increases if the demand increases. This might implicate a scale effect, i.e. the fleet of SAV is utilized more efficiently for higher levels of demand. However, such effects are expected only if such a system covers an appropriate level of the existing car traffic.

Boesch et al. (2016) argue also that since the transport demand is influenced by new mobility offers and changes in mobility costs, such innovative mobility concepts will definitely have an effect on the overall mobility demand. I.e. SAV might generate more demand because the service will be more comfortable and cheaper than the usage of private cars or maybe even the public transit. Such undesirable shifts in demand could bring the existing infrastructure capacities to its limits and hence increase travel times provided by SAV. This would have a demand reducing effect leading to a new system equilibrium.

Case of Berlin

Bischoff, Maciejewski (2016) propose a large scale simulation of autonomous taxi services for Berlin, Germany. The authors were able to show that the city would require roughly 100'000 vehicles to cover the demand for car trips which is currently served by 1,1 million cars. Moreover, their simulation provides sufficiently good results at very high computational speeds. With this number of vehicles, the average wait time for an autonomous taxicab can be kept under three minutes at most times of the day. During peak hours it increases to approx. five minutes. The 95 percentile of wait time is just above 14 minutes.

The authors take account also of the issues of empty rides and the generated additional mileage. Both might have a significant impact on the traffic in the city. In total 16% of the overall drive time will be spent driving without a passenger. Traffic induced by empty rides is expected to be less than 10%. This additional amount of traffic might have a negative impact on travel flow especially in the outskirts where the authors expect an empty ride share of up to 45%. This arises from the fact that average pickup distances are considerably higher in the outskirts. It amounts up to 5 km in less densely populated zones, whereas it is generally around 1 km in most city center areas.

These outcomes suggest that autonomous taxi services will be working most efficiently in densely populated city areas. In some sparsely populated areas, empty driving can make up for almost half of the share of trips. In these areas the congestion level is expected to have a negative influence in particular on the living quality. Therefore, the authors suggest a 'mobility hub operation model' for fleets of autonomous taxicabs. They propose a limited service area (Berlin S-Bahn circle) which will enable a fleet operator to provide high efficiency levels with scenarios where a single autonomous car can handle as much as 26,8 trips during the day at the average distance of almost 7 km. There would be four mobility hubs around the city center where car travelers would be required to change from their car to an autonomous taxicab to enter the service zone. The resulting service quality (i.e. waiting time) would be constant throughout the city center, however, above average at the mobility hubs (Bischoff, Maciejewski 2016).

Another interesting finding from the Berlin case is that the fleet size will need to grow proportionally to meet the additional demand from the possible shift from public transit towards autonomous taxi services. This is based upon the assumption that such autonomous services are likely to compete with public transit systems.

7.3 Analysis and Limitations

The author of this dissertation is chiefly interested in the strategies for radical efficiency shifts in automobility and the possible reduction potentials of the total number of vehicles that consume the space in urban areas. From this perspective the studies that are presented above show some very optimistic prospects for the future trajectory of automobility with autonomous vehicles and shared principles at its heart. However, these prospects hold true only for a system functioning under some conditions, modelling limitations and behavioral assumptions that should be understood and considered when drawing specific conclusions and implications for the future. These aspects pose important questions with regard to the excessive optimism and confidence regarding the benefits of autonomous vehicles and shared mobility concepts. The author will outline and discuss the conclusions and the main limitations in the following sections.

7.3.1 Quality of Service

The efficiency benefits of a mobility system based on autonomous vehicles, carsharing and ridesharing come at a certain price. In order to offer shared services the users of the system need to accept lower levels of the quality of service, i.e. waiting time and the maximum delay that a customer tolerates in a shared service trip. It is mainly due to the fact that shared mobility options need to allow for accepting:

(1) Start time window:

- carsharing: an autonomous vehicle needs to reach the location to pick up a customer that required a trip,
- ridesharing: an autonomous vehicle waiting a fixed amount of time for additional passengers to join the ride that aim at the same or similar destination.

(2) Longer travel time:

- this specifically refers to the ridesharing option where an autonomous vehicle makes a detour to collect additional co-passengers,
- such detours add up to the trip time.

The findings from the simulations indicate that there are trade-offs between fleet sizing and the quality of service (Spieser et al. 2014; Rigole 2014; International Transport Forum 2015). This means that increasing the number of vehicles can bring about higher quality of service for travelers. On the contrary, the acceptance of extra waiting or travel time can yield additional benefits with regard to the further reduction of the required fleet size.

7.3.2 *Average Vehicle Occupancy*

Shared autonomous vehicles in the basic scenario, i.e. without ridesharing, aim at eliminating the inefficiencies of car usage but do not address the efficiencies associated with the unused space in the cars. This type of scenario raises the frequency of the usage of single vehicles. There is no impact on the occupancy rate. However, in simulation scenarios where ridesharing is implemented the occupancy rate is obviously affected, as this is the main rationale behind this mobility concept.

The ridesharing scenarios indicate that the occupancy rates increase along with the acceptance of longer waiting and travel times. This makes sense as relaxing the travel time constraints increases the chance that another passenger will join the trip. Furthermore, simulations conducted for Lisbon by International Transport Forum (2015) reveal that peaks in mobility demand in the morning and early evening enhance the ability to form larger ridesharing pools. The Lisbon case also shows that popular geographic areas produce satisfactory average occupancy even in periods of low average demand, such as late evenings. This would suggest that the potential for higher occupancy rates increases during peak hours and in locations such as railway stations (International Transport Forum 2015).

Additionally, accepting higher occupancy rates can lead to further reduction of the required fleet size. Santi et al. (2014) investigated the current taxi demand on Manhattan and came to the conclusion that if 80% of the today's taxi trips on Manhattan were shared (only by two passengers), the entire size of the current taxi fleet of 13'000 could be shrunk by 40%, without introducing autonomous cars. This indicates how a collective benefit can be achieved if individuals accept a certain discomfort (sharing the ride and a slightly longer travel time).

7.3.3 *Implications on Total Distance and Empty-Vehicle-Performance*

One of the possible drawbacks of the discussed mobility concepts based on SAVs is the possible increase in distance driven (often referred to as Vehicle Miles Traveled, or VMT) by the SAV as opposed to total distances driven today. It is a valid critique point as the increased mileage can cause rebound-effects with regard to the total energy consumption of mobility and to the increase in environmental impacts (Rigole 2014).

Also in this case, there is a difference resulting from the specific configuration of the mobility system, i.e. with or without ridesharing. An autonomous system considering only carsharing as the underlying mobility concept will probably indicate additional VMT. This is due to the fact that such a mobility system needs to meet the entire demand that is being covered today by privately owned cars. Additionally, it needs to allow for the relocation of SAVs between the customers. Hence, it will inevitably lead to empty-vehicle-trips and, hence, to more traffic. For example, Fagnant, Kockelman (2014) show for their model city that while the number of car decreases to the level of 10% of the number of private cars, the VMT increases by 11%. Several scenarios for Stockholm imply that a SAV fleet without sufficient ridesharing might increase congestions even up to 71,6% (Rigole 2014).

Allowing for ridesharing could address this important issue, but without certainty. For example, Rigole (2014) concludes that in his mileage minimizing scenario for Stockholm (assuming 10 minuntes waiting time and 30% increase in travel time) the VMT can be reduced by 11%. On the contrary, cases of Lisbon and Austin suggest that even ridesharing will not prevent increase in VMT. In Lisbon for example the best case scenario with ridesharing results in + 6% more car-kilometers travelled than today (International Transport Forum 2015). Whereas, the moderate ridesharing scenario for Austin (with a max. increase of 30% in travel time) leads to + 2,67% increase in total VMT (Fagnant, Kockelman 2015b). In conclusion, ridesharing might offer a reduction in total mileage traveled by vehicles but at the cost of a significant decrease in quality of service for the users, i.e. increased waiting and travel time.

Another important aspect is the latent demand for mobility services. It might be the case that the implementation of a new highly convenient mobility mode could actually generate additional demand for travel. Given these competing forces, it remains still unclear what the effect of SAV-based mobility systems will be on congestion levels in cities (Spieser et al. 2014).

7.3.4 Reduction in Parking Infrastructure

Shared vehicle fleets are expected to free up significant amounts of space in a city. In all studies, self-driving fleets would contribute to the significant elimination of the need for on-street and off-street parking. Rigole (2014) highlights the implications for a reduction of the necessary parking lots for Stockholm by claiming that the required on-street parking space could be reduced by the rate the fleet size is reduced. For example, if the amount of cars can be reduced by the factor of 10, then similarly parking requirements could be throttled by the same factor. This approach makes sense for two reasons: (i) only the remaining cars would require parking lots and (ii) the cars would be utilized much more frequently without the need to search for parking in between the trips. Only in idle phases or if recharging (or refueling) was required would the vehicles be relocated to the dedicated off-street hubs. The case study of Lisbon suggests that the on-street parking could be eliminated completely and the off-street parking by 80% (International Transport Forum 2015). In Lisbon it would be an equivalent of 210 football fields or approximately 20% of the kerb-to-kerb street space. This released space could be regained and transferred for alternative purposes. For example it could be allocated for recreational usage, delivery bays, bicycle tracks, enhanced public transport or enlarged footpaths, facilities which are difficult to accommodate in today's city road network (Rigole 2014; International Transport Forum 2015).

7.3.5 Environmental Impacts with regard to GHG Emissions and Energy Use

Given the possible negative implications regarding the total VMT of such an automated mobility system it is essential to consider the rebound effects with regard to the energy consumption and the greenhouse gas (GHG) emissions. For example, Rigole (2014) takes the calculated total mileage as a basis and compares the resulting GWP100 (in ton CO_2-eq)[8] and the energy consumption (in GWh) for every simulated scenario. The basic assumption is that the vehicle fleet consists of a mix of diesel and gasoline cars. The best case scenario with the lowest total distance (i.e. with significant portion of rides-haring) indicates that the GWP100 and the energy consumption can be reduced to 76% of the baseline level. For example, in the current situation the total energy use is 1,5 GWh and the emission amounts to 650 tons CO_2-eq per operative day. With the new automated mobility system the respective values are 1,18 GWh and 494 tons CO_2-eq. On the contrary, in less optimistic scenarios where the new mobility system generates greater VMT both environmental parameters increase up to 172% of the baseline levels.

More detailed examination of the environmental implications is delivered by Fagnant, Kockelman (2014). The impacts are estimated based on not only vehicle operation (VMT-based) but also on vehicle production (embodied energy), vehicle parking infrastructure (via parking space maintenance), and trip-start emissions as all of these categories would be influenced by changes of the fleet. Not only is GHG calculated but also other pollutants are included: sulfur dioxide (SO_2), carbon monoxide (CO), oxides of nitrogen (NOx), volatile organic compounds (VOC), and particulate matter (PM_{10}). The results suggest reductions for all emissions species when shifting to the automated mobility system; however, only under the condition that the mobility demand remains the same as today. The most significant reductions are expected with regard to VOC and CO emissions, whereas GHG and PM_{10} show rather negligible potential due to resultant empty driving.

Another interesting consideration is that the total production rates for new autonomous vehicles might remain about the same as today because SAVs will be utilized much more frequently than conventional cars. Hence, it might result in a much greater turnover rate of the fleet (1,5-2 years) leading to much faster introduction of much more environmentally friendly technology. Such considerations suggest considerable potential for further energy and environmental savings (Fagnant, Kockelman 2015b).

---

[8] Global warming potential over 100 years.

However, from the environmental perspective an interesting outlook is the implementation of autonomous electric vehicles (EV). Already today it is being suggested that sharing concepts for mobility could have an accelerating impact on the adoption and diffusion of EV on the market. Therefore, it seems self-evident to assume that the fleet of SAV will be completely electrified in the long run. With that in mind, Rigole (2014) conducted an analysis for a SAV fleet consisting completely of EVs powered by Swedish electricity mix, which is characterized by relatively low emissions, i.e. 56g CO_2-eq/kWh. The assumed lifetimes are 150'000, 200'000 and 400'000 km. The evaluated GWP100 reduction potentials range between 14-65% of the baseline case where most of the privately owned vehicles are powered by fossil fuel. Again, the differences are dependent, on the scenario configuration and the assumed lifetime of the EVs. The longer the lifetime of the vehicles is, the lower the total environmental impacts of the mobility system are. However, it needs to be noted that the introduction of EV technology is associated with some fundamental obstacles: consideration of much shorter ranges, implementation of a network of chargers, management of charging times, skepticism among users (Rigole 2014).

In conclusion, based on the analyzed publications and simulations, it seems that the congestion and environmental issues can be addressed by a mobility system based on autonomous vehicles; however, the reduction potential in this field is rather moderate. The beneficial impact will likely depend on the configuration of the system, i.e. underlying mobility concepts and implemented vehicle technology. On the other hand, an easy accessible, convenient and cheaper individual door-to-door transport service could generate increases in the total mobility demand posing the risk of the occurrence of environmental rebound effects (Chakravarty et al. 2013). Therefore, further research will be required to analyze whether an automated mobility system could address and circumvent these barriers.

7.3.6 Costs of the System

Implementing groundbreaking innovations such as autonomous vehicles and introducing disruptive amendments in the underlying mobility concepts have a potential for opening up a new system trajectory and establishing a novel techno-economic paradigm for urban mobility. The prospect of such a radical and disruptive shift within the mobility domain, which is an important functional system from the societal and economic perspectives, will inevitably raise also fundamental questions regarding the costs of the possible transition. This is a valid aspect which needs to be addressed along with the other essential challenges which are being discussed here. The investigated literature includes several attempts to quantify the costs of a mobility system based on autonomous vehicles. All in all, three different cost perspectives have been identified.

Costs of implementing the system

The only rough estimate of the costs of implementing such a mobility system which takes advantage of autonomous vehicles is that provided by Kornhauser (2011). It needs to be stated, however, that the estimates do not refer to a fully flexible mobility system of SAV as proposed and discussed here. Kornhauser (2011) designed an area-wide Personal Rapid Transportation (PRT) network capable of providing high- quality, non-stop, and demand-responsive mobility services to the entire state of New Jersey. Such a PRT-based mobility service would require establishing a completely new infrastructure, as opposed to a flexible SAV-based mobility system which aims at taking full advantage of already existing infrastructures. The proposed system would encompass 10'000 stations, interconnected by 10'000 miles of guideways, and used by 750'000 driverless PRT-vehicles. The implementation costs were estimated to be of the order of 150 billion dollars and the operating costs less than the marginal operating cost of today's car. However, it was later admitted by the author that the demand data used for the calculations was insufficiently precise which made the simulation inaccurate and hence not reliable. Therefore, these estimates were rejected (Kornhauser 2013).

Costs for the system operator and mobility provider

Another more viable approach has been recently proposed by Fagnant, Kockelman (2015b). The provision of mobility services by means of SAVs could be outsourced to a private system operator. Such an external party would implement a business model of a service provider. In such an approach the risks and costs associated with implementing, operating and maintaining the system would lie with the operator. Fagnant, Kockelman (2015b) proposed a financial calculation framework for a hypothetical operator and mobility service provider based on the data from Austin, Texas. According to these authors the goal of such a system operator will be the optimization of the size of the fleet in order to maximize profits, while providing a relatively high level of service to the users. For that simulation the authors deploy the concept of return on investment (ROI). The investigation demonstrates that mobility concepts based on SAVs have the potential to be a quite profitable business: assuming purchase prices at 70'000 USD per autonomous vehicle, operating costs at 0,50 USD/mile, travel fares at 1 USD per trip-mile, no competition, and stable demand, the simulated ROI for a new mobility provider in case of Austin could amount to 19%.

However, the authors disregard some other important aspects. For example, Spieser et al. (2014) points out that high utilization rates and the shared nature of the proposed mobility system will require significant maintenance and cleaning budgets to uphold high levels of customer safety and satisfaction. This will obviously significantly contribute to costs of maintaining the system. Also further aspects such as insurances, parking establishments, service stations or charging stations for EVs will substantially influence the cost structure. This will need to be included into more detailed financial calculations and forecasts. This poses of course the question of the influence of these costs on the final service price. Hence, the assumption of 1 USD per trip-mile might be greatly underestimated.

Costs for users

As of today, the costs of private car ownership are limited to the financial investment in the purchase and the operation costs (expenditures in service, parking, insurance, and fuel). Spieser et al. (2014) note that beside the financial costs, the value of time, attributed to the time invested in various mobility-related activities, also needs to be quantified. Since automated mobility systems can induce time savings and enable alternative usage of time during the trip (c.f. chapter on new business models for autonomous cars) it is completely reasonable to include the value of time into the calculation. In order to explore and measure the hidden costs of mobility the notion of total mobility costs (TMC) has been developed. It encompasses (Spieser et al. 2014):

- costs of service (COS), the sum of all explicit costs associated with accessing mobility, i.e. retrofitting the vehicles with sensors, actuators, and computational power required for automated driving, and
- the value of time (VOT), the monetary valuation of the total time invested in mobility related activities, i.e. time for requesting, waiting, entering, traveling, and exiting the vehicle.

For quantifying the value of time Spieser et al. (2014) deploy the notion of the value of travel time savings (VTTS) which is expressed as a fraction of the median income. According to the calculations conducted for Singapore total mobility costs for a SAV-based mobility system would amount to 0,92 USD/km as compared to 1,72 USD/km in the system of privately owned cars. Spieser et al. (2014) conclude that the savings stem largely from the ability to split the hefty cost of car ownership and to eliminate parking activities.

To sum up, from the economic perspective the mobility solution discussed here shows potentials for financial sustainability. It would effectively eliminate the costs for a driver, substantially cut the cost for parking lots, and release users from many time consuming and costly activities such as driving the car, dealing with insurance and legal requirements, conducting frequent car services or paying traffic tickets. Eventually, the investment in obtaining a driving license could be also eliminated completely. Accepting the ridesharing option would further distribute the costs among the users leading to lower mobility fares. Finally, the costs and the risks for maintaining the mobility system would be passed on to the institution or company that operates the fleet and provides the mobility services. This could potentially lead to the realization of beneficial economies of scale.

7.3.7 Further limitations

Many other barriers remain for implementing such a mobility system. They include (Fagnant, Kockelman 2014):

- technological barriers: fully automated vehicles, able to operate in all urban environments safely and without backup drivers, are not yet on the road,
- regulatory barriers: complex questions remain relating to legal, liability, privacy, licensing, security, and insurance regulation,
- costs: affordability is a key issue.

It may also not be completely correct to consider that the main reason that consumer values personal mobility is because of its ability to get them to a specific destination, i.e. from A to B. There may be other reasons that could impede users from choosing SAV. These motives could be (Kornhauser 2013): the glamour of a car, the privacy of a car, the convenience of a car, or the car as a status symbol. The SAV mobility system along with effective policies could potentially address these issues and effectively attract a significant number of commuters.

7.4 Next Steps for Further Research

The discussion of the strategies for the radical increase in the efficiency of cars has identified three main concepts, which will now be elaborated: carsharing, ridesharing and SAV. During this first part of the dissertation the following questions arose (see also Table 9):

- What are the technological platforms that enable shared automobility services? The main field of interest: digital technologies.
- What are the organizational and managerial concepts that make it possible to offer these shared automobility services to the users? The main field of interest: business models.
- How do these models look like? How are they different to traditional approaches? What are the possible business model innovations? The main field of interest: digital business model innovation.

In Part II the author will draw his attention to developing the required body of knowledge about the possible implementation and diffusion of these innovative mobility concepts. Therefore, the goal of the further research is to explore the arena of technology-enabled business models. In particular, the research interests lie in generating the possible prototypes of digital business models for mobility services and showing how they can contribute to the factor 10 scenario proposed in this thesis.

Table 9: Summary of findings and further research areas.

Mobility Concepts	**Carsharing**	**Ridesharing**	**Shared Autonomous Vehicles**
Possible Strategies	Increase the frequency of car usage (more car trips)	Increase the intensity of car seat usage (more car journeys)	Increase both: the frequency of car usage and the occupancy rate
Technology Availability	What are the technological platforms for shared automobility services? Main interest: Digital Technologies.		
Business Models	How do the current organizational and management models for carsharing look?	How do the current organizational and management models for ridesharing look?	How do the future organizational and management models for managing fleets of SAV look?

PART II
Digital Technologies and Business Model Innovations for Urban Mobility

8 Part II: Introduction

8.1 Objectives

Cities have long been at the forefront of sustainable, multimodal mobility due to the transportation demands placed on a city by a large, densely located population. There is a considerable movement towards a more advanced and intelligent approach to urban mobility. Cities are moving toward a model of on-demand mobility in which citizens can take advantage of clean transportation options that meet their immediate needs, increase accessibility and contribute to much higher quality of life in urban areas.

Recent socio-economic trends such as the growing internationalization and pluralization of governance or individualized lifestyle patterns are leading to remarkable consequences in the field of transportation and mobility. Travel patterns are becoming much more complex, individualized and flexible. Also a few key technology developments over the last decade underpin this movement. Chiefly the fast rise of the availability of mobile digital devices (such as smartphones), their omnipresent connectivity to the Internet, the rise of plug-in electric vehicles (PEVs) and the ability to connect vehicles, infrastructure, transportation managers, and end-users have led to the emergence of new and more flexible forms of mobility supply and demand. These technological innovations extend not only the possibilities of transport planning (transparent information availability) but they enable additional travel mode alternatives and their flexible combination to get the highest value. These developments have started touching upon the surface of the private car usage especially in urban areas. The automobility system seems to be on the verge of transformation, even though many mobility rationalists claim that the future mobility system will still be based on automobiles. The author of this thesis is of the opinion that this transition can be as spectacular as it was in the case of the carriage and the automobile in the 19th century.

In that respect the author aims at fostering the understanding of the recent advancements in the arena of digital technologies and the value proposition of digital business models for new mobility concepts. His focus lies on strategies that could eliminate radical inefficiency in automobility.

Based on the Factor 10 scenario described in Part I further research questions have arisen that relate to the following aspects:

(1) What are the technological platforms that enable new mobility services? The main field of interest: 'Digital Technologies'.
(2) What are the organizational and managerial approaches that make it possible to offer shared automobility services to the users? The main field of interest: 'Business Models'.
(3) How do these models look? How are they different to traditional approaches? What are the possible business model innovations through digitization? The main field of interest: 'Digital Business Model Innovation'.

The author has recognized that in these three areas in particular there has been a substantial gap in academic research thus far. Current contributions chiefly represent the applied research stream and give fresh and new ideas. However, they are often characterized by limited academic rigor and methodological discipline. Therefore, the motivation of the researcher is to conduct a systematic desk research followed by a structured primary research approach. In doing that he aims at closing the identified gap in research and contributing to the overall academic body of knowledge in the mobility sector.

8.2 Research Design and Methodology in Part II

Centered on these important questions the author sets up an exploratory research design to gain familiarity with the phenomenon of digital technology and to develop the understanding of the recent developments in technology-enabled mobility innovations and associated business models. He aims at acquiring and synthetizing new insights into these areas and creating a comprehensive body of knowledge for interested academic peers and mobility experts. The research approach will be separated into two main phases: desk research and primary research. Figure 11 shows the overview of the research work flow.

Firstly, the author applies a systematic literature review. The aim of the literature review is to collect knowledge about mobility technologies and innovative mobility services as well as to build up a general understanding of latest advancements in the arena of digital technologies. Based on the examination of the literature the researcher develops knowledge clusters to systematize and present the results. These clusters encompass: mobility value chain, mobility innovations, state-of-the-art digital technologies, relevant actors in mobility, and business model archetypes.

Secondly, the author explores the notion of a business model. The aim is to develop a deeper understanding of this phenomenon and to establish a framework for analyzing business models of innovative mobility concepts which are based on digital technologies.

In the next step the researcher focuses on developing knowledge about the mobility area of shared automobility services by applying primary research approaches. Firstly, the researcher evaluates recently emerged digital business models in the area of carsharing and real-time ridesharing. For this purpose the researcher explores and analyzes two relevant case studies: *smexx* and *TwoGo by SAP*. The data for developing the case studies is acquired by means of a questionnaire which is derived from the underlying business model framework which has been proposed by the author during the desk research.

Finally, the author sets up an exploratory research approach to explore further innovations in the mobility sector which can have the capability to radically shift the paradigm in urban mobility. The additional focus lies on developing prototypes of business models for such innovative mobility services. For this purpose the author seeks to access subjective points of view, in order to generate new ideas for car usage in urban mobility. Hence, the author relies on formal data collection in the form of semi-structured in-depth interviews with experts from the mobility sector.[9]

According to this approach ten selected mobility entrepreneurs and visionaries from Switzerland and Germany were interviewed throughout 2014 and 2015.[10] The interviews were recorded and transcribed. The collection of all transcripts has been stored in a separate file in digital format.[11] Subsequently, the researcher conducted qualitative text analysis by means of QSR NVivo in 2015. NVivo is a software for qualitative analysis of field data. The tool was used to structure the field data and to develop prototypes of future mobility concepts and associated business models that are possible.

---

[9] The detailed approach is stored in Appendix 11 and can be accessed via OnlinePLUS.

[10] The list is of selected mobility entrepreneurs is stored in Appendix 7 and can be accessed via OnlinePLUS.

[11] Due to the length (464 pages) the collection of transcripts has been attached as a digital file and can be accessed via OnlinePLUS.

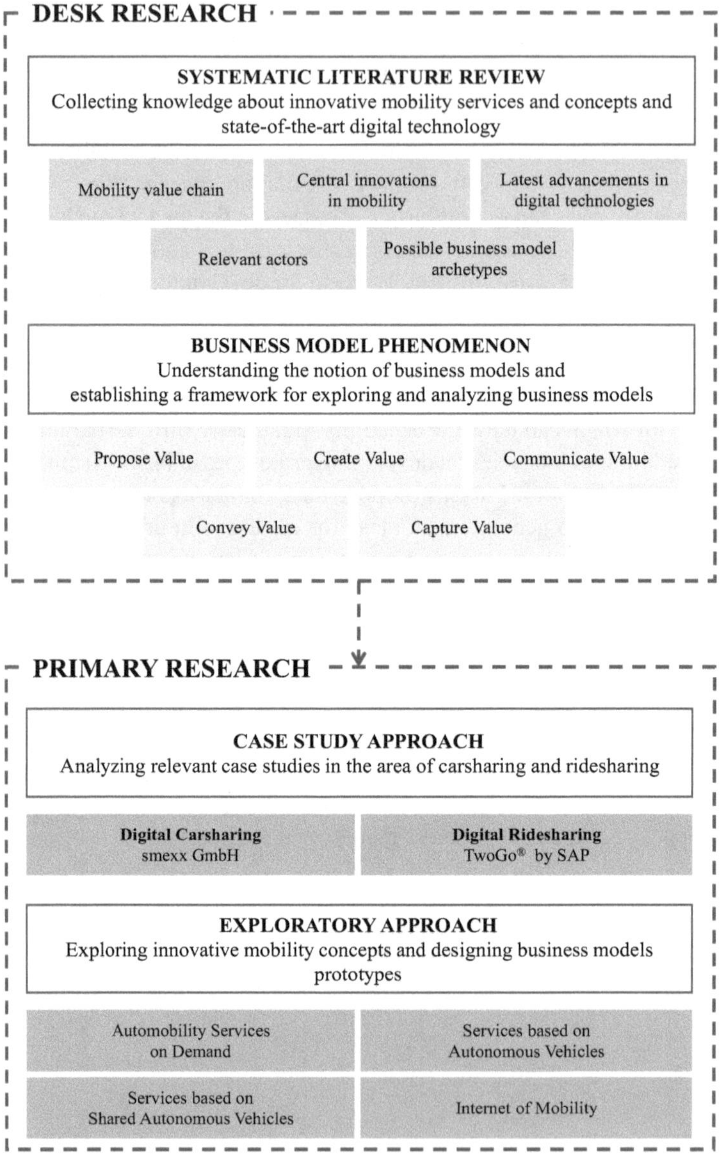

Figure 11: Research Workflow.
(Diagram by author).

9 Literature Review

9.1 Literature Review Strategy

9.1.1 Areas of Interest

The transformation towards a sustainable mobility system which on the one hand provides good alternatives to energy-inefficient but highly individual cars and on the other hand offers an environment-friendly and flexible transportation modes for people, represents a major challenge for cities nowadays. This challenge requires from the city authorities advanced capabilities to balance the expectations from involved parties. An even greater challenge, however, is posed by the incorporation of rural agglomeration regions where mobility strategies are chiefly based on automobility (see chapter 22.2).

Advancements and innovation in technology have been considered to be key success factors in meeting the challenges of urban passenger transport. Especially with regards to decreasing the environmental impact, the focus of previous research has been mainly placed on alternative drive technologies, including improved technologies for fuel efficiency of internal combustion engines, alternative fuels, and propulsion systems (Spickermann et al. 2014). Currently, several further technological innovations are presented and discussed, which might have a considerable potential to radically redesign the system of the urban mobility. These innovations include:

(1) Digital technology: highly innovative networking technologies, information retrieval systems, or new access and billing systems are increasingly affecting mobility patterns and schemes such as car- and bike-sharing. In this regard, the technologies for system scalability (Cloud Computing), processing high data flows (Big Data management) and the issue of data security are critical.
(2) Advanced car technology: by a progressive combination of laser, radar and camera sensors the dream of fully automated car usage is coming closer to reality. Although this solution may lie in the distant future, this innovation in combination with other advancements could lead to a radical transformation of the urban mobility structures as the society knows them today.
(3) New usage and ownership paradigms: through information and communication technology and advanced car technology the mobility concepts of the future can become more diverse, multimodal and individual. Based on the omnipresence of the Internet and the high maturity of digital technologies, carsharing and car-pooling schemes are becoming widely accepted. If they get adopted area-wide this new usage paradigm can considerably change the cityscapes.

So far these innovations have been somehow neglected in favor of the exploration of the alternative propulsion systems. Only on the edge of the mobility research can one observe indications that these technological innovations bear a potential for a system change. Currently, these advances are being slowly recognized and further explored. Most of all their transformation impact on the existing mobility system via completely new mobility concepts is of high importance. They seem to be technologically viable and economically feasible for mass-implementation. However, it seems that a comprehensive view and understanding of these enabling technologies and the resulting digital business models are still somehow missing. Therefore, the goal of the researcher is to explore these new arena of technology-enabled business models.

9.1.2 Research Domains and Limitations

Research domains that are relevant for the present design of the literature review comprise digital technologies (e.g.: information and communication technology or internet technology), new mobility concepts (e.g.: innovative carsharing), and technology-enabled business approaches focusing on the marketability and scalability of these mobility concepts in urban areas (e.g. platform businesses). Secondary importance will be given to the impact of these technologies on industry structures. Finally, the arena of sustainable mobility research will be included as well. Therefore, the substantive literature analysis shall focus on digital technologies that enable advanced forms of mobility concepts. Therefore, the literature review is carried out based on two questions:

- Whether there are fields of academic or non-academic research that address digital technologies (such as advanced information and data processing technologies) and new mobility concepts or services?
- Whether there are fields of academic or non-academic research that address innovations in business models and new mobility concepts or services?

The review aims at systemizing the present research and revealing concrete digital technologies and technology-enabled business models. It is not the intention of this research to consider technologies for alternative propulsion systems for fostering the energy efficiency such as: electromobility, hydrogen fuel cell or photovoltaic. Since the main research goal of the author is a substantial reduction of inefficiencies in car usage in urban conurbations, the literature review will be limited to mobility concepts such as carsharing, ridesharing or multimodality in cities. Furthermore, the review will also focus on the notion of sustainable urban mobility.

9.1.3 Strategy for the Literature Review

The strategy of the literature review will be twofold:

(1) The author applies the method of a database search by keywords.
(1) The author includes also the literature review conducted by Spickermann et al. (2014) as they provide a comprehensive selection of relevant academic and applied research on future-oriented urban mobility publications that have recently emerged in this field. This approach will be further explained in section 9.1.3.2.

The results will be shortlisted and further revised by means of developing synthesis matrices to evaluate the research that has already been undertaken. Therefore, the articles will be analyzed with regard to their contextual setting and the general coverage of the topics under investigation, i.e. digital technologies and business model innovations. Based on that the researcher will:

- draw out the key points and trends,
- present them in a logical way and
- show the relationship to his own research.

This literature review provides the readers of this work with the necessary background knowledge and establishes the boundaries to the research question.

9.1.3.1 Literature Review via a Database

Initially, the researcher decided to limit the literature review only to peer-reviewed journal publications, using the Scopus database which is the largest abstract and citation database of peer-reviewed literature. The database encompasses scientific journals, books and conference proceedings. Scopus is owned by Elsevier B.V., a Dutch academic publishing company that publishes scientific literature and it covers journal titles from over 5'000 publishers, of which 21'000 are peer-reviewed journals (Elsevier 2015).

Not very surprisingly the initial general queries in Scopus in Keywords such as (KEY(technology and "sustainable mobility")) or (KEY(technology and "urban mobility")) have shown that research on innovative technologies and sustainable urban mobility is dominated by disciplinary perspectives on technological, social and economic issues relevant for the diffusion and adoption of electric vehicles. The author considered it as an indicator, albeit a weak one, that the current research in the field of sustainable mobility may focus on energy efficiency of the car. As this is not the purpose of this dissertation the author decided to conduct a systematic literature review which would address his main fields of interest.

The literature review of peer-reviewed journal paper was therefore extended by a search in a database which is strictly dedicated to transportation research - the Transportation Research Integrated Database (TRID).

TRID is the world's largest and most comprehensive bibliographic resource on transportation research information. The TRID Database contains more than one million records of references to books, technical reports, conference proceedings, and journal articles in the field of transportation research. It is produced and maintained by the Transportation Research Board (TRB) of the US National Academies with the sponsorship by State Departments of Transportation, the various administrations at the U.S. Department of Transportation (Transportation Research Board 2015).

The literatures is searched by a purposeful combination of key topical terms on technologies (e.g. digital technology, Internet technology), business models (e.g. business strategy, business model) and mobility (e.g. mobility concept, carsharing). The author applies two methods of a database search:

- by 'Titles, Abstracts and Keywords', which should deliver a broad perspective on the general topic in question,
- by 'Keywords', which should narrow down the perspective to specific topics of interest.

Hence, a search query by 'Titles, Abstracts and Keywords' is applied to the area of mobility concepts and sustainable mobility. An additional search query which will be limited only to 'Keywords' relates either to the area of digital technologies or business models. This strict limitation makes sense since only contributions are to be considered that are very relevant to the topics under investigation. To be as broad as possible a Boolean operator "OR" is used between the terms that have been defined for the searches, which should deliver documents that contain any of the search terms.

Figure 12 depicts the design and the strategy for the literature review and gives the list of search terms that have been used.

Altogether, four queries have been conducted:

(1) Sustainable Mobility and Digital Technologies via SCOPUS.
(2) Sustainable Mobility and Digital Technologies via TRID.
(3) Sustainable Mobility and Business Models via SCOPUS.
(4) Sustainable Mobility and Business Modes via TRID.

The literature review has been executed in August 2015. The detailed queries and the results are summarized in Table 10.

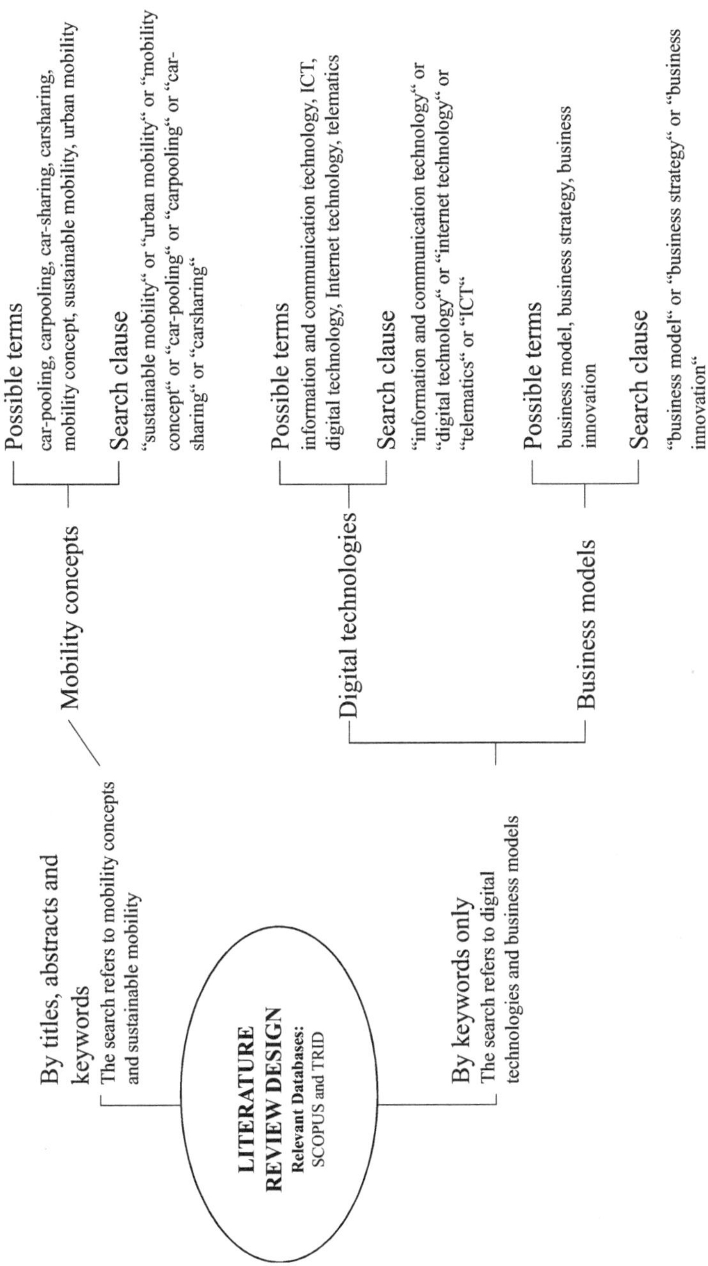

Figure 12: The Design of the literature review on urban mobility, digital technologies and business models (Diagram by author).

Table 10: Definition of the queries for the literature review and their initial results.

Topic of the Query	Source of Knowledge	Query	Initial Re-sults	Highly rel-evant
Digital Technolo-gies	SCOPUS	(KEY("information and communication technology" or "digital technology" or "inter-net technology" or "telematics" or "ICT") AND TITLE-ABS-KEY("sustainable mobil-ity" or "urban mobility" or "mobility con-cept" or "car-pooling" or "carpooling" or "carsharing" or "carsharing"))	28	26 highly rele-vant and available
	TRID	("information and communication technol-ogy" or "digital technology" or "internet technology" or "telematics" or "ICT") AND ("sustainable mobility" or "urban mobility" or "mobility concept" or "car-pooling" or "carpooling" or "carsharing" or "carsharing")	37	
Business Models	SCOPUS	(KEY("business model" or "business innova-tion" or "business strategy") AND TITLE-ABS-KEY("sustainable mobility" or "urban mobility" or "mobility concept" or "car-pool-ing" or "carpooling" or "carsharing" or "car-sharing"))	20	18 highly rele-vant and available
	TRID	("business model" or "business innovation" or "business strategy") AND ("sustainable mobility" or "urban mobility" or "mobility concept" or "car-pooling" or "carpooling" or "carsharing" or "carsharing")	11	
TOTAL			**96**	**44**

The four search queries delivered 106 potential documents with possible relevance for the research. In the next step the researcher refined the results by manually analyzing the titles, keywords, specific publication domain and abstracts. Ten positions turned out to be duplicates and were excluded. Then the researcher evaluated the articles and publications by rating them on the following scale: 'high relevance', 'limited relevance', and 'low relevance'. This step excluded 15 articles that are either not relevant at all or have no direct relation to the research fields. Of the remaining papers 57 have been judged highly relevant and 15 only limited relevance. Due to resource constraints the researcher decided to focus only on highly relevant publications for the further examination. Finally, in 13 cases the author had no access to the full-text documents and hence has ignored them as well.

The remaining 44 articles are regarded to be highly relevant for the research field; 25 are related to the topic of 'Sustainable Mobility and Digital Technology' and 19 to the topic of 'Sustainable Mobility and Business Innovation'. They have been included into the literature review.

9.1.3.2 Literature Review on Future-Oriented Urban Mobility

For the sake of completeness the author has also included parts of the literature review of future-oriented urban mobility research conducted by Spickermann et al. (2014) in their article "Heading towards a multimodal city of the future?". The authors of this article have reviewed various forms of 'foresight approaches' with respect to the future of urban mobility. They have provided a comprehensive selection of academic and applied research on future-oriented urban mobility publications that have recently emerged in that field. The key benefits of including the literature by Spickermann et al. has been twofold:

(1) It has extended the review to non-academic reports from agencies and governmental institutions.
(2) The authors have categorized the literature by different research scopes, such as: technology and new business models.

Spickermann et al. have derived these focal clusters for 'research scope' by applying multidimensional scaling (MDS). Following their classification the researcher has included only those positions from their literature review which have related directly to the research scope 'technology' and 'new business models'. He intentionally has excluded literature which covers other topics such as: customer preferences, cross-sector synergies, regulations, incentives or structural changes. In order to focus on most recent findings publications before 2010 have been excluded.

Both academic and non-academic positions have been considered. The reason for including non-academic research is logical. Recently, also governmental institutions, automotive industry and consulting agencies have been increasingly attracted to investigate the arena of urban mobility. On the one hand they explore new possible urban mobility patterns for citizens in the near future to overcome emerging challenges like increasing urbanization. On the other hand they inspect innovative business models that emerge due to the rapid digitization of societies. Based on that, they derive innovative business strategies for incumbent industries (e.g. automotive). The authors argue that these applied perspectives will reveal some interesting advancements at the frontier of digital technologies and technology-enabled business model innovations.

Therefore, after excluding duplicates which have been already found in the previous Scopus and TRID database inquiry 10 additional papers have been incorporated into the relevant list of papers that have been reviewed.

9.2 Initial Literature Discussion

The initial results of the literature review have indicated that research at the frontier of innovative mobility concepts for sustainable mobility and digital technologies is still rather limited and therefore provides a wide range of opportunities for scholars and business practitioners to undertake further research studies. The review has unveiled that most of all the arena of innovative business models for mobility services in the context of digital technologies is in an emergent stage and the relevant discussions in the most recent academic and non-academic literature has just started. Admittedly, recent contributions have recognized and investigated the value of advanced information and communication technologies (ICT) and to some extent also referred to their possible applications for the transportation system. However, they tend to focus on efficiency improvements of existing elements of the mobility system and not on possible system innovations. For example one of the most researched topics is the contribution of ICT to the further development of intelligent transportation systems (ITS). ITS aims at optimizing the usage of existing infrastructure and not at changing the prevailing mobility paradigm. Moreover, the ICT is often described as kind of a 'black box', with no reference to the deeper comprehension of underlying technologies and structures. Only some authors offer deep-dives into the single technologies. The reviewed literature also fails to deliver a common understanding of what exactly digital technologies are, how they are categorized and in what way they contribute to the development of innovative mobility concepts and services in the urban context.

With regards to the area of particular business models for mobility concepts and possible business model innovations in this field there have been only few papers that have explicitly addressed these topics. Admittedly, these contributions chiefly represent the applied research stream. In this way fresh and innovative business ideas for the mobility sector can be identified. However, they show limited academic rigor and methodological discipline. For that reason it can be claimed that there is a substantial gap in academic research within these areas.

Hence, in order to synthesize the knowledge about digital technologies, innovative mobility concepts and business models for future urban mobility a purposeful integration has been required. In the author's opinion this would contribute to the better understanding of the field of technology-enabled urban mobility concepts and support their dissemination and implementation throughout the society.

In the attempt to overcome the high level of fragmentation of the recent literature on this topic and to achieve a logical knowledge synthesis and integration the author proposes a holistic framework which is based on conceptual elements that have emerged from the literature analysis. In particular, the researcher conceives urban mobility as constituted by five main elements which are in mutual interaction:

- starting from the main pillar which is the value chain, i.e. the sequence of activities that create products or services which customers are willing to obtain and pay for,
- central mobility services and innovations,
- latest advancements in digital technologies and digital infrastructure that support the implementation and the functioning of innovative mobility services,
- relevant actors to be considered and involved and
- possible business models that describe the processes for value creation, value communication, value distribution and value capture.

Figure 13 depicts the summary of findings that have been obtained during the literature review. This is only a high-level summary of the conducted research. In the following sections each building block of the emerged body of knowledge is analyzed and discussed in-depth.

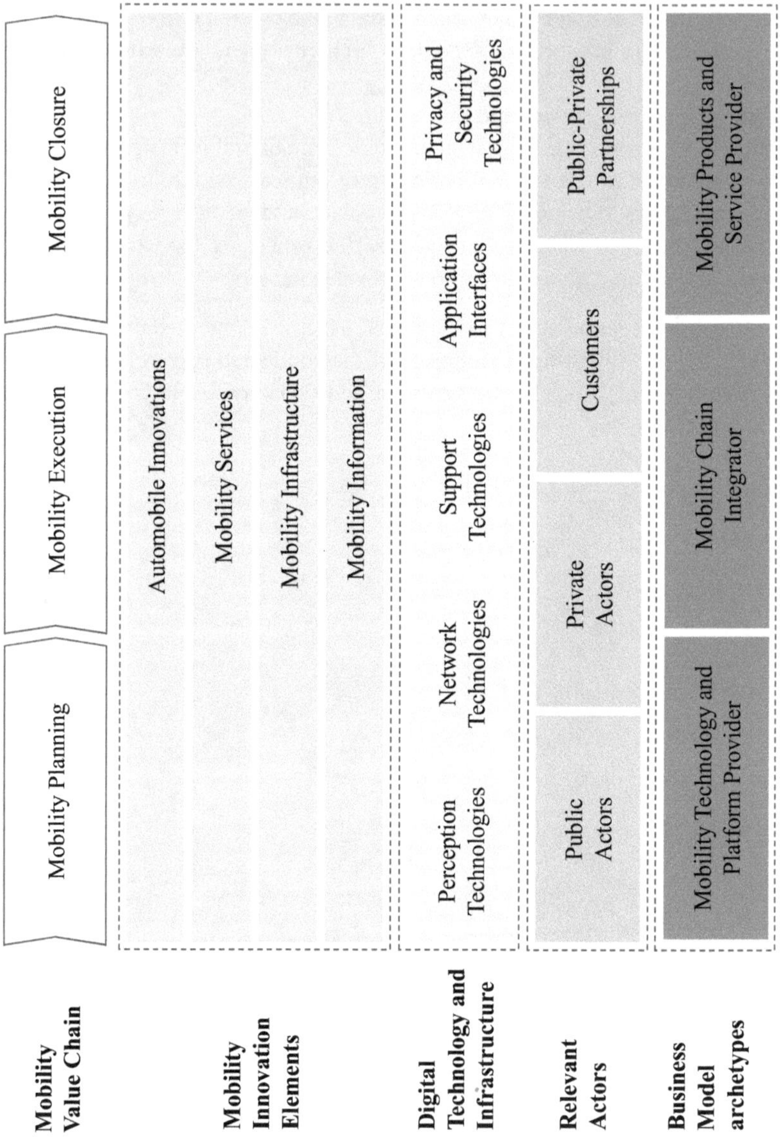

Figure 13: Body of Knowledge about the Innovation in Mobility. (Diagram by author).

10 Results of the Literature Review

10.1 Mobility Value Chain

To organize the key activities of companies providing mobility services the author will refer to the traditional definition of value chain model as described by Porter (1998). Porter's notion of value chain is a standard tool used in the academia and business. According to Porter the value chain is a tool of strategic planning applied to identify the competitive advantage of companies. It investigates the critical activities connecting the supply and demand side of organizations. The value adding activities can be organized internally and conducted within the firm or they can be provided by external partners. Moreover, the concept aims at developing an understanding of their impacts on value and cost of offered products or services (Porter 1998). The value chain concept by Porter also provides a definition of value and the understanding of how the value is created. According to that, the definition of value is simply the willingness to pay for a product or service which is offered via the value chain to the customer (Peppard, Rylander 2006).

Based on this definition of the value chain concept the researcher was seeking to understand the value chain for urban mobility services. However, in the reviewed literatures it has not been clearly defined what the end-to-end value chain for such services or products is and what it might look like. Some authors refer directly to the concept of value chain (Beutel et al. 2014; Franchi, Malpezzi 2013; van Audenhove et al. 2014). However, they describe it in many different ways or only some parts of it. Other authors describe some value chain activities but do not refer to the notion of value chain at all (Boehm et al. 2013).

In the first case it depends clearly on the field that the researchers are interested in. For example Beutel et al. (2014) use the notion of 'value chain' to define a specific activity configuration of a business model of an 'information broker' for heterogeneous mobility services on virtual markets. In this respect they only refer to one explicit domain required for providing mobility services, which is: gathering, organizing, selecting, synthesizing and distributing required information (Beutel et al. (2014). Authors state that important value-added activities such as: user registration, authentication, reservation, billing and clearing can be outsourced to an information broker which increases the effectiveness and efficiency of mediating between other activities in the mobility value chain. They conclude that new technological solutions can contribute to reshaping existing business models.

Another example is the characterization of the value chain for 'infomobility' by Franchi, Malpezzi (2013). Their value chain describes information management, availability and accessibility for mobility services and is represented by the flow of following processes: data collection, data elaboration, data integration and data usage. This information from and about these processes can be then applied for different application areas such as: fleet management, traffic management, mobility payments, and information services.

Also other authors describe what may be viewed as significant parts of the value chain of mobility services, even though they do not directly refer to them as such. For example, Boehm et al. (2013) precisely describe activities for smart, clean and efficient urban mobility and calls them 'emerging ICT services'. These services are then categorized into specific service bundles. The service bundles help to manage the complexity related to a large number of identified mobility services and to allow their detailed analysis. One of these service bundles is described 'multimodal mobility services'. Within this service package the following services are identified: multimodal pre-trip planning, multimodal on-trip services, social traffic, and incentive-based mobility services in the form of new mobility concepts.

Another example is the concept of 'extended mobility ecosystem' proposed by van Audenhove et al. (2014). Such an ecosystem consists of several important components which to some extent constitute important elements that are necessary for the process of creating and delivering urban mobility services. The proposed mobility ecosystem can be described as holistic because it exhaustively encompasses most of the parties involved in the urban mobility value chain:

- system integration providers: providing technology platforms, apps and terminals that enable overall system integration through standardized interfaces,
- connectivity providers: responsible for the network connectivity and secure data exchange via fixed line, mobile or near field communication,
- data provision providers: in charge for maps, real-time congestion info, time schedules, etc.
- end-user equipment providers: providing mobile handsets and smart cards or chips,
- integrated mobility platform operator: responsible for value adding services for urban mobility such as: planning, booking, payment and billing,
- mobility service operators: actually providing modes for transport such as motorized-individual, public individual, public, non-motorized or stationary,
- value added services providers: such as retail, culture, sport, food and beverages or tourism.

However, the author of the contribution at hand aims at developing a general comprehension of an end-to-end value chain for mobility services, which holistically describes the complexity of such a service. He seeks to develop a general structure of innovative urban mobility service with main activities that are involved in providing these services to the citizens of an urban area. Considering previously discussed findings regarding the mobility value chain, 'urban mobility service' can be described as a straightforward chain of the following value-adding activities:

(1) Activities for mobility planning, e.g.: planning and booking.
(2) Services for mobility delivery and consumption, e.g.: bus service, carsharing service or taxi service.
(3) Journey closure services, e.g.: payment, billing, evaluation.
(4) Services during the journey, e.g. real-time information about the journey such as delays or changes in the itinerary, parking search or other cultural and retail offers.

The ability to provide such an end-to-end mobility process to end-users requires several supportive components such as: network connectivity, end-user equipment and infrastructure, technology platform for system integration, platform for mobility service integration, mobility services and additional value-added services.

10.2 Mobility Innovation Elements

Recent research on technologies and innovations for the sector of transportation and mobility embraces several areas of application. For example Lerner et al. (2012b) summarize innovative applications according to the following categories: transport, infrastructure, traffic management, and information, planning and payment. European Commission proposes a similar classification of innovative technologies: vehicles, infrastructure, transport organization and information technology (Transport Research & Innovation Portal 2015). Research on new vehicle and infrastructure technologies targets sustainability, efficiency and safety, and covers all transport modes and new types of transport infrastructure. Transport organization includes several developments and advancements in the area of intelligent transportation systems (ITS). While information technologies include real-time mobile information, real-time tracking systems, and vehicle-to-vehicle communication.

In the study "The Future of Urban Mobility: Towards Networked, Multimodal Cities in 2050" (Lerner et al. 2012b) the authors identify 39 crucial and innovative technologies for urban mobility. This overview is seemingly one of the most comprehensive collections of currently available innovations for urban mobility services in the recent literature.

Detailed examination by the author of all contributions showed that while some concepts are repetitive and overlapping in general the research to date concentrates on four main topics (see Figure 14):

- Automobile Innovations,
- Mobility Services,
- Mobility Infrastructure,
- Mobility Information.

In the next step the author briefly elaborates on each innovation category and provides insights into the most interesting areas.

AUTOMOBILE INNOVATIONS

- Alternative Propulsion
- Keyless Access
- Car sensors and digitization of the car
- V2V, V2G, V2I Communication
- Autonomous Vehicles
- ...

MOBILITY SERVICES

- Traditional Urban Transportation Services
- Slow Mode Mobility Services
- Emerging Digital Urban Automobility Services
- Unconventional Urban Transportation Services
- Urban Freight and Logistics
- Electromobility Services
- ...

MOBILITY INFRASTRUCTURE

- Parking Infrastructure
- Traffic Infrastructure
- Tolling Infrastructure
- Railway Infrastructure
- Roadway Infrastructure
- ICT Infrastructure
- Electromobility Infrastructure
- ...

MOBILITY INFORMATION

- Multimodal Information Services
- Mobility Payments
- Fleet Management
- Traffic Management
- Safety and Security
- Information Cross Service
- ...

Figure 14: Areas of innovation in mobility.
(Diagram by author based on the literature review).

10.2.1 Automobile Innovation

Automobile technology encompasses several innovative developments. The most recent and prominent one is the exchange of the power train by alternative propulsion systems such as electromobility, hydrogen fuel cells or solar panels. Another innovation area is the ongoing semi-automation of cars. Several improvements are incorporated in commercially available vehicles (e.g. Tesla, Toyota Prius, Lexus RX-450h, Nissan Leaf). One example is the Intelligent Speed Adaptation (ISA) which dynamically informs the drivers about the current speed limit and has the capability to automatically limit the speed of the vehicle. Another one is the Intelligent Parking Assist System (IPAS) (van Audenhove et al. 2014).

However, the most radical innovations are associated with the increasing digitization of cars such as the digital car access and the technology of fully autonomous vehicles. The technology can be regarded as already available as many research programs, such as Google's Self-Driving Car Project (Google 2016) or Daimler's Mercedes-Benz F 015 Luxury in Motion (Daimler AG 2016), have been developing and testing it in the recent years, some also in everyday traffic situations. Furthermore, the concept of 'connected mobility' has also emerged in the research and the industry. It seeks to establish wireless links between cars and traffic infrastructure to exchange real-time data about the street, parking or weather conditions to compute appropriate trip routes and driving behavior for fleets of autonomous cars.

Digitization and Connectivity

By enabling vehicles to communicate with each other via vehicle-to-vehicle (V2V) or with roadside base stations via vehicle-to-infrastructure (V2I), digital technologies can contribute to safer and more efficient mobility (Dimitrakopoulos et al. 2012). Such communication technologies will allow a car braking abruptly to alert the vehicles behind it to automatically trigger their emergency brake. It will also support safe navigation, pollution control and traffic management. For such applications, however, connectivity is an essential factor. Cars will need to extend their features to become ICT platforms which absorb information from the environment and other objects and transmit their own data to the infrastructure. Gerla et al. (2014) label it the Intelligent Vehicle Grid. In order to support this development cars' internal networks need to be able to communicate (e.g. via CAN-bus) with external sources using communication standards such as: USB, Bluetooth, Wi-Fi or 3G/4G networks (Koscher et al. 2010).

This clearly indicates that car manufacturers are required to join forces with tech companies. A good example of such a vehicular grid is the recent alliance between Samsung, SAP and SEAT which aims at establishing new car based services around such communication and data exchange. The cooperation has resulted in developing a future concept for parking in urban areas. With this concept car drivers get access to a global parking inventory of connected on-street and off-street parking spots which can be reserved from any location through fingerprint recognition. The system then navigates the drivers to the specified location and automatically raises the access gate when the car approaches. When the driver exits the car garage, payment is made directly from the app without leaving the car. Such seamless integration can make urban parking simple for drivers and significantly reduce the search time and the associated traffic.

Fully Autonomous Vehicles

Advancements in autonomous or more precisely driverless cars, which operate using a combination of sensors, video cameras and artificial intelligence software, can bring about some radical innovations in this specific transport area. Autonomous car technology shows a tremendous development. It is expected that the technology will mature within the next decade (The Economist 2014). The hardware used, for example, in Google's self-driving cars includes LIDAR (Light Detection And Ranging), radars, cameras, and GPS sensors. The LIDAR data is combined with high resolution maps to create a detailed 3D and 360 degrees map of the environment (Thrun 2010). The system of sensors is provided with a tremendous amount of information, around 750 MB/s, which is far more than a human driver could ever acquire (Shankland 2013). The software is essential to robotic driving as it conducts tasks in six areas: sensor data preprocessing, localization, obstacle tracking, path planning, behaviors and control of the vehicle (Thrun 2010).

The advances in the arena of car digitization and automation are not only interesting in their own right. Most important they provide the necessary foundation for further and more innovative vehicle centric applications, which are already being pioneered, for example, by Google or Uber. It has been argued that the next step in this evolution is the Internet of Autonomous Vehicles, a network of Internet-connected autonomous vehicles (Gerla et al. 2014).

10.2.2 Mobility Services

The area of mobility services includes the vast and flourishing possibilities how to move people and goods throughout cities. It ranges from traditional privately and publicly organized collective urban transportation services, such as bus and rail services, car or van rental and taxi services; slow mode mobility concepts, such as bike-sharing schemes; emerging shared automobility services, such as carsharing and ridesharing; unconventional transportation systems, such as water services and personal rapid transportation; to urban freight logistics, electromobility services and virtual mobility services.

Alternative Pubic Transportation

The area of Alternative Pubic Transportation encompasses technologies developed for both individual and collective modes of transport. Lerner et al. (2012b) state that there are new radical technologies under development that can revolutionize travel in the cities of the future. For instance, solar-powered buses or trains would be self-contained from the perspective of energy provision and would eliminate the need to build new infrastructures. Another interesting example is the 'Green Wheels' project, which was developed by the MIT Mobile Experience Lab. Green Wheel is an innovative in-wheel regenerative electric motor that can be adapted to any sort of bicycle. This solution can be retrofitted to existing bikes (MIT Mobile Experience Lab, Smart Cities Group 2014).

Personal Rapid Transportation

Personal Rapid Transportation (PRT) is a relatively new and innovative mobility service. It is being implemented only in specific situations, such as: airports, business parks, university campuses or national parks. Such systems consist of pods which can carry up to six people and which move on fixed tracks or guideways. There exists a high potential to fully automate the PRT-systems to provide round-the-clock availability of such a system. Key partners for such systems are providers of network infrastructure and vehicles, system operators, and local governments. The cost side of such a transportation system consists of the establishment of an area-wide network infrastructure, provision with an adequate number of pods and operation costs (e.g. maintenance, electricity and labor). Revenue side of the service includes ticketing the passengers for mileage or journeys, charging for freight services and collecting subsidies from local governments for offering advanced public transportation services. Lerner et al. (2012b) state that PRT-services could have a highly positive impact on issues associated with current transportation system inefficiencies such as congestion and parking.

Emerging Shared Urban Automobility Services

Carsharing and carpooling have been recently introduced as relatively novel mobility concepts with regard to the car usage in urban areas, although the concept has been already known for almost 30 years. However, it is noteworthy that carsharing and carpooling has experienced an exceptional come-back in the recent years. It is thought that the high urbanization and the digital revolution of the society has favored the revitalization and flourishing of this mobility concept (Lerner et al. 2012b). In Chapter 12 (Typology of Digital Business Models for Emerging Shared Automobility Services) the author will explicitly focus on this field of innovation. In this respect, he will discuss the impact of the advances of digital technologies and the resulting business models.

10.2.3 Mobility Infrastructure

This innovation sector covers technological applications in several areas related to the mobility infrastructure. These infrastructures incorporate: parking, traffic, tolling, railway, roadway, ICT, and electromobility (Lerner et al. 2012b; Boehm et al. 2013; Abdelkafi et al. 2013). Within this mobility domain the following business models are existent or conceivable: operators of road and rail networks, parking space operators, charging station operators or ICT infrastructure providers (Lerner et al. 2012b).

Interesting and innovative mobility concepts in the domain of infrastructures are 'Automatic Parking Garage Providers', both for cars and bikes. Automatic Parking Garage is an innovative space-saving solution. Thereby, a vehicle or a bicycle is left on an automated lift which then moves it to the nearest parking lot in a multi-story structure. Some additional advantages of this solution are: very low in-garage accident rate, reduced carbon emissions, and greater convenience for drivers. This solution will be attractive to customers in dense urban areas where the parking space is very limited and the land is at premium. The operating and maintenance costs will be covered by parking fees and from additional possible revenue streams such as cleaning services or on-site advertising (Lerner et al. 2012b).

The arena of Mobility Infrastructure incorporates conventional technologies and structures such as roads, parking facilities and energy supply stations for individual transportation modes and rail tracks, stations, and energy supply centers for collective modes. For example, the existing infrastructure is being already adapted for electric vehicles with implementation of fast-charging stations but can be extended by hydrogen highways, chains of hydrogen-equipped filling stations along roads and motorways (Lerner et al. 2012b). However, there are also some radical technological developments that could lead to advancements in the infrastructure. Prominent examples are automatic robotic parking systems or solar-powered Wi-Fi bus stations and roads. The latter ones are being prototyped in the form of solar panels made of toughened glass which is strong enough to be installed instead of asphalt on the roads. The technology combines a transparent driving surface with underlying solar cells, electronics and sensors to act as a solar array with programmable capability (Solar Roadways 2015). Other innovative infrastructures are evacuated tubes, pipelines, Maglev and Personal Rapid Transit systems described above (Transport Research & Innovation Portal 2015).

10.2.4 Mobility Information

The area of innovative technologies that enable highly advanced information services for integrated modality in urban areas can be also referred to as 'infomobility'. A precise examination of infomobility is delivered by Franchi, Malpezzi (2013). They segregate them into four main categories which correspond with the information value chain, i.e.: information collection, information processing and integration, information transmission, and information usage. Data collection technologies are, in principle, monitoring systems, for example vehicle on-board-units such as controller area network (CAN-bus) and radio-frequency identification sensors (RFID). Data processing and integration technologies include data translation and homogenization software and databases. Data and information transmission technologies comprise network infrastructures, transfer supports and communication protocols. Usage technologies are portable devices such as notebooks, palms, mobile phones and smartphones, using technology standards such as GSM, WAP or GPS. Other relevant technologies that can support the information value chain are: weather sensors, facilities for measuring pollution levels, electronic payment systems and systems for vehicle control and assistance (Franchi, Malpezzi 2013). Intelligent integration of these technologies and ensuring the availability of required data can contribute to the establishment of integrated mobility platforms for advanced information applications based on information collection, transmission and usage. The relevant application fields encompass: Fleet Management, Traffic Management, Safety and Security, Multimodal Mobility Services, and Information Cross Services. The author will briefly elaborate on the most interesting developments.

Traffic Management

Technologies for Traffic Management include several advancements, chiefly in the area of intelligent transportation systems (ITS). Advanced Traffic Management Systems (ATMS), which are based on real-time traffic data from cameras and sensors, have the capabilities to efficiently reroute the traffic and message the road users through Dynamic Messaging Systems (DMS). Lerner et al. (2012b) propose some additional technologies for urban mobility such as: automated fare collection, real-time info panel, collaborative applications, or automatic and mobile payments.

Traffic Management includes services like: individual urban mobility management, road infrastructure management, modal transport integration, park and ride services, economic sanctions management, management of incidents data statistic, tolling services, cooperative traffic signal control, speed management, and dynamic and predictive parking services (Lerner et al. 2012b; Boehm et al. 2013; Franchi, Malpezzi 2013). One of possible business models in this area is 'Traffic Management Operator' which aims at more efficient use of the infrastructure, safer journeys and lower emissions (Lerner et al. 2012b). Traffic control depends on a network of detection and enforcement systems distributed throughout the city. This information is processed and transferred to traffic control centers. Traffic Management Operators need to rely on a number of key partners including: highway authorities, data providers, ICT operators, emergency services, vehicle recovery organizations, and enforcements agencies such as police. According to

Lerner et al. (2012b) the revenue for offsetting the costs comes from infrastructure owners in the form of regular fees based on the amount of traffic handled or toll revenue raised. Additional revenue stream could come from selling raw or processed data to other providers of intelligent mobility services such as multimodal journey planning systems.

Multimodal Mobility

A prominent new mobility concept based on information includes multimodal mobility or the Mobility-as-as Service (MaaS) concept, which encompasses such elements as 'Intermodal Routing', 'Smart Mobility Cards' or 'Multimodal Information Services'. They aim at offering their users access to a large network of transportation possibilities. For example, the advantages of smart cards are their multimodal nature and highly convenient, seamless and cash-free mobility execution. The partner network can be extended to retail outlets, car parks or cinemas. A noticeable example is Hong Kong which relies on a highly integrated system which has a smart multimodal card, the Octopus card, at its heart (Lerner et al. 2012b).

However, the backbone of multimodal mobility is 'Multimodal Information' and 'Intermodal Routing' (Gruel, Piller 2016). It enables the provision of highly personalized and interconnected mobility services to the travelers. Multimodal Information seems to constitute one of the most important service category. These services include: multimodal pre-trip planning, multimodal on-trip planning, integrated ticketing, payment execution and billing (Boehm et al. 2013; Lerner et al. 2012b; Urban ITS Expert Group 2013). Geographical location and navigation or location-based information services are also relevant (Franchi, Malpezzi 2013; Urban ITS Expert Group 2013; Boehm et al. 2013).

However, the provision of multimodal information is strongly dependent on solid data sources which are rather difficult to access and reuse, as they are highly dispersed among many institutions and organizations (Urban ITS Expert Group 2013; Gruel, Piller 2016). The other main issue with the operational deployment is the absence of sustainable business models. Such concepts are often not viable without public support. The reason for that is that the users usually take information for granted and are not willing to pay for this kind of added-value services (Urban ITS Expert Group 2013).

10.3 Digital Technology Developments for Application in Urban Mobility

10.3.1 Introduction

The above outlined overview of innovative technologies for urban mobility covers four crucial technology areas for urban mobility. In this chapter the author aims at exploring current developments in the arena of information technology (IT) and more precisely within the field of information and communication technology (ICT). IT and ICT are two different notions and should not be confused with each other. The IT includes computers, software, networking and other IT infrastructures. ICT, on the other hand, is a term which stresses the role of communicating data by electronic means. This communication is achieved digitally, i.e. via networks of sending and receiving equipment, wires or satellite links (Zuppo 2012).

As a matter of fact, ICT has long been attracting research interest. This is reflected in the development of complex network infrastructure, efforts in international projects and standardization activities, as well as discussions which aim at the provision of innovative services and applications in order to address individualized user needs (Dimitrakopoulos et al. 2012; Hasselbring, Reussner 2006). A significant proportion of recent articles, publications and reports focus on telematics and ICT in the field of transportation. However, much of the literature is strongly related to one specific field of application, the field of intelligent transportation systems (ITS). ITS encompasses applications aiming to provide innovative services for traffic management to enable various users to be better informed and make safer, more coordinated, and smarter (meaning more efficient) use of transport networks (European Parliament 2010). One prominent area of these innovative services are Multimodal Information Systems (MIS), as described above. They represent a combination of new information tools that support the integration of different networks and the optimization of transport systems as a whole. In that respect MIS is providing information on all modes of transportation allowing users to choose any combination of mobility modes from A to B (Urban ITS Expert Group 2013). This in turn can considerably contribute to a much higher efficiency of the transportation system. It has been suggested that this kind of multimodal traveler application has an important role to play in incentivizing and stimulating shifts in modal share. According to Urban ITS Expert Group (2013) some studies have estimated the potential contribution of MIS to modal shift as approximately 5%.

Furthermore, with regard to sustainable mobility ICT is also often referred to as technology that can alter human behavior in numerous areas of social life and therefore considerably change the mobility patterns. For example, Banister (2005) defines ICT as a new technology that changes people's life style patterns and therefore influences their travel behavior substantially. Important life spheres that are impacted are life styles (e.g.

shopping, e-business), working (e.g. teleworking) or production (e.g. just-in-time logistics, freight distribution) (Banister 2005).

However, the author of this dissertation seeks to extend the comprehension of ICT. He is aiming at exploring and including one of the most recent stream of disruptive technologies which can be summarized under a general, however not yet clearly specified and defined, term of 'digital technologies'. The author claims that this field of technology has not yet been fully taken into account and exhaustively explored with respect to innovative mobility concepts. It is due to the fact that the domain of digital technologies is still at the early stages in the field of urban mobility. At least there are only few research papers that simultaneously introduce digital technologies and discuss their contribution to the development of innovative urban mobility concepts (e.g. Schade et al. 2014; Beutel et al. 2014; Hayashi et al. 2014; Vaidyanathan 2014; Roland Berger 2014). These authors mention several recent technological developments and describe their possible disruptive character for urban mobility systems that could potentially induce the transformation of the existing mobility patterns in the near future. Moreover, previous studies have also tended to focus just on a fraction of these emerging technologies and therefore fail to offer a holistic understanding of the underlying structures and purposes of these digital developments.

The author suggests to structure the identified ICT by capturing their general purpose, i.e. the digitization of the physical world. Hence, he will categorize the ICT and the associated emerging technologies under the umbrella of digital technologies. Therefore, in the following sections the focus will lie on specifying the definition of digital technologies, and identifying and briefly describing these technologies.

10.3.2 Digital technology: What is it?

The notion of digital technology is rather vague and difficult to grasp. There is no single agreed upon definition of digital technology. It is viewed from different perspectives. From the technological standpoint it is defined as a process which makes the handling of vast amounts of information possible. For example Schafer (2003) gives following definition: "Digital technology is a base two process. Digitized information is recorded in binary code of combinations of the digits 0 and 1, also called bits, which represent words and images. Digital technology enables immense amounts of information to be compressed on small storage devices that can be easily preserved and transported. Digitization also quickens data transmission speeds. Digital technology has transformed how people communicate, learn, and work."

Another viewpoint on digital technologies is the application perspective, i.e. what can be done by means of digital technologies, as described in the following definition in the learning context (The Ministry of Education of New Zealand 2006): "The term Digital Technologies is used to describe the use of digital resources to effectively find, analyze, create, communicate, and use information in a digital context. This encompasses the use of web 2.0 tools, digital media tools, programming tools and software applications."

Furthermore, digital technologies can be referred to as a set of specific ICT and appliances that enable direct interaction with people. For example McDonald, Rowsell-Jones (2012) describe the possible advantages of digital technologies for businesses which aim at fostering the interaction with their customers: "Digital technologies such as mobile, social media, smartphones, big data, predictive analytics, and cloud, among others are fundamentally different than the preceding IT-based technologies. Newer technologies touch the customers directly and in that interaction create a source of digital difference that matters to value and revenue".

Finally, there is also the perspective on the fierce cultural transformation that has been taking place due to the adoption and diffusion of digital technologies. According to Rückriem (2009) digital technology has been radically affecting the nature of everyday life human activity and it transforms reality in a fundamental way (Rückriem 2009, p. 88): "No societal development within the past 50 years or so has been more fierce or far-reaching than that related to information and telecommunication technology. The digital technology on which it is based has penetrated every societal process and every societal activity system. It not only laid the foundations of the World Wide Web, including its derivations, but built a new global network of communication systems. No matter how we may judge the consequences of this technical development, we cannot but concede that digital technology has entered most things in everyday life, and it increasingly determines the activity of people even if they avoid using it. In more general terms, it has become the basis of an emerging globalization process that is not only economic but cultural, not only universal but irreversible. There is nothing outside it. Reality itself has changed fundamentally".

Based on these ideas the author proposes a general notion of Digital Technology which describes the variety of existing and emerging digital technologies as enablers for:

- collecting, processing and transmitting vast amounts of data and providing real-time, customized and purposeful information,
- providing network-based connectivity anytime, anywhere and on any device (e.g. stationary and mobile),
- providing generalized applications, such as one-stop-shop services (e.g.: identification, planning, booking, payment and billing),
- interacting directly or indirectly with people and transforming their way of conducting everyday life activities by adding value to these activities.

A possible categorization could be based on the general architectural concept of the 'Internet of Things' (IoT). The reasoning behind this is that the IoT aims at enabling the digital flow of information between physical objects and/or humans, making it possible to create and offer new classes of intelligent applications and services (Miorandi et al. 2012; Atzori et al. 2010). This is to some extent what the author of this work understands under the underlying technological structures for intelligent mobility services. For example such a structure would encompass the entire spectrum of digital technologies which, if logically combined and integrated with each other, would enable the digitization process of vehicles. This could possibly contribute to much higher utilization or more precisely efficiency rates of cars than today.

Therefore, the author suggests using the structure proposed by Suo et al. (2012) and Boehm et al. (2013), for intelligent transportation systems in smart cities:

1) Perception technologies: obtain information of all components of the infrastructure with sensors, actuators, tags and readers.
2) Network technologies: enable the data transmission between sensors and the support layer by using either wired or increasingly often wireless connections.
3) Support technologies: provide massive data storage and processing capabilities by using the capabilities recent advances in IT infrastructures.
4) Application technologies: analyze, process and present information related to intelligent mobility.
5) Security and privacy layer: overcomes the physical threats, mobile network security risks and eliminates malware.

In the following sections the digital technologies associated with each category will be listed and briefly discussed.

10.3.2.1 Perception Technologies

The most basic level is the perceptual layer also known as the recognition layer. The physical world is being identified by collecting all kind of relevant information through physical equipment and representing it in the digital form. This information includes for example object properties or environmental conditions (Suo et al. 2012). Boehm et al. (2013) suggest that intelligent mobility concepts are highly dependent on both energy-efficient sensing and processing technologies. In that respect they list beside smart sensors additional basic digital technologies such as: advances in semiconductor and processors technologies, memory technologies and display technologies. Since the physical and digital world are increasingly converging it is important to consider these key technologies also with regard to future mobility concepts.

Processors and memory

Processors are technologies for all computational processes with information and data that are applied for all subsequent applications and services. Boehm et al. (2013) state that until 2020 the transistor counts and densities will still be doubling every 3 years (according to Moore's law) and that the performance of available processors will also increase substantially. These developments have always resulted in some significant adjustments in the underlying technologies since the limiting factor in achieving required performance levels is the energy consumption. Therefore, parallelism, accelerators, heterogeneous processor cores and tighter software-hardware partnerships are required (Boehm et al. 2013). Beyond silicon-based technology some other innovative technologies have been currently under investigation, such as: compound semiconductors, carbon nanotubes or bio-computing. However, they are still not commercially viable for mass production.

It is also crucial to briefly mention the development in the arena of memory technologies. The reason is that emerging intelligent information services around mobility are dependent on the flow of gigantic amounts of data (also called Big Data), which need to be collected, stored, processed, analyzed, transmitted and presented to end users (Romph 2013; Franchi, Malpezzi 2013; Urban ITS Expert Group 2013). Additionally, this information needs to be repeatedly observed, collected and evaluated over time and space.

Additionally, also the 'instant-on' concept has been introduced. In essence it describes the ability to use specific applications immediately without waiting for the operating system to boot. With that in mind the associated need for memory and power consumption becomes a real issue. Hence, critical applications are becoming data-centric (and less compute-centric) and memory performance is forming a considerable bottleneck that limits the overall system performance (Boehm et al. 2013). Currently, the most common memory technologies are hard drive disks (HDD) and NAND-based flash memory, but these have some fundamental physical limitations. Massive changes are expected in the memory market over the next couple of years, with more reliable technologies challenging the dominant NAND flash memory used in so called solid state drives (SDD) and embedded in mobile devices (Meena et al. 2014). Researchers estimate that NAND-based SSDs will be too slow, i.e. at the data capacity of 5TB when access delays will surge dramatically (Grupp et al. 2012). There are several alternate technologies available, however. The most prominent in respect to energy efficiency, access time, endurance and retention are perfect RAM (PCRAM) and Spin Transfer Torque RAM (STTRAM) (Meena et al. 2014; Boehm et al. 2013; Kryder, Kim 2009).

Smart Sensors

Smart sensors are one of the key components in this layer as they capture the physical information from the surrounding world (Suo et al. 2012). With regard to mobility some important data collection and monitoring technologies include physical equipment such as: vehicle on-board-units, radio-frequency identification (RFID) readers, weather sensors, facilities for measuring pollution levels or controller area networks (CAN-bus) in vehicles (Franchi, Malpezzi 2013; Lerner et al. 2012b; Suo et al. 2012).

The latter constitutes an interesting case in relation to intelligent mobility services. In modern cars there are as many as 70 electronic control units (ECU) for various vehicular subsystems and the CAN-standard enables the communication with and between them (Studnia et al. 2013). Typically the biggest processor is the engine control unit. Other ECUs are used for transmission, airbags, antilock braking system (ABS), cruise control, electric power steering, audio systems, power windows, doors, mirror adjustment, battery and recharging systems for hybrid/electric cars (Koscher et al. 2010). The communication among these subsystems is essential, as they need to control and receive feedback from actuators and sensors.

The vehicle access via CAN-bus is essential for a variety of potential innovative mobility services. Carsharing and pooling services need access to a large amount of vehicle data provided on the CAN-bus, such as distance driven, odometer readings, and fuel level. CAN-bus enables also locking and unlocking the car. Some have taken this concept even further by proposing a 'car-as-a-platform' model for third-party development (Koscher et al. 2010). For example Hughes Telematics described plans for developing an App Store for automotive applications (Mollman 2009) while Ford announced that it will open its telematics system (Sync) as a platform for third-party applications (Goodwin 2009). Indeed, Ford did introduce its own infotainment system SYNC AppLink in 2014. It offers a selection of compatible apps that can be used safely in selected Ford cars. SYNC AppLink deploys voice-activated technology to build a hands-free bridge between the drivers and their smartphone applications (Ford Motor Company 2015). Even though technology journalists report several drawbacks and limitations (Riofrio 2014), yet these are only teething problems in the complex digital upgrade process in the car technology.

Localization Systems

Another digital ability at the perception level, which is of foremost importance for intelligent mobility services, is the possibility to determine the location of humans and vehicles. The access to satellite-based geo-localization systems with the associated flourishing of digital maps services (e.g. navigation devices or web-based Google Maps) have considerably influenced the development of innovative mobility services (Coldefy, Lyon 2014).

The most recognized and used system today is the Global Positioning System (GPS) which is an element of a Global Navigation Satellite System (GNSS). The technology originates, as does every such technology, from the military arena – more precisely from the space race competition between USA and USSR (Wilson 2012). However, GPS was released for civil usage and allows technology-enabled representation of the global space (Boehm et al. 2013; Wilson 2012). The GPS is a constellation of satellites that broadcasts time signals. The interpretation is done by GPS receivers which compare these time signals to measure the distance traveled by various signals, and thereby fix a location (Harvey 2008). Another available and operating GNSS is the Russian GLONASS which is currently the only alternative to GPS. Other systems currently emerging (Hegarty, Chatre 2008): Galileo (European Union) include BeiDou/Compass Navigation Test System (China), Quasi-Zenith Satellite System (Japan) and Indian Regional Navigation Satellite System (India).

In the context of intelligent mobility services it is highly significant, that GNSS and cellular technologies enable "a new generation of mobile electronic devices that are capable of measuring their position in the Earth's surface, and of modifying the information they collect and present based on that knowledge" (Goodchild 2001, p. 1). Today location systems are widely available and accessible from smartphones for free or at considerably decreased costs (Urban ITS Expert Group 2013). This is due to the fact that the GPS receivers can be quite small (size of a postage stamp) and embedded in many devices (Wilson 2012).

By combining a satellite navigation systems such as GPS and user equipment, added-value personalized services can be provided such as: mapping services to drivers, freight vehicles tracking or detection of blockages along routes.

Another interesting recent development is mobile phone location determination or cellular positioning as a universal positioning method in the areas where the smartphone penetration is high and the infrastructure almost ubiquitous (Boehm et al. 2013). This technique is dependent on location data from the Global System for Mobile Communications (GSM), which is location-based information retrieved from mobile phones. Each mobile phone is at all times connected to a certain GSM cell site antenna. Such a cell, provided by a mobile provider, knows what mobile phones are present in that cell. The most advanced cells can return an indication of the distance from the mobile phone to the cell antenna which results in fairly accurate positioning of a phone. When the phone moves, for example during a car ride, the mobile phone switches over from one cell to another cell. Monitoring the movement of an anonymized mobile phone through the provider's network gives the desired data on mobility. This is considered as an additional source of data that feeds into the concept of Big Data (Romph 2013).

Machine-to-Machine Communication (M2M)

M2M is, in principle, a specification of IoT. The M2M concept refers to the communications between computers, embedded processors, smart sensors, actuators, and mobile devices without or with limited human intervention. M2M is a superset of technologies that use Extensible Markup Language (XML) and Web services enabling computers to automatically view and share information on the Internet and to communicate with each other (Watson et al. 2004). The main idea behind M2M communications is twofold. Firstly, a networked object is more valuable than an isolated one. Secondly, when multiple objects are interconnected, more autonomous and intelligent applications can be generated (Chen et al. 2012b). Various M2M applications have already started to emerge in several fields, such as: healthcare, robotics, manufacturing systems, home technologies, or energy grids. Obviously automobiles also constitute an interesting area of focus for M2M developers by enabling vehicles to communicate with each other via vehicle-to-vehicle (V2V) or with roadside base stations via vehicle-to-infrastructure (V2I) – see chapter 10.2.1.

10.3.2.2 Network Technologies

Network technologies enable the data transmission between sensors and actuators and the application support layer by using either wired or increasingly often wireless connections (Boehm et al. 2013). The network is responsible for the reliable transmission of information from perceptual layer, initial processing of information, classification and polymerization. In this layer the information transmission relies on several basic networks; i.e. the Internet, mobile communication network, satellite nets, wireless network, network infrastructure and communication protocols are also essential to the information exchange between devices (Suo et al. 2012).

Communication Technologies

Currently, the most widespread wide area mobile communication technology is Universal Mobile Telecommunication System (UMTS or 3G). The initial release of UMTS was in 2000 and since then it has undergone many evolution steps. Long Term Evolution (LTE or 4G) initiated in 2004 is the enhancement of UMTS (Boehm et al. 2013). Other advanced communication technologies include satellite communication, short range devices such as Bluetooth, radio-frequency identification (RFID), local area wireless computer networking (Wi-Fi), ZigBee or Near Field Communication (NFC) and wireless sensor networks (WSN) such as WirelessHART (Kaufmann 2011).

Internet of Things (IoT)

IoT is a concept that stretches beyond the traditional Internet, the mobile network and the sensor network. It aims at connecting every 'thing' and enabling these things to communicate with each other (Suo et al. 2012). Technological advancements of recent decades have considerably decreased the costs of sensors, actuators and processors making it possible to implement them in basically any physical thing (Boehm et al. 2013). According to Boehm et al. (2013) 'things' refer to everyday objects that are readable, recognizable, locatable, addressable, and/or controllable via the Internet, RFID or other means. In the IoT-vision these physically distributed smart objects with sensing and actuation functionalities are becoming a part of the Internet and will be able to communicate with each other and with humans, enabling a whole new class of applications and services (Miorandi et al. 2012; Atzori et al. 2010; Boehm et al. 2013).

The main building blocks of the IoT concept are RFID, NFC, WSN and new Internet Protocols (IP). The main challenge to implement the IoT vision is to orchestrate these innovative technologies and make them work together. It also needs to be born in mind that with the IoT new security and privacy problems will arise. Therefore, more attention should be paid to the issues of confidentiality, authenticity, and integrity of data in the field of the IoT (Suo et al. 2012).

Future Internet

Mobile broadband subscription counts are rapidly increasing and users are generating large amounts of data traffic on mobile networks by using web-based applications. Most likely, future mobile traffic will increase dramatically due to streaming types of services such as entertainment (e.g. music and video). Another source of tremendous mobile data traffic growth is predicted through M2M-communication, as described above. However, current mobile network architectures are not well prepared to cope with these amounts of mobile data, chiefly because of poor or non-assured service quality of the Internet connection. The latter is the glue that holds the Internet together via bilateral network interconnection agreements (Ghezzi, Dramitinos 2016). Hence, the research is ongoing to restructure and redesign current network architectures to meet the requirement of providing increasingly high network performances. Therefore, it requires a significant redefinition and realignment of the basic concept of interconnection at both a technological and business level, adopting a 'Future Internet' perspective to cope with these changes in the service demand and offer (El-Gendy et al. 2003; Gu, Luo). New concepts and design principles for the Future Internet are believed to meet new qualitative requirements in critical services such as e-health applications, clouds of services and clouds of sensors, new social network applications like collaborative 3D immersive environments, new commercial and transactional applications, new location-based services and so on (Future Internet Architecture Group 2012).

10.3.2.3 Support/Infrastructure Technologies

Support technologies constitute a reliable computing platform, which is a required resource for the application layer. On this platform all kinds of intelligent computing and storage technologies are deployed and organized in order to combine the upper application layer and network layer downward (Suo et al. 2012). However, as mentioned above the gigantic amounts of generated data from all kind of perceptional technologies and the requirements for real-time (ad-hoc) data analysis put high pressure on memory and computing performance. In that respect massive data management will be at the heart of intelligent mobility services that are based on the holistic view on urban traffic (Boehm et al. 2013). For overcoming this challenge an efficient, secure, scalable and market oriented computing and storage resourcing is essential (Gubbi et al. 2013). The research to date has tended to focus on technological trends such as cloud computing, Big Data platforms and business intelligence and analytics (Gubbi et al. 2013; Suo et al. 2012; Boehm et al. 2013; Lyndon 2014; Chen et al. 2012a). The author will now unravel the notion of Big Data, since in recent times it has been one of the most popular and overused marketing terms in transportation-related circles.

Big Data Paradigm

Big Data is a term that has been coined for the vast amount of data on virtually every facet of human activities and characteristics. The National Institute for Standards and Technology (NIST) defines Big Data as follows (NIST 2015, p. 5):

> "Big Data consists of extensive datasets – primarily in the characteristics of volume, variety, velocity, and/or variability – that require a scalable architecture for efficient storage, manipulation, and analysis."

In that respect the notion of Big Data refers to the need of overcoming the inefficiencies of traditional data architectures in handling extensive datasets and developing system architecture that can scale to achieve the needed performance and cost efficiency in relation to the characteristics of Big Data. Features that force new architectures are the size of the dataset (volume), data from multiple repositories, domains, or types (variety), the rate of flow (velocity) and changes in other characteristics (variability) (NIST 2015). Put simply, what really makes big data Big is the frequency of recurring observations over time and space (Jacobs 2009) that need to be stored and often saved for several years due to legal compliance and/or business requirements.

From the business perspective Big Data stands for advancing trends in technology that open the door to a new approach to understanding the world and making decisions. According to Professor Brynjolfsson, an economist from Massachusetts Institute of Technology, decisions in business, economics and other fields will be increasingly based on data and analysis rather than on experience and intuition, which will make decision-making more scientific (Lohr 2012). McAfee et al. (2012) found that companies in the top third of their industry in the use of data-driven decision making were, on average, 5% more productive and 6% more profitable than their competitors. However, Big Data needs to be taken with a pinch of salt. Reid (2012) cautions against the excessive optimism about Big Data. Firstly, it is not evident that having more data leads to better information or better decision-making. Secondly, even if Big Data promises to reduce the problem by purposeful data analysis the proliferation of data might have a rebound-effect and, indeed, add to the problem. Thirdly, regarding the analysis of Big Data as 'scientific' might lead to 'black-boxed facts' that bear a compelling, yet deceptive, scientific stamp for their approval.

Also there are several technological challenges that need to be considered with regard to Big Data, such as: data accessibility and integration, consistency and synchronization across the data sources, high-performance data analytics, legal compliance and data security (Loshin 2014; Kaisler et al. 2013). These issues are being addressed by the development of advanced Big Data platforms and real-time analytics tools.

Big Data Platforms & Real-Time Analytics

An unprecedented amount of data is a critical outcome of the emerging field of IoT, M2M-communication. Not only do the storage capacity, data security and energy efficiency of energy-consuming data centers become a significant issue but also the analytical capabilities of these centralized data centers (Gerla et al. 2014). The collected data does not add value itself. The value-added process is the meaningful analysis on multi-structured and heterogeneous data to make sense out of that data. A technique that helps discover new patterns from large data sets is called data mining. However, until recently these types of analytics have been difficult to process by using traditional analytical processing technologies (Maitrey, Jha 2015). Unlike the structured data that can be handled repeatedly through traditional rational database management systems (RDBMS), semi-structured data calls for ad-hoc and real-time extraction, parsing, processing, indexing, and analytics in a scalable and distributed environment (Chen et al. 2012a).

For that purpose the arena of investigative computing platform has emerged reflecting the magnitude of data-related problems to be solved in contemporary organizations

(Chen et al. 2012a; Maitrey, Jha 2015). Currently the most popular computing paradigm for the analysis of gigantic amount of data are frameworks that are based on MapReduce algorithms, such as Hadoop. The MapReduce algorithm was developed by Google for searching millions of pages and return the results in milliseconds or less. It is an evolutionary new platform for large-scale data access and optimized analytic data processing (Maitrey, Jha 2015; Patterson 2008). Hadoop on the other hand is the most popular open source software framework for developing Big Data analytical capabilities and is inspired and based by MapReduce approach. The Hadoop software framework is very successful and has been widely acclaimed by the industry and academia alike (Maitrey, Jha 2015; Agrawal et al. 2011). For example, Hadoop has been adopted by the top traditional data warehousing software suppliers, such as: IBM, Oracle and Microsoft for their custom solutions to collect, store and analyze multi-structured data masses (Chen et al. 2012a). For further advancements in this area it is being suggested to foster automated decision making with innovative fusion algorithms. Modern non-linear, temporal machine learning methods based on evolutionary algorithms, genetic algorithms, neural networks, and other artificial intelligence techniques are proposed and investigated to support this development (Gerla et al. 2014).

Real-time analytics refer to decision tools that enable superfast and so called 'on-the-fly' analysis of vast amounts of multi-structured data. The goal is availability at the push of a button, i.e. in real-time. To achieve this kind of availability it is required that data is stored and processed directly within the main memory of the database and not on a traditional storage such as hard disk drive. Such capabilities are provided by so called 'in-memory databases'. Real-time analytics have several advantages: visualization of analyzed metrics in real-time, facilitating highly personalized experiences, or highly increased response during emergencies (Kejariwal et al. 2015).

The public transportation sector has actually for a long time been at the forefront in utilizing and implementing Big Data and real-time analytics. Transportation applications associated with Big Data range from urban planning activities with computerized processing of massive amounts of demographic and geographic data, to complex signaling and train dispatching or control systems, to communications, train tracking, and passenger information operations using increasingly common modern technologies like GPS, Wi-Fi, and cellular phone systems (Lyndon 2014).

The importance of Big Data and real-time analytics in the arena of mobility is expected to grow in the coming years. Along the development and implementation V2V and V2I concepts, described above, Big Data will lead to exponential growth in transferred data from and to vehicles. For example, Ford Motor Company is now looking to collect masses of relevant data, in order to develop new intelligent vehicle functionalities, and is currently conducting a 'Big Data Drive' experiment in Detroit with its own employees who agreed to participate in the project (Ford Media Center 2015). Each of 200 test cars is equipped with in-vehicle smart actuators and sensors which can capture up to 25 Gigabytes of data per hour (Ford Motor Company 2013). By applying big data analytics the carmaker believes it can provide its customers with added conveniences such as assistance in finding a parking space, based on GPS data (Chapron 2015).

These massive amounts of produced data are a tasty morsel for both public and non-public companies. The industry, whichever is involved (automotive, IT, telco, energy), desires the access to the information that is of relevance to it. By harnessing and evaluating data from diverse sources - including vehicle data, and data from the social media and customer communication - closer contacts with potential customers can be built. In business terms closer contacts obviously mean commercialization. Good examples for these developments are Ford's AppLink, Google's Android Auto and Apple's CarPlay (Mossberg 2016).

Advanced IT Infrastructure - Cloud Computing

The computing world is facing a rapid transformation in its traditional paradigm - towards developing software for masses to consume as a service, rather than to possess and run on individual computers. The new paradigm denotes that users are able to access applications from anywhere in the world on demand, i.e. when they need it (Buyya et al. 2009). The general infrastructure technology which facilitates this is called cloud computing and constitutes a new technology platform for both enterprise and personal computing (Cusumano 2010). Cloud computing commonly refers to the utilization of shared computing resources, both hardware and software, that are available typically over the Internet. More precisely, according to the NIST "cloud computing is a model for enabling ubiquitous, convenient, on-demand network access to a shared pool of configurable computing resources (e.g. networks, servers, storage, applications, and services) that can rapidly be provisioned and released with minimal management effort or service provider interaction" (Mell, Grance 2011, p. 2). There are five essential characteristics of cloud computing: on-demand self-service, broad network access, resource pooling, rapid elasticity, and measured service. The infrastructure for the provision of these requirements encompasses both a physical layer and an abstraction layer. The physical layer consists of the hardware resources that are necessary to support the cloud services (such as: servers, storage and network components). The abstraction layer consists of the software deployed across the physical layer (Mell, Grance 2011). Three most popular cloud service models include: Software as a Service (SaaS), and Platform as a Service (PaaS), and Infrastructure as a Service (IaaS). The concept, however, can also be extended to 'Database as a Service' or 'Storage as a Service' (Agrawal et al. 2011).

Concepts based on sensor network technologies (e.g. IoT, M2M or V2V) and the associated data flows, management and processing are posing new challenges to existing IT infrastructures. For the realization of intelligent functions and services for the society (such as new mobility services) the challenges relate chiefly to efficient, secure and scalable computational power and storage resourcing (Gubbi et al. 2013). The cloud computing paradigm seems to offer solutions for such computing- and data-intensive tasks by providing scalable storage, computation time, developers' environment, and other tools and integrating them in such a way that the development of new services and businesses is possible (Buyya et al. 2009). For example, Aneka, a PaaS, is a platform and framework for developing distributed applications on the cloud. It offers a developers' environment and a set of application programming interfaces (so called APIs) that enable developers to build customized applications by using multiple programming models such as for example MapReduce Programming (Manjrasoft Pty Ltd.). Applying the cloud computing paradigm enables combining services provided by multiple stakeholders and scale to serve number of end users in a reliable and distributed manner, as they use the innovative services in both wired and wireless setting (Gubbi et al. 2013).

10.3.2.4 Application Interfaces

The application layer is the top level of the digital architecture and aims at offering personalized services taking the needs of the end users into consideration (Suo et al. 2012). A broader definition is provided by Boehm et al. (2013) who states that on this layer the data related to the monitoring and mobility services is analyzed, processed and presented to the users (Boehm et al. 2013). While the possible digital services will be discussed in a separate chapter (see chapter 10.2) the author will discuss here the technologies for user interactions. According to Suo et al. (2012) on this layer users can access the required information to the application layer via interfaces such as television, personal computer or mobile equipment (Suo et al. 2012). The latter one encompasses Internet-enabled mobile devices such as smartphones, tablets or e-readers. This corresponds with the idea of 'multimodal interaction' which means that the users are given multiple possibilities to interact with a system, application or a mobile service (Boehm et al. 2013). Mobile equipment already has a high and increasing market penetration and offers a variety of capabilities for users (Yelton 2012). This is the reason why the author will further discuss some of the recent developments in this field.

Mobile Devices

Button- or menu-based interaction styles are outdated user interfaces with respect to mobile devices. Furthermore the mouse and keyboard are being replaced by touch and motion based interfaces (Kratz et al. 2011). The current trend is to move towards more direct techniques which involve rich sensory input and output. For example in the most recent mobile devices such as smartphones advanced input techniques in the form of multi-touch technology has been adopted (Kratz et al. 2011).

Natural User Interfaces (NUI) refers to user interfaces that are effectively invisible and remain invisible as the user continuously learns increasingly complex interactions. The word 'natural' refers to an objective in the user experience, which means that the interaction with such interfaces comes from naturally interacting (Boehm et al. 2013).

Kratz et al. (2011) claim that there is a shift in mobile technology away from the predominantly utilitarian notion of interaction towards more playful and socially relevant forms, which makes the principles of NUI relevant for mobile user interfaces.

Augmented Reality

Another development in this arena is augmented reality (AR) which is a variation of virtual reality. AR aims at supplementing the surrounding reality so that the user can experience that the virtual and real objects coexist in the same space (Boehm et al. 2013). In that way the information provided by the virtual objects supports users in conducting their activities in the real world. Current smartphones already include the technology that enables AR.

Another interesting AR-application is the head-up display (HUD) which is already being adopted in vehicles on the windshields. The HUD displays additional driving-relevant information (e.g. augmented night vision view) without disturbing the driver (Boehm et al. 2013).

10.3.2.5 Security and Privacy

One key challenge of the integration of networked environments is the fact that the critical infrastructure is increasingly connected to the Internet and public networks (Boehm et al. 2013). With the growing amount of wirelessly connected devices, objects, sensors and use of public cloud platforms the digital environment is getting more and more complex, unsecure and vulnerable. As with every ICT intelligent digital environments (e.g. IoT or V2V) are exposed to risks. The current research findings suggest that using applications and services in digital environments is chiefly associated with security and privacy concerns (Suo et al. 2012; Gidoin et al. 2013). Both are of critical importance for gaining user trust and acceptance. Security and privacy are complimentary concepts, each including important facets in their own right. Nonetheless, there is a significant overlap with regard to the protection of personal data (Gidoin et al. 2013). In the following paragraphs the author will briefly discuss both security and privacy risks and the possible mitigation measures.

The common expectations about security in such highly vulnerable environments with personal information and use of public networks, are data confidentiality, integrity, authenticity, non-repudiation (traceability), and access control (Li et al. 2011; Gerla et al. 2014; Gidoin et al. 2013; Suo et al. 2012). Every single technology layer discussed above is affected and needs to be properly protected. At all levels the fulfillment of all security requirements is necessary to prevent illegal access and to protect the data transmission. Most of all, data encryption is an absolute necessity. Lightweight encryption technology (lightweight cryptographic algorithms and protocols) offers strong safety measures. Further security mechanisms encompass identity authentication and key agreement, communication security, and mechanisms against network attack (such as commonly applied 'distributed denial of service'). The infrastructure layer requires highly secure multiparty cloud computing, which can be achieved by strong security systems, encryption methods and antivirus. Additionally, the application layer requires protection of the end user's privacy. For that reason password management and privacy education are of high importance (Suo et al. 2012).

With regards to privacy Gidoin et al. (2013) identified three main privacy risks of digital applications for mobility services:

- Use of personal data for purposes other than agreed upon, such as: surveillance, trade of personal information or unsolicited marketing.
- Lack of transparency and a lack of options for users to amend or delete their personal data, mostly in a complex and relatively new organization or system.
- Insufficient security for databases and web-based services leading to large-scale leaks of personal data (e.g. personal location data over longer periods of time).

Privacy risks may be mitigated or avoided by combining both technical and organizational methods. The technical approach includes: anonymization of personal information, use of pseudonyms, data minimization, and other information security means (as discussed for security). Providing users with an accessible web interface in which they can adjust their personal information can considerably increase transparency. On the other hand organizational means focus on raising privacy awareness within the organization providing a service, and implementing checks and procedures that help identify and avoid decisions that harm privacy (Gidoin et al. 2013).

10.4 Actors of Urban Mobility

The research indicates that the main actors of the mobility arena can be grouped into three general categories: public, private and customers. They represent different players who manage, provide or consume different activities of the value chain of mobility services. Van Audenhove et al. (2014) name three main stakeholders – the city administration, the private sector and the citizens – that lay out the purpose and objectives of the mobility system. Hanley et al. (2013) suggest a slightly different categorization of mobility stakeholders and split them into: infrastructure providers, city administrators and transport modes operators. However, they could also be grouped either into public or private actors, as suggested by Urban ITS Expert Group (2013). They additionally include users of mobility services and state that these can contribute to the refinement of the services by providing their feedback. Similarly Franchi, Malpezzi (2013) present three macro categories: consumer, business and public. Cohen, Kietzmann (2014) speak of agents and principles for sustainable mobility and define them as service providers and local governments. Furthermore, some authors point to public-private partnerships as increasingly important actors in the mobility sector (Urban ITS Expert Group 2013; Cohen, Kietzmann 2014). However, they refer to them rather in the context of a strategy for developing and providing innovative mobility services. Nonetheless, they shall be also discussed within this chapter as possible cooperation schemes between users, public and private stakeholders for collaborative innovation in the mobility sector.

The author briefly discusses the four main actors of mobility services that have been identified in the literature.

Public Actors

The public category includes actors such as the civil transport authorities, urban development boards and public transport providers (Hanley et al. 2013). Similarly Boehm et al. (2013) name actors such as the municipal traffic management department, the transportation authority or the public transport operators. A more precise register is provided by Urban ITS Expert Group (2013). Accordingly, the relevant stakeholders of the public sector involved in providing innovative mobility services encompass: public decision makers in a city or region, administration of the city or region, public transport operators or associations such as bike services operators, public road operators and other public services (such as police). Current thinking suggests that public actors bear a key role in the management of the mobility system. They can directly act on the system or appoint different private companies to manage various mobility areas, in order to provide people with an effective mobility service (Franchi, Malpezzi 2013, 2013). They are in charge of securing the public interest (e.g. public transport, parking lots, road infrastructure) and providing the required information for providing innovative mobility services (e.g. datasets for multimodal traveler information systems) (Urban ITS Expert Group 2013).

Private Actors

Historically the arena of transport infrastructure and public transit systems was exclusively the core competence of local and regional governments (Cohen, Kietzmann 2014). If there are autonomous business models that are economically viable, then mobility services based on digital technologies can be carried out by private actors (Urban ITS Expert Group 2013). The private sector is crucial because it feeds on its high technological capacity and implementation competences (Urban ITS Expert Group 2013). Boehm et al. (2013) note that the responsibilities for technology-enabled mobility services are distributed among various local pubic actors. However, the research to date has identified that the structure of the ecosystem for innovative mobility services progresses radically. Researchers discuss and propose the inclusion of numerous further actors that need to be considered as well, since the emergence of new technologies extends the list of stakeholders considerably (Urban ITS Expert Group 2013). Franchi, Malpezzi (2013) define private actors as business actors, i.e. privately owned firms operating in transport, communication, IT and other correlated areas. These companies play an increasingly important role in the development of new mobility ecosystem. A few years ago nobody would have considered them as directly relevant for providing mobility services. Nowadays, they provide real-time mobility information, connectivity instruments and network services for interaction with external environment, and e-commerce solutions for online payment and account management (Hanley et al. 2013).

Customers

This category includes those actors that utilize mobility services (Franchi, Malpezzi 2013). They take part in, obtain and are charged for the provided mobility services, either through taxes or they pay directly to a private service provider. Additionally, they can also assess the services and provide feedback, e.g. through social media (Urban ITS Expert Group 2013). The customers' mobility needs evolve with the advancements in digital technologies. Hanley et al. (2013) state that customers increasingly demand real-time mobility information and planning, single payment interface and connected transport modes.

Public-Private Partnerships

Numerous studies have argued that all these actors will need to cooperate closely with each other in the future in order to integrate innovative mobility solutions and hence deliver the strategic vision of more sustainable mobility in cities and regions (van Audenhove et al. 2014; Urban ITS Expert Group 2013). These developments offer a window of opportunity for new market players to deliver creative and entrepreneurial mobility solutions. Public transport authorities and operators will need to open up and take a much more holistic view on public transport than they have done before in order to exploit innovation power of technology for overcoming the current deficiencies in the mobility system (van Audenhove et al. 2014).

An additional interesting aspect for providing innovative mobility solutions is that multiple actors from public and private space seek to develop and implement new business models which address deficiencies in public infrastructure and public transportation systems (Cohen, Kietzmann 2014). For example, the sharing economy for cars has recently seen entrants from both startups and multinational corporations (Cohen, Kietzmann 2014). However, this coexistence of public and private subjects creates a remarkable complexity (Franchi, Malpezzi 2013). The literature suggests that the common interest in sustainable mobility among these different types of agents does not necessarily lead to harmony. On the contrary, it gives a rise to agency conflicts that can reduce the positive sustainability impact of their individual and collective initiatives (Cohen, Kietzmann 2014). Franchi, Malpezzi (2013) state that this might be caused by the necessity of integrating both economic and managerial behavioral criteria of the market with management mechanisms of the public space.

City authorities need to cope with this challenge to provide innovation for more efficient mobility and become smarter through the use of new digital technologies. Since the technological capacity lies with the private sector they need to rely even more on public-private collaborations to implement a wide array of technology innovations and solutions (Paskaleva 2011). Therefore, the innovation in mobility and the provision of future mobility services will require the implementation of collaborative projects that bring together public sector, private actors and customers. Each party needs to contribute its expertise in order to study, develop, implement, and test new mobility services (Urban ITS Expert Group 2013). Urban ITS Expert Group notes also that the current system is clearly moving from provision by public authorities to targeted partnerships with private actors. These public-private partnerships should rely on the advantages of each involved group of actors and optimize their benefits. Furthermore, the paradigm should move from producing mobility services for users to one of co-producing services together with users. By taking the individual needs of customers into account the new flexible mobility approaches based on digital technologies can be developed. (Urban ITS Expert Group 2013).

10.5 Business Models for Urban Mobility

10.5.1 Initial Considerations[12]

While the necessary technologies seem to be available to address the needs of integrated and intelligent urban mobility services, there are challenges in the technological interfacing of different transport modes and infrastructures, the seamless integration of technology as well as the underlying management mechanisms (van Audenhove et al. 2014). Hence, the real innovation potential from the available technology is still rather untapped. One of the main reasons might be the overregulated and hostile environment for innovation in which organizations and managements of urban mobility still operate (Lerner et al. 2012b). The notion of environment encompasses various characteristics of a system, such as: "groups of stakeholders, the relationships between these, the rules and incentives that govern their behavior, and the assets and capabilities through which they seek to achieve their objectives" (Lerner et al. 2012a, p. 16). Confronting the challenges of urban mobility will require the adoption of new business models that would bring demand and supply into a natural balance (Lerner et al. 2012b, p. 5).

Similarly Cohen, Kietzmann (2014) state that an interesting aspect of innovative mobility solutions is that multiple actors seek to develop business models which address deficiencies in the private and public transportation systems. They contend that the mobility market place has experienced a market failure due to several reasons, such as: increased congestion in cities, lack of sufficient access to quality transit alternatives and lack affordable private and clean vehicles for consumers. Chiefly the private sector has recognized the challenges associated with overcoming this failure and started developing business models to address them (Cohen, Kietzmann 2014).

Further literatures also indicate that one of the emerging research fields for the future of urban mobility relates to the potentials of establishing new business models for providing intelligent mobility services. Abdelkafi et al. (2013) state that technology innovation and business model innovation are strongly linked to each other. Furthermore, they assert that business model creation and innovation is crucial for a high diffusion of any new technology, since the necessary prerequisite for the industry to provide specific innovative applications of the new technology is to gain profits. Commercial companies will contribute and commit to the development and implementation of system-level innovations in urban mobility only if a fair return on investment is assured, commensurate with the financial risks taken. A good example are the fast-charging stations for electric vehicles: it will require reassurance that there will be a sufficient number of electric vehicles on the roads (Lerner et al. 2012b).

[12] This section is partially reprinted in Janasz, Schneidewind (2017). Courtesy of Springer.

It has been suggested that new business models are also a key megatrend within the automotive industry which currently has been facing many structural challenges such as market stagnation, high requirements regarding sustainability and the integration of electromobility in its product and service portfolio (Spickermann et al. 2014; Peter Wells, Paul Nieuwenhuis 2012). Therefore, it is argued that highly integrated strategies are becoming increasingly important and that greater public and private sector synergies need to be pursued and encouraged (Jones 2012; Spickermann et al. 2014; Cohen, Kietzmann 2014). For example, the growing importance of carsharing and multimodal information provisioning is expected to greatly support changes in mobility patterns (Firnkorn, Müller 2015; Cindy Costain et al. 2012; Spickermann et al. 2014).

Similar conclusions have been drawn by Augenstein (2014) in her comprehensive and exhaustive study regarding the adoption of electromobility (e-mobility) in Germany. In particular, the study focuses on this innovative, albeit not that novel, propulsion technology as a sustainable system innovation which could lead to a less car-dependent mobility system in Germany. By applying the concepts of transformative capacity and system adaptability, Augenstein has shown that the system-innovative potential of electric vehicles still remains limited. This is based on a high transformative capacity of electromobility (which means that it does not fit the current mobility system and cannot compete with conventional cars) and simultaneous low system adaptability (due to powerful influence of incumbents, conflicting political goals and traditional science approaches). Due to this misfit the considerations will need to go far beyond the mere diffusion of the new technology throughout the market, if electromobility is to address sustainability concerns and car dependence in a comprehensive way. Hence, a system innovation (i.e. a paradigm shift) for a less car-dependent and more sustainable mobility system in Germany will be dependent on the emergence of new functionalities in the form of intelligent mobility services based on electromobility. In essence, this means embedding the electric car in the overall mobility and energy system of Germany and 'intermodalizing' it with other transport modes. For such a shift fundamental changes in infrastructures, regulations, user practices and business models will be required in the long run. For that to happen actors from outside the prevailing mobility system constellation (regime), typically small innovative niche actors (for instance from the ICT sector), will need to create and provide new and innovative mobility functionalities. However, if the innovation system remains dominated by regime actors, the system-innovative potential of electromobility will be diluted and the more substantial transition to the paradigm of sustainable mobility will be blocked (Augenstein 2015).

These considerations seem to indicate a need for the reorganization of the existing industry structures, the development of new innovative business concepts and the encouragement of synergies between private and public sectors. This would be consistent with what has been also proposed by Cohen, Kietzmann (2014) who suggest that new mobility concepts and business models for innovative urban mobility can have positive effects on urban areas if synergies between private service providers and the local governments are pursued. Therefore, in order to come up with highly integrated and intelligent urban mobility concepts, innovative business models need to be introduced and a system-level collaboration between all stakeholders of the mobility ecosystem needs to be achieved (van Audenhove et al. 2014).

To understand the arena of business models for emerging mobility concepts the author first presents the emerging business model archetypes that can be reused by both private and public sectors for business model generation and innovation in their specific context. Later he draws his attention to currently emerging business models in the field of shared automobility services (see chapter 12).

10.5.2 Outcomes from the Literature Review

While most of the contributions deliver an extensive comprehension of mobility concepts and service innovation for urban areas, only a few explicitly address the commercial nature of business models and examine them from the value-oriented perspective. However, the main problem is the fact that almost no detailed elaboration on the nature of the underlying business model patterns is provided. This is a gap which the author of this work is willing to close, at least to some extent.

Lerner et al. (2012b) offer a comprehensive list of 36 possible business models for the future of urban mobility. They cluster them into five distinct areas: Transport, Infrastructure, Traffic Management, Integration, and Information, Planning and Payment. Although the authors label them with the term business model, they actually provide an extensive overview of possible urban mobility concepts.

Another typology is delivered by Boehm et al. (2013), albeit they do not call them business models but emerging mobility ICT services for smart, clean and efficient urban mobility. These mobility services have been clustered into 'service bundles': electric mobility services, multimodal mobility services, urban logistics services, urban traffic management services, virtual mobility services, booking and payment. Further Franchi, Malpezzi (2013) concentrate on services for infomobility and present several application areas where economically viable business models can be developed and implemented. Information is also a focal topic for Urban ITS Expert Group (2013). They coin the term of Multimodal Information System (MIS).

Another set of business model patterns has been delivered by Cohen, Kietzmann (2014). They draw attention to various business models in the arena of shared mobility. They cover concepts such as carsharing, carpooling, and bike-sharing and provide an insightful discussion on the emerging agency conflicts between private mobility service providers and the service recipients, i.e. local governments. However, even though they provide an extensive overview of possible business scenarios in these areas, they do not really examine their business nature, i.e. how the value is created, delivered and captured.

An outstanding review of generally applicable business model patterns has been delivered by Abdelkafi et al. (2013). However, they have focused their discussion on the transferability only to business services for electromobility. Nonetheless, their work constitutes an invaluable source of knowledge which can be transferred to other areas of business models for urban mobility.

Finally, Lerner et al. (2012b) propose three general business model archetypes for networked, multimodal urban mobility systems of the future (discussed in the next section). Interestingly, Lerner et al. label them with names of renowned global companies from industries that have already successfully implemented similar business models archetypes in their context. By doing so they essentially imply the transferability of business models to the mobility sector. However, it needs to be noted that transferability is only one of possible systematic approaches to generate or innovate business models, which will be further elaborated in chapter 11.2.

10.5.3 Business Model Archetypes for Urban Mobility

Business model archetypes for urban mobility are based on the study conducted by Lerner et al. (2012b, pp. 23–25).

Mobility Service Platform Provider

This archetype describes a provider of single point of access for mobility and cross services, such as: identification, information, booking and payment. It requires the involvement of many actors: policymakers, public transport operators, banks and payment firms, telecommunication companies, and ICT suppliers. The latter ones are crucial since this archetype is based on the generation, processing and transmission of significant amounts of data, and on high penetration rates within the society.

An actor adopting a business model based on this archetype provides a medium for any user who seeks to receive travel information, plan a journey, make a booking and pay for the journey. His challenge is to aggregate, source and contract the underlying third-party services, such as: operators of parking lots, public transportation, bike-sharing schemes or providers of location-based services. The providers of such a platform aim at reaching as many users as possible, since the revenue stream would result from partner transactions, advertising or interest income from e-wallets of the customers. Lerner et al. (2012b) label this archetype as *Google of Mobility*.

A closer look reveals that this archetype is an existing business model pattern of a multi-sided platform (Osterwalder, Pigneur 2010). Multi-sided platforms apply to many e-commerce companies, as long as the platform involves two types of groups such as service providers and users of the medium or buyers and sellers – for example the auction-based e-Bay platform. A specification of a multi-sided platform is bundling. It is an archetype that aims at making purchasing simpler and more complete for customers by packaging related services together (Johnson 2010). Moreover, bundling increases the quantity of services that may be provided to the users (Abdelkafi et al. 2013).

Mobility Chain Integrator

This business model archetype focuses on the integration of the entire mobility value chain. There are two possible characteristics: B2C and B2B. The B2C approach aims at delivering integrated mobility services for end costumers, i.e. services which provide seamless and multimodal journey experience. The B2C integrator offers personalized journey from A to B, whatever modal mix it requires. Providing integrated and multi-modal mobility solutions at 'turnkey basis' for cities and mobility service providers would be the B2B approach. The B2B integrator could include parking infrastructure, charging infrastructure, automated fare collection, bike-sharing scheme, city buses, financial services, mobility planning etc.

Andrew et al. (2013) describe this archetype as an Integrator. Integrators are companies who choose to do it all themselves. They distinguish themselves by a high level of vertical integration and by performing almost all value adding activities in-house. According to Lerner et al. (2012b) premium car manufacturers could apply this business model archetype, since they are in the position to provide integrated mobility services from one hand. This is in line with Abdelkafi et al. (2013) who assert that car manufacturers are a good example for a high level of vertical integration, albeit the level of this integration has decreased considerably in recent times.

Because of a high vertical integration Lerner et al. (2012b) term this urban mobility business model archetype, not surprisingly, as *Apple of Mobility*. As is common knowledge Apple has implemented a highly integrated business model which allows to control the production from beginning to end. However, it needs to be noted that vertical integration requires to focus not only on the core business, but also on several other complex areas, such as sourcing materials, manufacturing, and finally selling the product to the end user (Andrew et al. 2013).

Mobility Products and Service Provider

This archetype refers to many facets of urban mobility ranging from mobility offerings e.g. car- or bike-sharing, through technology providers such as key-less access for cars, to travel planning and information. Although, multimodal connectivity and networking is not the key aspect in this business approach, the mobility products and service providers are the prerequisite for the integration and multimodality in cities. In principle, such a supplier delivers standalone solutions to municipal administrations or to mobility chain integrators.

Lerner et al. (2012b) label this archetype *Dell of Mobility*. In fact Dell has pioneered a direct business model in the computer industry by removing the need for the mediator, i.e. a salesperson. Johnson (2010) names this business model pattern 'Disintermediation'. It denotes that the product, service or information is provided directly to the customer. However, more appropriate is the notion of 'Unbundling the business model', a business model pattern which was defined by Osterwalder, Pigneur (2010). It assumes that enterprises operate much better if their attention is drawn only to one type of commercial activity. This can relate for example to product innovation, service delivery or infrastructure management (Osterwalder, Pigneur 2010). For instance, mobile phone companies that would combine all sorts of business areas, now tend to focus only on one specific domain (Abdelkafi et al. 2013).

A prominent example for this kind of business model in urban mobility are carsharing and ridesharing mobility services. In chapter 12 the author delineates relevant business models in these two areas as not all business models for carsharing and ridesharing services are created equally. There are literally dozens of unique business models in the arena of shared mobility (Cohen, Kietzmann 2014).

11 Innovating and Developing Business Models for Urban Mobility

11.1 Introduction

While the described mobility concepts constitute a good overview of possible urban mobility innovations, they do not offer a general understanding of the exact nature of their business models. The author, therefore seeks to understand the general nature and structures of possible business models to be able to describe them in a comprehensible way. This should give a clear guidance for the private and public sector about how to approach the implementation of such business models in the real world. For that purpose he first establishes a value-focused definition of a business model and derives a business model framework as a general approach to discuss business models. Subsequently he will elaborate on possible systematic approaches to business model innovation. Finally, possible business model prototypes will be discussed which will be then used for further investigation of business approaches for urban mobility concepts.

11.2 Business Model Innovation

Companies in general have three possibilities to generate and/or innovate business models in a systematic manner. Firstly, they can look for successful business model patterns within the industry they operate and implement them with respect to their specific context. Secondly, they could transfer business model patterns from other industries than their own and adapt them to their specific context. The transfer of patterns from one context to another, however, only leads to the improvement of a single value dimension, but not of the whole business model. Thirdly, a comprehensive business model innovation is possible by combining different patterns for each value dimension, to reengineer a completely new business model. This recombination of patterns might generate radical innovations, because the modification will affect more than one value dimension of the business model structure. For the purpose of describing the operating business models of companies an adequate framework is required (Amshoff et al. 2015).

11.3 Developing a Business Model Framework

An abstract explanation and a high-level classification of business models can be carried out by using a value-focused business model framework. Several frameworks have been proposed to date. One of the most prominent ones is the business model framework proposed by Osterwalder, Pigneur (2010). It is abstracted into nine central business dimensions: value proposition, target customer, distribution channel, relationships, value configuration, capabilities, partnerships, cost structure, revenue model. Their concept is often used as a conceptual tool which contains different building blocks that constitute a so called 'business model canvas'. Another example is the framework developed by Köster (2014) who also suggests to work with building blocks that answer concrete key questions of a sound business model, such as: supply model (Which product or service do we offer and what kind of value do we bring for which costumer?), customer model (How do we design the interface to our customers?), value creation model (How do we create the product or service?) and financial model (Which costs does the business accompany?). Such a general concept has been also proposed by Abdelkafi (2012). Based on previous recognized literature in this arena (Osterwalder 2004; Osterwalder, Pigneur 2010; Johnson 2010) he provides a general value-focused framework, which incorporates: value proposition, value creation, value delivery, value capture and value communication, and deploys it for the investigation of possible business models in the arena of electromobility (Abdelkafi et al. 2013).

Having studied the proposed concepts the author has come to the conclusion that all presented frameworks have the same foundation as they all refer to the work by Osterwalder (2004): "The business model ontology: A proposition in a design science approach". At heart, Osterwalder's meta-model emphasizes following four areas that a business model has to address (Osterwalder 2004):

(1) Product: What business the company is in, the products and the value propositions offered to the market.
(2) Customer interface: Who the company's target customers are, how it delivers them products and services, and how it builds strong relationships with them.
(3) Infrastructure management: How the company efficiently performs infrastructural or logistical issues, with whom, and as what kind of network enterprise.
(4) Financial aspects: What is the revenue model, the cost structure and the business model's sustainability.

Based on these works the author synthetizes previous findings to a comprehensible and concise business model framework for his further investigations in the field of innovative concepts for urban mobility. His framework is based the definition provided by Abdelkafi (2012, p. 300):

> "A business model aims at revealing the value-focused nature of every business endeavor and therefore should answer three basic questions: what, whom and how. What value does the company propose? Whom is the value communicated and conveyed to? How is the value being created and captured?"

Based on this notion the author proposes 5 basic business model elements. He deliberately describes these key elements with action verbs to emphasize that these denote activities that not only need to be described but also need to be undertaken and executed by a company to deliver value to end users. These action elements include: Propose Value, Create Value, Communicate Value, Convey Value and Capture Value. Together they constitute a 'P4C Business Model Framework' (see Figure 15). Beside Propose Value every element of the framework has its own two distinct variables which can explicitly describe a certain business model.

Propose Value

Value proposition represents a general understanding of a company's bundle of products and services that propose a value to the customer. It denotes an offering that addresses and satisfies customers' needs (Osterwalder 2004; Johnson 2010; Abdelkafi 2012). The variable is: Jobs-to-be-done.

Create Value

Value creation can be understood as a process of resource transformation with regards to the provision of a valuable product or service (Huff et al. 2009). Resources encompass tangible (e.g., production facilities, materials, financial capital, etc.) and intangible (e.g., knowledge, reputation, etc.) goods (Abdelkafi 2012). Two variables include:

- Organizational Structure,
- Strategic Partners.

Communicate Value

Value communication translates the distinct value proposition as a message to the target groups, such as customers or investors. The value proposition has to be conveyed by a story which should be understandable and coherent. It needs to be annotated that different target audience needs to be approached with different information (Abdelkafi 2012). Two variables include:

- Marketing Channels,
- Customer Segments.

Convey Value

Value conveying implies how the value, i.e. products or services, is distributed or delivered and to whom exactly. It also defines the channels and instruments with support of which the enterprises interact with their customer base in order to transfer the value proposition (Bieger, Reinhold 2011; Abdelkafi 2012). Two variables include:

- Distribution Channels,
- Customer Relationships.

Capture Value

Value capture encompasses the revenue stream and the resulting profit from the value delivery. The profit depends on the cost structure, which includes direct costs and overhead (Johnson 2010). The revenue stream depends on the offering price and the quantity of sold products or services. The enterprise's profit results from the difference between the revenue stream and costs (Abdelkafi 2012). Two variables include:

- Cost Structures,
- Revenue Model.

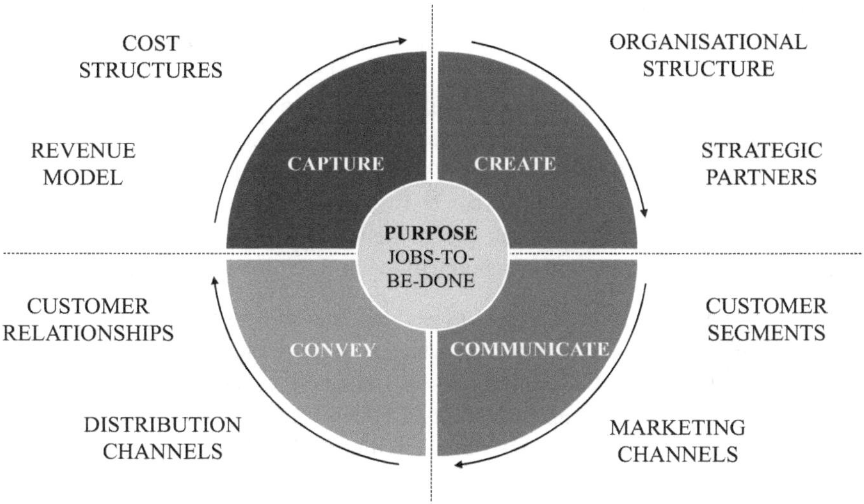

Figure 15: P4C Business Model Framework.
(Author's own framework based on Osterwalder 2004, Abdelkafi et al. 2013, p. 12, Köster 2014 and Osterwalder, Pigneur 2010).

11.4 Business Model Patterns

In this section the author introduces a range of business model archetypes and patterns. The goal is to give an overview of possible taxonomies for business models which the author will utilize for his further research with regards to digital business models for innovative shared automobility services.

The fast development, diffusion and adoption of the Internet has had a major influence on the generation of entirely new business models. The reason is that the Internet created completely new ways how to organize businesses differently, without necessarily changing the core value proposition. Therefore, the term business model is found in numerous variations, such as 'new business models', 'e-business models' or 'internet business models' (Osterwalder 2004). However, Osterwalder claims that these additional attributes, such as: 'e-' or 'new' will disappear in time because most business models will be based on ICT components and Internet connectivity.

It is thought that in order to benefit from technologic advancements innovative business models are required (Chesbrough 2010; Christensen et al. 2009). It seems that the capability to design viable business model tends to be a key aspect for remaining competitive in technology driven markets. However, the main challenges in developing business models are managing the complexity of the technology and anticipating the business logics in the promising markets. One of the approaches to overcoming these challenges is the usage of prototypes and patterns (Gassmann et al. 2013). According to Alexander et al. (1977) patterns describe recurring problems in the environment and the core of the solution to that problem. The solution can be then reused again and again. According to Buschmann et al. (2007) patterns can contribute to the reduction of complexity and to the increase in effectiveness and efficiency of the problem-solving process.

In the context of business models prototypes, patterns and taxonomies have been discussed quite frequently in the recent literature. Capturing prototypes and patterns is beneficial because it enables the reduction of the different types of business models encountered in practice to a few recurring patterns (Abdelkafi et al. 2013). There have been numerous authors that undertook research activities in this field (Timmers 1998; Weill et al. 2005; Andrew et al. 2013; Johnson 2010; Osterwalder, Pigneur 2010; Gassmann et al. 2013; Abdelkafi et al. 2013; Bonakdar 2015; Stähler 2002). These authors provided various taxonomies of business model and classified these business models in a set of different categories using a number of common characteristics.

One of the best known classifications and definitions of business models is the one conducted by Timmers (1998). Timmers' research focused chiefly on electronic business models. He distinguishes between eleven generic e-business models and classifies them according to their degree of innovation and their functional integration. The models are e-shops, e-procurement, e-malls, e-auctions, virtual communities, collaboration platforms, third-party marketplaces, value chain integrators, value-chain service providers, information brokerage and trust and other third-party services. Stähler (2002) categorizes the business models by the possible cooperation scheme between ditinct business partners which can act either as suppliers or purchasers. There are three business partners: Consumer, Business and Government, from which the following cooperation models can be derived: C2C, C2B, C2G, B2C, B2B, B2G, G2C, G2B and G2G.

Weill et al. (2005) define a taxonomy of business model patterns based on two characteristics. The first represents the type of asset involved: financial, physical, intangible or human. The second refers to the rights that are being sold, which can be: creator, distributor, landlord, or broker. Their typology encompasses 16 business model archetypes and which is then used to classify the business models of the top 1000 firms in the US economy. Johnson's (2010) taxonomy compiles 19 patterns that are used analogously across industries as a tool for business model innovation. These patterns are: affinity club, brokerage, bundling, cell phone, crowdsourcing, disintermediation, fractionalization, freemium, leasing, low-touch, negative operating cycle, pay-as-you-go, razors/blades, reverse auction, reverse razors/blades, product-to-service, standardization, subscription club, and user communities. Osterwalder, Pigneur (2010) deliver a more general overview with five business model patterns: unbundling business models to three core businesses types (product innovation, customer relationship management and infrastructure management), long tail business models, multi-sided platforms, free business models, and open business models. Andrew et al. (2013) define three business model patterns: orchestrators, integrators, and licensors. Weill, Vitale (2013) describe eight atomic business models. Each model describes a different way of conducting business in electronic way. The most recent and probably the most extensive classification thus far has been provided by Gassmann et al. (2013). They identified 55 universal business model patterns, described them in detail and made them available for the purpose of constructing new business ideas.

Below the author will give a more detailed overview of such business model taxonomies. Table 11 to Table 13 provide an explanatory descriptions of business model patterns based on the work of Timmers (1998), Weill, Vitale (2013) and Tapscott et al. (2000). The reason for shedding the light on these taxonomies is the fact that they do strongly refer to electronic business models. Therefore, they are highly applicable for the work at hand which deals with digital technologies and their application to innovative urban mobility concepts. However, for the further investigation activities the author will resort to all taxonomies and classifications that were identified during the literature review process and could fit better for his research needs.

Table 11: Patterns of business models (source: adapted from Timmers 1998).

Archetype	Business Model Description
E-shops	Denotes web marketing and promotion of a company or a shop and increasingly includes the possibility to order and to pay.
E-procurement	Describes electronic tendering and procurement of goods and services.
E-malls	Consists of a collection of e-shops, usually enhanced by a common umbrella, for example a well-known brand.
E-auctions	Stands for the electronic implementation of the bidding mechanism also known from traditional auctions.
Virtual communities	This model brings together virtual communities that contribute value in a basic environment provided by the virtual community operator. The revenue stream is generated by membership fees and advertising. It can also be found as an add-on to other marketing operations for customer feedback or loyalty building.
Collaboration platforms	Companies of this group provide an environment for collaboration between enterprises.
Third-party marketplaces	A model that is suitable when a company wishes to leave the web marketing to a third-party. Third-party marketplaces offer a user interface to the product catalogue of the supplier.
Value chain integrators	This pattern represents companies that focus on integrating multiple steps of the value chain, with the potential to exploit the information flow between those steps as further added value.
Value-chain service providers	Stands for companies that specialize on a specific function for the value chain, such as electronic payment or logistics.
Information brokerage	Embraces a whole range of new information services that are emerging to add value to the huge amounts of data available on the open networks or coming from integrated business operations.
Trust and other third-party services	Stands for trust services, such as certification authorities and electronic notaries and other trusted third-parties.

Table 12: Patterns of business models (source: adapted from Weill, Vitale 2013).

Archetype	Business Model Description
Content Provider	Content providers are firms that create and provide content (information, products, or services) in digital form to customers via third-parties.
Direct to Customer	In this model, the buyer and seller interact directly often bypassing traditional channel members.
Full-Service Provider	Firms in this category provide total coverage of customer needs in a particular domain, consolidated via a single point of contact. Domains cover any area where customer needs cover multiple products and services, such as financial services or health care.
Intermediary	The intermediary links multiple buyers and sellers. Usually the sellers pay the intermediary listing fees and selling commissions and it is possible that the buyer

Archetype	Business Model Description
	may also pay a purchase or membership fee. Advertisers also provide revenue for intermediaries. There are six major classes of intermediaries, namely electronic mall, shopping agents, specialty auctions, portals, electronic auctions and electronic markets.
Shared Infrastructure	In this atomic business model a firm provides infrastructure shared by its owners. The shared infrastructure generally offers a service that is not already available in the marketplace, and it may also be a defensive move to thwart potential domination by another major player.
Value net Integrator	The value net integrator coordinates product flows from suppliers to allies and customers. He strives to own the customer relationship with the other participants in the model, thus knowing more about their operations than any other player. His main role is coordinating the value chain.
Virtual Community	In this model the firm is in the center, positioned between members of the community and suppliers. Fundamental to the success of this model is that members are able to communicate with each other directly.
Whole-of-Enterprise /Government	The single point of contact for the e-business customer is the essence of the whole-of-enterprise atomic business model. This model plays an important role in public-sector organizations but also applies to the private sector.

Table 13: Patterns of business models (source: adapted from Tapscott et al. 2000).

Archetype	Business Model Description
Agora	Applies to markets where buyers and sellers meet to freely negotiate and assign value to goods. An Agora facilitates exchange between buyers and sellers, who jointly 'discover' a price. Because sellers may offer a wide and often unpredictable variety or quantity of goods, value integration is low.
Aggregator	In Aggregation b-webs there is a leader that takes responsibility for selecting products and services, targeting market segments, setting prices, and ensuring fulfillment. This leader typically sets prices in advance and offers a diverse variety of products and services, with zero to limited value integration.
Integrator	In a Value Chain, the so-called context provider structures and directs a b-web network to produce a highly integrated value proposition. The seller has the final say in pricing.
Alliance	An Alliance strives for high value integration without hierarchical control. Its participants design goods or services, create knowledge, or simply produces dynamic, shared experiences. Alliances typically depend on rules and standards that govern interaction, acceptable participant behavior, and the determination of value.
Distributor	Distributive Networks are b-webs that keep the economy alive and mobile. They play a vital role in ensuring the healthy balance of the systems that they support. Distributive Networks service the other types of b-webs by allocating and delivering goods.

12 Typology of Digital Business Models for Emerging Shared Automobility Services[13]

12.1 Introduction

12.1.1 Focus area

The challenges of automobility in urban areas arise from both (i) their over-engineered characteristics, e.g. a typical car can reach speeds of well over 160 km per hour, whereas typical urban driving speeds range from between 24 to 40 km per hour (Mitchell et al. 2010), and (ii) their radical underutilization as discussed in chapter 6. Even though these problems have been widely recognized the challenge remains to keep the benefits of privately-owned cars while removing the dependence on non-renewable resources, minimizing pollution, and avoiding the need for additional road infrastructure and parking space in the urban area.

In this respect, sharing concepts, such as car- and ridesharing, have been recently introduced as a novelty with regard to the patterns of car usage. Even though these concepts have been known and implemented for more than 30 years, it needs to be stated that car- and ridesharing have experienced an exceptional come-back in recent years. It is thought that high urbanization and the digital revolution of society have favored their revitalization and flourishing (see chapter 5).

Therefore, the report below examines key mobility innovations in the sector that can be labeled as 'Shared Automobility Services', a sector which has emerged at the frontier of sharing concepts, car digitization and vehicle automation. In particular, the study analyzes the development in the following niche areas of mobility services based on cars:

- Carsharing mobility concept,
- Ridesharing mobility concept,
- On-demand mobility concept,
- Mobility services based on autonomous vehicles,
- Mobility-as-a-service concept.

It needs to be stated that the author has initially introduced carsharing and ridesharing concepts in chapter 5. In the sections below he further elaborates on them from the perspective of digitization.

[13] Several sections of this chapter were partially reprinted in Janasz, Schneidewind (2017). Affected sections will be marked in the footnote.

12.1.2 Research Methodology

According to the nature of this thesis the particular interest goes to innovative business models based on digital technologies. The author aims at identifying business model patterns for innovative mobility concepts that can be applied in the practice.

To achieve this goal the researcher has set up an exploratory research approach which has relied on two qualitative research methodologies:

- Acquiring knowledge by developing and analyzing two relevant case studies for the mobility concepts of car- and ridesharing from the field: smexx and TwoGo by SAP, both from Germany.
- Semi-structured in-depth interviews with selected mobility experts in order to develop further possible prototypes.

During the data collection phase (in the period from 2014 to 2016) 10 selected mobility experts and startup entrepreneurs from Switzerland and Germany were interviewed. In these interviews access to subjective points of view has been sought to generate new insights into the emerging urban mobility field of 'Shared Automobility Services'.

The outcomes have been analyzed by means of qualitative methods of data analysis. For the specific analysis and design of business models the author has applied a value-oriented approach which he has developed in the previous chapter: the P4C Business Model Framework.

Six business model prototypes are proposed to guide and support mobility specialists and policy makers. On the one hand, the generic prototypes should help understand the influence of the most recent advancements in digital technologies on the provision of urban mobility services. On the other hand, the prototypes should depict the value proposition of digital business models for overcoming automobility dependence.

12.2 Prototype 1: Digital Carsharing

12.2.1 Carsharing: Business Concepts

With reference to the underlying business concept carsharing programs seek to shift personal transportation choices from asset ownership to a service provided 'on-demand' (Fagnant, Kockelman 2014). This business model is referred to as product-to-service, servitization or rent instead of buy pattern (Abdelkafi et al. 2013; Johnson 2010; Gassmann et al. 2013). To be more precise, a number of past studies have attributed carsharing as a use-oriented and product-service system (Mont 2002; Tukker, Tischner 2006; Williams 2007). In that sense the value proposition is not the product itself but the 'job-to-be-done' (Christensen 1997). According to Weill et al. (2005) selling the right to use assets might be more profitable and more highly valued by the market than selling the ownership of assets. This conclusion is based on the analysis of 1000 US enterprises which revealed that the most popular business models such as manufacturers (46% of all analyzed enterprises) are less profitable (Weill et al. 2005).

The financial model of a carsharing organization is based on member revenues, sponsorship, government subsidies and grants (Cohen, Kietzmann 2014). Carsharing institutions may be organized as a commercial business or the users may be organized as a public agency, cooperative or an ad-hoc grouping (Tietenberg 2007). In general, there are four possible organization schemes for a 'Carsharing Service Provider': private end-user (B2C), business internal (B2B), customer-to-customer (P2P) and nonprofit (Lerner et al. 2012b; Cohen, Kietzmann 2014).

Business-to-Consumer (B2C) Carsharing

This type of service is defined as an economic and environment-friendly mobility option which is complementary to the public transportation systems. The users hire a vehicle on demand rather than invest in a privately owned car (Cohen, Kietzmann 2014).

Business-to-Business (B2B) Carsharing

This carsharing variant operates as a closed system within a specific company, where vehicles are not provided to the staff in the form of company cars but they are shared among the staff. According to Lerner et al. (2012b) it contributes to savings on parking spaces and to the reduction of company's carbon footprint.

Nonprofit/Cooperative Carsharing

In cooperative carsharing schemes members collectively contribute resources and manage the carsharing organization. They also have no expectation regarding positive financial results. Some examples are: the Swiss co-operative 'Mobility' in Europe or the Metro Vancouver carsharing co-operative 'Modo' in North America (Canada). It is the traditional carsharing approach with its roots in Europe in the 1960s and 1970s where it was established as more affordable alternative to owning and maintaining a vehicle.

Peer-to-Peer (P2P) Carsharing

The fourth carsharing scheme is the peer-to-peer approach (P2P). In this model individuals who need a car constitute the demand side of the market. The supply side is created by private owners of underutilized vehicles who are willing to share their cars. Both parties are connected and matched via an online platform which acts as a trusted intermediary partner. Once this intermediation process is completed the private car can be used by the end user who declared the interest in the vehicle. Clearly, the P2P carsharing service strongly relies on the digital technology in order to provide a reliable intermediation process and service (Cohen, Kietzmann 2014). Examples for such P2P services are the German company Tamyca (from 'take my car') or US American RelayRides.

The ubiquitous access to the Internet, wide-spread diffusion of mobile devices and other digital technologies can further contribute to the development of the carsharing paradigm. A purposeful integration and implementation of digital technologies could lead to the establishment of a mobility system with open access for every market participant, which is globally scalable and does not require capital intensive investments. The global goal would be to connect as many as possible underutilized cars to a global system and offer mobility services to the market. One possible resolution option could be a provision of such a technology that would enable a network of brand-independent carsharing programs that are integrated across each other on a single and global platform. The following case study of the smexx GmbH, a start-up company from Berlin (Germany), will illustrate that in more detail.

12.2.2 Case Study: smexx GmbH[14] [15] [16] [17]

12.2.2.1 Introduction to smexx

The smexx GmbH is a company that offers hardware and software for keyless access to vehicles and other electronic locks. The business was established in the beginning of 2016 as a new formation of carzapp GmbH. Carzapp was an award-winning start-up from Berlin (Germany) that aimed at revolutionizing the carsharing market with its patented hardware solution ZappKit, an installed bit of hardware that enables smartphone-based access to any car. It was carzapp's CEO, Oliver Lünstedt, who stated that ZappKits implemented in 100'000 cars would have the potential to replace 1 million cars on the roads (Mechnich 2014). The carzapp company was originally founded as a peer-to-peer carsharing platform provider (similar to GetAround or RelayRides) based on its technology stack: ZappKit access unit, software and online platform.

The special features of this toolkit enabled this approach. It allows spontaneous renting of cars without the need to hand over the keys, since the hardware enables digital car

[14] GmbH (Ger.) stands for limited liability corporation (Amer.) or private limited company (Brit.).
[15] The case study has been published with permission from smexx GmbH.
[16] This section is partially reprinted in Janasz, Schneidewind (2017). Courtesy of Springer.
[17] In 2017 smexx was acquired by Valeo S.A. The case study presented in this book refers to the period before the acquisition.

access, i.e. keyless opening and closing of vehicles, via smartphone. It can be installed in all kinds of vehicles which have a central locking system. With other embedded digital technologies such as GPS and GSM the solution offers some further unique features such as: forwarding of all necessary information to the police in case of attempted theft or vehicle location as well as route calculation. In addition to the hardware, the company offers a scalable and comprehensive software solution, including a white label platform for the fleet management of vehicles equipped with the ZappKit. After the company had originally developed its hardware for motor vehicles, now also heavy equipment, garage doors and electronic door locks can be equipped with the ZappKit. The solution is also ECE certified which makes it applicable possibly to almost every vehicle. Although, the carsharing platform still exists, it is currently only one of the pillars of smexx. The company has recently shifted its business strategy and re-launched as a provider of variety of applications and services.

The carzapp company participated in several financing cycles. In the initial phase of the start-up the company was financed from owners' own capital and external 'angel' investors. The first investment (2012-2013) amounted to 280'000 Euros. The second financing cycle took place in 2013 by means of a crowdfunding initiative. The amount of this investment was 250'000 Euros. In 2015 the company received a 'made in.de' award for an innovative digital business model and product in the amount of 25'000 Euros. The grant has been awarded for efforts to achieve sustainable value creation and to contribute to the future competitiveness of Germany. Even though, the company achieved a break-even in the operating cash flow for the first time in December 2015 it had to file for insolvency at the end of 2015. The reason for that were overdue liabilities and an unexpected capitalization flap which resulted from failed investments by two potential partners. This situation might have been induced by deliberate actions as both investors were aware of each other's intentions. Nevertheless, the severe situation was staved off through a buyout by founders along with the support from previous and new private investors. The company has been reestablished as a new formation – smexx GmbH. Since then the company has been fostering a new strategic reorientation on the market by extending its value proposition from a carsharing enabler to a provider of the technology for remote control and key-less access to every possible electronic lock. Therefore, the name smexx stands for 'smart access'. The company has set a goal to achieve a dynamic growth, however, under a strict condition of financial stability. The prerequisites for that is securing existing and establishing new partnerships as well as full customer satisfaction. The brief start-up history of carzapp/smexx is depicted in the Figure 16 below.

12.2.2.2 Possible Use Cases

Peer-to-Peer Carsharing

Car owners and renters are brought together via the smexx online portal. Owners of vehicles set an ask price (for the car hire). The renters of the vehicle pay a fixed fee based on the duration of the car usage. Owners would typically rent their cars while they are on holiday or at work, when the car is underutilized. For the renters the scheme provides an opportunity to flexibly source a car in the proximity of their location. If a renter needs a vehicle he or she can request it from the vehicle owner. The vehicle owner has the option to approve or to decline the request. However, once the owner approves a request, the renter uses their smartphone to unlock and access the car. The ZappKit mobile application enables the deal without the need to hand over the actual keys. For the duration of the deal both parties are completely protected via a usage-based insurance option. It is possible thanks to a novel hour-based insurance provided by R+V.

Owners benefit financially from utilizing their cars, while they do not use them. For renters it is about flexible access to cars on-demand and about convenient access. This carsharing scheme has significant environmental benefits. Carsharing means fewer cars on the roads. Car sharers can reduce their carbon dioxide (CO_2) emissions by up to one ton per year or roughly ten per cent of average German emissions per head (Climate-KIC 2011). Additionally, in 2011 smexx partnered with Renault, Peugeot, Vodafone, E.ON and Capgemini in a pilot program to foster the development of electromobility in Germany. It was concluded that by combining the advantages of carsharing with electromobility the vehicle operating costs could be reduced by up to 70 per cent, whilst optimizing the underutilized usage of private vehicles (Climate-KIC 2011).

Independent Carsharing Schemes

It is interesting that smexx with its entire digital infrastructure (i.e. telematics equipment, online platform, and the end-user mobile app to locate and select vehicles can provides) provides the possibility to set up an independent carsharing scheme, in principle, from the scratch. The 'white label' strategy makes it possible for every community, private company, public institution or any other organization to establish their own carsharing program.

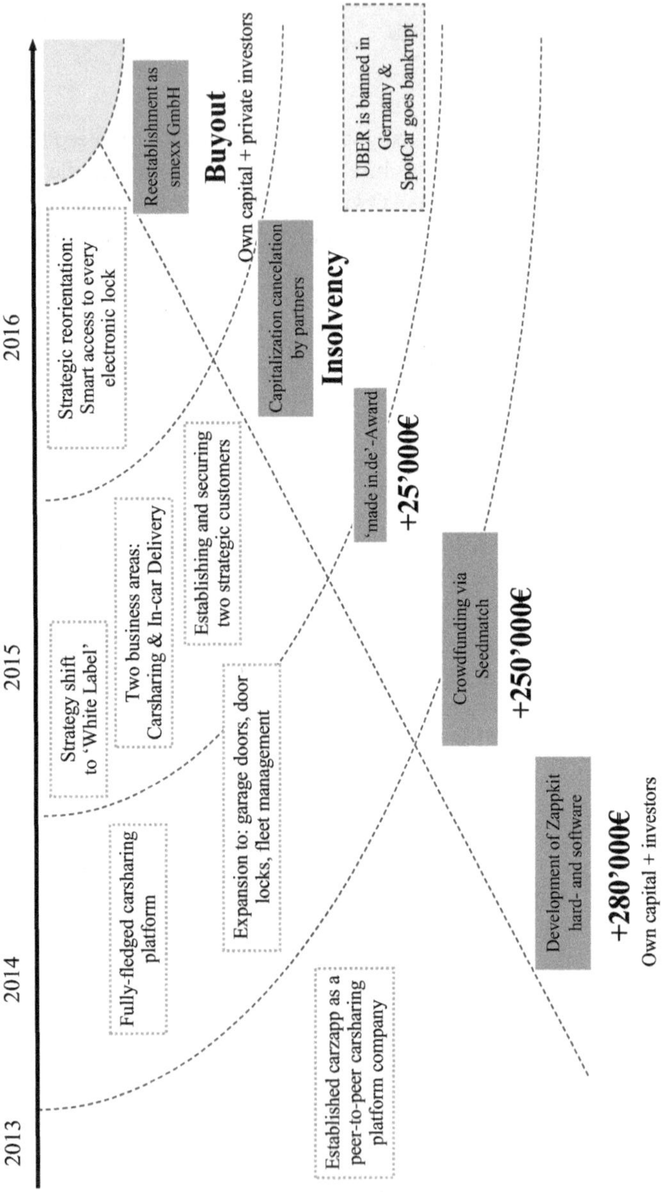

Figure 16: The brief history of smexx/carzapp. (Diagram by author).

An example of such prominent organizations are car dealerships who, in fact, could be the best adopters of commercial carsharing business. They can approach it in different ways. Some may use unsold vehicle inventories. Others could focus either on specific models or on a mixed offer. It is up to the dealership to determine the best suited approach. Once there is an idea to provide a carsharing service, smexx would provide the required infrastructure. The car dealer receives the access to the technology infrastructure and a toolkit with marketing materials such as flyers, car decals, and parking space signage. In addition, marketing consulting, financial processing, and call center support could be provided by additional partners who can be also included into the carsharing program.

The benefit for the dealers is as obvious as trivial. They could foster the utilization of their extensive car fleets that they anyway need to maintain. They can do it because they have access to an immense customer base that they serve locally or regionally. On the other hand the smexx carsharing platform users are able to access the vehicles across all dealers that are participating in the program, allowing for a wider range of choices and locations. However, the cars must be picked up and dropped off within their local area, since they do not allow for point-to-point usage at this time.

In-Car and In-Night Delivery

The combination of the ZappKit and the smexx mobile app enables also the implementation of completely innovative special services, such as freight delivery services. This innovation is called 'in-car delivery' and it aims at overcoming the inefficiency resulting from package delivery at fixed times. This often leads to the problem that the same packages need to be delivered several times before they are eventually picked up by the addressee. Hence, this contributes to the traffic generation on the roads. The idea behind in-car delivery is that cars, in particular their trunks, can be utilized as smart lockers for freight delivery. This would happen while the car is parked. Across the world cars seem to be parked at least 92% of the time and typically about 96% of the time (Barter 2013). In that time the packages could be delivered directly to the car without the need to actually interact with the courier. It can be enabled by digitally tracking the parking routines of car drivers. A smart matching-platform would be then able to automatically send the delivery service to a specific place where the car is currently parked. The trusted delivery partner can access the trunk of the car by using a keyless electronic authorization process with the mobile app. This would make it possible to pop the trunk and deposit the package inside. After that the car can be securely locked and the car owner is updated via SMS. Besides offering customers greater flexibility, the in-car delivery service promotes efficiency since it avoids unsuccessful attempts to encounter customers at the specified address. In that way the in-car delivery service could contribute to the reduction of the amount of traffic on the roads. There are already several attempts to implement this kind of innovative services (Popken, NBC News 2015; Cardrops 2016).

There are also similar use cases in the B2B-sector. To name just a few: unlocking of containers and accessing freight trucks. In the first case for example, cooling containers in grocery shops could be directly accessed to deliver fresh food. In the latter case the warehouse employees could easily access every truck at night shift to load them before their daily touring begins without the need to carry around dozens of keys. This setup gives the customers several benefits, chiefly faster availability of goods and a better utilization of drivers, technicians or tradesmen. The professional staff can then effectively spend time on their value-adding activities and not on waiting for spare parts or tools to become available. This kind of service can be referred to as same-day or in-night distribution/ delivery.

12.2.2.3 Business Model Analysis

The author has analyzed the business model of smexx by means of his P4C Business Model Framework (see Figure 17). Subsequently, he will take a closer look at the characteristics of the underlying patterns and illustrate smexx's business model in accordance with the current theory in the field of business models.

Purpose and Value Proposition

Two questions arise here: what is the value proposition and what are the possible relevant digital use cases that can be offered based on the intelligent implementation of digital technologies? Even though smexx has been established as an organization that provides peer-to-peer carsharing scheme essentially the company is an ICT and service provider. The proprietary technology stack encompasses: ZappKit hardware, software components and an online platform. By combining these technology elements the company is in position to propose an innovative value to the market. The purpose smexx serves can be described as follows:

> Electronic remote control of every possible electronic lock and the enablement of key-less access.

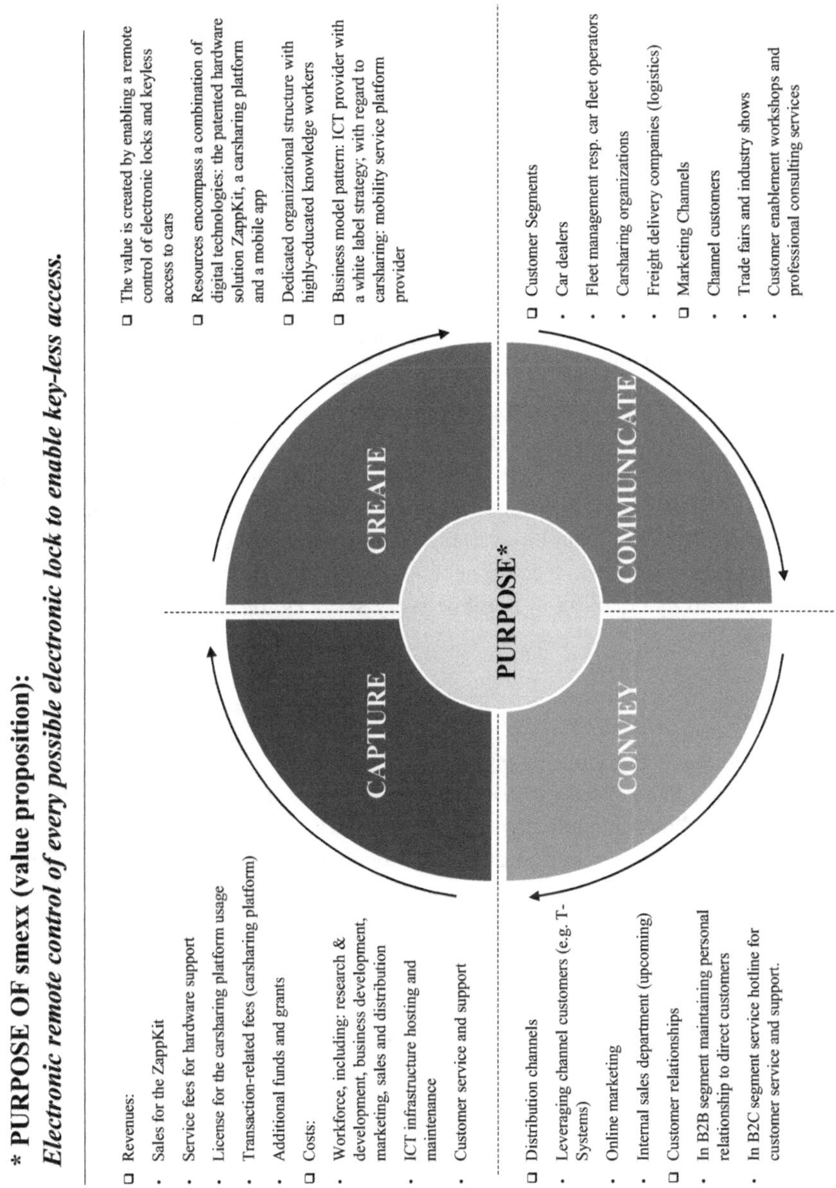

Figure 17: The P4C Business Model Framework applied to the smexx company. (Diagram by author).

This statement represents a general understanding of smexx's underlying bundle of products and services offered to customers to satisfy their needs. Based on this unique value proposition there are several digital use cases, in other words digital 'jobs-to-be-done', that have been designed prototyped, tested and launched by smexx's engineers:

(1) Carsharing platform provider

Smexx does not directly act as a carsharing service provider. It enables the provision of manufacturer-independent carsharing services. This means that every fleet operator, such as a company fleet or a car dealer, can establish a carsharing scheme based on the vehicle fleet they possess.

(2) Freight delivery enabler

Several applications are possible for freight delivery. Especially, in-car delivery, same-day and in-night delivery are innovative services that are enabled, chiefly in situations where there is no personnel to receive the deliveries. By deploying the smexx solution the delivery is made possible without the need to interact with the addressee or a dedicated staff member. The technology can be implemented in cars, garage doors, access locks for goods or other heavy equipment. Currently, the B2B freight delivery segment is being explored by enabling in-night delivery services for spare parts or construction components.

Create Value

As described above the value is created by enabling an electronic remote control of electronic locks and a key-less access, for example, to cars. Besides the proprietary technology developed by the company there are several other important factors that enable the value creation. The most important components for the value creation process are described below.

(1) End-to-end value chain

Smexx's technology solutions and partnerships set the foundation for providing an end-to-end set of value adding activities. These activities are both (i) organized internally and conducted within the firm and (ii) some of them are provided by external partners. In general, smexx aims at offering a one-stop-shop concept which should give the possibility to carry out all the necessary steps that lead to the provision of the specific digital job-to-be-done from a single location or device.

With regard to the white-label carsharing platform, smexx technology offers a single point of access and control for following main and supplementary services:

- identification via an automated web process (own capabilities),
- booking platform (own capabilities),
- key-less vehicle access (own capabilities) and
- billing, accounting and payment (in cooperation with a third party partner).

With respect to the in-car or in-night delivery enablement the required one-stop-shop process steps encompass: identification and key-less access.

(2) Resources and Organization

Obviously, the key resources that enable creating the value is the matured technology stack, i.e.: software elements such as online booking platform and the mobile application, and the hardware element, i.e. the ZappKit access technology. However, beside the technology there is a professional organizational structure that leverages the business potentials of the underlying innovation in technology. The smexx organization includes two distinct divisions: technology and management. The former is responsible for software and hardware and encompasses such activities as:

- software and hardware development,
- research and
- technical support.

The latter includes business-related activities, such as:

- strategy development and implementation, e.g. securing further investments,
- business development, e.g. expansion to other business areas and new markets,
- customer relationship and end-customer support and
- consulting services.

(3) Partnerships

Smexx has established several partnerships. These partnerships can be distinguished into: operational and strategic ones.

- Operational partnerships

Not all value chain activities are provided by smexx alone. Some activities, which are not directly related to the core competence, which is providing electronic key control and keyless access, are provided by third parties. These non-core activities include: call center for end-customer support, payment and identification and are sourced from external partners.

- Strategic partnerships

As of 2015, smexx has been maintaining two strategic partnerships in order to provide innovative services in the area smart access to a wide range of customers. The company partners with the largest independent leasing bank for car dealers in Germany as well as with T-Systems, one of the largest German IT services company. The partnerships are designed to provide services based on the ZappKit technology to the end customers of involved partners. However, they should not be perceived as customers in a classical sense of the end consumer of products and services. They should be rather to as 'channel customers' who provide marketing channels to the end-customers who receive and consume the services from smexx. From that perspective the strategic partners can be also labeled as gate-keepers to the end consumer.

The partnerships with the independent leasing bank aims at providing 'carsharing-ready' cars to dealers and their end-customers. Car dealerships can extend the range of their services by becoming carsharing service providers. For that purpose smexx provides and operates the platform and additional cross services such as payment, billing and the call center. In addition, in accordance with the leasing bank smexx connects the carsharing-ready cars and additional end users with its own carsharing platform to achieve scale effects.

T-Systems is the strategic partner for providing the ZappKit technology to freight delivery companies which supply components and spare parts to professional tradesmen at nighttime. With regard to this customer segment smexx offers innovative 'in-car' and 'in-night' delivery services. The idea behind in-car delivery is that cars, in particular their trunks, can be utilized as smart lockers for freight delivery. This happens while the car is parked. In the case of in-night delivery the warehouse employees can easily access every truck during their night shift to load them before the daily touring begins. For example, T-Systems has more than 10'000 cars in which spare parts for service technicians are being delivered during the night. Additionally, there are also warehouses (such as containers, garages), which still operate based on physical key solution. Process costs occur due to key management (e.g. ordering a spare key or lost keys) and car searching by logistics provider. By installing ZappKits T-Systems considerably simplifies the process for the freight delivery companies by enabling following digital functionalities:

- tracking cars' locations via GPS,
- unlocking via cards with near field communication (NFC) sensors,
- logging who has accessed which car at what time to avoid problems due to cars being left open after delivery etc.

Current pilot customer has expanded from 30 to 850 equipped access points for the in-night delivery service. In this case, the benefits encompass faster availability of goods and a much better utilization of drivers, technicians or tradesmen.

(4) Additional value adding services

As an ICT company with extensive know-how in digital technology smexx is also obliged to deliver a know-how transfer to their customers. The knowledge transfer is organized in the form of professional consulting services. These services can be divided into following categories:

- Technical Consulting: to provide expertise about the technology stack and how to implement and operate it,
- Management Consulting: training in customer acquisition for carsharing services, correct localization of cars for optimal utilization, establishing marketing campaigns for carsharing, integration of carsharing with other services of car dealers.

Communicate Value

(1) Customer segments and customer communication (Story)

Smexx translates its unique value proposition into understandable messages. These messages are coherent stories that are directed to company's specific customer segments. Smexx approaches different target audience with different stories. The consumers of smexx technology can be divided into following customer segments:

- Car dealers

Car dealers aim at establishing and providing additional carsharing services to their end-customers. With that they further extend their service portfolio and they can also utilize their car fleets in more efficient way. The story for car dealers can be described:

> Smexx technology supports the product-to-service shift. It enables car dealers to establish a forward-looking business model with innovative mobility services such as carsharing. Not only can the automatic access control lead to a development of a new business pillar but also to the expansion of the existing business model, as the vehicles can now be accessed outside of the normal business hours. With that car dealers can become mobility service providers of the future.

- Fleet management and car fleet operators

Fleet management and car fleet operators are companies or corporate divisions who seek to implement a corporate carsharing scheme based on the available fleet of pool cars. The communicated story for this customer segment is as follows:

> Corporate carsharing enables the company to provide efficient mobility services to its employees. With that instrument the fleet manager can achieve

the reduction in costs and size of the fleet which lead to the optimization of the entire corporate fleet.

- Carsharing organizations

Smexx offers its technology also to the traditional carsharing operators who operate in the B2C segment. Smexx's offering includes the end-to-end service enablement technology and price advantages in comparison to the competition on the market of carsharing technology.

- Logistics companies

In the logistics industry smexx addresses in particular the freight delivery companies who offer, for example, express delivery services. The offering for this customer segment is to expand their range of services by options of in-car, same-day and in-night delivery. The message to be communicated is defined as:

> Smexx technology enables the deployment of additional services such as in-car and in-night delivery by means of electronic key-less access to storage spaces. The deliveries can be carried out outside of the business hours and therefore no human interaction is required. This creates a considerable cost reduction potential in the process areas of key management and tracking of the deliveries.

(2) Marketing channels

As mentioned above, in terms of the marketing channels smexx currently uses its channel customers (i.e. the leasing bank and T-Systems) as a contact channel to the consumers of its platform technology and services. Furthermore, smexx presents its technology at various trade fairs and industry shows. Moreover, also professional consulting services and customer enablement workshops in the B2B segment can be used as a form of marketing instruments.

Convey Value

(1) Distribution channels

Both channel customers are currently the main sales and distribution channels of smexx. With regard to the carsharing platform there are currently 40 car dealers participating in the pilot phase of the bank's carsharing scheme. However, the car dealership base of the bank encompasses approx. 30'000 dealers in Europe and 14'000 dealers in the U.S. Currently, smexx is working on establishing an online marketing strategy in order to be able to reach this base of mass customers. The strategy is to be introduced after the pilot phase with the selected car dealers of the bank has ended.

With regard to freight delivery companies smexx is currently cooperating with T-Systems. However, for this business pillar smexx is planning to establish an internal sales department in order to further expand the business beyond pure inbound business development. Internal sales will address the logistics service providers. This will include, for example, tele-sales in order to start pro-active customer acquisition process in this business segment. Potential customers are: logistics services, express delivery, and automotive companies for in-car delivery enablement.

(2) Customer relationships

Currently, smexx manages the relationships to its customers by customer segments, i.e. B2B and B2C. In the B2B segment the main instrument of customer care is maintaining personal relationship to direct customers, i.e. chiefly managing the key channel customers. In the segment of B2C the end-customers are covered by the service hotline for customer service and support. Otherwise, there is no direct contact with the end-consumers, but through channel customers. Once smexx has established online marketing and outbound sales departments, the company will need to consider consolidating and automating its marketing, sales and distribution by means of an integrated customer relationship management (CRM).

Capture Value

(1) Revenue flows

In general, the model for revenue generation at smexx comprises four components:

- hardware sales, i.e. the ZappKit technology,
- fix monthly service fee for the hardware,
- license for the carsharing platform usage, and
- transaction-related fee - however, only in the field of carsharing services.

In the logistics business line the revenue model has been limited to hardware sales and the fix service fee. However, smexx has been considering the implementation of a further cost for access component in the future. This will mean that a fee for every key-less access transaction would be imposed.

(2) Cost structure

The main cost element is personnel. However, this cost covers the most critical parts of the business, i.e.: solution development, research, business development, project management, customer support and marketing. Further cost elements are production costs (e.g. materials) for the ZappKit hardware. Other none-core activities are sourced from external service providers. It includes all ICT-related costs, such as server hosting and maintenance, and first-level service and support hotline. The costs for this external services are directly posted into the company's books.

12.2.2.4 Business Model Patterns

In this section the author takes a closer look at the characteristics of the underlying patterns and illustrates smexx's business model in accordance with the current theory in the field of business model design.

With its ZappKit the company has been deploying a white label business strategy. White label products or services are produced by one company, i.e. the producer. Other companies, the marketers, rebrand these products or services and let them appear as if they have made them (Gassmann et al. 2013). The producing company can direct its attention to further optimization of its products and services. Thus the company has better opportunities to achieve economies of scale (Gassmann et al. 2013).

The business model pattern which applies to smexx's business approach is the *intellectual landlord model* (Weill et al. 2005). This business model can take two distinct forms: *licensor* or *franchisor* (Andrew et al. 2013). In the case of a franchising system, the franchisees would be allowed to carry the name of the franchisor and apply its processes and technology (Abdelkafi et al. 2013). This is clearly not the case with the business model of smexx because the company delivers white label solutions. The smexx technology, which encompasses the white label ZappKit hardware, the associated white label software platform and the white label mobile app, has been licensed to the leasing bank and to its customers, i.e. the car dealers. The licensees use the digital technology, processes and the intellectual property of smexx, however, under the label of the bank. The system involves fees that should be paid to the licensor as described in section "Capture Value". With that in mind, smexx is de facto an ICT platform provider offering a scalable end-to-end carsharing platform.

However, it needs to be noted that smexx is not only a pure technology provider but also provides a range of value-added services. The smexx all-round carefree package includes both (i) one-stop-shop digital processes such as: identification, information brokerage, booking, payment and billing, and (ii) professional services such as: customer services and professional management consulting. With that in mind, smexx can be denoted as the *mobility service platform provider* or the *Google of mobility* in Lerner et al.'s terms (Lerner et al. 2012b).

This unusual venture between a financial institution and a technology supplier smexx has demonstrated a completely new approach to providing carsharing mobility services. The business concept behind it has not been offered in this form by any other institution before. The pioneering idea about this particular carsharing approach is that it offers a possibility to set up a brand-independent carsharing service. The car dealerships can provide a carsharing service to their end customers, independently of the OEM, by deploying both the smexx technology and their available vehicle fleet. Additionally, the service can be used by customers across the entire smexx system which contributes to the possibility to scale the carsharing system area-wide. With that in mind, smexx can be also denoted as the *mobility service platform provider* (Lerner et al. 2012b). If this approach succeeds the growth potential can be remarkable.

12.2.2.5 Business Model Innovation

As mentioned above, smexx company started as pure peer-to-peer carsharing platform. However, although Berlin has been often referred to as the 'world city' of carsharing, some recent examples indicate that the peer-to-peer carsharing market can be volatile and shows some weaknesses. For instance, a relatively new carsharing system in Berlin, SpotCar, went bankrupt in May 2015 (GetMobility 2015). Also Uber's low-cost taxi service, has been recently banned in Germany after a court in Frankfurt decided it violates the German transportation law (BBC 2015; Spiegel Online 2015).

The decision to re-launch its strategy to become a white label technology provider with its ZappKit access unit seems to be a clever and rational strategic move which addresses the current market developments. Not only can the company further expand its share within the carsharing market, but the ZappKit can now be deployed also for other purposes, such as: heavy equipment, garage doors and door locks (Carzapp 2015). This shift has immediately led to a strong demand as the rapidly growing client base indicates. Currently smexx's customers encompass, e.g.: StarCar, ZF's Openmatics, eMio, Entega, EnBW and T-Systems (Carzapp 2015).

With regards to the carsharing service the company has decided to become a white label carsharing technology and platform provider with a main focus on car dealers and major car fleets. Smexx has launched a partnership with 70 car dealerships in Germany (Automobilwoche 2015). With this move smexx is entering the untapped and unexplored market of B2B carsharing for car dealers. However, one of the most interesting aspects of this realignment is the establishment of a strategic partnership with an independent leasing bank. It is rather an unusual situation, at least in the carsharing sector. Therefore, the question arises: where does the business model innovation come from?

It needs to be noted that the car dealers usually tend to work with three institutions to cover their financial needs. This includes the OEMs (car manufacturers) and usually two banks (Bacco 2015). A closer look at the leasing bank reveals that it is the largest financer of car purchases among Germany's independent financers. It has held a market share of 70% in this segment. It has possessed also 13% of the overall market for financing automobile purchases in Germany, ranking second only to Volkswagen Bank (Tschoegl, Guillén 2008). Additionally, it needs to be also noted that the bank specializes in subprime lending. Subprime lending is a type of loan that is offered to individuals who do not qualify for prime rate loans because of their rather low credit ratings. That is why the credits are offered at a rate above prime (Investopedia 2015). Furthermore, according to recent press reports the subprime loans for vehicle purchase are booming. It seems to result from the observable increase in new cars sales (Lanctot 2015). It is clear that the leasing bank aims at leveraging its relationships with their clients from the dealership sector. The bank has lending relationship with 30'000 dealers in Europe and 14'000 dealers in the U.S (Lanctot 2015).

According to some industry experts this puts the bank in a unique position and creates intriguing new opportunities. One of them is the provision of the innovative carsharing program. The bank supports the dealers with the set-up of the entire carsharing scheme. In the first step only location-based carsharing is possible. The dealer will receive the smexx hardware and software technology, marketing materials and a billing service. The installation of the ZappKit hardware solution allows model-independent keyless locking and unlocking of the vehicles via a smartphone. The associated white label software, an online booking platform, enables easy and flexible management of carsharing vehicles and it also fulfills the intermediary task of connecting car dealers with their end customers. The actual rental process runs completely digitally thanks to the white label smartphone app. This makes it possible to use the carsharing service also outside business hours. In addition to supplying the necessary hardware and software components, the smexx company maintains the online platform and the end customer support (Carzapp 2015). The carsharing service is primarily aimed at tier-two cities as the carsharing competition and diffusion seems to be still limited there. However, smexx will also support dealers with entering tier-one markets, if they so wish (Bacco 2015).

With this approach the bank has decided to offer a novel and innovative business option for car dealers – a carsharing service which is actually completely unrelated to the bank's core competency. However, this is actually a logical move if one takes into consideration that many subprime loans borrowers might have problems with the payments for their vehicles. As a matter of fact in some cases the financial institutions have already been deploying similar telematics solutions. The reason for that was the need for a mechanism which would enable disabling the vehicles in case of clients' disability to settle the payments. This has caused severe damages to the industry's reputation in the past, however (Lanctot 2015). The cooperation scheme with smexx puts the bank in the position to innovate its services to its partners in the dealership sector. The bank can offer innovative rental and lease programs as well as new car financing options. Additionally, the dealers can now effectively become fleet operators and establish carsharing programs. As a next step in 2016 the bank might also expand to corporate carsharing by offering the service for companies that are not large enough to establish a dedicated company fleet program. Furthermore, taking into consideration the current advancements in the field of usage-based discounted insurance options based on tracking devices installed in cars, the deployment of further innovations based on the present business model is possible. Some industry experts acknowledge that the business model innovation proposed by smexx and the bank has the potential to change auto lending dramatically. However, the adoption of this business model will happen gradually as it will need time to be adapted according to customer preferences (Lanctot 2015).

There are several other conceivable innovative use cases for smexx technology. In the future the service portfolio of smexx could be extended to the private sector: remote management of rental apartments or sharing keys in the family. The ZappKit could be also deployed into truck vehicles to simplify the management of big professional car fleets in logistics.

12.2.3 Proposition: Digital Carsharing

Sharing cars is an entrepreneurial approach which is built on the recognition that an idle car is an immense wasted asset, which means that it is greatly underutilized. Understanding this perspective could lead to the application of this business model by every single car owner.

As the case of smexx indicates, dedicated technology can enable a network of manufacturer-independent carsharing programs that are integrated across each other on a single and global platform. Such a business model prototype can be defined as Digital Carsharing which offers next-generation shared mobility through a digital and key-less access to every car and the possibility to synchronize their usage in a timely manner. The focal point being addressed here is the increase of productivity of available vehicle fleets in terms of the number of car-trips that are provided by a car on a single day. Therefore, the business model serves the purpose of eliminating the car-usage inefficiency in urban areas, i.e. extending the time cars are actually utilized for travel.

The purpose of a Digital Carsharing provider is to connect underutilized cars to a global carsharing system. This prototype is based on a range of digital technologies and instruments that enable the provision of carsharing services based on existing car fleets and privately owned cars:

- multi-sided platform and mobile apps for virtual communication and transactions between car owners, car users and other involved partners (e.g. insurance institutions, payment platforms),

- key-less digital access to every vehicle with a mobile device (e.g. smartphone),
- automatic mobile payment options,
- provision of viable insurance options,
- establishment of trust mechanisms.

Digital Carsharing business model offers quality segmentation, full price transparency and low transaction costs by overcoming physical intermediaries. With that it re-envisions the entire customer experience and makes carsharing schemes convenient, appealing and scalable. The following mobility concepts are possible to implement:

(1) Business-to-customer carsharing, i.e. manufacturer-bound.
(2) Corporate carsharing, for a specific corporate fleet.
(3) Private carsharing and peer-to-peer carsharing.
(4) OEM-independent carsharing.
(5) Optimized Fleet Management.

12.3 Prototype 2: Digital Ridesharing

12.3.1 Ridesharing: Business Concepts

Since the infancy of the Internet numerous ridesharing schemes have integrated the Internet, mobile devices, and social networking into their services making them much more efficient and convenient for the users (Chan, Shaheen 2012). Today, there are various ridesharing concepts in place which are much more advanced in their functionality compared to the previous approaches to carpooling. Generally, ridesharing can be categorized into two distinct forms: long-distance and short-distance ridesharing. The first one refers to journeys above 200 km and covers inter-city trips, whereas the latter approach focuses on car rides below 200 km and aims chiefly at daily commuter journeys. The author of the work at hand will focus on short-distance ridesharing since his focus lies at mobility concepts within urban areas. Based on the literature review he categorizes them as follows: traditional carpooling, flexible carpooling, vanpooling, taxi services (however, only to some extent), shared taxi services and P2P real-time ridesharing (Chan, Shaheen 2012; Cohen, Kietzmann 2014; Martinez et al. 2015; Arnould et al. 2011; Kelly 2007; Ferreira et al. 2009).

Traditional Carpooling

Traditional carpooling refers to several ridesharing schemes that have been known and implemented already for decades. They encompass subcategories such as: acquaintance-based and ad hoc carpooling. The first one encompasses shared car journeys among members of families, friends or co-workers. These schemes are typically self-organized and door-to-door. This carpooling form is rather less flexible as it is strictly prearranged and aims at bundling journeys with the same origins and destinations. Carpooling among co-workers is often incentivized by the employer to reduce the necessity to provide parking space or to contribute to sustainability goals of the company. The majority of carpooling service providers are nonprofit, community-based services or organized as social enterprises (Cohen, Kietzmann 2014; Chan, Shaheen 2012). There are several mechanisms to organize shared rides such as: self-organized, incentivized, based on notice boards or various computerized ride matching products (Chan, Shaheen 2012).

Flexible Carpooling

Flexible carpooling is also referred to as ad hoc ridesharing. This form is a much more flexible approach to organize shared rides as it is realized through casual carpooling (Chan, Shaheen 2012). Firstly, it enables the use of designated meeting places which makes it easier to match routes which does not necessarily have exactly the same origins and destinations. Car drivers and potential riders can meet there and arrange the further journey (Cohen, Kietzmann 2014). Secondly, it requires little relationship between participants and usually does not require any membership (Chan, Shaheen 2012). It can also be referred to as 'slugging'. Car drivers stop along a so called 'slug line' at a designated location where they can pick up casual passengers. A benefit for drivers can be substantial as vehicles with higher occupancy rate are allowed to use the high occupancy lanes (HOV) on motorways (Chan, Shaheen 2012). This gives the car drivers the opportunity to overcome the traffic jams in peak-hours and in this way simultaneously save time and costs.

Vanpooling

Vanpooling can be also listed as a kind of carpooling service, even though it differs slightly from the classical ridesharing approach with cars. Nonetheless, the underlying idea of gathering more people in one vehicle in order to utilize it in a more effective way is the same. Vanpooling focuses specifically on transporting larger numbers of passengers who share a van (Cohen, Kietzmann 2014). Passengers may board them at designated stops along their route or hail them as share taxis. In that respect, vanpooling can be seen as a hybrid mobility service between ridesharing, share taxi and bus services. It was introduced in the 1970s as forward-thinking transportation service and has been eagerly encouraged and supported by federal governments in the USA, as it has offered flexible and low-cost access to transit service for low-income populations (Kircher, Wapensky 1978). Today, a range of vanpools exist, including corporate-sponsored vanpools for employee use, privately operated vanpools for commuters or trips to airports and hotels, and publicly subsidized vanpools (Chan, Shaheen 2012).

Taxi Services

Taxis are one of the best transport options when convenience, comfort and safety are considered. They offer point-to-point trips along flexible routes (Martinez et al. 2015). However, the traditional understanding of ridesharing does not apply here, albeit taxi services enable higher occupancy of cars. According to Chan and Shaheen (2012) ridesharing should be organized as a nonprofit service, whereas typical taxi services are commercial profit-making organizations. Clearly, this disqualifies taxi services from being a ridesharing service. Nonetheless, some recent developments based on the implementation of digital technologies imply that this nonprofit notion of ridesharing is rapidly changing and the meaning of ridesharing is being also extended to the definition of traditional taxi offerings. A case in point is Uber Technologies Inc., a company from the IT sector that has introduced novel vehicle dispatching methods based on digital technology and mobile connectivity to the Internet. Several governments and the taxi industry claim that Uber is a taxi service provider (Spiegel Online 2015; Bonaventure 2014; NSW Government 2015). Therefore, from the legal perspective the company should be subject to existing local regulatory frameworks for the taxi industry. Uber, however, affirms that it is not a taxi service but a platform provider that offers an on demand ridesharing platform (Uber Technologies Inc. 2016). The differences between these mobility approaches appear to be very controversial. Therefore, technology-enabled platforms that aim at dispatching vehicles are subject to a broad public debate. Moreover, they are under heavy governmental and regulatory investigations in many countries of the world. The author aims at addressing these controversies later in this thesis. However, for the purpose of this work he will further refer to the ridesharing concept as a nonprofit mobility alternative as defined by Chan, Shaheen (2012). Therefore, traditional taxi services should not be categorized as ridesharing services.

Shared Taxi Services

Another interesting development is the field of shared taxi services. This approach denotes the use of taxi cabs by more than one person (or by a small party) serving to bundle multiple trips on the same taxi route (Teal et al. 1980). The concept is not entirely new and there have been experiences in different countries of the world (Martinez et al. 2015). For example in Istanbul, Turkey, where this kind of mobility alternative is very popular, the taxis run a pre-determined route, with each passenger paying only a portion of the normal fare (Feibel 1987). Even though a shared taxi is a low-capacity mode, it is being recognized as a possible feeder system for other public transportation systems.

Furthermore, advanced initiatives are being tested that aim at taking advantage of digital technologies in order to support the implementation of an intelligent shared taxi mobility concept (Martinez et al. 2015). Some recent simulations indicate that such an area-wide system could bring about a substantial contribution to the reduction of the total travel times served by taxis and also to a radical decrease of the size of taxi fleets in cities (Santi et al. 2014; Martinez et al. 2015). Despite the fact that this approach is a taxi service and therefore it does not meet the nonprofit condition in author's opinion it can be referred to as a ridesharing system. From the perspective of the user such a system offers a clear cost sharing option. From the system perspective it might contribute to the higher utilization of the vehicles by collating the taxi requests and hence to the elimination of undesired low-occupancy journeys from the roads. For these reasons the author is including this mobility form into the ridesharing classification.

Dynamic Peer-to-Peer Ridesharing Services

While there have been numerous attempts to provide carpooling services in the past, the real quantum leap in the mass adoption has not yet really occurred. Chiefly it is directly associated with the lack of flexibility and monetary incentives (Arnould et al. 2011). First of all, drivers and passengers are required to register their travel preferences in advance. It has resulted in a highly static approach to ridesharing (Ferreira et al. 2009; Kelly 2007). Therefore, a great deal of effort has been put into adding more flexibility and dynamicity to resolve the inefficiencies associated with traditional carpooling services (Correia, Viegas 2009). Dynamic P2P ridesharing has emerged as a substantial mobility alternative in cities around the globe and can be referred to as a further development of the traditional carpooling approach. It has been stimulated by the development of the Internet and advancements in digital technologies (Cohen, Kietzmann 2014). By combining mobile devices with instant network connectivity, mobile geolocation technologies and the power of social networks so called real-time ridesharing has been enabled among the participating members (Kietzmann et al. 2011). Real-time ridesharing uses Internet-enabled smartphones and highly automated ride matching software applications. In this way shared rides can be organized dynamically, i.e. in real-time. Real-time means that participants can be matched either minutes before the trip takes place or during the trip. Passengers can be picked up and dropped off along the way. These offerings are highly flexible and convenient for both drivers and riders as they overcome the inconvenience and inflexibility of traditional carpooling schemes. However, a critical mass of subscribers is required to provide a reliable matching service. Otherwise, the participants can quickly get discouraged if the application does not deliver the promised service (Cohen, Kietzmann 2014).

Not surprisingly, recent innovations in digital technology have played a crucial role in enhancing ridesharing services and made them appealing to a wider group of users (Cohen, Kietzmann 2014). Its greatest contribution is overcoming the barrier of reaching the critical base of service subscribers and addressing the issue of interoperability as both aspects have heavily limited the potential of this transport mode in the past (Chan, Shaheen 2012; Gorringe 2009). In the next sections the author describes a case study of a of technology-enabled business model that have been recently established with the goal of providing digital ridesharing offerings to a wider audience: TwoGo by SAP.

12.3.2 Case Study: TwoGo® by SAP[18] [19]

12.3.2.1 Introduction to TwoGo by SAP

The German Institute for Economic Research (Institut der deutschen Wirtschaft) forecasts that there will be 40 million commuters in Germany in 2015, which will set a new record in the German history. Two third of them will use cars for their commutes (Institut der deutschen Wirtschaft 2015; Frankfurter Allgemeine Zeitung 2015). It adds up to 1,5 billion driven kilometers and 700 million euros in costs a day. It is approximately 22 euros per day and capita (Schmid 2013). In addition to increasing congestion and pollution, the traffic causes stress and psychosomatic illnesses such as headaches or back pains. At the same time many car commuters travel solo along almost identical routes within urban or industrial areas, often very likely to the same employer (Schmid 2013). A case in point is the company SAP SE, the world's largest provider of enterprise application software. Back in 2000, SAP was a company of roughly 24’000 employees, and in 2015 it has reached the level of almost 77’000 employees around the globe (SAP Global Corporate Affairs 2015). It is expected that the staff of SAP will be still growing due to the company’s positive growth in the recent years and the promising prospects associated with emerging high-growth markets such as cloud computing and big data management. The company is aware of sustainability issues related to such an unprecedented growth and therefore aims at embedding sustainability in its core culture. Therefore, it has established a sustainability department with a dedicated Chief Sustainability Officer. One of the main goals of SAP is to roll back its emissions’ levels to those of 2000 by the year 2020 (SAP SE 2014). Among others, one of the main activity areas with regard to this ambitious goal is the field of mobility of its employees, especially the mobility associated with the usage of company cars. Unsurprisingly, the fleet of company cars at SAP is placed second to air travel as it regards the carbon dioxide emissions (Schmid 2013).

---

[18] This section is partially reprinted in Janasz, Schneidewind (2017). Courtesy of Springer.
[19] The case study has been published with permission from SAP SE.

The headquarters of SAP SE are located in Walldorf (Germany), a small city in the Rhein-Neckar district 80 km from Frankfurt. There are 25'000 company cars in operation globally (SAP internal source). At headquarters in Walldorf there are 10'000 company cars distributed among the staff, which in 2016 numbers approximately 13'000 employees (SAP internal source). In 2014 approximately 75% of them used cars for their journeys to the campus (SAP internal source). Additionally, according to the SAP Sustainability Dashboard the average distance of all commuters in that year was 46,1 km per day and the occupancy rate of the cars used for these trips was as low as 1,1 persons per car (see Figure 18). This state of matters had been already recognized before at SAP. Therefore, an internal corporate ridesharing program was considered to generate savings in gas emissions and costs related to commuting. The idea was first initiated by two SAP developers back in 2009. They had been allowed to spend a fixed share of their working time on the development of an intelligent solution and were soon supported by other colleagues and external consultants. After several months of the development phase, the first version of TwoGo was announced and introduced. Since July 2011 SAP has been using the solution internally. After the test phase TwoGo has been deployed to other countries: Austria, Brazil, Mexico, Belgium, Canada, France, Germany, Hungary, Ireland, Italy, Singapore, India, Spain, Switzerland, Portugal, Bulgaria, UK and the US. Further locations are also being scheduled for deployment.

The company claims that in the period until April 2013 TwoGo created 36'000 carpools and more than 5 million dollars of value for SAP which can be attributed to following tangible and intangible benefits (SAP News 2013):

- Cost savings related to commuting to work; for example, reducing fuel consumption and maintenance costs and increasing the resale value of company cars,
- Expense avoidance related to employee travel such as reimbursements for fuel, limo services or parking,
- Increased networking among employees by matching employees into carpools more than 36'000 times and adding 2'200 additional days of networking time among employees,
- Reduced greenhouse gas emissions by helping to eliminate 400'000 miles of driving and 88 tons of greenhouse gases.

Since 2013 TwoGo is also commercially available to the external market as a cloud offering. As of 2014, also individuals can register for free at the TwoGo platform and find a ride to work or back home in a dynamic and flexible way.

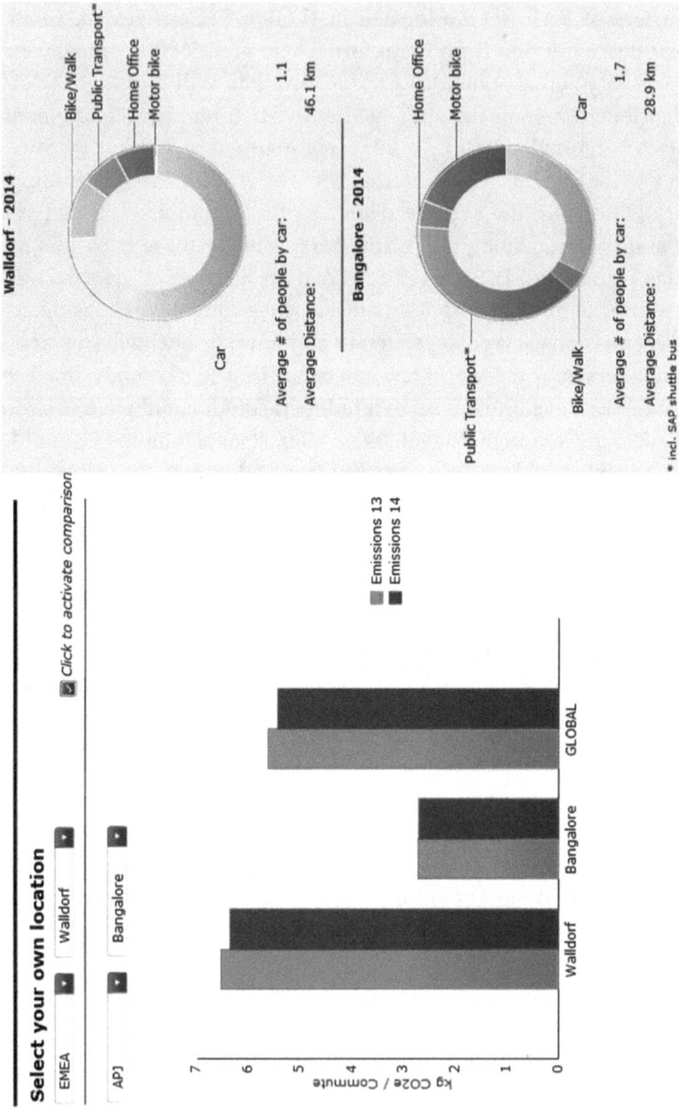

Figure 18: Commuting Dashboard.
(Source: SAP's internal documentation)[20].

[20] Courtesy of SAP SE. All rights reserved.

12.3.2.2 Possible Use Cases

Essentially, TwoGo by SAP is a mobile, cloud-based carpooling service. Drivers register online and specify the requirements such as the desired radius of the place of residence and the time for departure and arrival. The same applies to riders who can specify the pick-up location and their timing preferences. TwoGo automatically matches the demand with supply and offers suitable rideshare option for both parties. Specifically, one can provide TwoGo with highly individual details regarding following possible parameters (source: SAP internal documentation):

- roles: one can act as a driver or passenger or both,
- flexible route determination: a driver can decide on the route by himself,
- flexible time determination: one can set the earliest departure time and latest arrival,
- detour time determination: drivers can make an approximation of the detour time (in minutes) they are willing to make to pick up or drop off a passenger,
- detour route determination: no matching if there is a need to leave the highway,
- flexible passenger determination: for example no matching with specific individuals or with people from other organizations. One can also invite specific friends to rides,
- gender flexibility: women can decide to be matched only with other women,
- tracking: drivers can enable TwoGo to track them via GPS five minutes before the calculated meeting time.

Since the matching algorithm is fully automated, TwoGo proposes suitable rides only if the entire set of these individualized criteria are met. If there is no exact match available according to personal settings one can also see potential rides that are close to original settings. Users are required to maintain these data only once. Hence, there is no need to spend additional time (e.g. during work) to search lists in order to find suitable ride matches, a drawback which is often criticized in case of other ridesharing solutions.

There are several ridesharing scenarios that are covered by the TwoGo software. The author will give an overview of possible use cases that are likely to be beneficial for every organization with respect to economic, ecological and social aspects of mobility.

Corporate Ridesharing

TwoGo was designed specifically for the scenario of daily commuters and business travelers of an enterprise. By means of this software solution an organization can assist their employees in forming carpools for their daily trips. It aims at automatically connecting employees who look for car rides, based on a very specific set of criteria. Once an enterprise licenses the solution, employees can sign up online and enter ride-sharing preferences such as proximity, timing to and from work and willingness to leave the highway to pick up passengers. After preferences are entered, rides are instantly matched and communication is handled automatically via email, push messages or short text message (SMS).

The solution is available online as a website and can be also downloaded as an app for smartphones running on iOS and Android. Additionally, it can be used from any electronic calendar application, allowing employees to interact with the system without leaving their normal work environment. It is operated and maintained solely by SAP. It is delivered over the cloud, i.e. as a software-as-a-service (SaaS). Therefore, TwoGo can be instantly rolled out across organizations, allowing employees to be matched into carpools automatically and according to their individual preferences that they have previously set.

Moreover, TwoGo employs sophisticated algorithms designed to ensure that employees do not get stranded at work. To help locate desirable matches in an easy and clear way, TwoGo is powered by HERE, Nokia's location cloud, which delivers one of the leading map and location experiences across multiple screens and operating systems. In the case of Corporate Ridesharing the matching is possible only within the company.

By corporate carpooling (other term for ridesharing), employees may recoup some of the lost productivity by encouraging networking and brainstorming on the road. In addition, TwoGo may create a more networked culture, helping employees to feel better informed and involved with their peers.

Fleet Management

It is thought that business trips represent a huge leverage for companies to save costs and contribute to sustainability goals. For example, many employees (such as consultants) often work for the same customer at its premises. This inevitably creates a need to travel back and forth every week. Without transparency every employee travels on his own. As a consequence it can happen that several consultants go by their cars to the same airport and leave their cars there at very high daily parking charges. If one realizes that it is not unusual that some customer engagements can last up to 2 years or longer the saving potential through transparency and proper fleet and travel management becomes clear. In order to intelligently increase the efficiency of the car fleet for business trips, in terms of the car seat usage intensity, a travel manager of a company could consider adjusting travel policies in such a way, that ridesharing is compulsory. Otherwise, other more effective transportation modes would need to be taken. Companies can use ridesharing instead of investing in new car fleets by leveraging the latent efficiency potential of the existing fleet. The vivid example of SAP's fleet of 10'000 vehicles and the associated occupancy rate of 1,1 clearly depicts the existing redundancies. Establishing a transparency can lead to a more efficient usage of the available fleet of vehicles.

Private P2P ridesharing

TwoGo is not only limited to commercial organizations. It is applicable for cities, non-profit institutions and also to everybody interested in sharing their vehicle seats with other commuters. For example, it is worth mentioning that in the case of SAP the city administration of Walldorf is actively contributing to the establishment of an area-wide ridesharing scheme in the region. The goal of the city is to raise awareness regarding the issue of sustainable mobility and thus contribute to the reduction of the automobility dependence of its residents. In 2010, Walldorf had around 14'500 inhabitants and the district offered 18'000 jobs (Stadt Walldorf 2010). The city maintains an industry area which has become a magnet for the entire region. The most important employers are SAP (IT), Heidelberger Druckmaschinen (printing industry), Ikea (furnishing articles), or session GmbH (music industry). The city proactively provides the ridesharing option to its residents and in this way promotes ridesharing among the commuters regardless of their company affiliation (Stadt Walldorf).

The openness and the inclusion of all interested parties who could be interested in using the service is completely plausible for one basic reason: only those ridesharing platforms are successful which reach a critical mass of users in the respective area of operation (Kühn 2014). For that reason SAP has decided to offer a private peer-to-peer carsharing. Since mid-2014 all private commuters have received the access to the TwoGo platform. The main goal is to involve as many potential drivers and riders as possible who reside in the same region or work in the same industry area and wish to profit from a flexible and dynamic ridesharing service. Most importantly, private commuters are not being charged for using the service as it would discourage them from using the platform. Some previous examples of ridesharing platforms in Germany, such as carpooling.com, clearly show that demanding fees for using such services can be disastrous for the user base (Wagner 2013).

Calendar Feature

TwoGo aims to manage the rides in a way that is most convenient and efficient for the users. One of the distinct and interesting features is the direct connection with the calendar function. TwoGo is seamlessly integrated with corporate calendars such as Outlook, Lotus Notes or Blackberry. If the TwoGo system finds a suitable match for a collective ride an automatic entry is made into the calendar of both participating parties. As a consequence one can see this entry along with other daily meetings. Another, more convenient option is to create an entry for a ride in the calendar by oneself and invite

TwoGo as a dummy participant. In this case registered users do not need to use the user interface (web or app) and can flexibly move or remove rides if necessary. For example, if there is an important meeting coming from the manager one only needs to move the TwoGo entry to a later point in time or decline it directly in the calendar. In this case TwoGo by SAP will move or cancel the ride and take care of potential changes in the background and automatically inform the involved participants. For that the system sends a push message and/or an SMS about the matched ride to all associated mobile phones.

Surprisingly, this small feature might have a considerable impact on behavioral patterns of employees. Since corporate calendars are one of the most important tools of today's office workers automatic entries into the calendar can ensure that matched rides cannot be replaced by a spontaneous meeting requests from colleagues. In this case the colleague will see that this time slot is already reserved for something else. On the other hand it can positively contribute to the regulation of the working time of employees. If one is aware that there is a ride at 18 hours he or she will leave the office premises exactly at the specified time and will not stay longer, as often happens in the corporate settings nowadays.

Analytics

In the 21st century more and more companies include Corporate Social Responsibility (CSR) as a main strategic goal along with financial imperatives. CSR refers to the general belief held that modern businesses need to actively take responsibility for society and environment that goes beyond the investors' interests. Therefore, organizations take proactive steps to realize and manage activities related to sustainability initiatives. To report on these initiatives outside of the organization companies require reliable transparency with respect to such aspects like the GHG footprint, diversity management or employee retention. In the case of SAP, the sustainability department uses analytical tools to measure and report on the impact of its CSR activities. The tool developed by SAP is referred to as the Sustainability Dashboard. One important part of it is the Commuting Dashboard. The dashboard is based on a yearly, global survey on emission monitoring that collects required data. With roughly 35% of global employee participation the survey results are highly significant. The sustainability department of SAP can draw interesting conclusions by means of the analysis tool. In 2014 there were following observable changes in the commuting patterns of SAP employees as compared to 2013 (source: SAP internal):

- Commuted less by car: -5,3%,
- Worked more from home: +6,1%,

- Commuted more by bike or walk: +3,5%,
- Used more public transport and corporate vanpooling (shuttle buses): +5,8%.

These behavioral changes have led to a decline in global emissions per commute by 4,1%, i.e. to 5,4 kg CO_2/commute (see Figure 18).

Furthermore, the TwoGo solution can be interlinked with the Commuting Dashboard in order to provide the actual usage data out of the ridesharing platform. Based on that detailed analysis and comparisons between locations are possible, for example with respect to the average modal shift, commute distance or car occupancy rate (see Figure 18). TwoGo also offers advanced analytical features. For example, fleet managers are provided with data on the utilization rate of the company vehicles, while travel managers receive insights regarding employees' travel behavior by car for business trips. Based on that information they can derive corrective measures to optimize the usage of the fleet or to adjust the travel patterns of employees.

12.3.2.3 Business Model Analysis

The author has analyzed the business model of TwoGo by SAP by means of the P4C Business Model Framework (see Figure 19). Subsequently, he will take a closer look at the characteristics of the underlying patterns and illustrate TwoGo's business model in accordance with the current theory in the field of business models.

Purpose and Value Proposition

TwoGo by SAP is in essence a ridesharing solution. Therefore, the proposed value is most simply the enablement of ridesharing services. However, it needs to be noted that it is not the ridesharing service that is being provided but the platform which enables the matching of drivers and riders. In this sense TwoGo is, technically speaking, a contact-matching tool, albeit a very sophisticated one, that provides an automatic service for coordinating drivers and riders who commute every day on the same or similar route. It needs to be clarified, however, that due to its high automation the TwoGo scenario is most suitable to regular trips such as commutes or business trips under 200 km distance. Trips above 200 km can be covered as well, but they are probably better served by tools that specialize in long-distance journeys. Taking a more detailed look at the value proposition, i.e. the job-to-be-done of the solution, one can obtain three distinct perspectives: that of the driver, of the rider and of the company.

(1) Drivers and Riders

Obviously, the main motivation of the driver is the willingness to utilize the free space that they have available in their cars. However, this is the value proposition of ridesharing service itself and not of the TwoGo software. It needs to be clearly distinguished between these two views. From the drivers' perspective the main job-to-be-done of TwoGo is finding the right people according to their specific personal preferences with whom they are prepared to share their private space in their private cars. Furthermore, they want to preserve the flexibility of changing their plans spontaneously. As it regards the riders, their main goal is similar. Their job-to-be-done is finding a driver who corresponds with their personal preferences to reach the desirable destination on time and get back home. However, they want to be sure that they will get the ride back home, even though the driver preserves the right to flexibly change his plans. Obviously, a joint ride is only feasible if the preferences of the driver and that of the rider match exactly with each other. Hence, the value proposition of TwoGo can be described as follows:

> The TwoGo by SAP system offers a fully automatic matching service, however, without any obligation. I.e. all participants preserve the full flexibility until the ride begins.

(2) Companies and Institutions

The third actor in this setting are companies who provide the TwoGo service to their employees. Their perspective is slightly different to that of the users. According to SAP the TwoGo solution creates value for companies and institutions in following areas (source: SAP internal):

- spending less on fuel, maintenance, and parking facilities for both corporate and employee's vehicles (financial aspects),
- higher resale value of company cars due to lower mileage during the depreciation phase,
- reduction in employee travel expenses for taxi cabs, limos and car rentals (financial aspects),
- contribution to employee satisfaction by increasing information sharing and collaboration among employees, especially among the 'new hires' (social aspects),
- reduction in greenhouse gas emissions (environmental aspects),
- engaging employees in sustainable thinking (environmental aspects),
- brand and image enhancement as a sustainable company and attractive employer (reputational aspects),
- more safety and fewer accidents for the employees and as a result less sick leave days for the company.

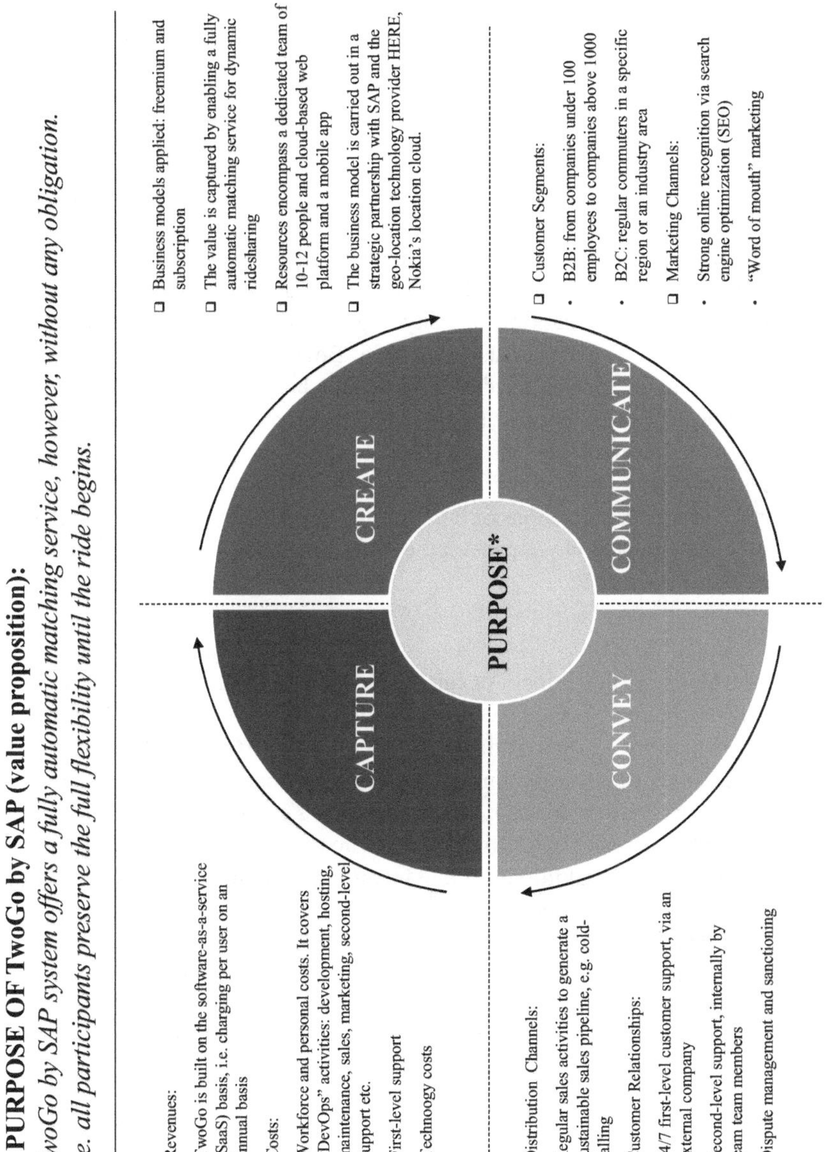

Figure 19: The P4C Business Model Framework applied to the TwoGo by SAP. (Diagram by author).

In general it can be noted that the value proposition of TwoGo by SAP corresponds with the commonly accepted triangle of sustainability, i.e. TwoGo aims at contributing to economic vitality, environmental integrity and social equity. In the following paragraphs the author will briefly explain how TwoGo adds value for a company in those specific areas by looking closer at the departments that are likely to directly or indirectly benefit from this solution.

(3) Economic Vitality

Financial advantages can be harvested in the financial areas of facility management, fleet management and travel management. In the area of facility management the positive impact is attributed to less parking capacity required for cars. It brings about fewer rented parking spaces and smaller areas to manage. Both result in lower costs. In the field of fleet management corporate ridesharing means less money spent for fuel and maintenance and possibly also a higher resale value of company cars as they suffer less wear and tear. For travel management the cost savings come primarily with reduced travel expenses for shared rides to a customer side, hotels or airports. In companies, these domains are usually subdivisions of the financial department. Therefore, the office of the CFO can register a positive impact on the P&L (profit and loss) statement and on the balance sheet.

(4) Environmental Integrity

Environmental integrity is the domain of internal sustainability departments which are typically also held accountable for aspects associated with Corporate Social Responsibility (CSR). The value proposition of ridesharing for this department is the contribution of the company to lower the overall number of cars on the roads. As a consequence the direct benefit is the substantial reduction of the company's carbon footprint. An indirect benefit for the society can result in less road construction and less costs for infrastructure maintenance. There are some additional, albeit intangible, benefits for a company. Even though they are rather image-related they can play an important role for environmentally aware companies. Through integrating ridesharing benefits into the CSR strategy a company is fostering a sense of unity in the internal communication and thereby increases positive brand recognition among customers and investors. Commuting Report can be included as an important element of annual reporting as part of the environmental performance of the company.

(5) Social Equity

Social aspects are also addressed by SAP's ridesharing solution TwoGo by SAP. Maintaining social equity among employees is usually the domain of HR departments. Three main benefits relate to: networking, integration and time savings (for commuting). Employees sharing a ride have a chance to socialize and discuss ideas as they would do at the office for example at the coffee corner, which tend to be a place of social exchange in corporate settings. It may be also the case that the user meets completely new colleagues as TwoGo matches the rides automatically. In that way the business network of participating users gets extended what can lead for example to new job opportunities within the company. Especially, for new recruits and young employees, ridesharing can support their integration into the company much faster and help them build up the required network. Another positive impact can be registered in the field of occupational health and safety. Without the need to drive a car employees arrive at the office in a more relaxed state of mind. This might have a positive impact on their productivity. Searching for an available parking slot in the morning tends to be very frustrating and annoying for commuters in the long run. Therefore, offering preferred parking spaces for ridesharing users can extrinsically motivate the employees to participate in the corporate ridesharing program.

It needs to be stated, however, that rational aspects such as cost and time savings and networking prevail against the ecological integrity. The case study of SAP in Walldorf indicates that for the users the rational goals are of upmost importance. The TwoGo power users, i.e. those who frequently use the service, state that they primarily aim at utilizing the advantages of well-located parking slots in the garages, followed by networking possibilities and savings in car costs. The positive ecological impacts of ridesharing are rather of secondary importance for them. Nonetheless, there is a clear tendency that people with already established sustainable life styles integrate ridesharing in their behavioral patterns much easier and more often.

Table 14: A detailed overview of value propositions of TwoGo by SAP for the company and employees along the triangle of sustainability.
(source: expert interviews and internal materials of SAP).

Affected Departments	**Proposed Value**
Sustainability domain: Economic Vitality	
Facility Management	- Less parking capacity required - Fewer rented parking spaces - Smaller areas to manage - Lower costs
Fleet Management	- Higher resale value of vehicles. Company cars suffer less wear and tear in companies that operate ride-sharing schemes. - Less money spent on fuel and maintenance - Lower repair costs / insurance premiums - Fewer replacement vehicles required
Travel Management	- Employees can share rides between a company's locations, so fewer rental cars are required.

Affected Departments	**Proposed Value**
	- When employees share rides, the company pays out less in 'kilometer allowances' for car journeys. I.e. reduced travel expenses. - Employees can share Taxis instead of booking one per employee - Employees have an alternative to traveling by train or other means of public transportation.
Sustainability domain: Environmental Integrity	
Sustainability Department	- Fewer vehicles on the roads - Lower emissions (e.g. in particulate matter or CO_2), i.e. lower carbon footprint of the company - Less road construction
Corporate Social Responsibility, Marketing	- Fostering a sense of unity in internal communication - Sustainability Report as an element of annual reporting - Image increase and positive brand recognition not only among customers and investors but also among local communities and citizens, as firms are often responsible for externalities associated with the local traffic they induce.
Sustainability domain: Social Equity	
Employees	- Employees can use their commute to extend their business and personal networks. - A ride-sharing scheme may encourage employees to decide against buying and running their own car. - Greater flexibility for employees who otherwise rely on public transportation for their commute. - Useful tool when plans change at short notice; rides are set up automatically and 'on the spot'. - The 'match-finder' function displays alternative options if there is no 'perfect match' available. - Employees are transported direct from their front door to their chosen destination. - Cost savings in fuel and repairs for privately owned cars.
HR, Occupational Health and Safety	- Employees have a chance to extend their networks during the commute. - They arrive at work in a more relaxed frame of mind. - New recruits become integrated more quickly. - The company shows interest in issues that affect employees outside the workplace (the journey to work and back home). - Employees appreciate the company's interest and feel a stronger bond between themselves and their employer. The retention rate of employees might be positively impacted. - Ride-shares are safer. Fewer accidents happen when two people commute together in the same vehicle. - Employees trust the SAP brand.

Create Value

(1) Organizational Structure

SAP maintains a dedicated team that manages the operations and further development of TwoGo. The team is a sub department in the development division of SAP. Interestingly, in case of TwoGo a lot of non-core development activities are covered and carried out directly from the team. These activities encompass following aspects: design, development, quality assurance, operations (e.g. hosting), developing go to market approach, pricing, business models, acquisition of customers and partners (e.g. cold calling), and customer support. This approach is rather unusual for a global IT corporation such as SAP. There are of course legal, marketing or sales departments in place, however, their focus lies chiefly on providing big ERP software to large customers. Paradoxically, this seems to bring about a great deal of simplification and flexibility and allows the TwoGo team to run like a start-up company.

(2) Strategic Partnerships

The organization and the investor behind TwoGo is SAP. Clearly, this provides some considerable advantages for the development team. Most of all the TwoGo team has access to the know-how, technology, data centers, and to limited extent also to the customer base of the IT giant. Apart from that, the main external strategic partner is the solution provider HERE (formerly known as Navteq), a company owned by Nokia. It supplies TwoGo with advanced map and geo-location data. Furthermore, strategic cooperation is sought with other ridesharing platforms. The goal is the interoperability among the platforms in order to establish an area-wide critical mass of ridesharing users. This is an ongoing endeavor and no collaboration has been started as yet. Partnerships with mobility providers such as car rentals or car manufacturers, and other commercial transportation services such as taxis or shuttles are also being considered.

(3) Flexibility

The convenience and usability of the platform is the upmost rationale with respect to value creation. Therefore, the usage of TwoGo by SAP solution needs to be highly elastic. The goal is to create such circumstances for the TwoGo users which would be comparable with the situation while driving the car alone and not being dependent on anyone else. Thus, the value that is being offered here can be described as 'flexibility' the drivers are given the option to be able to change or cancel their journeys until the very last minute before the journey. On the other side, however, the riders need to be sure that if such a case occurs they will be able to get to work or return home as previously planned. Therefore, there is a need for a kind of contingency insurance, a warranty that ensures that nothing will go wrong. Such an insurance needs to be provided by a partner. Therefore, TwoGo is currently preparing such an insurance package together with one of the

German insurance providers. It can be seen as a further strategic partnership which creates the value in terms of flexibility of participating in ridesharing service. For the time being, SAP is offering a taxi service as a warranty, however, only for their employees.

Communicate Value

(1) Customer Segments

There are two different segments that TwoGo by SAP currently operates in: business (B2B) and customers (B2C). After the launch and the successful test phase internally at SAP in 2013 it was decided to begin with the commercialization of the product directly within the B2B segment. This approach was unlike other rival ridesharing platforms which usually had been operating in the B2C segment first before subsequently changing their strategy towards the B2B sector. This was a logical move since it is the B2B sector which is likely to yield profits. Beyond any doubt positive cash flows support the further development and survival of such start-up endeavor.

Within B2B customers range from companies under 100 employees to companies above 1000. Evidently, the bigger the company the easier it is to establish a ridesharing program, since the more employees participate the easier the critical mass can be reached. For smaller companies it is therefore purposeful if there are other bigger companies participating in the ridesharing scheme in the same region. This implies that a ridesharing scheme is likely to succeed in areas were industries are densely concentrated. The threshold for implementing a ridesharing system such as TwoGo by SAP lies at around 500-1000 employees. As of September 2015 there are 30 B2B-customers of TwoGo. Interestingly, they were established by only one dedicated sales person from the development team.

For the B2C segment SAP offers free access to the TwoGo by SAP platform via a website, the mobile app or an online calendar. The target group are other regular commuters in a region or an industry area. This approach aims at reaching the critical mass of ridesharing users. There will be no attempts to charge these users for using the platform in the future.

(2) Communication Strategy and Marketing Channels

The communication with the users from the B2C segment is rather limited. SAP as the solution provider and operator does not need to focus on this customer segment. The communication to this segment can be conducted by the local administration or the participating companies. As outlined above the much more important segment for TwoGo are the B2B customers as they generate the revenue stream. Furthermore, in particular attracting new companies can be beneficial for setting up a ridesharing scheme with TwoGo. Establishing a relationship with a company adds an additional big user group at once. In terms of reaching the critical mass of users this seems to be a more effective strategy than setting up and conducting marketing and awareness campaigns directed at the end users.

It is also worth mentioning that TwoGo by SAP uses neither the regular SAP marketing and sales channels nor the traditional promotion approaches such as advertising. As a matter of fact, the team tested the effectiveness of end user marketing campaigns. A two-week long radio advertisements were broadcasted after every traffic messaging and posters were distributed in the entire region. The impact on the user base was rather limited.

Apart from generating a sustainable customer pipeline the TwoGo team draws special attention to a strong online presence. In case of web-based platforms such as TwoGo, the main imperative is to be detectable on the Internet. Thus, the team puts a considerable amount of marketing effort into so called search engine optimization (SEO). Search engine optimization can be described as a cluster of strategies and techniques used to increase the amount of visitors to a website by obtaining a high-ranking placement in the search results page of a search engine such as Google Search (Parikh, Deshmukh 2013).

Some further interesting facts about TwoGo by SAP with regard to communication and marketing strategy are (source: SAP internal documentation):

- 'get-back-home' guarantee: the company pays a cab back home if a previously arranged shared ride does not take place,
- ride with senior management, e.g. Jim Snabe, the former Co-CEO of SAP,
- reserved parking slots in garages in favorable spots, i.e. near the entrance,
- win the lottery: the company raffled off one iPad per week for the first half year,
- carpool for a cause: the company has donated $1 per mile shared during one month of the year to charity organizations.

(3) Corporate Identity Design

Nowadays, innovative services like TwoGo by SAP that are affiliated with recognized enterprises such as SAP need to develop an appealing and holistic design for the website and the mobile app. In this way they can distinguish themselves from the existing brand and attract the right consumer group. For that reason TwoGo has been developing its own corporate design and identity. In this context TwoGo used its SAP affiliation and resorted to the Design and Co-innovation Center (DCC) in Heidelberg. The DCC is an 'app-house' of SAP specializing in developing novel user interfaces (UI) and user experience (UX). The app-house has developed an innovative design for TwoGo's website and mobile app.

Convey Value

(1) Distribution Channels

As TwoGo by SAP is a comparatively new service, active sales is very useful. Especially, in the first phase of growth it is important to reach a certain market position and to be recognized for the unique selling points that are being offered with the solution. Hence, in terms of distribution channels TwoGo has placed a great emphasis on regular sales activities to generate a sustainable sales pipeline. The main sales approach has been cold-calling, which has turned out to be the most effective way of approaching B2B clients. Second is the 'word of mouth' marketing which is conducted by already established customers.

In the long run, once the online platform is well established active sales will not need to be that important. The main distribution activities will shift towards demand generation. The brand recognition should reach a point where the customers will obtain the product on their own based on the idea of one-click shopping: visit SAP store, add to cart, and check-out. In this maturity phase, maintaining proper customer relationships and securing the brand reputation are much more important facets of running the business, in particular when providing added-value service via web platforms.

(2) Infrastructure Requirements

TwoGo by SAP is a cloud solution. No further adjustments in the existing IT infrastructure of the customer company are required. TwoGo is not an isolated application which needs to be installed every time a new organization joins the ridesharing program. Hence, it is possible to match everyone with everyone to reach the critical mass of users. TwoGo is running on one server instance only and all data sets are stored in one data base. The installation and data bases are hosted in the datacenter of SAP. SAP guarantees very high standards of data privacy and security. Additionally, a Data Privacy Statement has been issued by the German Federal State of Baden-Württemberg after a very thorough and meticulous examination procedure. TwoGo is also compliant with EU data protection standards.

The components that are needed for providing the service are the TwoGo website and the mobile app. The latter needs to be downloaded and installed. The calendar feature and integration is possible without any adjustments in the current customer infrastructure. Additionally, customers who are already running the SAP cloud solution for travel management, i.e. Concur, can integrate TwoGo by SAP for travel planning purposes. In this scenario TwoGo can for example access the itineraries of travelling employees making it easy to integrate ridesharing within the travel planning process. However, TwoGo by SAP is entirely a standalone solution and does not require any other solutions from SAP.

(3) Customer Relationships

TwoGo maintains a 24/7 first-level customer support which is outsourced to an external call center. The second-level support (e.g. issues with functioning of the system, downtimes) is provided by the TwoGo team directly. The team has also established dispute management and sanctioning. In the future these will be the most important areas to strengthen customer relationships, brand recognition and secure the image. The team is preparing also an insurance package to cover all possible risks that can be associated with ridesharing, e.g. ride cancellation and taxis service back home.

Capture Value

(1) Current Pricing

Generally, the access to the TwoGo platform and its ridesharing features is free of charge. Principally, everyone can register and use the service. The aim is to encourage people to adopt it. Furthermore, TwoGo recommends each passenger a 'fair cost-share' amount to be paid to the driver. Fair cost-share means that the driver does not receive any premium which would otherwise need to be declared at the tax office. This approach sets TwoGo apart from other vendors who usually recommend a fix amount for 100 km. There is also a revenue model implemented behind TwoGo in order to generate profit for SAP. TwoGo by SAP is built on the software-as-a-service (SaaS) basis. Hence, SAP aims at selling licenses to enterprises who are willing to implement a ridesharing scheme. The company employs a business model of charging per user on an annual basis. The catalog price is 10€ per employee at the specific location and per year. However, as a new player on the market SAP offers first-time user discounts.

(2) Cost Structure

The highest cost elements are by far the personal costs. However, the personal expenditures cover almost all relevant aspects of business operations and the further development of the TwoGo solution. This approach is referred to as 'DevOps'. It covers development, hosting, maintenance, sales, marketing, second-level support etc. The first-level support is outsourced to an external call-center. The use of DevOps is a prerequisite for implementation of continuous delivery.

Total costs of ownership (TCO) are held at a comparatively low level by taking advantage of SAP's datacenter. The entire solution is hosted in the cloud environment of SAP. To preserve low TCO and ensure high maintainability of the solution the team depends on reliable and proven technology. As a consequence almost no downtimes occur which is a guarantee that the TwoGo platform is always available online for its users.

(3) Insurance

An important aspect of every ridesharing service is the question of liability. TwoGo by SAP acts as an online platform for matching drivers and riders. Therefore, everything that occurs after the ride has been successfully matched is outside of TwoGo's or SAP' responsibility. The ride which then takes place is a private endeavor of the driver and the ridesharer. Therefore, the liability remains with these parties. For example, in Germany the driver's liability insurance covers also passenger protection. Hence, no further insurance for the trip needs to be obtained, neither by the driver nor by the rider. However, this is the case only if the journey is carried out privately. I.e. once the driver receives a premium for his ridesharing service (beyond the 'fair cost share'), the ride's status is commercial and hence the Passenger Transportation Act takes effect. Private liability of the driver loses validity.

(4) Future Pricing

TwoGo by SAP considers to change the current pricing model which is traditionally based on the 'per user' approach. One possibility would be the introduction of package sizes such as: S, M and L depending on the size of the company (i.e. number of employees). The idea behind that is not to limit the customers in the usage of the platform. Current pricing has an upper boundary as the companies obtain a certain amount of licenses. Customers who do not want to pay further licenses for additional users will not actively promote ridesharing within the company. However, the more users the better. If a company obtains a specific package which fits to the size of the company it can invite as much users as possible. It positively contributes to the achievement of the required user base in the region.

12.3.2.4 Business Model Patterns

The general business model pattern behind TwoGo by SAP can be referred to as a multisided platform. In the classification of Osterwalder, Pigneur (2010) the multi-sided platform business model aims to bring different groups such as buyers and sellers together and to facilitate the interactions between them. TwoGo bundles the supply of and demand for ridesharing services on one platform and enables easy and convenient matching. Such platforms are only successful, if a critical mass of users is reached. This is referred to as network effects (Abdelkafi et al. 2013). It corresponds with the goal of the TwoGo team to reach as wide-ranging audience as possible.

Additionally, TwoGo by SAP is currently characterized by the combination of two further patterns, which, however, relate to the underlying pricing models, i.e. the generation of the cash flows. The first one is akin to a 'freemium' business model. It consists of giving the access to the platform free of charge and finding other sources to generate profits (Johnson 2010). The second pricing model implemented by TwoGo is the subscription approach. Subscription is a type of fixed pricing, in which the customer pays a fixed amount of money to use the service for longer periods at any convenient time or amount (Al-Roomi et al. 2013). It is also a model which has been implemented for providing cloud applications (or in other words software-as-a-service). As opposed to the freemium model it aims at generating positive cash flows. While paying a regular fee, customers gain access to an advanced service, which allows convenient use of the offering and high price transparency (Johnson 2010).

12.3.2.5 Business Model Innovation

Possible areas for Business Model Innovation

Having an advanced solution and technology in place TwoGo is in a position to reconsider its strategic direction for the future. There are further conceivable possible patterns of business models, which could be applied in order to facilitate the expansion of TwoGo in the ridesharing market. In the following paragraphs the author will elaborate on some possible directions for business model innovation for TwoGo.

One possible approach for TwoGo by SAP is becoming a 'technology provider'. The unique advanatage of TwoGo is the 'matcher' solution, i.e. the innovative way in which the drivers and riders are matched with each other. There are various potential customers who could be interested in adopting the advanced software of TwoGo. For example, the existing and established ridesharing platforms which would avoid further investments in developing their proprietary solutions. In this way they could focus their efforts on the growth of their customer base. Other conceivable customers could be the car manufacturers who could implement the TwoGo matching solution directly in their vehicles. This would create an added value service for the owners of these cars who would automatically participate in the ridesharing program, if they wished so. In that way they could utilize their cars and offset their costs for owning the car. As a technology provider TwoGo by SAP could deploy a white label strategy, similarly to smexx.

Another opportunistic business scenario for TwoGo to generate complementary revenue stream is the reseller scheme. Multipliers such as car rental companies, who are already well established mobility service providers, could serve as potential strategic partners in this arena. This business model might be intriguing for both TwoGo and the car rental companies as it can be applied in both directions. The one direction is when TwoGo provides a car hire service as an add-on option on their platform. In this scenario TwoGo offers a rental car as a fallback solution for those TwoGo users that have not been successfully matched. In this case TwoGo would receive a premium for moderating, if the rental process should be successful. The second direction consists in integrating the ridesharing solution into the car rental platform. In this scenario the customers of the car rental company would have an additional option to take ridesharers. The TwoGo platform would match the drivers and riders with the same trip itinerary and according to personalized preferences. This is an additional opportunity for TwoGo to expand the ridesharing user base. Therefore, TwoGo considers establishing partnerships with car rentals in the near future. A supplementary strategic reselling partnership is possible with the insurance companies, which refers chiefly to corporate customers. While obtaining the TwoGo licenses they would receive an additional option to source a contingency insurance for their employees.

There are also alternative options for generating further revenue flows. Both options are associated with some changes to the mobile app. For example, it is technically possible to make premium features of the app billable for the end users. Furthermore, it is also feasible to incorporate advertisements into the mobile application. Alternatively, the app users could obtain an ad-free usage of the app. However, they seem not to be realistic options for TwoGo, because it is very likely that these approaches would have an opposite effect on the user base.

Next wave of innovation in ridesharing

However, the most interesting innovation field is related to the cooperation with the emerging ICT platforms for cars. This approach bears a potential to overcoming the barrier of using the smartphone for accessing the ridesharing platform. Drivers using the mobile app via the mobile phone during the journey bears some considerable safety risks. Therefore, there were attempts to integrate the ridesharing software into to navigation system. However, the main issue with that approach was the need for establishing a partnership with every single navigation system provider. Today, it is conceivable that the ridesharing service will be fully integrated into the car, without the need to use a personal mobile device or a navigation system. There are emerging ICT providers on the market that are attempting to establish special ICT platforms for accessing the car with additional services (e.g. weather, parking or multimedia services). Currently, the two major car platform providers are Apple (i.e. CarPlay) and Google (i.e. Android Auto). Once a car has direct access to such a platform it is easily possible to provide the ridesharing service into this car. However, currently every manufacturer needs to decide whether to use one or the other platform. In this case, technology providers such as TwoGo by SAP will need to provide and maintain the service for both platforms.

How does it work? Apple and Google provide operating systems which are installed on dedicated hardware which is originally mounted and connected with the car by the OEMs themselves (e.g. via CAN-bus). Interestingly, the service could automatically recognize how many seats are available and based on the user preferences dynamically decide whether to share them or not.

Additional added value services could be: weather information, hotel bookings, parking services, etc. This opens the possibility for using services such as games and information services (newspapers, books) during the journey.

Interoperability among numerous ridesharing databases could achieve a notable step in this direction. Open source data sharing among ride matching companies could enable members to find matches across all databases. This would require a standard protocol that shares data, while still maintaining competition among firms. OpenTrip is one proposed protocol format, which is still in development (Gorringe 2009). Another idea is a 'ride match aggregator' – a website or other interface that searches all ridesharing databases. The online travel agency industry already employs such aggregator websites.

12.3.3 Proposition: Digital Ridesharing

By combining mobile devices with instant network connectivity, mobile geolocation technologies and the power of social networks a so called real-time ridesharing mobility concept has recently been enabled. Real-time ridesharing uses Internet-enabled smartphones and highly automated ride matching software applications. In this way shared rides can be organized dynamically, i.e. in real-time.

The business model prototype categorized as Digital Ridesharing offers a next-level of shared mobility through technology-enabled access to every car-seat and its effective utilization. The model aims at optimizing the efficiency of car seats for every car-journey. Hence, it serves the purpose of eliminating the seat-usage inefficiency in vehicles. Classical ridesharing systems are inefficient because they require:

- pre-defined relationships,
- both parties must be in proximity of each other, and
- passengers must arrange return trips.

As opposed to these traditional ridesharing services Digital Ridesharing intelligently and dynamically matches drivers willing to share journeys with travelers who need a ride. The specifications of the Digital Ridesharing business model include (Arnould et al. 2011):

- users specify their intended journeys and are matched with other users with similar intended journeys. It enables a carpool between people who do not have predefined relationships,
- Digital Ridesharing is a dynamic carpooling transport system, reacting in real-time to events and user transport requests. Hence, the ridesharing service can be

provided to random users on the move, whether they are in their cars or simply walking by,
- digital technology (e.g. applications via smartphone) enables a comprehensive wireless communication and fully automated booking procedures. The Digital Ridesharing platform enables establishing vehicular networks and seamless integration with other transport modes,
- the service gives flexibility and transparency in the form of price and quality segmentation, and low transaction costs,
- it saves money, reduces the number of cars on the road, striving to reduce accidents and traffic congestion. Hence, the service is environmentally friendly.

However, some further critical issues are still open and need to be considered in future research (Arnould et al. 2011; Le Vine 2014):

- a clearing service needs to be implemented to solve the inherent compensation issues,
- clarification regarding the usage of surge pricing is needed. For example, it has been strongly disputed whether UBER is a ridesharing service or an ICT platform provider that offers regular transportation services for fees,
- as with ridesharing apps, the capacity and legal powers of public sector institutions to regulate a secondary-exchange market in shared-mobility is still an open question,
- further research is needed to identify such legal and institutional issues, as well as the implications of the various possible public-private relationships which are characterized by a range of types and intensities of interactions.

Companies assuming this business model prototype aim at commercializing the inefficiencies associated with the current low occupancy rates of private cars. They can provide dynamic matching services at almost zero marginal costs and very low transaction costs. The following mobility concepts are possible:

(1) Business-to-customer ridesharing.
(2) Corporate ridesharing, i.e. limited only to one company.
(3) Private ridesharing, i.e. peer-to-peer mobility.
(4) Shared Taxi Services.
(5) Optimized Fleet Management.
(6) Provider of integrated systems for operating fleets of SAV.

12.4 Further Prototypes

In the past century, mobility has been based on the dominance of cars. Private automobiles have dramatically changed the paradigm of personal urban mobility by enabling fast and anytime point-to-point travel within cities. However, fractions in the 'system of automobility' have become more and more visible (Urry 2008). Today, ecologic and economic considerations as well as technological advancements challenge the way people move. Apart from the innovations in mobility technologies and concepts, as described above, another developments which are considered as revolutionary, or at least evolutionary, for the nature of urban mobility systems are automobility on demand (MoD), autonomous vehicles (AV), shared autonomous vehicles (SAV) and the Internet of mobility. Taking into consideration the nature of this chapter the author will further discuss possible business models for these (auto) mobility services.

12.4.1 Prototype 3: Automobility on Demand[21]

Mobility Service Description

One promising strategy for urban mobility is the concept of one-way carsharing schemes which utilizes small-sized and electric cars. Such a concept is also referred to as free-floating carsharing or mobility-on-demand system (MoD). The system aims at providing a network of light electric vehicles which are distributed and accessible to subscribed citizens throughout a city, however, it is often limited to a central urban zone (Mitchell et al. 2010). The usage is based on the on-demand principle: travelers use a smartphone application to find a car in their immediate proximity; if it is available they reserve it for the next 15 minutes; they walk to the vehicle, swipe a card to pick it up, drive to the selected destination, and they drop it off at an available public parking spot (parking spaces are usually provided in close cooperation with municipalities).

Such MoD fleets, which are additionally equipped with electric vehicles, are directly targeting the problems of oil dependence, energy efficiency and pollution (assuming renewable energy sources), and parking spaces via higher utilization rates and less need for parking. Furthermore, they ensure more flexibility with respect to the conventional two-way or station-based carsharing. Hence, they provide personal, anytime mobility, in contrast to traditional taxi systems or alternative one-way sharing concepts such as ridesharing or vanpooling (Pavone 2015).

MoD systems are being advocated as a key step toward sustainable personal urban mobility (Mitchell et al. 2010). On-demand carsharing mobility concepts may offer substantial benefits to both users and local transportation networks. Shaheen et al. (2006) indicate that carsharing membership reduces vehicle miles travelled (VMT) by 44% on average in the US and by between 28% and 45% in Europe. Martin et al. (2010) reports that every shared vehicle can result in the removal of approximately 9 to 13 private

[21] This section is partially reprinted in Janasz, Schneidewind (2017). Courtesy of Springer.

vehicles from the roads, either by members selling a privately owned vehicle or by postponing a car purchase. Based on the Carsharing City Ranking 2015 in Germany one carsharing vehicle replaces up to 10 private cars (bcs 2015a).

MoD systems, however, present a number of limitations. For example, due to the spatio-temporal nature of urban mobility, trip origins and destinations are unevenly distributed and as a consequence MoD systems inevitably tend to become unbalanced, i.e. vehicles build up in some parts of a city, and become depleted at other locations. Additionally, it needs to be noted that further possible rebound effects may occur and need to be taken into account. For example, some experts explicitly criticize the free-floating carsharing approach for actually increasing the traffic in cities rather than reducing it (civity Management 2014; Harder 2014). They would not directly contribute to a reduction of congestion, as the same number of vehicle miles would be traveled with the same origin-destination distribution. Indeed, more vehicle miles would be conducted, considering trips to rebalance the fleet (Pavone 2015). A recent study of a free-floating carsharing program in Berlin revealed that the cars are mainly used for leisure activities and chiefly in the evening hours. Accordingly, this would not contribute to the relief of the rush hour traffic in Berlin. Rush hour is caused mainly by commuters and they would not use carsharing for their journeys. Hence, it is likely that free-floating carsharing schemes could rather contribute to more overall traffic in Berlin, since it is much more convenient than the public transportation system (Harder 2014). In that sense the free-floating carsharing concept would actually directly compete against the environment-friendly public transportation system.

One of the current challenges with carsharing programs is also their fragmentation. There is an increasing number of organizations that offer carsharing services, however, they are not integrated and are chiefly based on proprietary systems. Some estimates suggest that currently there are more than 600 different carsharing providers around the globe (Cohen, Kietzmann 2014). Additionally, establishing an area-wide carsharing scheme is a challenging endeavor since the carsharing service provider needs to operate and maintain its own car fleet (unless it is a P2P scheme which does not require a vehicle fleet). Currently, it seems that the provision of such unilateral carsharing systems is only possible for big market players. Such players are, for example, automotive manufacturers that are in a position to provide the required number of vehicles and that have the capital for setting up their services in major tier-one cities of the world, i.e. cities with a population in excess of 600'000. Such examples are Daimler's Car2Go (a one-way rental company operating over 10'000 two-passenger vehicles in 26 cities worldwide) and BMW's DriveNow. Hence, such area-wide services are limited to very dense urban areas. This might pose a severe limitation to the wider spread of carsharing services to tier-two cities, i.e. mid-sized towns with a population of 250'000- 600'000 people, or to less dense suburban areas. The fragmentation of the carsharing market can also lead to a limited and localized use of carsharing service, since the overarching integration of different carsharing services is not yet in place. Interestingly, these deficiencies open new opportunities for further innovations by implementing digital technologies. For example, CarJump, a start-up company from Berlin, aims at consolidating all possible carsharing services in the specific area within one mobile application. CarJump allows the location of available vehicles in the neighborhood, to compare them, select the best one and directly book it via an app (CarJump 2015).

Definition of the Business Model Prototype

The business model prototype 'Mobility on Demand' assumes the product-to-service shift, i.e. establishing a use-oriented mobility concept. The mobility service proposed here is based on a fleet of shared and city-friendly vehicles which are distributed area-wide. These vehicles are on-demand which means that the mobility service can be obtained fully flexible and spontaneously. Companies pursuing this strategy act as 'Mobility Service Providers'. They focus on the core competence which is the delivery of a standalone solution to municipal administrations or to mobility chain integrators. The high-level analysis has been conducted by the elements of the previously proposed P4C Business Model Framework (see Table 15).

Table 15: Definition of the business model prototype 'Mobility on Demand'.

P4C Business Model Framework Elements / Description
Propose Value
Flexible on-demand and key-less access to vehicles on the city streets in order to satisfy the situational mobility need.
Create Value
Provide on-demand automobility by: - Owning or operating a fleet of city-friendly cars, - Enabling key-less access to cars, preferably in a digital way, - Ensuring rebalancing and realigning of the fleet throughout the city perimeter. Establish strategic partnerships with: - Carsharing technology and platform providers, - ICT platform operators, - Public transport operators, - Public authorities, - Payment operators, - Provider of geo-localization and location-based services.

P4C Business Model Framework Elements / Description
Communicate Value
Mobility users: - Get flexible on-demand access to vehicles, - Perform a trip according to your situational requirement, - All-inclusive charging (e.g. maintenance, insurance, fuel/electricity, parking), - Eliminate the first mile/last mile problem, - Leave the cars on the public parking space, - Secure urban mobility without the need of car ownership. Municipalities and Society: - Provide additional mobility alternative, hence increase the accessibility and locational attractiveness, - Establish a necessary building block for multimodal urban mobility, - Potentially help reduce car ownership, automotive emissions and parking requirements, - Redesign traffic infrastructure and make space for new land-use patterns, - Be recognized as an innovative and sustainable city.
Convey Value

- Location management (appropriate sizing of fleet of urban vehicles, zoning, manage relationship to local municipalities),
- Providing fleet access via well designed and user-friendly mobile apps,
- Digital B2C relationship management on all channels:
    o E-Mail-Marketing,
    o Online campaigns (e.g. AdWords, web banners),
    o Landing pages and mobile apps,
    o Social media marketing (e.g. YouTube, Tweets, Facebook),
    o Content marketing.
- Multichannel B2B-marketing for the corporate segment,
- Appropriate management of the business network and partner structures.

Capture Value
- Pay-per-use operating model, for example, pay-per-minute and/or kilometer, - Subscription model.

12.4.2 Prototype 4: Autonomous Vehicles[22]

Mobility Service Description

Autonomy with respect to the automobile means an ongoing automation and interconnection of vehicles and traffic infrastructures with the ultimate aim to enable a mobility system which will depend on fully self-driving cars (Baber et al. 2005). In such a system tasks and decisions previously allocated to a human driver are now to be entrusted to a computer driver. The embedded technology for the automation extends the capacity of the human driver, i.e. the agency of the driver, to act more independently within the car. Thus, the driver is being converted to a passenger (Weber et al. 2014).

The technology can be regarded as already available, as many research programs, such as Google's Self-Driving Car Project (Google 2016), have been developing and testing it in everyday traffic situations in the recent years. Furthermore, also the concept of connected mobility has emerged in the research and the industry which seeks to establish wireless links between cars and traffic infrastructure to exchange real-time data about the street, parking or weather conditions to compute appropriate trip routes and driving behavior for the fleets of autonomous cars.

The shared opinion is that traffic safety would increase considerably since it is also believed that the driving abilities of computers outperform those of humans. The technology also promises more comfortable car journeys, lower insurance costs and better fuel-efficiency (Marks 2012). Another prominent advantage of autonomous driving is offering automobility to non-drivers who have been excluded from automobility. For example, according to Google, blind and disabled people could be strong beneficiaries of autonomous driving (medGadget 2012). Some experts also expect the resolution of the congestion issue in urban areas because the autonomous technology is considered to be able to optimize the efficiency of the transport infrastructure (Kornhauser 2013). However, this argument has been debated as there might be possible rebound effects. There is a general awareness that improvements in energy efficiency, safety or quality of driving may lead to an increased demand for such autonomous mobility which could actually generate additional car travel. In consequence, this could lead to a substantial increase in external costs caused by cars and could also put the public transportation systems under extraordinary pressure (Litman 2014).

[22] This section is partially reprinted in Janasz, Schneidewind (2017). Courtesy of Springer.

Definition of the Business Model Prototype

For the providers of autonomous cars, i.e. the manufacturers, the business model will further rely on selling cars to specific customer segments. The author believes that further business models appear to be viable.

Assuming that such development will take place in the not-too-distant future it is worthwhile to consider what human drivers, who are to be degraded to the role of passengers, will do with the spare time gained during a lengthy car journey. It is argued that the motivation for companies to provide such autonomous technology does not lie in altruistic impulses such as contributing to road safety or enhancing parking space utilization, even if these are likely to be major benefits for the society, but rather some other more opportunistic aspects. Instead, industry experts claim that actors, such as Google, are interested in freeing up spare time for passengers to give them additional opportunities to be connected to the Internet. This would enable the provision of additional services and products during the journey (Austin 2016). In that respect, there are several commercialization ideas that would be conceivable:

- the ability to work or rest while traveling would enable the provision of services in the vehicle, such as consulting services, online shopping, video streaming, playing games etc. Experts claim that also ill-conceived marketing strategies would emerge such as commuter sex (Litman 2014),
- using cars for local deliveries of goods during vehicle's idle time. For example, UBER already offers on-demand delivery services such as lunch or ice delivery for free, albeit not yet fully autonomously (Spector 2015),
- other services that can be run mobile, for example, delivery of the laundry or flu shots.

The condition for providing a range of value-adding services is that OEMs undertake a full digitization of their vehicles and to also establish access to car data for third parties via application interfaces and external digital platforms. Therefore, the OEMs would need to extend the car to become an environment for collaboration between different service providers. In that sense companies with this business model will not provide a mobility service per se, but rather act as intermediaries linking multiple buyers and sellers on their car platforms. An optional business strategy would be Vertical Integration, i.e. providing vehicles, integrated mobility services and value-adding services from one source. Premium manufacturers pursue such an approach. A case in point is Tesla which is bypassing traditional dealerships to sell its cars directly to the consumer while also building the world's largest battery plant (Favaro 2015). Table 16 depicts the proposition of a business model prototype for delivering additional services for owners and passengers of autonomous vehicles.

Table 16: Definition of the business model prototype 'Autonomous Vehicles'.

P4C Business Model Framework Elements / Description
Propose Value
Full autonomy in the car as well as stress-free and safe automobility
Create Value
Sell cars that feature the following characteristics: - Equip vehicles with autonomous self-driving technology, - Open up the vehicle to full digitization. Provide value-adding services (e.g. connected parking) in the car by: - Establishing an ICT platform and providing proprietary value-added services (e.g. Ford's ApLink), - Enable third party digital services delivery (e.g. via Google's Android Auto or Apple's CarPlay). Establish strategic partnerships with: - ICT platform operators, - Public transport operators, - Payment operators, - Providers of geo-localization and location-based services.
Communicate Value
Car owners and passengers: - Full autonomy: transformation from a driver to a passenger, - Full journey safety and trip comfort, - Freed up time for other activities during a car journey: work, relax, online shopping, consulting services etc., - Utilize the car for other less valued activities such as: delivery and pickup of packages and other assignments (groceries, laundry etc.), - Yield earnings from the car by enabling P2P carsharing and dynamic ridesharing service. Municipalities and Society: - Enable an additional mobility alternative, hence increase the accessibility and locational attractiveness, - Ensure high road security standards with almost no accidents and fatalities, - Potentially provide more efficient traffic flow. However, questionable due to additional empty vehicle miles and more convenience as compared to public transport, - Redesign traffic infrastructure and make space for new land-use patterns, - Be recognized as an innovative city that supports and ensures high standards of quality of life (by minimizing road hazards).
Convey Value
- Direct marketing with no intermediaries (level zero) or authorized reseller distribution channels (level one),

P4C Business Model Framework Elements / Description
- Value-added resellers (VAR) responsible for integrating appropriate warranty, support and licensing of additional products and services, - Multichannel B2C and B2B relationship management, - Content marketing, - Appropriate relationship management towards the business network and partner structures.
Capture Value
Possible business operating model are for example: - Pay-per-use, - Provision-based models, - Subscription.

12.4.3 Prototype 5: Shared Autonomous Automobility Services[23]

Mobility Service Description

Further innovation based on the convergence of self-driving technology and sharing concepts are mobility services labeled 'Shared Autonomous Automobility Services'. Autonomous driving would address many current carsharing and ridesharing barriers, such as the need to travel to access carsharing vehicles. It is believed that autonomous car technology will enhance resource utilization by enabling entirely new ridesharing and carsharing schemes, i.e. mobility-on-demand concepts (Thrun 2010; Fagnant, Kockelman 2014). The promise is that robotic vehicles can relocate themselves thus eliminating the rebalancing problem at its core, autonomously reach charging stations when needed, and enable system-wide coordination aimed at throughput optimization (Pavone 2015). As described in the previous section, they would free passengers from the task of driving, provide a personal mobility option to people with disabilities or non-drivers, and potentially increase safety. Some advocates claim that autonomous vehicles will dramatically cut travel costs by allowing crossover mobility concepts between on-demand schemes such as Car2Go, taxi services and public transportation (Burns et al. 2013). It is argued that this in turn could lead to the reduction in vehicle ownership, parking costs and parking space consumption by eliminating the need to own a personal vehicle in favor of a mobility service offered by a shared self-driving taxi (Fagnant, Kockelman 2015a; International Transport Forum 2015; Schonberger, Gutmann 2013; Burns et al. 2013). These benefits have recently prompted a number of companies and traditional car manufacturers to further develop the SAV concept, with activities ranging

[23] This section is partially reprinted in Janasz, Schneidewind (2017). Courtesy of Springer.

from the design of vehicles specifically tailored to such operations (Motavalli 2010; Induct Technology 2014), to the launch of first trial programs (Google 2014).

The rapid technological advancements in this field and the increased commercial interest in on-demand transportation systems have started eager discussions about the design of mobility systems which would be based on SAVs and their potential societal value or its destruction (Pavone 2015). Key points addressed include: How many autonomous vehicles would be needed to achieve a certain quality of service? What would be the total cost of their operation? Who would operate them and what are the regulatory requirements? Would such mobility systems decrease or rather increase the congestion in cities? Would such solutions be technologically feasible, economically viable, sustainable, and societally acceptable to the future of personal urban mobility?

These considerations have also encouraged the academic world to develop dedicated research agendas to provide viable answers to these questions. For example, several research teams have recently undertaken the development of theoretical frameworks for modelling and simulating such systems. The author has outlined and discussed the current state of the research in chapter 7. His attention has been directed towards the potential impacts on the fleet size – more precisely on answering the question whether *factor 10 of automobility* in the urban context is possible, and on understanding and depicting the associated rebound effects that may occur.

Definition of the Business Model Prototype

Fleets of SAVs are the most advanced mobility concept of cooperative autonomous driving. This paradigm enables a plethora of autonomous vehicles to coexist on the roads, autonomously drive in cooperation with each other and provide on-demand mobility services. It is the prospect of an additional transportation mode which would be fully flexible and would offer a door-to-door mobility service. The business strategy would combine all previous prototypes of digital carsharing, digital ridesharing, mobility-on-demand and autonomous vehicles. It would mean a full servitization of cars. Companies pursuing this strategy will act as 'Mobility Service Providers' who deliver fleets of autonomous vehicles to cities. However, to operate in such a market, cutting-edge ICT capabilities will be necessary in the form of advanced platform solutions. Therefore, 'Mobility Platform Providers' will also emerge to integrate different mobility service providers. Table 17 depicts the business model prototype 'Shared Autonomous Automobility Services' in more detail.

Table 17: Definition of the business model prototype 'Shared Autonomous Automobility Services'

P4C Business Model Framework Elements / Description
Propose Value
Fully flexible on-demand and door-to-door mobility service, also for disabled people and non-drivers
Create Value
Provide shared autonomous services by: - Owning or operating a fleet of autonomous cars in different segments (e.g. compact, limousine), - Operating a highly-advanced ICT platform for efficient routing and matching depending on the current mobility demand as well as rebalancing the fleet throughout the city perimeter, - Ensuring the maintenance of the entire fleet, e.g. everyday service: cleaning and repair. Build strategic partnerships with: - Carsharing technology provider, - Carsharing platform providers, - ICT platform operators (Google, Apple etc.), - Other mobility operators, - Public transport operators, - Public authorities, - Payment operators, - Provider of geo-localization and location-based services.
Communicate Value
Mobility users: - Receive fully flexible on-demand access to shared vehicles, - Perform door-to-door journey without changing the mode of transport, - All-inclusive charging (e.g. maintenance, insurance, fuel), - Much lower mobility costs, - Eliminate the first mile/last mile problem and the need for parking, - No need for car ownership. Municipalities and Society: - Fundamentally redefine the mobility system of the city, e.g. combine with public transportation for resolving first/last mile issues, - Dramatically increase road safety, accessibility and hence the locational attractiveness, - Radically reduce the need for car ownership for the citizens, - Redefine public parking space requirements, - Potentially reduce automotive emissions by more efficient use of the traffic infrastructure, - Completely redesign land-use patterns (e.g. there is no need for parking), establish shared spaces, livable neighborhoods and hence foster compact city development, - Be recognized as highly innovative, future-oriented and sustainable city.

P4C Business Model Framework Elements / Description
Convey Value
- Mobility service providers responsible for integration, customizing, consulting, implementation and location management (appropriate sizing of the fleet, zoning, relationship management to local municipalities), - Providing fleet access via well designed and user-friendly mobile apps, - Multichannel B2C and B2B relationship management, - Appropriate management of the business network and partner structures.
Capture Value
- Pay-per-use operating model, for example, pay-per-minute and/or kilometer, - Subscription-based models, e.g. sell mobility packages, - Fees for premium services, e.g. no ridesharing, high-class limousine service etc., - Provision-based model for services provided to the passengers during the journey, - Freemium models, e.g. get a ride for free to a commercial institution (e.g. shopping mall) or accept advertisement during the journey (YouTube-like), - Advertisement.

12.4.4 Prototype 6: Internet of Mobility

Mobility-as-a-Service

Thus far, the author has chiefly concentrated on questions relating to overcoming automobility dependence in urban areas by implementing innovative mobility concepts based on digital technologies, advanced car technology and new business models. This is in line with the overall research agenda of the author. However, the future of sustainable urban mobility is regarded to be rather multimodal. Such a system would not be oriented to favoring one major transportation mode – regardless whether it would be car or public transport – but it would rather focus on the key issue of urban mobility which is a high level of accessibility. From this perspective, it is claimed to design such urban mobility systems which aligns the balance between every possible mode of transport in the urban space and intelligently utilizes their benefits where appropriate. It is claimed that this would contribute to more sustainability and higher levels of life quality for city residents as it would potentially lead to minimization of negative externalities associated with transportation.

Certainly, it can be claimed that mobility systems have been multimodal already, as citizens can use whatever mode of transport they require: cars, bicycles, public transportation systems, taxis or advanced carsharing services. However, it is recognized that the current organization of urban mobility systems usually does not sufficiently allow for flexible multimodal mobility. By flexibility, the author means an interconnected and highly personalized combination that is most suitable for a specific situation of a citizen.

In this respect, a prominent and innovative mobility concept includes Multimodal Mobility Services (see also chapter 10.2.4), which aims at enabling an optimized interconnection between several modes of transport depending on personalized parameters of the system users. The organization of such an urban mobility system would be based on the establishment of one additional layer of service organization and provision which is labeled 'Mobility as a Service' (MaaS). MaaS refers to a system, in which a comprehensive range of mobility services are provided to customers by dedicated mobility operators. Multipurpose and flexible services offered by these operators aim at satisfying all mobility needs of travelers, regardless of the mode of transport and if required in a multimodal way (Heikkilä 2014).

In such a setting the 'MaaS-level' represents an interface between the user and the actual transport service (see Figure 20). Transport companies would provide mobility services and offer them in large numbers to the mobility operators. The divergent, originally separated transport services would then be combined into practical service supplies by the mobility operators. Hence, customers would receive ready complete packages of services in the form of easily accessible service supplies.

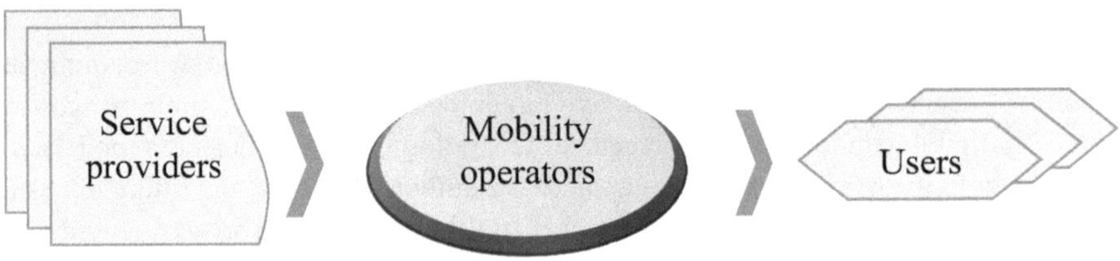

Service providers produce services and sell them to mobility operators

Mobility operators buy services from service providers and bundle and deliver them to customers

Users consume mobility services in the most valuable way for them

Figure 20: The conceptualization of Mobility-as-a-Service (Maas). (Source: adapted from Heikkilä 2014, p. 71).

It is believed that this development would be similar to the process of liberalization of the telecommunication market in Europe (Heikkilä 2014). There would several advantages of such a system reorganization. Firstly, the mobility operators would be commercial in their nature. With that in mind it is expected that they will be able to acquire an extensive knowledge about their users' mobility patterns and therefore will design their operation methods user-centric. In addition, they would operate on a competitive market and thus, strongly focus on the level of their service quality. Service provision would be made attractive for example by providing individual services, packaging services according to customer desires, informing, and marketing (Verband Deutscher Verkehrsunternehmen VDV 2013). Secondly, from the perspective of the user several current disadvantages of mobility provision could be eliminated. These are currently associated with both (i) car possession (e.g. high capital costs, maintenance, parking costs) and (ii) the use of public transportation systems (e.g. insufficient service supply, low availability). In contrast, users will receive a comprehensive and affordable supply of all transport modes with a creditable level of service and the possibility to utilize the travel time (see Figure 21). In addition, also the transport of goods could be integrated into the city logistics system.

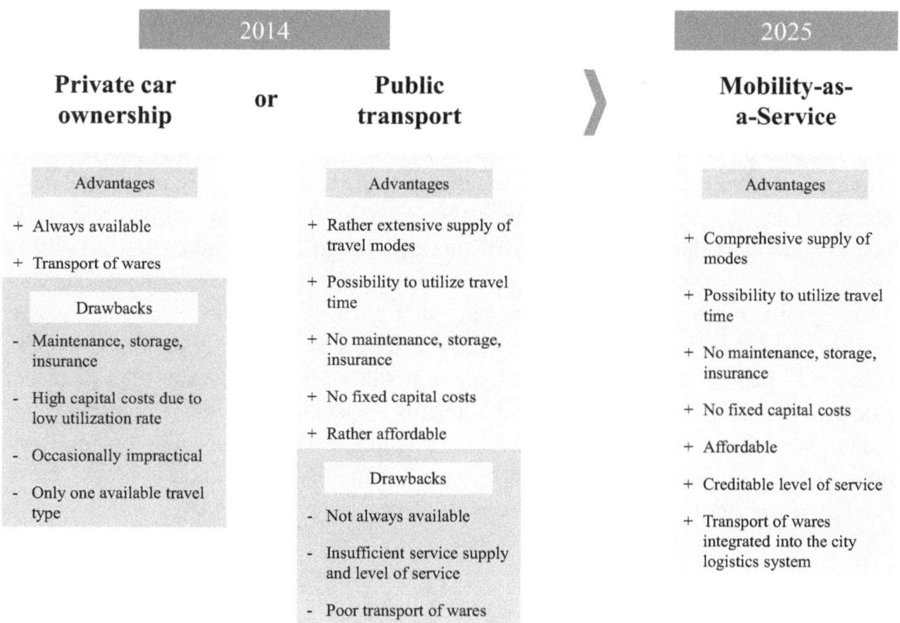

Figure 21: The transformation of the mobility service use from the user's point of view. (Source: adapted from Heikkilä 2014, p. 56).

A critical prerequisite for implementing such MaaS concepts, however, is a robust multimodal journey planner which is an IT system able to propose a set of one or more transport services answering at least the question: "How can I go from location A to location B at a given departure/arrival date and time under which conditions" (Rapp, Tempier 2011, p. 4). The common points of access to journey planners are via a specific web site or a smartphone application (Boehm et al. 2013). Multimodal information has an important role to play and is an incentive for the users to change their mobility routines from exclusive use of car to non-exclusive use. With additional supporting policy measures (such as parking supply management by municipalities or mobility pricing - see 0 for details) such a system is likely to decrease the need of owning a private car by city citizens. In that perspective, some studies have estimated the potential of multimodal information provision on modal shift at approximately 5% (Urban ITS Expert Group 2013).

As of 2013 there were more than 100 journey planners in Europe (Boehm et al. 2013). One main challenge of these planners is the integration of data from various sources that represent different modes. Secondly, existing tools give their users options regarding the services offered by the mobility providers but do not consider specific needs of individual users. Providing any kind of customized mobility service will require considering the individual preferences of customers during the trip configuration and planning process (Gruel, Piller 2016). Hence, the ability of journey planners to provide personalized information on multimodal alternatives is the next major challenge, which is currently pursued by several projects (Boehm et al. 2013). The success will be dependent on highly interconnected ICT components that are able to exchange the required data in real-time. Two concepts that will support this integration are an operating concept labeled as 'one-stop-shop' and a 'mass customization' fulfillment process for mobility services. In other words, MaaS aims at combining mobility services from public and private providers through a unified interface that creates and manages the trip, which users can pay for with a single account. There can be several pricing options: travelers might opt to pay per trip or they could pay a monthly fee for a certain total distance. Some innovative actors in this area include: Xerox – a leading Intelligent Transport Systems provider, RideScout – one of the world's leading mobility consolidators, and ally whose journey planning app crowdsources urban mobility data which is processed to optimize the services of diverse mobility providers.

Collective Mobility Intelligence

MaaS services could, for example, enable users to better manage their overall transport needs, for example purchasing a combination of long-distance and commuter trips under one fare on the same ticket. As well as traditional public transport, MaaS could also cover various rental and sharing services.

A new vision for personal transportation has been recently proposed by the Media Lab of Massachusetts Institute of Technology. Gruel, Piller (2016) argue that applying smart data and the principles of mass customization to transportation ecosystems will enable new business models and fundamentally change the way mobility is conducted in urban areas. Essentially, they propose a MaaS system which would be based on multimodal journey planning (intermodal routing), as described in the previous section. However, the idea is to design systems that utilize and aggregate the needs of millions of individual users, by considering their specific situational context, in order to offer personalized services, yet with the efficiency associated with mass-produced ones. This concept has been established in other sectors under the umbrella of mass customization or mass personalization (Gruel, Piller 2016). In their vision of a mass-customized mobility system users would be able to express their preferences prior the journey, for example, that punctuality is more important than price (for example in case of business trip). The system would then propose an optimal journey based on the combination of a dynamically routed bus transfer for the first mile of the service, subway transfer and limousine service for the last mile of the service. The end-to-end mobility service would be synchronized with traffic conditions and the subway schedule, so transfers would be seamless and without any delay.

While such a sophisticated MaaS concept that efficiently integrates single modes of transport and innovative on-demand mobility services might lead to a dematerialization of physical problems associated with urban transport by increasing the productivity of the mobility system, it can make non-physical problems worse on the other hand. For instance, according to Heylighen (2002), increasing complexity and information overload of systems can make it difficult and stressful for those who must control them, possibly resulting in loss of control. This can surpass the advantages of dematerialization and effectively lead to rebound-effects in form of efficiency losses. Heylighen has developed a concept of 'collective intelligence' or 'global brain' to counteract these rebound-effects. He proposes three basic components needed to tackle the information overload: 1) individual human minds, 2) economic and social rules for the allocation of attention, and 3) computer systems to support human decision-making (Heylighen 2002, p. 30). The idea behind that is that different individuals, agents or computer systems contribute their specific knowledge to solve partial problems and share them with all other components in a coherent system - 'collective mental map'. Such a collective mental map would be a collection of cognitive resources (e.g. database records, computer programs, or human experts) that are linked by a network of associations. This network would be organized in such a way that minimizes the effort in getting any resource to the place where it is needed (Heylighen 2002, p. 30).

The author will focus on the aspect of computer systems to support human decision-making which would constitute a sort of a 'global brain' for providing highly personalized mobility services. For that he proposes an idea of 'collective mobility intelligence' which would enable an efficient one-stop-shop fulfillment process for all possible mobility options.

In public governance a one-stop-shop concept refers to the possibility to carry out multiple bureaucratic steps associated with administrative processes at a single location. It constitutes a single point of contact where information requirements for a certain activity or service are made available to the interested parties and where these parties can make certain transactions to fulfill their needs (OECD 2013). With regard to the multimodal mobility provision it would refer to a digital aggregation of value chain activities (journey planning, journey execution and journey closure), from a single location. It would require the integration of following processes among many partners involved in the mobility value network (see Gruel, Piller 2016, van Audenhove et al. 2014, Boehm et al. 2013, Urban ITS Expert Group 2013, Franchi, Malpezzi 2013):

- single point of access to information about single mobility services,
- sophisticated intermodal routing for dynamic trip planning,
- end-to-end integrated booking and ticketing,
- auxiliary services for monetary transactions between various actors, secure mobile payment and billing.

Such collective mobility intelligence based on the principles of mass customization could bear substantial benefits for many actors. It is argued that both (i) municipalities and (ii) businesses have vested interests in such multimodal mobility provision. For the former not only does the potential arise to reduce car traffic and to cut back on automotive emissions and required parking space, but also to radically redefine the transportation infrastructures they have provided thus far. For the latter such multimodality would mean optimized car fleets and substantially simplified bureaucratic process for travel management (planning, reporting, reimbursement, controlling and monitoring). Last but not least, there is a potential for organizing efficient and sustainable city logistics processes (goods and packages delivery).

It seems, though, that such a global approach to organizing mass-personalized multimodal travel chains and to offering one-stop-shop mobility service will require a complex technical integration of numerous information sources and comprehensive institutional alignment among partners in the value network. Gruel, Piller (2016) claim that the most critical success factors include identifying parameters that matter the most to the users and hence create the most customer value (e.g. time, price, environmental impact), and robust fulfillment processes that can handle the almost infinite volume and variety of customizable mobility options. This is associated with several roadblocks:

(1) Technical:

- open access to required information sources,
- communication protocols and application program interfaces (APIs) for real-time demand and capacity information among all elements of a system,
- electronic processing of payments and handling various currencies.

(2) Institutional:

- contract negotiations between the service providers and pricing agreements,
- legal and insurance liabilities that relate to the connected value network.

(3) Infrastructural and service-related:

- improved physical interfaces such as train stations or park and ride systems redesigned for multimodality,
- new highly flexible on-demand mobility concepts such as dynamic ridesharing and SAVs,
- new value-added service offerings that can be consumed during the journey.

Definition of the Business Model Prototype

The innovation categorized under the business model prototype 'Internet of Mobility' offers a platform for comprehensive data coordination, data processing and data access across many mobility services. The business model pattern can be described as 'Mobility Service Platform Provider'. Companies assuming this strategy would act as digital mobility brokers. They run integrated business operations by embracing a range of new information services that are emerging from the Big Data available on the open networks. The value adding activities encompass the integration of numerous information sources from many possible mobility services and ensuring high data transparency as well as consistency of information. The overall value proposition of the Internet of Mobility is the provision of mass-customized multimodal mobility services based on the specific preferences of individual users, preferably on a global scale.

Table 18 describes a possible business model prototype along the elements of the P4C Business Model Framework.

Table 18: Definition of the business model prototype 'Internet of Mobility'

P4C Business Model Framework Elements / Description
Business Model Framework Elements / DescriptionPropose Value
Provide mass-customized multimodal mobility services based on the specific preferences of individual users.
Create Value
Enable intermodal routing by: - Gaining access to all required information sources and mobility platforms, - Building a platform for real-time demand and capacity information among all elements of a system, - Operating a system that is able to manage the high volume of all possible multimodal connections which in addition depend on specific customer preferences. Establish strategic partnerships with: - Mobility service providers, - Public transport operators, - Public authorities, - Payment operators, - Provider of geo-localization and location-based services.
Communicate Value
Mobility Users: - Full transparency about all mobility options in the city, - Seamless multimodal mobility throughout and beyond the city, - Searching according to individual preferences, i.e. personalized travel options (price, time, environment health etc.), - One-stop-shop process: planning, booking, ticketing, payment and billing. Municipalities and Society: - Interconnect all possible transport modes and hence ensure high efficiency of the existing mobility system and traffic infrastructure, - Guarantee high accessibility without the need for car ownership, - Establish an important foundation for implementing mobility pricing for the entire city, - Reduce car traffic, the need for car ownership, emissions and parking requirements, - Redesign traffic infrastructure, make space for new land-use patterns, - Enable efficient city logistics. Businesses: - Optimize car fleets, - Cut back on required parking space, - Substantially simplify bureaucratic process for travel management.

P4C Business Model Framework Elements / Description
Convey Value
- Well-designed online landing page, - Extremely user-friendly mobile apps for multimodal travel planning and execution, - Multichannel B2C and B2B relationship management, - Appropriate relationship management with the business network and partners.
Capture Value
- Provision-based business model, - Subscription, - Advertisement.

12.5 [Excursus] The Smart Ways Project

Back in 2013 the author of this dissertation participated in a collaborative program - Podlaski Accelerator of Innovation, which is a platform for developing and presenting innovative ideas based on novel technologies. It has been offered by the Bialystok Science & Technology Park which aims at extending innovation and technological advancement in the north-east region of Poland (Bialystok Science and Technology Park). Based on his previous research on innovative mobility concepts the author has proposed an intelligent platform – Smart Ways – for an integrated and central trip planning in the city of Bialystok. The advanced system provides accurate information about all mobility options to get from any point A to any point B in the city and allows direct comparison to support more informed mobility decisions. For that purpose the idea has been designed to integrate single modes of urban transport such as car, bus, tram, bicycle and walking and to utilize their specific advantages in urban traffic. By doing so Smart Ways aims at offering an optimal arrangement of a journey to meet the personalized needs of every resident of the city.

The travel planning system has been envisioned to personalize and optimize the urban journey with regard to a set of parameters that matter the most to the users and hence create the most customer value. Smart Ways offers also a platform for business partners who can offer dedicated marketing campaigns for the citizens via a geo-localization service. Additionally, both intrinsic and extrinsic motivation mechanisms have been incorporated into the overall concept as well as a gamification approach and social network integration. The system and the associated mobile application have been based on several distinct elements which will be briefly described in the paragraphs below.

Analytical Module

The analytical module aims at calculating the detailed parameters of possible travel options for different modes of transport, i.e. public transport, bicycles, walking and cars. The calculation of travel variants should be conducted based on real-time information. The goal is to achieve full information transparency by the system's ability to immediately calculate, display and compare the travel options.

This module should be able to precisely identify the start and destination positions on a map and calculate the possible routes between these positions. In addition, it should automatically locate the current user location via a geo-localization service. For that, the module requires an integration of an accurate map of the city, including the road network, public transport network as well as cycling network. Most important, this module should be able to calculate various multimodal options by integrating single modes of transport: cycling, walking, car and public transport. For that purpose the system requires access to information about the local urban public transportation system and its up-to-date timetables. Alternatively a bike-sharing scheme could also be integrated, if available. However, the users should have the possibility to decide whether they opt for a single-mode or multimodal travel. In addition, the module should be able to regularly and automatically update itself with required data from established information sources.

An advanced algorithm is intended to provide not only planning information about potential travel routes, but also accurate information about the most relevant travel parameters which are believed to be of high relevance to users who seek to personalize their mobility options. These parameters encompass:

- total travel costs, including ticket prices in case of a public transport or fuel and parking charges in case of a car,
- total travel duration, also including time for the first and last mile,
- total distance to overcome,
- time to leave the start location to reach the first mode of transport,
- number of required interchanges,
- environmental impact, e.g. generated emissions,
- health impact, e.g. burned calories by using more bike and walking, and
- attainable 'O_2 currency' for using environment-friendly and healthier travel options.

O_2 Smart Store

The system features mechanisms to encourage the selection of certain mobility options, which potentially have a positive effect on the health condition and the urban environment, such as increased usage of bicycles or public transport. For this purpose virtual

O_2 currency has been introduced which can be attained for specific behavioral patterns. The amount of granted currency is proportional to the scale of avoiding CO_2 emissions and also is dependent on the number of burned calories during cycling or walking. The more public transport and slow transport modes are used, the more points can be earned. The collected O_2 currency can be used in the 'O_2 Smart Store', where users can purchase products, obtain coupons and receive discounts offered by participating business partners or local institutions. After reaching an appropriate amount of currency users will receive a code, which can be used to collect the products or services directly from the participating business partners.

O_2 Business Program

Interested businesses, local authorities or other entities will be able to participate as partners in the O_2 business program, an innovative marketing and event approach. The module allows the opening of an additional distribution channel for business partners to reach the end customer through specific establishing dedicated advertising and marketing campaigns. It is a kind of a customer relationship management tool (CRM) which aims at providing various mechanisms to reach potential customers. The business partners can start their campaigns which can be properly targeted to specific group of people, for example, commuters who regularly move on a specific route. The access to the platform is gained by paying a subscription fee or via a pay-per-use approach.

Dashboard, Gamification and Social Media Integration

The users of the system will be able to make in-depth analysis of the structure of their mobility. The application will collect data about users' journeys and will display aggregated data on a dashboard for a range of variables: time spent in the specific transport mode, cost savings compared to the use of car, avoided emissions, amount of burned calories, kilometers cycled, collected O_2 currency, etc.

Beside the extrinsic O_2 mechanism, Smart Ways applies also a range of intrinsic incentives to achieve user loyalty and to raise awareness of particular mobility behaviors by means of gamification. Gamification is a set of mechanisms that helps induce inner pleasure from competition and cooperation with other users as well as achieving next levels of proficiency. Such instruments include: individual and group rivalry (e.g. with regard to attained O_2 currency or burned calories), city rankings, difficulty levels with progress bars on the completion rate of a specific level or achievement badges. In order to support the gamification approach also a deep social media integration has been introduced. The users have the possibility to share their rankings with their social network or to submit comments about specific travel routes, modes of transport, facilities or participating business partners.

User Interfaces

Most of all, the users should be in the position to clearly understand and compare the possible intermodal options with each other. Janasz, Janasz (2013a) designed an innovative approach to request and to visualize multimodal travel options in the form of possible user interfaces for a mobile application. Five interfaces have been designed[24]:

- Route selection interface,
- Presentation interface,
- Information interface,
- Gamification interface,
- O_2 Smart Shop interface.

Business Model and Business Plan

A detailed business model and business plan has also been developed for the participation in the Podlaski Accelerator of Innovation (Janasz, Janasz 2013b). However, it is not intended to further elaborate on the detailed business model for Smart Ways in this dissertation. **[End of excursus]**

12.6 Conclusions

In conclusion, this chapter has presented the following key lessons:

(1) Innovation areas in mobility encompass: Automobile Innovation, Mobility Services, Mobility Infrastructure and Mobility Information. Innovative activities and applications can be observed in all these fields. If a radical increase in efficiency of car usage is to be achieved, the coordination and integration of technological advancements is required in all these domains of the mobility system.
(2) Digital technologies are clusters of interrelated information and communication technology systems and applications which extend far beyond the boundaries of the digital industry they have introduced. Ubiquitous digitization has stimulated business innovation processes which recently have also affected the system of automobility .
(3) As opposed to the paradigm of private car ownership the product-to-service approach is an emerging option for overcoming extensive car ownership and car dependence in urban areas. Such business models aim at providing pay-for-use mobility concepts such as carsharing and ridesharing. Digital technologies have been seen as crucial assets to setting up innovative mobility concepts based on this servitization paradigm. This shift is being fueled by a growing range of innovative new

[24] The application interfaces are depicted in Appendix 1 to 5 and can be accessed via OnlinePLUS.

mobility service providers such as carsharing, ridesharing, e-hailing services, and bike-sharing programs as well as on-demand bus services.

(4) Two relevant case studies have been analyzed: smexx and TwoGo by SAP, which act as digital intermediaries who bring together the demand and the supply side of the market. Even though they do facilitate shared urban mobility, they can by no means be regarded in terms of classic mobility service providers. Indeed, these business approaches are rather to be classified as mobility platform providers.

(5) Mobility platform providers enable a single point of access, not only to mobility services but also to important cross services which considerably facilitate the obtaining of these mobility services: identification, information and planning, matching, booking, payment and billing.

(6) It seems, however, that offering such one-stop-shop mobility requires also the involvement of many additional actors such as: policymakers, public transport operators, banks and payment firms, telecommunication companies, and ICT suppliers. Such collaboration networks are necessary to be able to further innovate the service portfolio and to overcome the niche character of these mobility services. By doing so they aim to scale up to reach the required critical mass of users. If such innovative concepts and business models succeed the perceptions of car in general will be further changing possibly leading to less car dependence over time.

(7) There is also an observable convergence between these innovative mobility concepts and vehicle digitization and automation. An intelligent integration of digital technologies and recent advancements in the automation of cars could lead to the development of an integrated system of fleets of shared autonomous vehicles. Mobility service providers seem to anticipate the advent of the autonomous technology, which brings up the question about the value of owning a private vehicle over using shared autonomous automobility services, which are expected to become significantly more affordable once cars can drive themselves.

(8) Such a system will have the potential to radically increase the efficiency and intensity of car-usage which could lead to a significant reduction in the number of vehicles in the urban space. However, the premise for that seems to lie in the establishment of a Collective Mobility Intelligence which will enable a holistic data coordination, data processing and data access across many mobility services. This is also critical for the future vision of the Internet of Mobility.

Business model creation and innovation is crucial for a high diffusion of any new technology, since the necessary prerequisite for the industry to provide specific innovative applications of the new technology is to gain profits out of it. Commercial companies will contribute and commit to the development and implementation of system-level innovations in urban mobility only if a fair return on investment is assured to commensurate with the financial risks taken. Hence, technology innovation and business model innovation are strongly linked to each other (Abdelkafi et al. 2013). From this perspective, the author of this work has focused on the sector of mobility services based on automobility. He has showcased current developments in car- and ridesharing (cases smexx and TwoGo by SAP). Furthermore, he has developed possible mobility concepts and associated innovations in business models based on car digitization and automation.

The six ready-for-implementation prototypes of mobility services are based on a range of different business model patterns and digital technologies. They constitute innovative ideas reflecting how to commercialize and overcome the inefficiencies associated with private car ownership and usage. With that the author has created a body of knowledge and provided a source of information regarding the development and implementation of digital business models for Shared Automobility Services that can be integrated into a highly efficient urban mobility system of the future.

It is thought that the further development and deployment of these emerging technologies for personal urban mobility bears enormous benefits for the society. For example, autonomous vehicles promise safer and more comfortable personal transportation based on cars at lower insurance costs and better fuel-efficiency. The benefits could be much higher by enabling entirely new mobility concepts based on the hybridization of mobility services such as carsharing and ridesharing. Along with an efficient public transportation system and increased slow modes of transportation, such systems would aim at improving transportation security, radically shifting resource efficiencies and substantially reducing gas emissions (Sweeting, Winfield 2012).

However, these rapid technological advancements and the increased commercial interest by implementing business models for on-demand mobility have started eager discussions about the design of such mobility concepts as well as their potential societal value or disruption. Key points refer to technical, infrastructural, economic and institutional issues, as well as moral hazards that correspond with the uncertainty about the consequences and possible rebound-effects of implementing such innovative mobility concepts.

For example, with regard to autonomous vehicles following questions arise: How many autonomous vehicles would be needed to achieve a certain quality of service? What would be the total cost of their operation? Who would operate them and what are the regulatory requirements? Would such mobility systems decrease or rather increase the congestion in cities? Would such solutions be technologically feasible, economically viable, environmentally sustainable, and socially and politically acceptable? The author of this work regards these issues as critical for further research and development in this area. He also expects that this will encourage academic researchers and business practitioners to develop dedicated research agendas to provide viable answers in the near future.

PART III
Overcoming Automobility Dependence: Policy Interventions

13 Part III: Introduction

The purpose of this chapter is to provide familiarity with the phenomenon of sustainable mobility and the policies that are supporting and promoting this emerging paradigm. This chapter aims at creating a body of knowledge about possible policy interventions for gradually overcoming the structural auto dependence in urban mobility. The author aims at giving guidance to urban policy-makers and other involved parties who deal with the diversity of policy instruments and approaches in their specific urban context.

This chapter relies chiefly on reviewing available literature. However, also relevant insights from formal semi-structured in-depth interviews have been included. The interviews were conducted with 5 selected mobility experts from Switzerland in May 2014.[25] These interviews were intended to form a 'pilot study' for developing the case study of City of Basel in the subsequent next step. The knowledge acquired during these interviews has set an important pillar for drafting this chapter. A detailed approach to analyzing the data acquired during the interviews is described in chapter 16.3: Research Design, Methodology and Methods.

Therefore, the results of this chapter constitute the foundation for the development and in-depth analysis of the case study of the City of Basel. The case study is complementary to the work conducted so far and is presented and discussed in Part IV of this work.

---

[25] The list of experts is stored in Appendix 6 and can be accessed via OnlinePLUS.

14 Policies for Sustainable Mobility

14.1 Introduction

Sustainable mobility requires a clear and structured approach to all possible methods of delivering significant reductions in CO_2 emissions, congestion, pollution, and community disruption. One approach to the need for structure has been described as the ASI method (Dalkmann, Brannigan 2007):

(1) Avoid - through appropriate land-use and accessibility planning distances are kept short. Destinations are co-located within residential areas which leads to a lower level of car usage and a higher level of non-motorized mobility.
(2) Shift - wherever possible shift the mobility demand to public transport, mobility sharing concepts and slow modes. The modal shift aims at transferring the demand to more sustainable modes, i.e. less carbon intensive.
(3) Improve - so that vehicles are designed to be more fuel efficient, for example, by transitioning to electromobility.

It has been claimed that users should be taxed for the true costs of their actions to achieve more efficiency in transport. Imposing taxes, such as pollution taxes, would be in line with the core principle of economic policies for sustainability. However, the literature suggests that there are many other instruments that can be implemented to make sure that beside sustainability goals, such as reduction of GHG emissions, also social and economic co-benefits are generated. For example, Lah (2015) suggests that a combination of fuel pricing, differentiated vehicle taxation, vehicle standards must go along with the provision of additional modal choices.

Whitelegg et al. (2010) prposed a package of measures that covered spatial, fiscal, behavioral and technological interventions. The policy package aimed at producing a maximum impact scenario for a reduction in GHG for UK transport. Banister (2005) has addressed the important topic of combining policies and packages. Following Santos et al. (2010a) and Santos et al. (2010b) there are four distinct classifications of possible policy instruments for the urban transport sector that could lead to a sustainable mobility system: economic, physical, soft and knowledge policies. Economic instruments aim at directly passing on the negative externalities of the road transport to the emitters by direct policies such as taxes and charges. Physical policies mean infrastructural improvements to the road transport system and covers interventions in public transport and land use. Soft policies aim at inducing behavioral change by providing the required information to the public about the negative impact of their mobility choices and possible alternatives. Finally, knowledge policies underline the importance of investment in further R&D in the arena of low-carbon mobility technology and incentives for demonstration projects, and their large-scale implementations.

Banister (2008) and OECD (2004) suggest the consideration of push and pull measures as ways to reduce car use, hence to support environmentally sustainable transport. Push and pull measures can be also referred to as travel demand management (Saleh, Sammer 2009). The interventions include regulatory, pricing, planning or persuasive policies. The primary objective is to influence the travel behavior of individuals through voluntary reduction or restriction on private vehicle use and ownership, and the provision of travel alternatives (Saleh, Sammer 2009). According to Banister (2008) both push and pull interventions should be combined in mutually supporting packages. Policies restricting car usage or raising its costs should be implemented along with the increase of alternatives and communicating their attractiveness as opposed to car alone. The objective is to encourage individuals to either make their trips outside peak hours, by a different mode of transport, or to find another way of carrying out the trip (Saleh, Sammer 2009).

Both policy categorizations can be combined. On the one hand, push measures encompass the economic policies as proposed by Santos et al. (2010b). On the other hand pull measures incorporate soft and knowledge policies since they aim at raising the awareness and providing alternatives to end users. Both should bring about desirable alteration in mobility behavior consumers and firms.

Therefore, in this work the author proposes the following categorization of policies for the reduction of car use and for the promotion of sustainable mobility (see Figure 22):

- Push policies (fiscal or economic policies): are government regulations, which force consumers and producers to change their behavior and rely chiefly on fiscal measures (Santos et al. 2010b). They can include parking charges, workplace parking levies, fuel taxes, vehicle excise duty, car ownership permits, public transport subsidies, and road-user charging (Saleh, Sammer 2009).
- Pull policies (soft policies): cover policy elements that aim at improving and extending mobility alternatives such as public transport systems, walking and cycling, or innovative mobility solutions. Also intangible policies are included. They aim at changing behaviors by informing actors about the consequences of their transport choices and persuading them to use more sustainable alternatives (Santos et al. 2010b).
- Physical policies (spatial structures and land-use policy): have direct influence on the physical infrastructure of a city such as land use, road construction, transport of goods and logistics.

Push and pull measures in the transport policy can be also referred to as carrot and stick. Especially in large cities, the combination of alternative mobility offerings and clear restrictive rules (for example, with regard to parking space availability) is promising. It promotes car independence and ensures better urban mobility (Hertel, Bührmann 2014). In the following paragraphs the author outlines the most relevant push, pull and physical policies. Some examples are also given to analyze their impact or lack thereof in places where they have been implemented.

14.2 Push Policies

In contrast to the benefits, the entire cost of the environmental impacts and externalities of transport is generally not borne by the transport user (for details see chapter 14.2.1). Efficient mobility model for the future must take the true costs of transport into account. Corrective policy intervention can ensure that users are aware of these external costs in making their transport decisions. Therefore, the regulatory framework needs to create incentives for people to make sustainable transport choices. Inevitably this should lead to the internalization of external costs in the context of urban mobility.

There are several economic instruments that can help correct road transport externalities. Economics offers two types of instruments for addressing the problem of these externalities: command-and-control and incentive-based. In the following sections the author briefly discusses the economics of transport externalities that support the legitimacy of and the need for establishing push policies. Then both types of push policies are outlined in more detailed and some policy examples are given.

14.2.1 Economics of Transport Externalities

If the demand for road space is greater than road capacity, traffic congestion occurs. This condition is characterized by slow speeds with impacts such as: longer and unreliable travel times and negative economic effects as a result of an inefficient distribution and delivery of goods, services and resources (Santos et al. 2010a).

Walters (1961) established a correlation between travel time on a given length of a road, as a function of number of cars (traffic flow), and average costs, as a function of the traffic flow. According to this relationship higher number of cars (traffic flows) leads to lower average speeds and hence to higher travel times and costs per km. Additional traffic imposes an external cost on all other road users. Under congested conditions, particularly in urban areas, and in the absence of efficient pricing strategies for road usage, traffic is undercharged and hence excessive (Walters 1961).

POLICY INTERVENTIONS FOR SUSTAINABLE MOBILITY		
PUSH «Command-and-Control»	PULL «Soft measures»	PHYSICAL «Spatial structures and land-use»
▪ Fuel standards ▪ Vehicle standards ▪ Fiscal policy instruments – taxes on purchase and ownership of vehicles – taxes on vehicle usage ▪ Mobility Pricing and Congestion charging ▪ Regulatory measures: – speed limits – low emission zone – quota systems for the number of vehicles (limitation of the amount) ▪ Establishing parking regime ▪ Pricing / ticketing ▪ …	▪ Public transportation: infrastructure and service expansion ▪ Promoting walking by a convenient network and traffic calming ▪ Expanding cycling infrastructure incl. Bike & Ride ▪ Offering alternative mobility services, ▪ Marketing and campaigns about sustainable mobility behavior ▪ Mobility management for private transport (information provision, consulting, etc.) ▪ Corporate mobility management ▪ Effective traffic control and traffic management ▪ …	▪ Increased space resistance ▪ The renaissance of compact cities and short distances ▪ Transit-oriented development ▪ Establishing districts with high quality of life ▪ Settlement compaction with attractive shared urban spaces ▪ Connecting urban nodes with highly frequent transport modes ▪ …

Figure 22: The structure of possible policy interventions for sustainable mobility. (Diagram by author).

The conversion from time into cost combined with a demand curve for transport resulted in the standard diagram of the economics of traffic congestion (see Figure 23). This approach has enabled an analysis of congestion and its externalities from an economic point of view. In this model traffic is assumed to be homogeneous, that is, all vehicles are the same and all drivers and owners are identical (good or bad) and differ only by the marginal willingness to pay for a trip. Estimates of congestion costs, if expressed in monetary units, are based on assumptions regarding the value of time and the value of reliability. In general, it is expected that a higher income leads to a higher value of time (working and non-working). Hence, the more important the trip purpose, the higher the value of time savings. The value of reliability also varies with income and trip purpose, although gender differences, reflecting childcare commitments, also have an influence (Walters 1961).

In the aggregated form the curve D depicts marginal private benefits (MPB) of the road users. The private cost of using a road is depicted by the curve called marginal private costs (MPC). The MPC rises with the traffic flow (q) because of congestion. If every driver takes account of only their MPC in making driving decisions, the market equilibrium is reached at the traffic level of q^m (point C), where MPC equals MPB (Santos et al. 2010a).

However, if there is an increasing number of drivers on the road, traffic congestion is caused. I.e. each vehicle unit increases the congestion and raises total costs by an additional factor called the social (or marginal) cost of a trip (Arnott, Small 1994). In Figure 23 these additional cost factors are depicted by the curve called marginal social costs (MSC). Clearly, at the market equilibrium (q^m) MSC exceeds MPC by the external social cost of a trip, as shown by the segment M-C. This segment represents the cost which is imposed by a driver on other drivers and the environment. If no driver takes account of these resulting external social costs, congestion externalities in the form of marginal congestion costs (MCC) occur. The resulting deadweight loss of the market through incorrect pricing is the area H-M-C (Santos et al. 2010a).

The actual maximum efficiency and the equilibrium is reached at the traffic level (q^e). If the demand curve is D the efficient solution would be at point H. At this point the marginal trip is just worth its external social cost of a trip, i.e. the segment H-E. This is actually the extra toll that, if charged, would shift the equilibrium from q^m to q^e and marginal social costs (MSC) would then equal the marginal social benefits (MSB). Interestingly, the desirable state of zero congestion or car freedom would not be an optimal solution at all. In that case the scarce road resources would be just wasted (Arnott, Small 1994; Santos et al. 2010a).

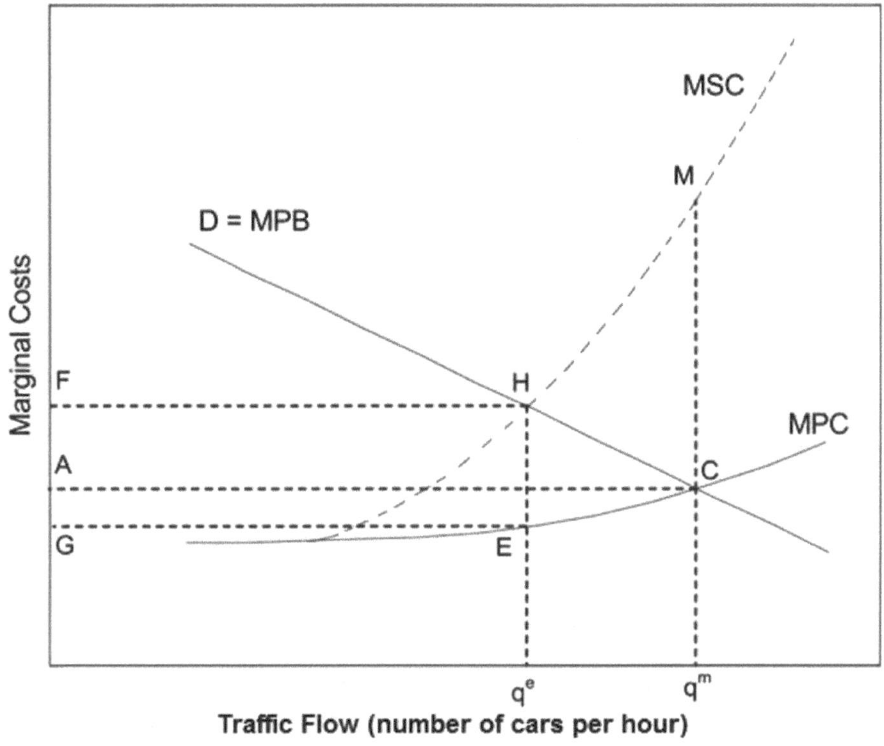

Figure 23: The economics of congestion.
(Source: adapted from Santos et al. 2010a, p. 6 and Walters 1961, p. 678).[26]

It is crucial to take external social costs into account when talking about the efficiency of the mobility system. Santos et al. (2010a) list various associated, externalities which pose high risks to the society and the environment such as: accidents, road damage, environmental damage (nitrogen oxides, carbon monoxide, sulphur dioxide, particulate matter), congestion or oil dependence. From an economic theory point of view, these severe problems can be solved by implementing corrective instruments to equate marginal social costs. In theory, they can help achieve efficiency, or at least reduce the magnitude of the deadweight loss. However, there are three main problems associated with their implementation in the mobility sector (Santos et al. 2010a):

[26] Courtesy of Elsevier Science and Technology Journals.

1) The marginal external cost imposed by vehicles is difficult to measure. Even when the marginal physical damage can be assessed, monetization is not always straightforward. Hence, typically, it is impossible to implement the objectively best policy.

2) Typically, new instruments are being implemented into a pre-existing system of corrective policies and regulations. Consequently, it may lead to double-internalizing the externality and therefore to inefficient outcomes that reduce welfare.

3) There is actually no guarantee of efficient outcomes of corrective instruments. There might be distortions in related sectors of the economy, which are not priced according to the approach of marginal cost. For example, inefficiencies caused by adverse selection in the insurance sector can affect the efficiency of the road transport sector.

In the next section the author discusses the main corrective instruments from the set of push policies.

14.2.2 Command-and-Control Policies

If there is an externality, the regulator can set a maximal level of the activity that causes the externality. The restrictions can be imposed on characteristics of products or on specific undesirable behavior of economic actors. These command-and-control policies are government regulations that aim at capping the total amount of the externality such as carbon emissions and force consumers and producers to change their behavior.

According to Santos et al. (2010a) these corrective policy measures seem to be the most widely used instruments. Even though, they are regarded as easy to implement, they are rather inflexible, as they do not go beyond the mandatory standard. They also may cause bureaucratic burden. In some cases the costs can exceed the potential benefits, thus replacing the failure of the market with a government failure. Nonetheless, often the implementation of command-and-control policies is justified by the severity of the underlying problem. A number of policies have been listed in table 19.

Table 19: A list of command-and-control policies and their description (based on Santos et al. 2010a, pp. 9–13)

Corrective Interventions	Description
Fuel Standards	These interventions are standards that countries impose on motor-vehicle fuels. The most prominent example is the ban on lead in petrol, which had a severe influence, for example, on the brains of children. It was phased out and finally banned all over the world as of 2009. By implementing these measures the emissions of benzene, sulphur dioxide, and other harmful pollutants have been reduced.
Vehicle Standards	These policies typically regulate vehicle safety, tailpipe emissions and fuel efficiency. Different countries set their own vehicle standards, although the EU sets standards for all its members. Notable examples of such regulations are catalytic converters or seat-belts.
Low or Zero Emissions Zones	LEZ or ZEZ are defined areas where access by certain polluting vehicles is restricted or discouraged. The aim is to improve the air quality. This intervention may favor vehicles such as hybrid electric vehicles, or zero-emission vehicles such as plug-in electric vehicles.
Parking Restrictions	Parking entails social costs because parked vehicles use public space. The space has opportunity costs, since the land could be used otherwise. This is a powerful approach to road space rationing. Quantitative restrictions on available parking spots indirectly reduce traffic levels and the most of traffic externalities. However, if not implemented wisely it can result in rebound effect, as search traffic for parking could be induced.
Restriction on Vehicle Circulation	The policies include the pedestrianization of streets, limited traffic zones (e.g. only public transport) or restricting license plates, where cars with even numbers are allowed to drive on even days only. This type of policy is equitable. It affects all drivers and does not differentiate by their willingness to pay for using the road (i.e. by their ability to pay). They usually do not harm the local economy, as is often suggested. They rather create a better environment for customers in the area.
Restrictions on Vehicle Ownership	Another capping policy is through restrictions on vehicle ownership. This is a direct quantity control system (e.g. Vehicle Quota System in Singapore). Prospective vehicle owners must purchase a certificate of entitlement, which is a license that lasts for a specific period of time (ten years). The government sets a quota of available certificates for different vehicle categories per year.

14.2.3 Incentive-Based Policies

Incentive-based policies include two distinct types of interventions: quantity control and fiscal instruments.

Quantity control policies give more weight to the problem of carbon emissions, pollution or waste from road transport. These policies are based on a cap-and-trade system of marketable (tradable) or transferable instruments such as permits, credits, allowances or property rights. The regulator sets an aggregated quantity for them. The distribution and allocation of the certificates among polluters is managed by the market. Consumers, firms and other entities trade these permits at an endogenously determined price (Baumol, Oates 1988, p. 59; Hepburn 2006). There are three main steps involved in establishing and maintaining such a system. First, the regulator sets the total quota. Under perfect information, the quantity is determined by the point where so called marginal abatement costs equal marginal social costs. Second, the regulator allocates the permits, which together do not exceed the limit. Third, emitters trade their permits. Usually, those with lower marginal abatement costs sell and those with higher marginal abatement costs buy permits. Permit trading establishes the market-clearing price (Santos et al. 2010a). It needs to be emphasized, however, that this form of quantity control system differs from command-and-control policies that also aim at capping the externality. Most of all, in the case of command-and-control instruments the level of emissions is regulated for every single source and no trading is permitted.

Fiscal control instruments, also referred to as price policies, put a price on an activity such as congestion. Fiscal tools include taxes or subsidies. Both aim at providing penalties and incentives to reduce the level of the externality. Taxes bridge the gap between private and social costs by internalizing an externality. In this case the corrective tax is set equal to the marginal external cost of the activity. Thus, the intervention brings the marginal private cost up to the level of marginal social cost. Theoretically, this should lead to an efficient market solution, i.e. the equilibrium. Subsidies, on the other hand, aim at encouraging the agents to reduce the level of activity by compensating for their loss (Santos et al. 2010a).

An important aspect of incentive-based policies is the handling of the revenues, which may lead to important welfare and distributional consequences. Moreover, purposeful tax revenue allocation is one of the determinants for the public and political acceptance of these corrective policies. Revenues can be redistributed in many ways: as subsidies to counteract the regressive impacts of the policy itself, as an instrument to cut income taxes or other distortive taxes, or for enhancement investments in other areas of the transport sector, for example the public transport.

Table 20: A list of incentive-based policies and their description (based on Santos et al. 2010a, pp. 13–29)

Corrective Interventions	**Description**
Quantity Control	A system of marketable (transferable or tradable) permits, credits, allowances or rights. The regulator determines a cap or an aggregate quantity of emissions, pollution or waste and leaves their allocation among polluters to be determined by the market.
Taxes on purchase and ownership of a vehicle	Many countries impose taxes on the purchase of vehicles and a periodic license fee on the ownership of a vehicle. Purchase taxes are direct tools to address CO_2 emissions generated during the manufacturing and disposal of vehicles.
Subsidies to efficient vehicles and carrot-stick systems	Subsidies for the purchase of fuel efficient or alternative fuel vehicles are an important economic instrument to encourage the purchase of low (or zero) emission vehicles. Subsidies may be effective in tilting preferences of consumers. However, they may also lead to an increase in the number of car ownerships, offsetting the beneficial effect of subsidies.
Scrappage incentives	These interventions are voluntary vehicle retirement programs that grant rebates to owners of old vehicles upon scrappage. The incentives aim directly at old vehicles that still circulate in the fleet and are responsible for a higher share of emissions than technologically advanced vehicles.
Taxes on usage of a vehicle	Usage taxes are imposed based on the usage of vehicle. If the vehicle is unused, there are no taxes to be charged. Examples of these charges include emission taxes, fuel taxes, vehicle km traveled taxation.
Congestion charges	The idea behind a congestion charge is to confront car drivers with the true social costs of their journeys. It reflects the external social costs of congestion. In theory, a congestion charge is set equal to the marginal social cost of congestion. A congestion charge ensures that only cost-justified journeys are made and the scarce road space is allocated to those who value it most. The effect of charging is to reduce travel demand and congestion, and to increase speeds and the total net benefits of travel.
Parking charges	The provision and use of the parking slot entails a marginal cost. Parking charges increase the total cost of a trip. This could reduce the attractiveness of a given urban area altogether, or discourage vehicle usage, resulting in a decrease in the inflow of vehicles. In addition, the introduction of parking fees could help matching demand with supply, thus reducing parking search time, and improving mobility.
Pay-as-you-drive insurance	Pay-as-you-drive (PAYD) insurance differs from standard insurance in that the premium is dependent on the annual distance traveled. Thus, insurance becomes a variable cost.

The main advantage of incentive-based instruments is their cost effectiveness. Agents such as producers or consumers with low marginal abatement costs rather reduce their level of externality than buy additional permits or pay charges. Whereas, those actors with high marginal abatement costs prefer to buy permits or pay taxes. Thus, the cost of reducing the externality is minimized as compared to the direct regulatory approach of setting standards (Baumol, Oates 1988). Another advantage is the self-revelation of private information through choices that are made by regulated actors. Hence, they help exploit the market's capability of private information aggregation, when the information basis is not complete and cannot be derived by the regulator (Santos et al. 2010a).

On the other side, incentive-based mechanisms can lead to market failures and considerable missing of objectives. This situation may occur, when the calibration of penalties and incentives is incorrect due to: difficulties in determining the level of marginal external cost, the system already having corrective regulations in place, and the presence of distortions in other sectors in the economy. One of the most significant barriers to the regulator is a state of imperfect information. In this case both permits and taxes yield inefficient outcomes. Finally, transaction and implementation costs may reach significant values due to the need for establishing advanced monitoring systems (Santos et al. 2010a).

14.3 Pull Policies

14.3.1 Integration of Public Transport

Public transportation systems are meant to serve the public, as the name indicates. They have set fares, run on fixed routes and utilize dedicated or shared infrastructures and facilities. Such systems encompass railways, buses or ferries and are provided by local authorities and usually operated by private companies under contract. It is widely acknowledged that public transport is a sustainable transportation mode, even though it also consumes energy and resources. Compared to cars, however, its impacts tend to be much lower. In case of high usage of individual motorized transport modes, the public transportation can contribute to the overall reduction of different traffic externalities (Santos et al. 2010b). With regard to achieving the reduction of the number of cars on the roads by factor 10, supporting any alternative to cars is beneficial. Therefore, strong public transport should be an imperative for those cities that aim at establishing the paradigm of sustainable mobility.

For public transport policy to be successful it is required that the policy is internally integrated, i.e. that it seamlessly combines different modes of transport (Santos et al. 2010b). Besides offering the extension of public transport, which obviously might require considerable investments into the new infrastructure, non-material measures of mode integration can be undertaken. Such interventions can include integrated ticketing and smart travel card systems, or increasing the availability of comprehensive information to make multimodal journeys more attractive (UK Commission for Integrated Transport 2009).

Especially the provision of real-time travel information is a vital factor for raising the attractiveness of public transport as an option relative to the car. The objective of such an information system is providing users with easily comparable and digestible information, for example, regarding the costs and schedule of different transport options. A multimodal traveler information system needs to be fully integrated to influence modal choice decisions with regard to public transport (Kenyon, Lyons 2003). An integrated multimodal information system would display information on different public transport alternatives together with comparable information for a car journey.

Integrated and technologically advanced ticketing and smart card systems help cutting costs and avoiding waiting time at interchanges. Hence, they support the perception of the public transport as a network system and contribute to making more multimodal journeys (UK Commission for Integrated Transport 2009). Introducing integrated tariff systems can have a positive influence on the demand for public transport (Abrate et al. 2009; Matas 2004).

As interchanges affect the comfort, reliability and total journey time of passengers, it is crucial that the interchange between the modes is as seamless as possible (Hine, Scott 2000). It can be achieved by providing interchange facilities such as park-and-ride systems, bike-and-ride, or establishing multimodal connections to airports (Santos et al. 2010b). The objective of such interventions is to integrate private and public transport modes and to encourage people to switch from using private cars to public transport.

One important aspect of public transport is that governments in many countries decide to subsidize public transport services, which could not operate under free market conditions otherwise. The reason for that might the steadily increasing car ownership in the developing world and also the relative increase in labor costs (Santos et al. 2010b). However, subsidies to public transportation can be justified by having several beneficial effects on the society. Firstly, there exist economies of scale with regard to the quality of service. I.e. the more frequent transport services and the higher the route density, the lower the waiting time and access costs for passengers are. This leads to the generation of higher demand (Small, Verhoef 2007). Secondly, subsidizing public transport is regarded as an efficient policy instrument to address the negative externalities of the transport, because public transport as an alternative to car contributes to the reduction of problems such as congestion, accidents and local air pollution (Parry, Small 2007). Thirdly, public transport has an important social function. Subsidizing public transport supports the social inclusion of disadvantaged groups such as those with low incomes or disabled people (van Goeverden et al. 2006).

14.3.2 Walking and Cycling

Establishing modern and sustainable urban environment requires to incorporate more walking and cycling as an integral and equal part of the overall transport system (Banister 2008). However, urban sprawling and low-density neighborhoods discourage people from walking and cycling and thus make them dependent on cars (Pucher et al. 1999). The reduction of travel distance through appropriate land use and the seamless integration slow modes with the public transport can generate substantial incentives for walking and cycling. These improvements can lead to sustainable travel patterns which can directly compete with the convenience of car usage (Santos et al. 2010b). Policies which support walking and cycling as an additional transport mode can be an excellent option chiefly for short-distance trips. A list of possible policies is depicted in Table 21.

Table 21: Policies which encourage walking and cycling for transport purposes (source: Santos et al. 2010b)

Area	Policies	Description
Cycling	Improving and building bicycle lanes and paths	Wider, color-coordinated and marked exclusive cycling lanes contribute to safer cycling, as safety risks are one of the main concerns of cyclists.
Cycling	Giving cyclists priority at junctions	Cyclists cannot properly indicate their movements in the real-life traffic. Therefore, separate traffic lights, opposite-direction lanes in one-way streets and priority at junctions are some solutions to make cycling safer and more attractive.
Cycling	Providing convenient and safe bicycle parking at popular locations	E.g. at shopping areas, train stations, or offices as cycling commuters put value on the ability to seamlessly interchange between several modes of transport.
Cycling	Showers in offices	Employers to provide facilities such as showers and locker at the office for employees to refresh and change once they get to work.
Cycling	Increased funding for cycling programs	Safety training programs for schoolchildren, bicycle repair workshops, bike weeks, etc.
Walking	Reducing crime in neighborhoods	Perception that crime rates are low encourage people to walk short distances instead of taking a car. E.g. regular police patrols make walking late in the evening or in a deserted neighborhood a safe experience.

Walking	Wider, well maintained and cleaner pavements	Aims at providing pleasant walking environment and experience.
Walking	Improved street furniture	Additional infrastructure such as flower-beds, trees, kiosks or benches can create a sense of safety and to encourage walking.
Walking	Safe crossings	Crossing roads quickly and safely reduces walking time, distance and leads to shorter waiting times. Especially important for surroundings of schools, offices and during peak hours.
Walking	Weather protection	Protection against disadvantageous weather conditions is relevant for cold and humid climates (e.g. proper clothing).
Walking and cycling	Less car parking	Restricting parking space makes car driving less possible, and hence walking and cycling more attractive. Additionally, it contributes to the environment being less congested, safer and more pleasant.
Walking and cycling	Lower speed limits	E.g. 30km/h zones have direct effects on the safety perception of cyclists and pedestrians. It can be implemented effectively in urban areas. On the other hand, introducing cycling lanes on high-speed roads can put cyclists in dangerous situations.
Walking and cycling	Accessible public transport	Providing seamless integration with public transportation systems and easier interchanges can contribute to better quality of service (shorter waiting times). E.g. cycle ramps on buses and trains could make traveling with bicycles much more convenient.
Walking and cycling	Grid layouts	Distinguishing the road space that is given to every type of road user can further contribute to the safety in the traffic. Grid layouts raise the perception of how much space is actually given to every mode of transport.

Walking and cycling as forms of urban transportation for short-distance trips can have some substantial benefits in terms of health, environment, safety and economy (Santos et al. 2010b).

With regard to health, walking and cycling, similarly to other physical exercises, can reduce obesity. The developed countries with strong support for walking and cycling tend to have lower obesity rates (Bassett Jr et al. 2008). For example, the UK government, has been integrating cycling promotion with the strategy for reducing obesity in the society (UK Department for Transport 2008).

With regard to the environmental benefits, walking and cycling produce neither carbon emissions nor pollution. Particularly, walking and cycling are beneficial because they can successfully substitute short-distance trips conducted by cars, which demonstrably have the highest emission rates (André, Hammarström 2000). Hence, encouraging people to switch from polluting forms of transport, such as cars, can have double positive effects: it can lead to the reduction of both car trips and carbon emissions.

With respect to safety benefits, studies have found that the likelihood of being involved in an accident as a cyclist or pedestrian varies inversely with the amount of walking and cycling (Jacobsen 2003). Jacobsen (2003) finds that doubling the number of people walking reduces the individual risk of fatality by 66%. Hence, a motorist is less likely to collide with a person walking and cycling, if more people walk or cycle. Policies that increase the numbers of people walking and cycling appear to be an effective way to improving the safety of people on the roads.

From the perspective of the economy there are several benefits that can result from improvements in walking and cycling (Santos et al. 2010c):

- improved health due to reduced healthcare costs and mortality and increased productivity,
- reduced road fatalities and disabilities caused by traffic injuries,
- generated positive economic effects on small business through pedestrianization and
- reduced costs of road, vehicle and parking maintenance and reduced pollution and carbon emissions.

14.3.3 Innovative Alternatives and Soft Policies

The policy area encompasses implementing novel mobility concepts, teleworking, online shopping, eco-driving and provision of general information and advertising campaigns. Even if they alone are regarded as insufficient for overcoming the auto dependence they are necessary to implement.

Carsharing

Carsharing is still not a widespread practice and hence its impact on the transport, pollution and congestion is regarded limited. However, carsharing mobility concepts may offer substantial benefits to local transportation networks. The reason is that carsharing members tend to abstain from owning or buying own cars and use more public transport instead (Santos et al. 2010b). Carsharing can lead to the reduction of personal vehicle miles traveled (VMT) and to a substantial decrease in private car ownership resulting in fewer cars on the roads.

Carsharing organizations are ususally not-for-profit. Recently there has been a growth in commercial enterprises, some of which, require initial public funding (Santos et al. 2010b) and privileged access to on-street parking lots (Le Vine et al. 2014). The parking space is typically managed by municipalities and local governments. These bodies are usually fragmented, each representing a relatively small geographic area, and under no obligation to reach agreements with carsharing operators. For carsharing service providers there is a risk of being unable to attain the required access to on-street space, Such a situation can effectively prevent them from operating. It creates uncertainty that constrains the ability of operators to invest the resources required for the provision of the carsharing service (Le Vine et al. 2014).

Firstly, governments are required to create appropriate regulatory frameworks to eliminate the uncertainties related to the availability of parking space (Le Vine et al. 2014). Secondly, there is evidence that carsharing services can have positive impacts on the local transport network, for example, by being complimentary to public transport. Therefore, incentives in the form of initial funding can be also provided to encourage entrepreneurs to step into the carsharing market (Santos et al. 2010b). Thirdly, investments in modern telecommunication infrastructure could foster the establishment of carsharing services based on digital technologies – a policy mostly required in developing countries (Santos et al. 2010b). Finally, Le Vine et al. (2014) propose that carsharing services must be represented by competent industry level bodies that can effectively mediate between individual operators and local governments. More information about modern carsharing concepts can be found in chapter 12.2.1.

Ridesharing

There has been a negative trend in car occupancy levels in developed countries in the recent decades. This downward development in car occupancy is due to decreasing fuel costs, improving vehicle efficiency, smaller families, increased time commitments and higher demands for privacy, comfort and convenience (Levin 1982; Ferguson 1997). Reduced occupancy of vehicles has contributed to increasing congestion and air pollution levels (Santos et al. 2010b). However, there is a considerable potential of supporting policies that raise occupancy rates in cars. For example, a recent study suggests that the fuel consumption in US could be reduced by 5,4% if one passenger was added to only one in ten cars. Not only can car occupancy rates be increased through dynamic ridesharing solutions (discussed in chapter 12.3.1) but also by implementing appropriate incentives and policies. These policies include push strategies such as increasing parking charges and road tolls, and pull strategies such as high occupancy vehicle lanes (HOV) and high occupancy toll lanes (HOT) on motorways. The HOV-approach allows vehicles with at least 2 or in some cases 3 passengers to use dedicated lanes. Supposedly, the incentive behind HOVs is the aspect of time saving. For example, a HOV in Washington, D.C. (the I-395) provides up to half an hour of time saving during peak hours (Santos et al. 2010b). However, no statistical significance has been found that time saving might be an incentive for ridesharing (Kwon, Varaiya 2008). Moreover, this approach might lead to the underutilization of HOV lanes (Dahlgren 2002; Kwon, Varaiya 2008). Another HOT-approach has emerged as an alternative to resolving the problem of underutilized HOV lanes. In general, HOT lanes allow single-occupancy-vehicles (SOVs) to pay a toll for using the HOV lanes (Li 2001). Although HOT lanes are better utilized they require expensive toll collection systems. Both require some sort of enforcement and more complicated and expensive lane configurations. HOV and HOT lanes can play a useful role in a well-managed overall freeway system, even though there is no clearance about their real contribution on occupancy. Kwon, Varaiya (2008) indicate that there are niche uses where HOV and HOT lanes can help. HOV lanes that carry a significant number of buses or vanpools can lead to a significantly higher person throughput. Also mixed HOV and HOT facilities can eliminate stop-and-go traffic and the resulting capacity losses.

Virtual Mobility

Teleworking is referred to as working through maintaining a direct linkage to the office network by means of telecommunication facilities. The virtual connection reduces the need to travel to the office (Bélanger, Collins 1998). Today, many employers offer some forms of teleworking to their employees. They use for it different terms such as: telecommuting, home office, remote work or virtual teams. Working away from the office has become increasingly available because of recent advances in digital technologies that enable mobile connections at ever-affordable rates (Allen et al. 2015). Potentially, this type of work could contribute to the reduction of congestion and to improved air quality: if workers do not commute to work, they obviously reduce traffic. However, the understanding of telecommuting is limited, as there are potential drawbacks as well. Possible rebound effects from teleworking include for example: alternative usage of cars by other household members and increasing urban sprawl by choosing to live further away from the office (Santos et al. 2010b).

Teleconferencing is yet another recent technological development that eliminates the need for several people to travel to the same location. The most prominent example is avoiding flying to another continent to have a face-to-face business meeting. In the meantime teleconferencing technologies are affordable and reliable, which makes them easily accessible for companies or institutions that provide Internet access to their employees. Adopters of teleconferencing solutions report considerable benefits (Santos et al. 2010b). A case study of British Telecommunications on teleconferencing showcased that in 2006 the company avoided 338'600 meetings a year and 42% trips which would have been made by cars. The result were CO_2 savings of more than 52'000 tons (James 2007).

Finally, e-commerce, which allows customers to compare and buy products online, by phone or post, has taken off dramatically in the last 20 years (Santos et al. 2010b). This development has affected the transportation system considerably. On the one hand, many products that have been digitized (e.g. books and music), do not need physical transport anymore. On the other hand, physical products (e.g. groceries) require physical delivery, however, only to the customer, eliminating the need for customers to travel to collect goods. However, the impacts of e-commerce on the modal split and environment are regarded ambiguous, since it causes direct changes in freight structures and logistic chains (Fichter 2002). For example, reducing the need to travel for shopping prompts freight traffic to deliver the goods to the customers. Another negative rebound effect is that the delivery trips caused by e-commerce can substitute those shopping trips that otherwise would be made by foot in the neighborhood (Santos et al. 2010b).

To conclude, the success of options for virtual mobility is not clearly evident in the literature. However, development in information and telecommunication technologies seem to remain the changing force with regard to how people conduct work, communicate and do shopping. Therefore, a careful and contextual empirical analysis for each case is necessary to determine successful policies for implementing virtual mobility measures (Santos et al. 2010b).

14.3.4 Smart Policies

In addition to the previous policy measures for a broader range of alternatives to cars, additional soft policies can be implemented. They aim at influencing behavioral changes by providing people with required information by means of educational and marketing instruments (Santos et al. 2010b). These policies address barriers to behavioral change towards sustainable mobility which might occur due to lack of information, complexity of available choices or upfront costs. Well-designed information policies should inform people about the economic and environmental implications of their actions and foster them to act in a sustainable manner (Stern 2006).

Information Provision and Education Campaigns

Dargay (2008) notes that car travel is relatively insensitive to changes in costs. This finding indicates that people might have a subjective attitude to car use and perceive it as a necessity, even if objectively this is not the case. Thus, information campaigns for raising people's awareness of travel alternatives and the negative environmental impact of their car use could change people's attitudes (Dargay 2008). Fujii, Garling (2007) show that especially personalized communication instruments can be effective in breaking habitual car use, as opposed to mass communications (Fujii, Garling 2007). For example, Personalized Travel Planning (PTP) provides a range of individualized, tailored information and incentives to encourage travel behavior changes within a concentrated population area. This instrument is regarded as beneficial in overcoming people's habitual use of the car and the associated psychological barriers to using sustainable mobility solutions (CIVITAS 2013).

However, the literature suggests that information is necessary but not sufficient for behavioral change. It might be due to the attitude-behavior gap, which seems to be a key issue with behavioral change towards sustainability (Anable et al. 2006). The attitude-behavior gap implies that even if the knowledge about the environmental issues is available the anticipated change in behavioral patterns fails to happen. Hence, information measures addressing attitudes and intentions might not be very effective, if implemented alone. On the other hand, classical economic push policies without a targeted information and education strategy might also be less effective, if not counterproductive (Anable et al. 2006). Therefore, the recommended optimal policy solution encompasses combination of both: enforcement policies and successful information provision (Santos et al. 2010b).

Advertising and Marketing for Behavioral Change

Public sector advertising and marketing strategies are increasingly being recognized and deployed by policymakers to motivate people to reduce their car usage and ownership. The main goal is to raise community understanding of environmental aspects of mobility and to increase the readiness to use more sustainable alternatives (Cairns et al. 2004).

An understanding of why people use cars and what provokes the desirable behavioral change in their mobility choices is crucial to design an appropriate communication instrument. It encompasses understanding the market, how it is composed and what are the driving forces behind car usage (Santos et al. 2010b). Furthermore, marketing campaigns should be tailored towards those population segments that are likely to increase their frequency of car use (Anable 2005). This requires a travel demand analysis regarding segmentation of users, number of trips, purposes, time of day, destination, mode and route, and their relationship with service attributes (Saleh, Sammer 2009).

One of the key instruments is proper market research. Techniques from conventional commercial marketing can be adapted, such as market segmentation, that is, dividing people into meaningful categories to be able to address purposeful marketing strategies. This segmentation requires knowledge about the socio-demographic, situational and psychological factors affecting travel choices. These factors can considerably differ among diverse groups of people (Anable 2005).

Banister (2008) refers to these instruments as dialogue-based techniques for promoting the use of public transport, cycling and walking as viable alternatives to the car. He also points out that this kind of communication must be based on a participatory and inclusive approach. This means approaching individuals, groups and localities, and explaining the need for behavioral changes and the importance of their contribution. Banister (2008) justifies individualized marketing and proactive information provisioning by referring to positive changes in travel behavior in several European and Australian cities (around 10% reductions in car usage).

Understanding Life Changes

There is evidence that changes in personal circumstances, such as changes in lifestyle or life events, are associated with reviews of available transport alternatives (Goodwin 2008). Major life adjustments such as change of home or job, retiring, getting married or divorced, or children leaving home, force a case-specific reconsideration of patterns of travel demand. This reappraisal can bring about a response in the form of changed travel behavior. Goodwin (2008) finds that people whose lives are stable tend to respond less to changes in the attractiveness of their preferable travel mode, regardless of whether their current mode gets worse or the alternative is better (for example, due to less costs, time savings, higher quality). Whereas people with important life events, tend to respond more likely to the changes in attractiveness of their mobility choices. The process by which the market adapts to changes might be influenced by the pace at which such life events occur in the population. This is connected with demographic trends, concerning the number of people who change jobs each year, change home, and so on (Goodwin 2008). In this respect, there are substantial implications for mobility marketing campaigns implemented by public authorities. Advertising and marketing for sustainable mobility are most effective, if aimed at people in the process of important life transitions. This is when they are most likely to respond with behavioral change (Santos et al. 2010b).

14.4 Physical Policies

Studies from across many countries have shown that denser urban areas with greater mixture of land use and better public transport tend to have lower car use than less dense suburban and ex-urban residential areas (Frank, Pivo 1994). For example, an influential study from 1989 by Peter Newman and Jeff Kenworthy compared 32 cities across North America, Australia, Europe and Asia. The main finding was that denser cities, particularly in Asia, experience lower car usage rates than sprawling cities, particularly in North America (Newman, Kenworthy 1989). These findings have been largely accepted, even though the study has been criticized for its methodology (Mindali et al. 2004).

Density, land use and public transport accessibility can influence travel behavior, even though social and economic factors, especially household income, might exert a stronger influence (Handy et al. 2005). Therefore, spatial developments in urban areas play a significant role in establishing policies for urban mobility. As cities grow and new cities are built, public authorities should be aware of some important land use policies that can reduce congestion and pollution, and may lead to a stronger switch to sustainable modes of transport. They can be incorporated into the patterns of urban form and layouts by (Banister 2008):

- increasing densities and concentration,
- mixed use development,
- appropriate housing location,
- the design of buildings, space and route layouts,
- public transport oriented development and transport areas,
- car-free development,
- establishing size thresholds for the availability of services and facilities.

Land use makes an invaluable and unique contribution to sustainable transport policy, as it can reduce the overall distance that people must travel. Thus, appropriate land use policies in existing cities can reduce aggregated travel demand as well as influence the uses of sustainable transport modes. In the following paragraphs the author introduces some of the most important physical policies for the paradigm of sustainable mobility.

14.4.1 City Design

The distribution of activities over space is one of the most important determinants of transport demand and so space must be explicitly considered (Enoch 2012). Therefore, the question about the general city design paradigm is significant. There has been a general polarization that distinguishes two city design approaches: polycentric and monocentric. Monocentric areas tend to have a unique center, termed the Central Business District (CBD). Employees living in the surrounding area are expected to commute to the CBD (Mori 2006). Whereas a polycentric city features multiple and dispersed subcenters and could potentially reduce commuting distances and improve live-work integration (Lin et al. 2012). At the heart of the debate is the idea that both concepts aim at reducing the frequency and distance of trips, overall traffic volumes and the associated energy consumption and pollution (Banister, Hickman 2006, p. 277). The main difference is that compact areas enable effective public transport, walking and cycling as compared to dispersed cities, which tend towards greater car dependence (Santos et al. 2010b). However, the research evidence is not clear about these relationships and sometimes even contradictory. Therefore, uncertainty remains over the most effective scale and structure of mixed-use centers within cities. On the one hand, it might be due to the impact of the spatial scale, that is, there might be other effects of decentralization in spatially large areas than in smaller spatial scale (Naess, Sandberg 1996). On the other hand, the dependencies between land use and travel patterns can have many other dimensions and hence cannot be explained in such a simplistic way (Crane 2000).

There are four factors that are important physical determinants of urban environments: development size, density, diverse developments, and city design. Based on that Santos et al. (2010b) draws some important conclusions for planning and transport policy measures that are under the control of urban planners and hence can be influenced.

Development size

Settlement size affects the range of jobs and services that can be supported. It influences also the quality of public transport that can be provided, and the length of trips (Banister 2008). In terms of transport the most energy-efficient population size for settlement is thus found to be between 25’000 and 100’000 or larger than 250’000.

Density, mixed-use developments and design

High densities tend to be associated with lower average trip distances for all modes, improved public transport and in particular, enhanced viability of walking and cycling (Kenworthy, Laube 1996). The design of neighborhoods plays also a significant role in establishing sustainable patterns for mobility. Mixed-use developments enhance density of land use and make it possible for people to live, work and do shopping in the close vicinity. Such developments lead to further reductions in trip lengths, and promotes walking and cycling (Santos et al. 2010b). Other prominent and extreme examples for sustainable neighborhood development are car-free districts. This kind of car-free zoning can be implemented in city centers but also in residential settlements (such as Floridsdorf in Vienna, for details see Sessa 2007). It needs to be supported by superior accessibility to the public transport towards the city center.

Combining the elements of land use and transport policy, as discussed above, can lead to a more sustainable model of urban mobility. According to Banister (2008, p. 73) there are several basic characteristics of a sustainable urban design that must be fulfilled:

- population should exceed 25’000, preferably over 50’000,
- medium densities: over 40 persons per hectare,
- mixed-use developments,
- preference given to developments highly accessible to public transport networks and interchanges.

14.4.2 Car Parking Provision

Transport demand is heavily governed by space (Enoch 2012). In that respect, providing free on-street parking is a huge incentive for car drivers to cruise at low speeds to find a free parking spot. This can considerably contribute to air pollution and congestion. Additionally, the availability of free parking makes pricing difficult to implement (Shoup 2006). The recommendation is to reduce free parking as far as possible. Knoflacher (2006) proposes an integrated approach by providing garaged car houses at public spots at relatively low costs and charging high rates for on-street parking, which should be three to four times higher. This approach could free up to 70% of city space from cars (Knoflacher 2006). A good example of such development is Copenhagen, which reduces its parking space in the city center by 3% every year (Newman, Kenworthy 1996). In that sense parking provision is one of the most powerful instruments to control the demand for car ownership and car journeys in urban areas.

However, the opposition to such interventions from various interest groups must be considered and carefully dealt with. For example, many private-sector employers in the UK meet resistance from employees if parking charges are raised (Rye, Ison 2005). People are also reluctant to give up car parking spaces at properties, because it is perceived that property without a parking space loses its value (Stubbs 2002).

14.4.3 Accessibility

Land use policies which promote sustainable transport must satisfy an important dimension: location and accessibility (Santos et al. 2010b). Accessibility is defined as the extent to which land use and transport system enable groups of individuals to reach activities and destinations (Geurs, van Wee 2004). Accessibility has become the main feature of policies that support the paradigm of sustainable mobility. Land-use policies which make walking, cycling, and public transport more accessible reinforce the demand for more sustainable transport modes (Santos et al. 2010b). However, the intention is not to prohibit the use of the car. This could be seen as being against free choice. It is rather recommended to design cities of such quality and at a suitable scale that people would not need to have a car (Banister 2008). The combination of clear planning strategies would allow a city design at the personal scale and would allow both high-quality accessibility and environment.

Private car use is negatively correlated with the distance to the nearest public transport station. Therefore, stops and cycling lanes must be located strategically that they connect residential areas and areas of interest, such as employment or shopping centers (Kitamura et al. 1997). Easily accessible transport has desirable effects on social inclusion and labor force participation (Sanchez 1999). Therefore, harmonized integration of policies for sustainable transport is crucial for accessibility. For example, physical integration of bicycle stands at railway stations or park-and-ride with public transport terminals enables people to organize their transport schedule in a multimodal way (Santos et al. 2010b).

14.4.4 Mixed-use Development

Strategies which emphasize mixed use are more likely to result in people living closer to work places and services they require for everyday life (Mindali et al. 2004). The car can then become an option rather than a necessity (Wegener 1996). Therefore, land use policies that promote mixed-use development can be significant in establishing and encouraging sustainable mobility patterns. Mixed-use development blends a variety of land uses together. It may encourage the development of small businesses, shops and restaurants in residential buildings (Santos et al. 2010b). The main goals of mixed-use zoning are increased intensity of land uses, increased diversity of land uses, and integrated segregated uses (Grant 2002). Such development can be achieved by variety of measures, such as (Ewing, Hodder 1998; Beyer):

- reduced distances between housing, workplaces, retail businesses, and other amenities and destinations for greater density,
- more affordable housing and life-cycle housing for greater housing variety (starter homes, apartments, larger family homes, senior housing etc.),
- more compact development and land-use synergy, e.g. residents provide customers for retail, which provides amenities for residents,
- walkable and cycle-able neighborhoods, increased accessibility via public transit, both resulting in reduced transportation costs,
- close and easy access to fresh and healthy foods, as an element of a livable, healthy community,
- sense of place and stronger neighborhood character by well-designed and mixed-use communities.

Prominent examples of mixed-use developments are Nyhavn (Copenhagen) or Canary Wharf (London). The former is the new harbor of Copenhagen, an area historically known as a red-light district and infamous for its high crime rate. Following a resident-led conservation program the area became a mixed-use residential neighborhood and established itself as one of Copenhagen's main tourist attractions (Roberts et al. 2006). The district is well connected by two metro lines. Furthermore, Copenhagen also offers a large bicycle-sharing network which makes cars almost obsolete. Canary Wharf is one of the world's most desirable business and commercial districts with a well established public transportation network. Even though the workforce of 80'000 people is one of the wealthiest in the UK, 75% of the commutes are done by public transport. The district provides only 3000 parking spaces in total (Metz 2012).

14.4.5 Planning Regulations

Fundamentally, the task of mobility planners is to match the demand for transport with the supply side, that is, the capacity of the transport system, in a given place and at a given time (Enoch 2012). It has been widely recognized that increases in travel demand can no longer be faced only by suppling further capacities. This is due to constraints on the available budget as well as natural resources. Hence, modern transport policies follow a demand-side approach. This approach influences the amount and pattern of demand flows (Gruyter et al. 2015; Saleh, Sammer 2009). Planning bodies can affect the demand, that is, transport choices of the society, through appropriate regulation. Local authorities can directly influence the 'trip generators', such as schools, workplaces or developers of new buildings to implement travel plans (Santos et al. 2010b). These plans work at the individual and organizational level. The aim is to achieve positive contribution to the community and the environment by managing car use, freeing up parking space, increasing accessibility and promoting active forms of transport (Gruyter et al. 2015).

A travel plan contains a mix of different strategies including (Petrunoff et al. 2015):

- policy: parking management policy, public transport ticket subsidies,
- infrastructure: provision of end-of-trip facilities, creation of maps,
- behavior change: cycling and walking programs.

Today, travel plans are increasingly being required for new and expanded buildings as a condition of planning permissions and approvals (Santos et al. 2010b; Gruyter et al. 2015). While results have been shown to vary considerably, travel plans have typically brought about a reduction in car use of 5–15% (Enoch 2012).

The need for more sustainable and integrative planning, as a way of managing the complexity of urban mobility, has been also recognized at the international level. For example, the European Commission supports local authorities across Europe in implementing new approaches that can stimulate a shift towards cleaner and more sustainable transportation. Sustainable Urban Mobility Plans (SUMP) promote balanced and integrated development of all transport modes (Eltis 2015b). A SUMP is a strategic plan designed to satisfy the mobility needs of people and businesses, and ensure better quality of life in cities. The SUMP-concept proposes specific guidelines with recommendations on how to prepare a strategy for sustainable urban mobility. It is based on existing planning practices and accounts for integration, participation, and evaluation principles (Eltis 2015c).

15 Sustainable Mobility in the Context of Consistency in Transport Policy

Integrated planning refers to collaboration, i.e. joint working within and across organizations to develop and implement a plan. Such cooperation may involve the alignment of objectives and policies and the sharing of knowledge, data, resources, finance and powers between several organizations (Heckley et al. 2014). With regard to mobility a belief is shared among researchers that policy integration is essential to produce synergies for several reasons: to gain further efficiency increases, to control the excessive production of negative externalities and hence to contribute to more sustainability in the transport sector (Saleh, Sammer 2009; UK DETR 1998; Santos et al. 2010b; Banister 2008). The author discusses the role of policy combination and integration. He also shows why consistency with other policy domains is crucial for avoiding pitfalls and achieving the desirable effects of sustainable mobility.

15.1 Policy Combination and Integration

Saleh, Sammer (2009) and Banister (2008) define integrated transport policy as a combination of pricing (i.e. push) and non-pricing (i.e. pull) measures in mutually supporting policy packages or programs. The goal is to assist local authorities and cities in developing appropriate schemes that meet their local objectives, solve the local transport problems, and are politically and publicly feasible (Saleh, Sammer 2009). The focus should not be only on pricing measures just because they generate revenues, as public acceptance could be jeopardized. Therefore, policies that lead to restricting car use or raising its costs should go along with well-publicized undertakings to improve accessibility, availability and attractiveness of alternatives (Banister 2008). For example, revenues from congestion charging can be used for funding investments in walking and cycling infrastructure. Such reinvestments increase public acceptability at the same time. Furthermore, policy integration can compensate those groups who end up worse-off as a result of any particular policy instrument and as such helps avoid loser-winner situations. For instance, free public transport passes may compensate low-income groups affected by congestion charges (May et al. 2006). Policy combination can be also helpful in overcoming any potential barriers for implementation, which are usually linked to financial, public acceptability and equity issues.

By integrating policies, financially unviable instruments that did not enjoy public support may become viable or more acceptable (May et al. 2006, p. 320). Therefore, combining policies is regarded crucial for increasing public acceptability, especially when push measures (making car use less attractive) and pull measures (improving alternatives) are implemented within the same policy package (Banister 2008; Eriksson et al.

2008). Saleh, Sammer (2009) claim that this approach might be the optimum solution to avoiding undesirable side effects of transport in urban areas. Similarly, Lah (2015) calls for a consistent regulatory framework with policy packaging and integration as a vital element. Such a framework minimizes possible rebound effects and significantly curb transport sector GHG emissions at low- or even negative cost.

There are four ways in which policies can be mixed with each other (May et al. 2006, p. 321):

1) Complementarity: the use of two instruments has greater impact than the use of either alone.
2) Additivity: the benefit from the use of two or more instruments is equal to the sum of the benefits of using each in isolation.
3) Synergy: the simultaneous use of two or more instruments yields higher benefits than the sum of the benefits of using either one of them alone.
4) Substitutability: the use of one instrument completely eliminates any benefits from using another instrument.

Even though there is a lack of research that quantitatively predicts side-effects of policy integration, there is evidence of the positive impacts of many transport policies (Santos et al. 2010b). The literature recommends the design of policy packages rather than individual policies to increase the chances of achieving the objectives of sustainable mobility. For example, Nash, Whitelegg (2016) conclude that effective urban transport policies require a consistently structured package of measures. The most urgent research concerns the design of such measures that achieve their objectives, while being financially sustainable and attracting public and political support.

15.2 Policy Consistency

It needs to be noted, however, that choosing policy measures for sustainable mobility requires weighing a set of conflicting concerns. These concerns include environmental effects, safety, oil security, tax revenue, competitiveness of domestic firms and consumer impact (Schäfer 2009, pp. 251–252). If applied in isolation, these interventions are unlikely to achieve their stated goals of reducing overall emissions and increasing energy efficiency of the transport sector. For example, vehicle standards alone are likely to increase the efficiency of the fleet. On the other hand, the gained improvement is likely to be offset by increased vehicle use, that is, a rebound effect. Similarly, increased fuel taxes, without transport alternatives and a supply of efficient vehicles, would impact negatively on mobility affordability (Lah 2015). In that sense, integrated policy implementation requires coordination and coherence, or at least no contradiction among these different instruments (Santos et al. 2010b). For that reason policies have to constitute a consistent framework (Lah 2015).

The consistency of policy-making across different (related) sectors is a vital element in making sustainable mobility politically feasible and publicly acceptable (Banister 2008). Successful transport policy must be internally consistent, i.e. combining different modes of transport, as well as consistent with government objectives in policy areas other than transport. Santos et al. (2010b) claim that policy integration goes beyond the idea of mere packaging of push and pull measures. Transport policies should be consistent also with other policy objectives across different government departments and social sectors (see Figure 24). Therefore, consistent policy integration should consider different modes of transport, different governmental objectives (such as the economy, health and the environment), different needs of social groups, and coordinate consistent actions between the relevant government institutions (Santos et al. 2010b). In that sense integrated transport policy means (UK DETR 1998):

- integrating different modes of transport by establishing reliable connections, safe interchanges, shared e-cards, or online payment technologies and timetables,
- Making transport policies consistent with objectives in the areas of land use planning, environment, health, economy and society,
- Social inclusion, i.e. including disadvantaged and those with reduced mobility,
- Institutional and administrative integration, i.e. cooperation between all relevant institutions and policymakers.

Hull (2005) claims that the success of consistent and integrated policies is dependent on the coordinated control of the delivery of transport services, local land use policies, clear policy specifications, and funding allocated according to targets. On the one hand, this requires new policy linkages and horizontal cooperation across local authority departments and service providers. On the other hand, there is a need for vertical cooperation. Vertical integration involves alignment of relevant legislation, guidelines and supporting policies between the different levels of government and other organizations operating at national, regional and local layers (Eltis 2015a).

Horizontal integration encompasses two types of cooperation: sectoral integration and territorial integration. The former concerns the coordination of cross-cutting issues in policy-making that do not correspond to the institutional responsibilities of individual departments in various policy areas (land use planning, social services, health, energy, education, enforcement and policing etc.). The latter concerns coordination of policies and activities between neighboring local authority areas. Depending on government responsibilities at local, regional and national levels, it may be necessary to involve also regional and national stakeholders, including transport network authorities (Eltis 2015a).

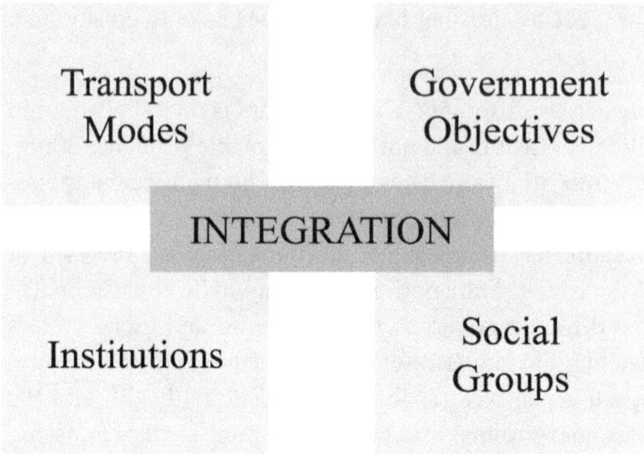

Figure 24: Dimensions of transport policy integration. (Source: adapted from Santos et al. 2010b, p. 49).[27]

However, the reality of the policy practice of local authorities is a complex field. Implementation deficits might result from the lack of integration, divergent agendas, and the lack of fit between different disciplinary and administrative policy areas (for example, land use, planning, transportation planning, and sustainability) (Hull 2005). Therefore, it is crucial to break down the complexity of local policy practice and understand how strategic policies are actually selectively combined and adopted. For that purpose Hull (2005) developed an analytic construct to describe the levels of policy integration. This model consists of a ladder of increasing levels of desirable integration. It is a typology that makes transparent the interconnections between policy issues and administrative responsibilities. The first level of the ladder is considered the most achievable, whereas the next levels mean the increase in the difficulty of integration (up to level 8). Table 22 describes the integration ladder.

[27] Courtesy of Elsevier Science and Technology Journals.

Table 22: The integration ladder for achieving policy consistency in sustainable mobility (source: adapted from Hull 2005, p. 322)

Level of integration	Description
Level 1: Physical and operational integration of public transport	Integration of fares, timetables, ticketing and physical interchanges between the different transport operators.
Level 2: Modal integration	The integration of the treatment of the different modes: walking, cycling, bus, rail, car and air through consistent regulation, pricing, appraisal criteria and budgeting.
Level 3: Integration with market needs	Focus on business concerns with efficiency, effectiveness and the costs of congestion.
Level 4: Integration with social objectives	Concerns with the needs of different social groups; issues of equity, distribution and social exclusion.
Level 5: The integration of environmental issues in transport policy making	Acknowledging and incorporating the environmental impacts of mobility and modal choice in transport policies and infrastructure development through appraisal models, pricing, and regulatory controls.
Level 6: Institutional and administrative integration	The integration of transport planning across administrative boundaries. The objective of Regional Transport Strategies is to address cross-boundary issues by identifing policy combination that produces an optimal transport strategy for each region and sub-region.
Level 7: Integration of policy sectors	The integrated management of transport, infrastructure, urban development and environmental protection. This can happen through the greater integration and coordination between the land use and transport systems, for example, for better accessibility.
Level 8: Integration of policy measures	Acknowledging the interdependencies between land-use, economics, the environment, sustainability and social objectives (such as health, education, affordability and inclusion). An integrated package of measures would include well-balanced mixes of fiscal, regulatory and other soft measures.

The ladder of integration illustrates how the conceptualization of integration can be differentiated into eight separate stages of achievement. Both horizontal and vertical integration are accounted for. On the one hand, the concept emphasizes that sustainable mobility interventions such as multimodal integration (level 2) are closely dependent on other publicly funded services such as education and health (level 4), environmental protection (level 5), and regional development (level 6). On the other hand, the ladder of integration draws attention to the fragmented nature of vertical integration. Without the translation of integrated national policies down the governance layers of city administration, local authorities are challenged to coordinate the relationship between sustainability, mobility and other governmental objectives. Such fragmentation, if not coordinated, can lead to unsustainable lock-ins. Car-oriented urban developments are typicall urban lock-ins. They have a long-life lasting and cannot be served other than by a car (Hull 2005).

The case studies investigated by Hull (2005) have demonstrated that the concept of policy integration is a very complex domain, which is often idealized. The notion of policy integration and consistency is distorted through the process of interpretation of government guidelines. There is also the need to align with the interests of different agents working within local arenas, structures and regimes. There is also a risk that the concept is weakened through the lack of ownership of government policy, the tensions between reducing car dependence and economic growth principles, the pressures from the competing professional agendas, and other local circumstances. Other problems with this concept include:

- reactive and fragmented approach to decision-making resulting from divided institutional responsibilities,
- constraints of finance,
- uncertainty over public acceptability and confusion over the appropriateness of policy initiatives.

These points are all barriers that potentially can result in conflicts between national, regional and local policies, and in discrepancy between the stated aspiration and the actual achievements. While a consistent combination of measures is vital to the success of sustainable transport policies, the policy environment and the institutional structures are equally important. Hence, creating the basis for coalitions between local authorities, national governments and other relevant veto players is crucial for achieving co-benefits of sustainable transport (Lah 2015).

In the next part the author describes the case study City of Basel (Switzerland). The local municipal authority has been introducing sustainable mobility innovations and policy interventions to overcome the car dependence and to increase the efficiency of the mobility system since the 1970s. The city has been pursuing a long-lasting reduction in mobility needs and car usage by consistently linking mobility to broader dimensions of sustainable lifestyles of its inhabitants. The author seeks to analyze the implemented policies and interventions based on the acquired knowledge in this part of the dissertation. The researcher intends to infer a 'mental map' of critical barriers and success factors for achieving policy consistency in the context of overcoming the auto dependence in urban areas.

PART IV
Transformative Literacy: Case Study City of Basel[28]

16 Part IV: Introduction

16.1 Objectives

Thus far, the author has been focusing on understanding and describing the dynamics related to the field of mobility from the following perspectives: digital technologies, innovative business models for shared automobility services and overarching policies for achieving the reduction of the car dependence in urban areas.

As discussed in the previous chapter the key element of the shift towards the new paradigm of sustainable mobility is the consistency of policy-making. Therefore, the policy for introducing sustainability in mobility must be internally coherent, i.e. combining different modes of transport, as well as consistent with government objectives in policy areas other than transport. However, the reality of the policy practice of local authorities is a very complex field. The process of policy development is not trivial to comprehend and policy implementation deficits might result. Therefore, in this chapter the author seeks to present knowledge about the dynamics that take place within the sociopolitical environment of modern cities that can lead to both their greater economic prosperity and the increased wealth of the city inhabitants.

In particular, he aims at creating a comprehensive understanding of the interplay of societal and political dimensions when overcoming car dependence and transitioning towards the paradigm of sustainable mobility. For that purpose he analyzes the case of the City of Basel, a Swiss progressive canton-city, which has been on the path of reducing car dependence since the 1970s and which has recently declared that it will transform its transportation paradigm towards a sustainable mobility system based on a consistent network of different interlinked transport solutions. Based on the acquired pool of knowledge, the researcher elaborates on barriers and enablers that influence the transition towards a sustainable mobility system for modern urban areas.

---

[28] The case study has been published with permission from the Canton of the City of Basel, Switzerland.

The author concludes that for an actual transition towards sustainable mobility in cities, three concepts need to be considered and effectively integrated: (technological) efficiency, (behavioral) sufficiency and (political) consistency. Based on that, the author develops his own notion of 'Integrated Sustainable Urban Mobility' which aims at integrating these three main concepts. With that the author proposes a holistic and innovative framework for sustainable mobility that also tries to incorporate other important sectors of urban activities, such as: land-use patterns, economy, environment, regional cooperation, health and sustainable lifestyles.

16.2 Why City of Basel?

The City of Basel is a particularly good example of an integrated and coherent policy development towards sustainable mobility that consequently has been focusing on reducing car dependence in its urban area.

The city already features a relatively balanced modal split. It is noteworthy that the sustainability objectives in terms of environmentally friendly mobility are being consistently pursued by the municipal administration. These developments take place along with clear objectives for increasing the competitiveness and locational factors of Basel as a life-sciences cluster, a finance center and a logistics hub (Kanton Basel-Stadt 2016). This might suggest that the economic strength of this region is not necessarily strongly correlated with the uninhibited automobility. A closer look at the local transport policy framework shows that the administration of the city aims at achieving rather a balanced transport system which should not be entirely based on automobility in the long run. It is based on the shared belief among the authorities of the city that such a balanced mobility system contributes to the attractiveness of the city as an industry location by providing an enhanced quality and standard of life for employees of industry sectors who reside in the city and in the agglomeration of Basel.

Secondly, the city shows the courage to systematically tackle the issues of the motorized transport to continuously increase the quality of life of its population. For this purpose, the city has taken advantage of many innovative policy measures and technologies, which are being implemented consistently, albeit not without any resistance from affected interest groups such as business centers or automobile clubs. Thus, Basel, along with other Swiss cities, has been assuming a leading position in reshaping the mobility system and in overcoming the car dependence among Swiss cities. Thus, it can act as a guide for other cities, who are struggling with similar issues related to urban mobility. For example, Basel is in many ways comparable to German cities, which is a characteristic that could allow for an easier transferability of good practices for transport policy planning, development and implementation.

Another argument for investigating the mobility system of Basel is the fact that Switzerland has no car industry in the traditional sense. While there are significant Swiss automotive suppliers, which are mainly concentrated in the cantons of Solothurn, Zurich and Bern, they do not carry a considerable weight in economic terms. For this reason, there are no strong vested interests among the actors as there are for example in Germany. The postulate of '*Factor 10 of Automobility*' thus exempts the researcher from the risk of being exposed to direct criticism of the affected industry representatives. In contrast, a strong support for the results of such research is expected due to the high awareness of the Swiss society and politics about the external social costs of automobility in Swiss cities.

For all these reasons, Basel is an ideal case study to gain important knowledge about successful practices in integrating and implementing transport policies for sustainable mobility. Firstly, policy measures towards a non-car-based urban mobility system will be described and analyzed. Secondly, a mental map of possible technological, institutional, cultural and economic barriers and enablers to overcoming auto-dependence will be developed and discussed. Hence, the results of this research will be an invaluable source of knowledge particularly for cities that have a significant reduction of car dependence on their future agendas.

16.3 Research Design, Methodology and Methods in Part IV

The purpose of this research is to gain familiarity with the phenomenon of sustainable mobility in industrialized urban areas. The importance is given to the reality of policy development and implementation as well as the resulting sociopolitical processes and dynamics. The author aims at acquiring and synthetizing new insights into these areas and creating a body of knowledge for decision-makers.

For the purpose of the analysis and the knowledge synthesis the author applies Transformative Literacy (see Figure 25), which was described in detail in chapter 1.3 of this work. Transformative Literacy constitutes a heuristic framework that aims at conceptualizing different important dimensions of complex transformational processes of socio-technical transformations to better understand them. It comprehensively covers technological, economic, societal, and political dimensions. By applying this framework, the researcher analyzes the critical success factors for the transition to sustainable mobility.

The research work is of explorative and hermeneutical character to generate new explanatory approaches about sustainable mobility in cities. A detailed description and explanation of the underlying research approach has been included into a dedicated research design document.[29]

[29] The research design is stored in Appendix 10 and can be accessed via OnlinePLUS.

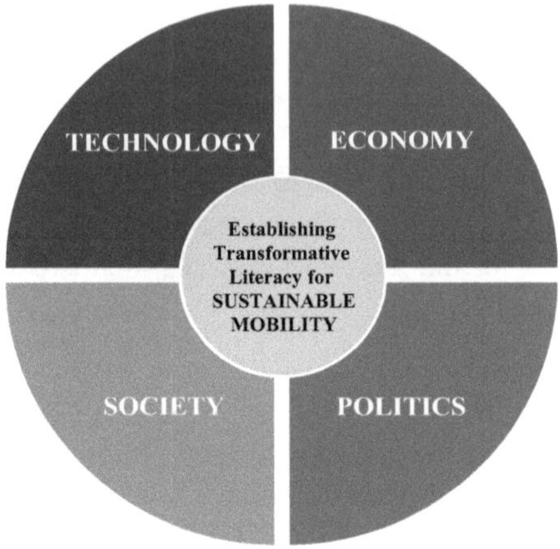

Figure 25: Transformative Literacy. Understanding the interplay between the contexts of: Technology, Economy, Society and Politics (diagram by author).

With regard to the research methods the author has relied on reviewing available literature, media articles, news bulletin and most of all on a formal qualitative approach in the form of semi-structured in-depth interviews with experts from the field under investigation. For collecting data, creating the case study, and developing the concept, 27 in-depth interviews with 23 selected mobility experts, municipal office workers, politicians and lobby representatives from the City of Basel, the canton of Basel-Country and Swiss academic institutions were conducted throughout 2014 and 2015.[30] For preparing the interviews the author developed a detailed questionnaire based on the analysis framework, and an interview handout for guiding the interviewees.[31]

Subsequently, every interview was transcribed.[32] The analysis was conducted by means of qualitative data analysis methods in 2015. The researcher applied QSR NVivo, a research tool for in-depth text analysis. Two coding cycles have been conducted. The first

[30] The lists of all conducted expert interviews for the development of the case study City of Basel are stored in Appendix 6 and Appendix 8, and can be accessed via OnlinePLUS.
[31] The relevant documents are stored in Appendix 12, Appendix 13 and Appendix 14, and can be accessed via OnlinePLUS.
[32] Due to the length (464 pages) the collection of transcripts has been attached as a digital file and can be accessed via OnlinePLUS.

one applied initial coding approach and the second one was based on axial coding. During the research the author developed numerous memos which were used for the final write-up. The report write-up followed at the beginning of 2016. For a consistency check the report was validated by the dedicated supervisor from the administration of the City of Basel in March 2016.

17 Case Study - City of Basel

17.1 Introduction

Today's challenges of a transition towards sustainable mobility in cities are multifaceted. Modern cities and their conurbations require a broadening of the scientific and political debate. They search for innovative solutions for urban mobility, which are technologically, financially, socially, and politically feasible. The focus seems to lie not only on the environmental issue and the energy efficiency of cars, but also on the economic and social aspects of urban mobility. Traffic and the heavy land use, which are caused by the individual motorized mobility, can lead to substantial losses in productivity - especially for regions with a significant level of economic activity. Moreover, accessibility is an important factor in terms of participation of city residents in social life. The significance of accessibility is highlighted by the fact that well-functioning mobility has a considerable economic and social function in modern societies. Therefore, not only should ecology and environment be the main concerns in terms of achieving sustainability in urban mobility. Additionally, one should consider social justice and the interests of important economic players in an equal manner. Finding a balance and harmony between partly contradictory objectives is a particular challenge for the policy-makers that operate in this area of conflict. With that in mind, the classical demand-oriented traffic planning and management seems to be only one-dimensional and therefore rather inadequate for the needs of modern cities.

How a new paradigm of a modern forward-looking traffic policy can be shaped, is exhibited by the efforts of progressive cities. Such progressive cities[33] implement improvement measures in diverse political and societal areas to enhance their attractiveness. As a consequence they aim at ensuring an ongoing willingness of existing and new citizens to reside there. Regarding urban mobility, they implement the principles of consistent mobility planning to provide sufficient accessibility to integrated mobility services. By that means, they strive to safeguard locational advantages and economic competitiveness, while increasing the quality of life and facilitating equal opportunities and social inclusion.

One such progressive city is City of Basel (Switzerland). The municipal authority has been introducing sustainable mobility innovations to boost the efficiency of the mobility system and to overcome car dependence. Furthermore, it has sought to link sustainable mobility to broader dimensions of sustainable and sufficient lifestyles, which have the

[33] Description is based on author's own conceptualization of the notion of a progressive city. The understanding has been obtained by studying the case of Basel-City.

potential of reducing the overall mobility needs of the inhabitants and hence also the extensive car usage.

The basis for this case study is the Swiss 'City Initiative' which was established and fostered back in 2008 by the environmental organization 'umverkehR'. This civic legislative initiative advocated for substantial reduction in car traffic in the major Swiss cities. The movement led to several referendums, among others also in the City of Basel. Even though the plebiscite failed, it led to a strategic adjustment of the Environmental Protection Law of the canton-city Basel, which was introduced in 2010. In general, it says that the volume of the motorized road traffic in Basel must be reduced by 10% by 2020 (excluding high-capacity roads).

The complexity of this requirement, however, lies in the fact that this canton-city already has a relatively balanced modal split. Measured by the number of routes, the share of the individual motorized traffic amounts to as little as 18% of the modal split (Bundesamt für Statistik BFS 2012d). In order to transform the mobility system according to this ambitious requirement the public authority is expected to introduce adequate policy adaptations and innovations in the near future. It is also required to reach a certain degree of behavioral change by users of the transport system.

The canton has prepared a set of strategies and measures that ought to foster the transition towards an integrative and car-independent mobility system. The authorities and the cantonal administration do not refrain from resorting to possible interventions in this field as described in Part III of this work. Basel places greater emphasis on developing and implementing both (i) promoting alternatives to motorized transport (soft policies) and (ii) further policy packages of fiscal or economic mechanisms (push measures). Last but not least, spatial structures and land-use patterns (physical measures) are being adjusted accordingly. Table 23 represents an excerpt from the set of strategic action areas and some examples of intervening policies in the field of urban mobility and transportation in the City of Basel.

The case study begins with a brief history of the transport policy developments in the City of Basel. With that the author aims at outlining the foundations for today's policy strategy which is intended to lead towards more car-independence in the city. This effort for achieving car-independence has not been a matter of course, but a result of public capacity, participative debate and political discourse of the entire society of Basel throughout several decades. Then, the researcher presents and describes the vision and strategy for sustainable mobility in Basel, and the measures to implement them in the near future. This leads to the analysis by means of the Transformative Literacy framework to derive the critical barriers and success factors for realizing the vision of sustainable, car-independent mobility for the City of Basel. The acquired experience and knowledge could be transferred to and used by other cities and conurbations world-wide.

Table 23: Excerpts from the set of strategic action areas in the field of mobility in Basel-City.

Policy	Action Areas	Description	Examples
Push	Road traffic:	Dosing of the urban car traffic within the city and redirecting the traffic onto the high-capacity roads (HLS)	Implementation of a regional Transportation Demand Management system
	Parking space	Implementation of an urban and regional parking management	Harmonized parking management in inner the agglomeration area
Pull	Walking and cycling	Further cycling promotion and development of attractive tri-national cycle route network	Establishment of an extended regional network of bicycle lanes
	Public transport	Infrastructure projects for a more effective public transportation system	Implementation Concept 'Tram Network 2020' Construction of 'Hetzstück' (centerpiece)
	Mobility management	Proactive mobility consulting and information	Action Program 'Basel on the Way'
Physical	Public space	Further traffic calming measures and the appreciation of the public road space	Establishment of attractive and lively city center with shared zones

17.2 City of Basel

Basel is a Swiss historic city on the Upper Rhine with about 175'500 inhabitants (Statistical Office of the Canton of Basel-Stadt 2015a). The city is the third largest in Switzerland, after Zurich and Geneva. The city center is divided by the Rhine River and consists of two main parts Grossbasel and Kleinbasel. The special feature of the city is that it is located at the border triangle of Switzerland, Germany and France. The tri-national agglomeration TEB, which stands for 'Trinational Euro District Basel' is distributed among the three countries (see Figure 26). In the district there are 250 cities and towns with altogether almost 900'000 inhabitants (Trinationaler Eurodistrict Basel TEB 2016). The urban structures go beyond the city boarders and reach other Swiss cantons such as: Basel-Land, Solothurn and Aargau.

Figure 26: Trinational Euro District Basel.
(Source: Lencer 2007)[34].

Undoubtedly, Basel is the economic center of the entire region. The city has a particularly important economic role due to its location in Central Europe and it is one of the most important centers of the pharmaceutical industry worldwide. Based on such an economic power Basel provides 20% of Swiss exports and accounts for one third of the gross national product. This is a cause for a high degree of mobility within the entire region. In 1990, the commuter balance from outside of Basel amounted to 47% (inbound commuters minus outbound commuters in relation to the entire workforce in the canton). This proportion had increased to 52% in 2011 (Bundesamt für Statistik BFS 2013c). For that reason Basel has been labeled 'the most typical labor canton' among Swiss cantons.

Another interesting aspect is that Basel is the capital of the Canton called Basel-Stadt. It includes the City of Basel and the municipalities of Riehen and Bettingen. As of 2015,

[34] "Topographische Karte vom Großraum Basel", first version by Wladyslaw Sojka, complete reworked version by Lencer. Distributed under a CC BY 3.0 license: https://creativecommons.org/licenses/by/3.0/deed.de

the canton has a total of 197'500 inhabitants (Statistical Office of the Canton of Basel-Stadt 2015a). The canton is the smallest in terms of the urban area (37 km²). However, it is the most densely populated canton in Switzerland, with 5'320 inhabitants per km². The population density within the perimeter of the City of Basel rises to 7'300 inhabitants per km² (Statistical Office of the Canton of Basel-Stadt 2015a). Throughout this chapter the author refers to City of Basel. However, all official documents that the author mentions stem from the administration of the Canton Basel-City.

It needs to be noted that the canton's population had been declining since the 1970s until the new millennium. The trend was continuing due to structural changes in the producing industries and the resulting job losses in the industry (Schneider-Sliwa et al. 1999). However, the population growth in the recent years and the current growth scenarios for the near future indicate that this trend has changed and that reurbanization is currently taking place (Statistical Office of the Canton of Basel-Stadt 2015b).

17.3 Transport Policy in Basel until 2010

17.3.1 Brief history of the Mobility in Basel

The growing demand for transport services between home and work was only one reason for the proliferation of the car as an individual mode of transport after the Second World War. Another reason was the wealth and the status symbol associated with the possession of car. The automobile had been reserved only for the higher-income society class due to its high purchasing and maintenance costs. This symbolism has been retained in the postwar society and it still applies also today, albeit not to the same extent as before (Epple et al. 2010c).

In the postwar period in Basel the ownership of the automobile was initially a question of income and not the derivation of the actual mobility demand. For example, the density of car distribution in the region around Basel after the war shows that the highest densities of vehicles did not occur in municipalities located far away from the public transport lines, as one would assume.

On the other hand, public transportation was primarily used by people from low income groups. For that reason public transport policies were initially understood rather in terms of social policy. The governmental interventions aimed at ensuring that the laboring class can reach their places of work at low rates. Therefore, the subsidies for the public transport operators (both rail and bus), which permanently ran into financial difficulties, targeted the reduction of prices for the annual ticket.

Once the economic prosperity took off, car ownership increased. Improved salaries in the lower social classes allowed for the purchase of a small or used car. The ownership of car was publicly perceived as a boost of the wealth status of the laboring class (Epple et al. 2010c). Similarly to other cities in Europe, in the second half of the seventies Basel was flooded with cars. Vehicles were parked literally everywhere: at the entrances, on the sidewalks or on the street corners. At the same time, the suburbanization trend has led to considerable reduction of the number of jobs and the trade activity in the city center (Wesołowski 2008).

Concurrently public awareness of the correlation between economic growth and its negative environmental impacts has grown. Two main factors have played a central role: (i) the awareness of the increasing pollution of the atmosphere by air pollutants and (ii) the assumption that the human activity may affect the climate also on the global scale. Society has realized that there is a possible trade-off between the unlimited use of resources and the healthy climate and environment it is living in. With that in mind, the post-industrial service economy and society has developed an understanding for the existence of the problem of the common pool resources, that is, the Tragedy of the Commons. It has become clear that these resources are a public good and that they can neither be divided nor privatized (Epple et al. 2010b). The need to prevent these negative trends led to a considerable reconsideration of the land use and transport policy by the City of Basel.

It was recognized that the further development of roads and the support of automobility would not diminish the increasing traffic problems. Furthermore, a set of problems associated with the oil crisis of the seventies was also acknowledged. Under these circumstances public transport experienced its renaissance. In the first step, the authorities merged a number of transport companies into one joint operating structure - the Baselland Transport (BLT) AG, in 1974. These efforts resulted in the implementation of the annual Environmental Subscription in 1984 (Umwelt-Abonnement or U-Abo). It allowed for an affordable and unlimited mobility on the entire public transport network in the region of Northwestern Switzerland (Epple et al. 2010a). From today's perspective, this unified rate for the public transport in the entire region can be regarded as a historic social achievement.

However, these rather favorable developments in the field of public transportation resulted in a long-lasting conflict between the supporters and opponents of the further development of the automobility system in the city and the region. It was mainly expressed in the so called 'battles for the parking space'. They took the form of recurring civic initiatives against the expansion of the underground parking garages in the Basel city center. For example, based on a public referendum held in June 1990, a bill was passed which strictly forbid the construction of public parking garages in the downtown area. This law has effectively blocked the further parking supply and has been in force until today. The shift has been considered as a clear precedent and has set a foundation for a new transport policy paradigm in the city and the region. The current policy aims at increasing the attractiveness and the accessibility of the downtown for the residents of the city and not at supporting the paradigm which can be expressed by the term 'free streets for free citizens'(German: 'Freie Fahrt für freie Bürger').

17.3.2 Policy Objectives until 2010

17.3.2.1 Parking Policy

By act of the Federal Law the city has already started implementing the 'blue parking zone' in 1986. The law aimed at rationalizing the use of available parking space. It resulted in the drastic reduction of the permitted parking time in this zone. The regulation eliminated also the car commuters, who left their cars in the city center, and promoted the residents and the businesses of the inner ring (Kanton Basel-Stadt 4/20/1986). Furthermore, in 1991 the Environmental Protection Act of the City of Basel prohibited public subsidies for construction and maintenance of private parking spaces within the City of Basel, excluding only 'P&R' systems and parking spaces for the residents. The city decided to cap the total amount of available parking lots in the downtown to the initial level of 10'300 (Wesołowski 2008). There is no limit on parking time in the existing underground parking garages. However, the level of fares effectively excludes the possibility of long-term parking (27 CHF for nine hours and 200 CHF for a monthly parking pass).

Another special feature of the parking policy is that the new retail-stores are allowed to build new parking spaces on their own property, but on a diminishing scale as compared to the available space on the property. Moreover, major investments, such as shopping malls, must anticipate a refusal from the authorities in this regard, if the surrounding road network does not have the required carrying capacity. Interestingly, while the neighboring canton of Basel Country dictates a minimum number of available parking space for new constructions, the City of Basel instructs a maximum amount of possible parking spaces (Regierungsrat des Kantons Basel-Stadt 12/22/1992).

Basel has been maintaining a parking guidance and information system, which helps to reduce the search for vacant parking spaces in the city center. The parking guidance in Basel is a dynamic information system, which dynamically indicates the number of available lots in all central parking garages (Center North, Center West and Center South). The system leads the car drivers from the suburban areas to the specific facility in the city center. There are 5'000 parking lots in the city managed by this system (Amt für Mobilität 2015b). Moreover, commuters are provided with extensive P&R facilities outside of the city, preferably on the outskirts of the entire agglomeration.

Another interesting fact about Basel is that by law the employees of the civil service, with only few exceptions, are prohibited to park their private cars in the public space designated for city authorities only. The officials of the city are expected to serve as role models for the usage of the public and slow modes of transport (Kanton Basel-Stadt 3/13/1991). For example, the Head of the Construction and Transport Department of the City of Basel commutes every day by bike.

17.3.2.2 Cycling Policy

The development of a network for cycling was enacted in 1975 (Tschopp 1997). Within only 5 years cycling as a transportation mode increased by 21%. Around the turn of the millennium, the implementation of a network has been completed with 140 km in total length (Baudepartement des Kantons Basel-Stadt 2005). Considering also the network of the neighboring canton of Basel Country the total range amounts to 425 km throughout the entire agglomeration.

There are several types of bicycle paths:

- completely separated bicycle lanes on the roads (including lanes in the opposite direction),
- lanes with combined bus and bike traffic and
- streets without transportation segregation in the 30 km/h-zones.

The integration of the TEB in recent years has also led to the development of cross-border cycle paths. Numerous parking facilities and parking garages for bicycle are available at the train and tram stations. A showcase of the new paradigm of sustainable transport policy is the bicycle bypass and parking garage under the main railway station (Basel SBB). This construction was one of the main achievements of the redesign of the central tram hub at the main station in 2001.

The promotion of the 30 km/h-zones strategy in all residential areas of the city is stimulating the share of slow modes of transport, and leads to the expansion of the paradigm of sustainable mobility in the City of Basel. Approximately 16% of all journeys in the city are covered by bikes (Städtekonferenz Mobilität 2012). Additionally, back in 2008 the number of bikes was already 50% higher than the number of cars in the city (Wesołowski 2008).

17.3.2.3 Tram Policy

The electric tram had been initiated and taken into operation in 1895 under the direction of the City of Basel. Even before the Second World War, the city had had a relatively dense network of tram lines to neighboring countries and the neighboring canton of Basel Country. It seemed that the tram would completely disappear during two decades of the complete car dominance (1950-1970). In a referendum in 1955, the citizens of Basel have rejected the liquidation of the tram.

Today, the municipal tram network is operated by Basler Verkehrsbetriebe (BVB). In 2010, BVB had 122 motor cars and 74 trailers which served on 9 lines on a network of 65,7 km. In the same year, the company operated 98 buses on 13 bus lines, with a total length of 107 km. The performance of trams expressed in passenger-kilometers was almost twice as large as that of the buses (Basler Verkehrs-Betriebe 2010).

Outside of the city, the agglomeration area is served by the company Baselland Transport AG (BLT), which was founded in 1974 after the merger of four local operators. The company operates five regional tram lines with 97 trams and 48 buses. All regional trams run cross the whole city of Basel, and are also connected with the main railway station Basel SBB. From the outset the BLT has been closely cooperating with BVB. For example, in 1987 both companies were the initiators of Tarifverbund Northwestern Switzerland (TNW), which builds a public transport association that covers the entire region of Northwest Switzerland. The centerpiece is the introduced U-Abo.

Further trans-border partnerships with German (Baden-Württemberg) and French (Alsace) transport associations have brought about the introduction of a new ticketing system. The system enables purchasing of cross-border tickets at all ticket machines. This has been achieved, even though there is no transnational coordination unit in place.

Dedicated traffic surveys of the regional commuters' traffic have indicated that the establishment of the TNW has considerably improved the modal split in favor of public transport. The modal split (=Share of public transport) in the period between 1980 and 2000 has developed as follows:

- in the City of Basel from 65% to 70%,
- in the agglomeration from 39% to 46%, and
- in the periphery from 35% to 37%.

What distinguishes the TNW transport association from other associations in Switzerland is that it has been established based on principles of effective leadership and corporate governance with a detailed business process map and clearly defined tasks, competencies and accountabilities as well as (TNW Tarifverbund Nordwestschweiz 2015a).

However, it needs to be stated that the well-regulated transport association is based on the provision of subsidies. The agreement stipulates that participating cantons subsidize each U-Abo with 25 CHF a month. As a result, the subscription fee is relatively low. An adult is charged only 70 CHF instead of 95 CHF (Heim 2011). The objective has been to convince as many people as possible to shift towards public transport for their daily commutes. In that way, a threshold of two million sold U- Abo subscriptions was exceeded in 2006 and since then has been on the rise. Approximately 30% of the population of the entire region have been using the U-Abo (TNW Tarifverbund Nordwestschweiz 2015b).

In 2010, the BLT AG received 22,6 million CHF and the BVB 64,5 million CHF from all vertical authority levels (i.e. federal, cantonal and local) in the form of service-level compensation. In addition, the 25 CHF subsidy for every U-Abo adds up to 49,6 million CHF p.a. (Heim 2011). Despite the popularity and the relatively good annual results the public transport in Basel and the agglomeration still remains heavily subsidized.

17.3.3 Interim Conclusions as of 2010

Due to the coherence in the mobility policy, thus far, it is difficult to find another city in Switzerland, in which the mobility function would be less stressful. A population survey of 2007 showed that 95% of the Basel population is satisfied with the public transport services delivered by the regional operators. However, the number has risen from 6,6% in 2005 to 8,3% of those who consider the traffic situation to be problematic (Government of the Canton Basel-Stadt 2007).

In 2010, according to the Swiss census for mobility and transport, the total number of journeys (German: Wege) traveled by car by the citizens of Basel, amounted only to 18% (Bundesamt für Statistik BFS 2012d). This constitutes the best result in the Swiss city comparison (Städtekonferenz Mobilität 2012).

Furthermore, 52% of households possess no car (i.e. only 48% of all households have at least one car). This is far above the national average of 21% and also better if compared to other urban centers such as City of Zurich with 47% and Bern with 50% (Bundesamt für Statistik BFS 2012d).

Finally, in 2009 the level of motorization (number of vehicles per 1'000 inhabitants) of Basel was at 30% only, i.e. 300 cars per 1000 inhabitants (Statistical Office of the Canton of Basel-Stadt 2009).

17.4 Mobility Strategy for the Future since 2010

17.4.1 City Initiative

The umverkehR is a Swiss-wide operating environmental organization for sustainable mobility, which has the form of an independent association. It is committed to promoting an ecological, socially responsible and forward-looking mobility. Therefore, the organization supports and promotes transport policies which aim at a significant reduction of traffic, especially of motorized individual transport (umverkehR Schweiz 2015b). At the origin of umverkehR lay a bold idea: the group umverkehR had launched a civic initiative that demanded halving of the total motorized individual transport in Switzerland. Stunningly, the group managed to promote a spectacular voting for that in year 2000. The idea also spectacularly failed, because 83% of voters rejected the initiative. Also no chance remained for the initiative of establishing car-free Sundays. It failed both in 1978 and 2003 to more than 60% negative votes (NZZ 2009). However, with these well-publicized but failed initiatives a nation-wide discussion started.

In spring 2008 umverkehR started promoting six similar 'City Initiatives' in Basel, Geneva, Lucerne, St. Gallen, Winterthur and Zurich. It had been ideologically based on the 'Alpine Initiative'. The initiative required legal protection of the Alps from the road traffic. It was accepted in 1994 by the Swiss population. Following that idea, also Swiss cities should receive the same legal protection (VCS Verkehrs-Club der Schweiz 2010). The initiators justify the initiative with the significant increase in traffic volume, costs and the environmental impact of transport in Switzerland in recent years. In fact, the mobility micro-census 2010 showed that the Swiss population is highly mobile. An average Swiss covered an annual distance of around 20'500 km - almost half of this amount by a motorized mode of transport (Bundesamt für Statistik BFS 2012d). The City Initiatives assume that public transport and non motorized traffic (slow modes) is much more efficient than motorized individual transport due to the high population density in urban areas. Therefore, the initiative requires that environmentally friendly and space-saving modes of transport are strictly preferred. Furthermore, additional road capacity extensions of high-capacity streets (HLS, i.e. Hochleistungsstrassen in German) must be prevented, since new roads lead to more traffic (umverkehR Schweiz 2015a). The ultimate objective of all City Initiatives in Switzerland has been the overall improvement of the quality of life in cities by radically reducing the car traffic in urban areas. Therefore, the main postulate of the City Initiative has been to increase the modal share of public transport and slow modes by 10 percentage points (umverkehR Schweiz 2015a). Even though the requirement does not directly address automobility it has a significant impact on the total share of car traffic.

17.4.2 Template for the City of Basel

In 2008, umverkehR submitted the City Initiative to the canton of the City of Basel-Stadt. It called for such cantonal law adjustments which would ensure the protection of the public from the negative impacts of the transport. Three main requirements were postulated (umverkehR Schweiz 2008):

1) Consistent commitment to public transport and to safe pedestrians and cyclists path network: The canton of the City of Basel must provide necessary policy measures for increasing the share of public transport and slow modes in the City of Basel. The share in the total traffic volume (measured in passenger-kilometers) must increase by at least ten percentage points within ten years after the initiative has entered into force.

2) No extensions and upgrades of highways and main roads: The construction of new or extension of existing high-capacity roads (HLS) and main streets within the canton boundaries can only be possible under the condition that the total capacity of the road network does not increase.

3) Annual reporting: The Executive Council of the City of Basel (Regierungsrat) should submit an annual report on the status of policy implementation to the Parliament of the City (Großer Rat).

Despite these noble objectives of the City Initiative, the requirements were criticized by the city administration for being far too restrictive. The postulates would imply radical interventions and therefore would pose huge risks to the consistency of the transport policy in Basel. The first main critique point was that increasing the share of environmentally friendly transport modes by 10% would imply a reduction of motorized private transport by as much as 25% (i.e. from 40% to 30%) within only 10 years. The representatives of the city found that this requirement was politically and technically not feasible within the required time frame, and eventually detrimental to the economy of the city. In addition, the other counter argument of the city administration was that the construction of high-capacity roads (HLS) falls under the federal responsibility and hence cannot be directly influenced by the government of the city (Kanton Basel-Stadt 2010b).

To avoid any radical interventions in the urban mobility system, the City Council and the Parliament prepared a counter-proposal for the voting. This counter-proposal called for following adjustments of the mobility system of Basel (Kanton Basel-Stadt 2010b):

1) Reduce road traffic by ten percent: The total volume of the individual motorized traffic must decrease by at least 10% until 2020 (compared to 2010) within the entire city area. Highways are excluded, however.

2) Promote traffic calming in residential areas: The extensions or new constructions in the highway network will be only permitted if the urban road network will be permanently relieved from traffic by means of implementing counter measures and policies for supporting traffic calming.

3) Implement traffic volume and performance controlling: The city administration must periodically collect data regarding traffic volumes by each road category to control the compliance with the reduction target.

4) Allow funding for supporting slow modes of transport: The City Council grants a credit line labeled 'Slow traffic'. The first installment amounts to 10 million CHF for the years 2011 to 2014 for investments such as further cycling network, construction of bicycle parking areas and establishing shared zones.

The cantonal voting took place on 28th of November 2010 with following results: 61,94% voted against the City Initiative, while 54,68% voted for the acceptance of the administration's counter-proposal (Kanton Basel-Stadt 2010a). This result has led to a substantial adjustment in the cantonal Environmental Protection Act which has taken the following form (Kanton Basel-Stadt 3/13/1991):

§13 Abs. 2:[35]

> "The Canton will ensure that the overall volume of private motor vehicle traffic will decrease in the canton-area by at least 10% by 2020, as compared to today. The traffic volume on the high-capacity roads has been excluded from this requirement. Any increase in traffic volumes through extensions of existing and constructions of new high-capacity roads must be compensated to the same extent on the remaining urban road network by supporting measures, also after 2020."

17.4.3 Towards the New Vision of Transport Policy in Basel

17.4.3.1 Cantonal Office of Mobility

The administration of the City of Basel has established and maintained the Office of Mobility, which is an integral part of the Municipal Construction and Transport Department. In general, it holds the responsibility for the strategic development of the transport system of the city. However, the Office of Mobility is not a strictly operative organization unit, but it is rather a municipal unit for strategic planning of long-term urban mobility development in close alignment with the entire region. In 2011, the office made an important step to align people, processes, and services by defining core statements for its vision and mission.

According to definitions, both the mission and vision serve important, yet different roles (Evans 2010):

---

[35] Based on author's own translation.

- mission outlines the reason why the organization exists, i.e. the present state and the purpose of an organization and
- vision defines which direction the organization is going, i.e. the optimal desired future state and the mental picture of what an organization wants to achieve over a long period.

Both are part of the normative management and provide a framework for deriving strategies, objectives and operational actions. Furthermore, they enable forward-looking planning, envisioning exciting and radical possibilities, and including others in a shared view of the future (Evans 2010). Even though, the process of defining the mission and the vision is usually associated with commercial companies, the Office of Mobility in Basel developed and established these core elements as a foundation for its strategic planning activities.

Mission of the Office of Mobility

The mission statement has been defined as follows (Stalder 2011, p. 2)[36]:

> "The Office of Mobility aims at optimizing the entire transport system, promotes urban and environmentally sound mobility, ensures the locational accessibility of Basel, and supports an efficient and reliable operations of the cantonal transport infrastructure."

Furthermore, the Office of Mobility seeks to ensure the balance between the interest groups, even if trade-offs exist, particularly in the following fields:

- increase public acceptance for environmentally friendly forms of mobility,
- provide a well-conceived and efficient public transportation network,
- promote walking and cycling by providing more attractive and safer infrastructure,
- provide traffic calming in the residential areas,
- prioritize residents for using the urban parking space to improve the quality of life for the city population,
- advocacy and lobbying for establishing appropriate national and international connections,
- channel the transit traffic on high-capacity roads and its liquefaction to minimize the negative effects,
- increase efficiency and safety of the urban road network.

[36] Author's own translation.

Vision of the Office of Mobility

The vision statement of the Office of Mobility assumes two main directions: internal and external. Internally, the vision provides orientation and motivation for the entire organization and for its individual members by creating the common organizational identity. Externally, that is, to the public and other institutions, it makes clear what the organization aims at. The current vision statement of the Office of Mobility says (Stalder 2011)[37]:

> We bring urban and regional mobility in coherence with the urban residential quality and the locational advantage of the economy.

The urban residential quality and locational advantages include several important characteristics derived from the cantonal legislative plan 2013-2017 (Regierungsrat Kanton Basel-Stadt 2013). These characteristics are listed in the table below.

Table 24: Important city characteristics for understanding the vision of future mobility in Basel (source: Regierungsrat Kanton Basel-Stadt 2013)

Locational advantages characteristics	**Urban residential quality characteristics**
Recognition as a hub for passenger and freight transport in Europe	Improving quality of life and safety in public places through: - greening of the urban area, - new residential areas with high amenity value, - revival of the urban centers.
Excellent multimodal and cross-border transport connections to the main European and national centers	Transport related: - traffic calming measures, - relieve heavily polluted residential areas from traffic by its rerouting towards high-capacity streets, - traffic management measures for noise protection.
Consolidated coordination between modes of transport and the political bodies	Land use related: - increasing urban density inwards, - establishment of attractive and lively city center with shared zones.
Further development of the infrastructure in rail transport	Social related: - high standards of living which cover heterogeneous requirements, - providing equal rights for people with disabilities to participate in the public life,

[37] ibid.

Locational advantages characteristics	**Urban residential quality characteristics**
	- care and assistance services adjusted to current demographic trends.
Economically and socially significant in tourism and event industries	Others: consistent planning in the field of housing, mobility, and safety.
Visible and well-perceived public services and efficient infrastructure	n.a.

17.4.3.2 Definition of Transport Policy Objectives and Strategic Priorities

Based on the legal implications of the City Initiative, the mission and vision, and the detailed characterization of desirable locational and residential advantages the Office of Mobility has defined clear imperatives for a forward-looking transport policy for the City of Basel. These objectives have been included into the strategic concept for the urban traffic policy, the *Verkehrspolitisches Leitbild* (Bau- und Verkehrsdepartement des Kantons Basel-Stadt 2015). The concept describes the transport policy and the measures planned for the next 15 to 20 years. There are four overarching goals:

1) Secure accessibility,
2) Increase quality of life,
3) Enhance traffic safety,
4) Ensure cost-effectiveness.

Based on these objectives seven strategic priorities for sustainable mobility in the city have been defined (see Figure 27).

Both, strategic objectives and priorities, have set the foundation for deriving a catalog of concrete policies and measures, i.e. the Action Plan. However, that strategic objectives and strategic priorities imply trade-offs. According to the mission, the Office of Mobility is obliged to resolve these conflicts continuously. The strategic concept is to be reviewed and updated periodically. In each case an aligned short-term action plan for the next four years must be derived (Bau- und Verkehrsdepartement des Kantons Basel-Stadt 2014b).

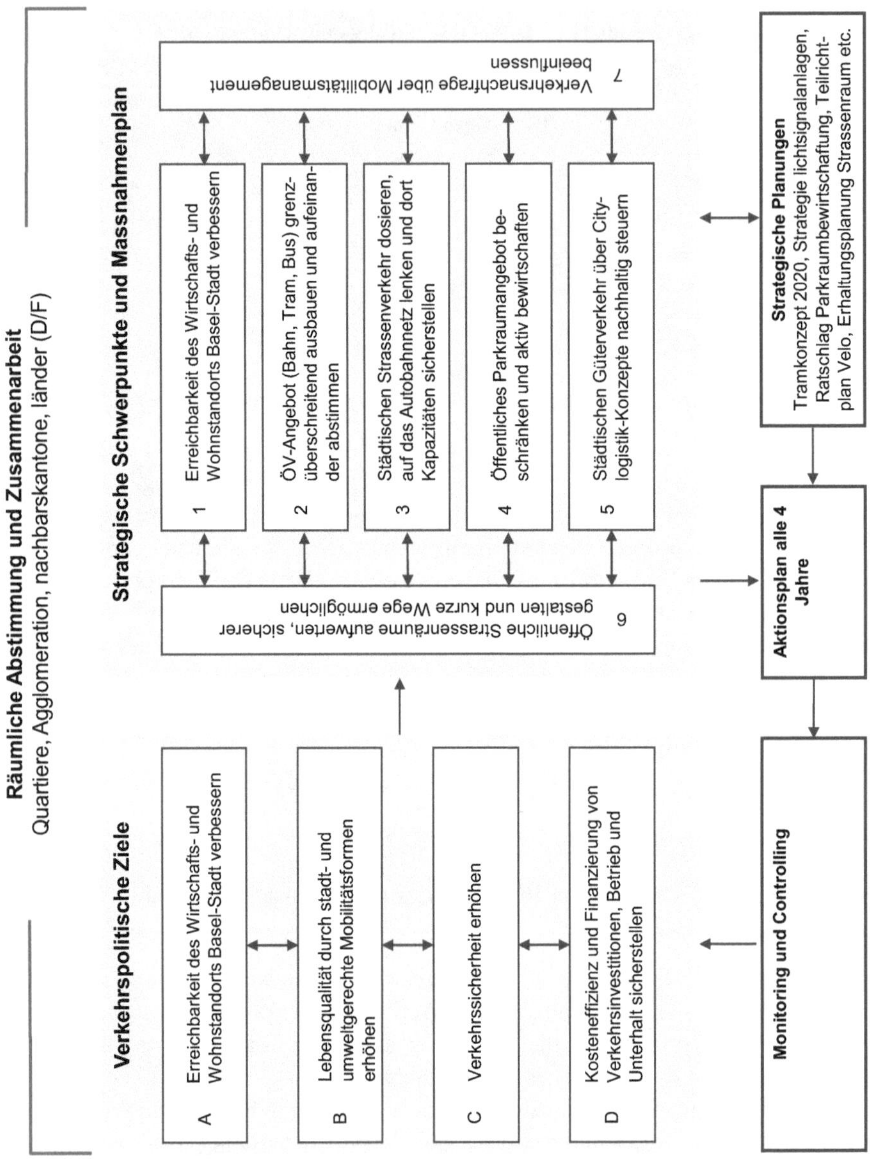

Figure 27: Transport policy objectives and strategic priorities.
(Source: Bau- und Verkehrsdepartement des Kantons Basel-Stadt 2015, p. 16).[38]

[38] Reproduced with permission from the Canton of the City of Basel, Switzerland.

17.4.4 Integrated Policy-Making for Sustainable Mobility[39]

17.4.4.1 Conflicts and Trade-Offs

Because the urban space and the municipal budget are limited, numerous conflicts arise. They occur because there are differentiating demands and objectives of the road users, on the one side, and the residents, employees or recreational visitors, on the other side. In addition, there are different implications of various modes of transport on aspects such as: space demand, emissions or speeds.

The following main trade-offs between the four transport policy objectives are to be considered, evaluated and balanced:

Accessibility versus quality of life:

This is the basic conflict of every urban transportation system. On the one hand, urban space needs to be opened equally for all and cities must be easily accessible by all means of transportation. Especially, the commercial traffic (deliveries, craftsmen, services, etc.) needs to have appropriate access. At the same time the residents of the city expect the least possible negative effects such as noise, air pollution or accident risks.

Traffic safety versus quality of life and accessibility:

Car traffic is often not adjusted to the specifics of urban spaces. Therefore, it is detrimental to traffic safety and quality of life in the cities. Mostly pedestrians and cyclists are greatly exposed to the road hazards. On the other side, slow modes of transport can make the biggest contributions to a safer and sustainable mobility. They consume the least space and cause least negative impacts to the traffic and the environment. Transport planning, which is oriented towards increasing the safety and infrastructure quality for slow modes, can lead to sustainability in the long term. Car traffic should be rerouted to high-capacity streets.

Cost-effectiveness versus accessibility and quality of life:

The budget claims of other policies areas such as education, healthcare, social, and culture are considerable. It creates conflicts and requires finding compromises and trade-offs among the various objectives. Conversely, affordable mobility, good accessibility

---

[39] This section is partially based on the "Transport Policy Concept" (Bau- und Verkehrsdepartement des Kantons Basel-Stadt 2015).

and high quality of life are important locational factors of Basel. Investments and developments in these fields promote the economy, prosperity and residential attractiveness of Basel.

17.4.4.2 Ensuring Coordination and Integration

The Office of Mobility of Basel continuously includes these considerations and trade-offs in all phases of transport policy development and implementation. Nonetheless, despite these universal principles, conflicts occur and cannot be always directly resolved. Hence, the administration of the city has recognized that any resulting conflicts must be approached in a coordinated manner on an individual case basis. In addition to the requirements of traffic policy, also locational land use concerns have to be integrated. Such locational aspects include desired changes in the current residential environment, concerns about open and shared spaces, greenery, existing gas, water, and power lines, and so on.

The overall model for sustainable mobility (the Traffic Policy Model) should be coordinated and integrated with other elements of cantonal strategic planning. This requires new policy linkages and joint working horizontally across local authority departments and service providers. There has also been a need for the vertical cooperation along the governance lines from the national down to the local level. The idea of consistency in mobility proposed in this book is based exactly on these considerations. In general, it is a purposeful coordination and integration of different policies on all levels of urban and national planning. The Office of Mobility has sought vertical and horizontal coordination and integration in order to ensure the consistency in Base (see Figure 28).

Political Alignment

The development of the Traffic Policy Model has been based on other already existing transport policy-related policies and laws. First of all, it has been anchored in the Environmental Protection Act (Kanton Basel-Stadt 3/13/1991) and in the Constitution of the Canton of Basel-City (Bundeskanzlei 3/23/2005). It interfaces also with the cantonal grand structure plan (Kanton Basel-Stadt 2015) and the cantonal legislative plan (Regierungsrat Kanton Basel-Stadt 2013) of the Executive Council of the City of Basel. In both strategic papers general aspects of transportation and mobility are included in a coherent way. The Traffic Policy Model picks them up and aims at going beyond the existing policy basics and extending them into consistent transport planning principles in a comprehensive and holistic way:

- it contains statements regarding the conflicts of objectives and how to address them in coordinated way,
- it is a binding Letter of Intent of the Executive Council of Basel and with that it replaces all previous transport plans,
- it is coordinated with the strategies of neighboring regions in the tri-national area TEB.

Spatial and Regional Policy Alignment

It is commonly recognized that the transport policy can be only successful if coordinated and integrated with the strategies and measures of spatial planning. The urban spatial planning policy has been comprehensively anchored and depicted in the cantonal grand structure plan (Kanton Basel-Stadt 2015) on both the strategic and tactical level (that is, overall strategy and action plan). Strategic development areas that have an impact on the field of traffic and mobility in Basel encompass:

- residential and urban development priorities,
- areas of economic priority,
- downtown appreciation,
- development of traffic intensive facilities,
- development of public buildings and facilities.

Spatial planning at the regional level is being coordinated in particular by the agglomeration program, so called 'Agglo Basel'. This federal instrument coordinates and complements the development measures of individual regional authorities with regard to the challenges of each Swiss agglomeration. The Agglo Basel program provides among other things, such as the development of the regional Rapid Transit System or the Road Strategy, the unique possibility for the tri-national alignment between the settlement developments and the overall traffic planning. The subsequent case study of Agglo Basel describes the principles of the federal Agglomeration Program and how it contributes to achieving the regional policy coordination and integration in TEB.

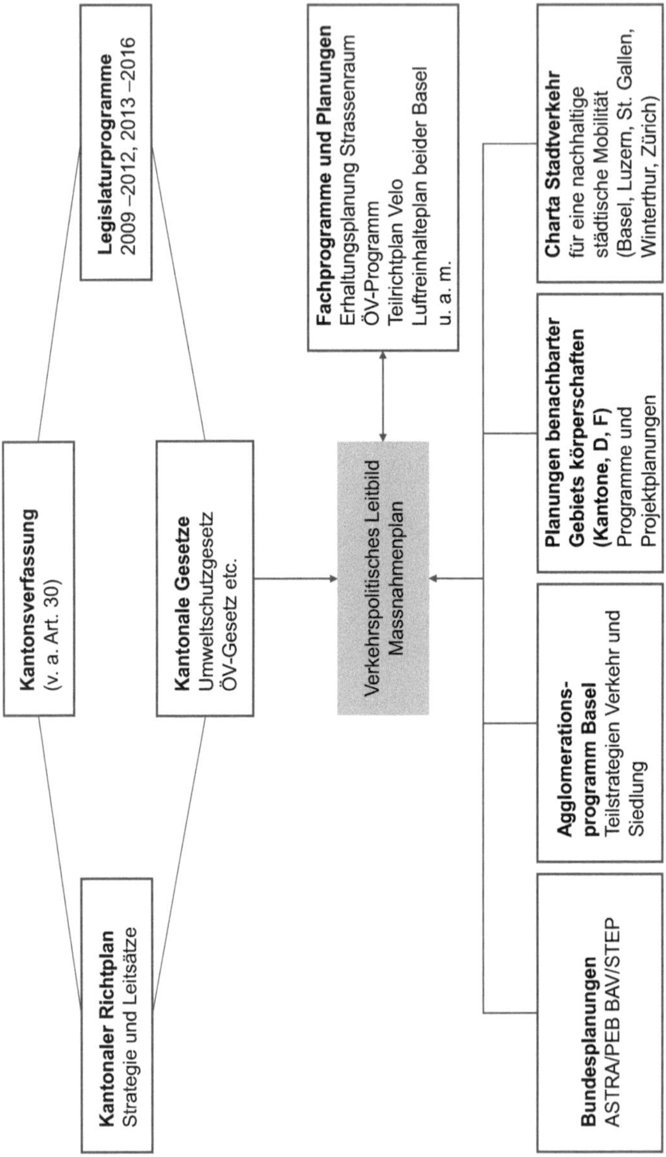

Figure 28: Strategic positioning of the Traffic Policy Model with measures plan. (Source: Bau- und Verkehrsdepartement des Kantons Basel-Stadt 2015, p. 12).[40]

[40] Reproduced with permission from the Canton of the City of Basel, Switzerland.

Agglo Basel

Approximately 75% of the Swiss population lives today in cities and urban areas. Around 80% of jobs are located in these areas, which encompass a quarter of Switzerland's total space - 9'000 km^2 (Neuenschwander et al. 2012). For that reason the Swiss Federal Government has established the Agglomeration Programs as an mechanism to coordinate sustainable spatial and transport development in Switzerland. The programs aim at achieving consistent planning of the infrastructure and land use developments for future transport and settlements in Swiss urban areas. It fosters the horizontal cooperation (between partners within the agglomeration) and vertical integration between the confederation, cantons and agglomerations (Neuenschwander et al. 2012). The program possesses a powerful instrument in the form of the infrastructure fund. It provides co funding (federal subsidies) to implement sustainable residential and transport projects; however, only infrastructure projects are subsidized. The federal government contributes up to 50% of the investment costs for eligible projects. Interestingly, also projects in neighboring countries can be funded. However, only under the condition that substantial benefits are accounted to Swiss communities. The program is implemented in recurring four-year cycles and as of today the third generation is being prepared (Bundesamt für Raumentwicklung ARE 2015).

One of the biggest subprograms is Agglo Basel which seeks to coordinate transport and settlement developments in the TEB. Since the Basel area is the only tri-national agglomeration, it faces particular challenges in integrating land use, settlement and transport politics (Agglo Basel 2015). The federal requirements for funding require precise statements, particularly regarding coordinated settlement and transport politics, technical feasibility, financial accountability, and priority setting. Therefore, the essential condition is the inclusion of all involved partners, also from France and Germany, in order to establish a consistent picture of the future development of the entire region and the political support for project implementations.

For that purpose the 'Future Perspective 2030' strategy has been developed with the representatives of the involved countries and cantons. Three strategic pillars have been established:

- landscape: establish, enhance and link the green spaces,
- settlement: foster consistent development inwards,
- transport: expand the network into the agglomeration.

This structure serves as the foundation for sub strategies. For instance, the transport pillar is further divided into four specific clusters. Operative instructions have been defined for each cluster to move towards the vision of Future Perspective 2030. Table 25 outlines the transport strategy of the Agglo Basel program. The clusters and the instructions form the foundation for the preparation, evaluation, prioritization and finally the application for funding of concrete measures and projects in the agglomeration.

There is an iterative process in place which leads to the selection of eligible projects for the funding application. In the first step, all ongoing projects have been collected from all involved territorial units (both cantons and communities) and new required measures have been derived based on the underlying overall strategy. In the second step, the examination regarding the coherence with the vision (Future Perspective 2030) and the sub strategies has taken place. In the third step, the maturation stage of planned measures has been verified and the measures prioritized according to specific criteria of the Swiss Federal Office for Spatial Development (Geschäftsstelle Agglomerationsprogramm Basel 2012, p. 177).

Since the first generation of the Agglo Basel program, whose planning started in 2007 and the implementation in 2011, eight projects have been completed, 7 are being implemented, 36 are nearing the construction phase and 31 are planned for the development (Agglo Basel n.d.b).

Table 25: Strategy clusters for transport and their instructions (source: Leypoldt 2012).

Transport Strategy – Clusters	**Instructions**
Cluster 1: Public transport and multimodal mobility	- Regio-S-Bahn: offer upgrades and new connections - Tram and bus: complement the network and boost the fine distribution - Combined mobility: reduce spatial resistance and expand offer
Cluster 2: Motorized individual traffic, traffic control and parking management	- Limit driving advent spatially differentiated - Channel and control traffic flow - Enhance road spaces and compensate any road extensions
Cluster 3: Walking and cycling	- Expand and link the regional cycle network - Improve and raise attractiveness of the local pedestrian and cycling - network - Expand intermodal interfaces public transport-slow modes
Cluster 4: Freight transport and logistics	- Ensure accessibility to regional business locations - Concentrate transportation hubs and promote intermodality

17.4.4.3 Stiig-Um

In 2013 the Office of Mobility commissioned an external expert study to develop measures and policies for achieving the goals for sustainable mobility that resulted from the adjusted Environmental Protection Act of the City of Basel (Kanton Basel-Stadt 3/13/1991) and the City Initiative. Three independent teams of experts have estimated the effects of the previously planned transport projects and proposed complementary measures. The results were summarized in a synthesis report Stiig-Um which was later presented and explained to the public. The Stiig-Um report includes following results (Frick, Belart 2013):

1) Assuming the growth of the motorized individual traffic of approximately 7% between 2010 and 2020 a total reduction of 16% will be required.

2) The predicted growth in traffic can be prevented with previously planned measures.

3) Required reduction of additional 10%, as incorporated in the Environmental Protection Act of the City of Basel (Kanton Basel-Stadt 3/13/1991), cannot be achieved with existing planned measures and policies.

The study has also reviewed the overall transport planning and policies of the City of Basel hitherto. The three teams concluded that the existing transport policies are consistent with the long-term strategy of the city and the region. It is noted that the transport policy consistently promotes alternatives to motorized transport via appropriate pull measures. For example, public transport has been extended and slow modes were continuously promoted. However, with an expected growth in population and economy in coming years, further significant interventions are inevitable. The support and promotion of alternative means of transport is still necessary. However, it is not sufficient to achieve the desirable total reduction of 16% in car traffic. Hence, the experts conclude that further policy packages with additional push measures (i.e. command-and-control mechanisms) must be considered, developed and implemented. With regard to the proposed measures the experts point to measures and policies that aim directly at limiting the car traffic, especially traffic demand management, traffic dosing, and parking space management. The expertise also argues that the implementation of such additional policy packages will require special conditions such as: political majorities in the parliament, the involvement of local and regional partners as well as great efforts in their implementation (Frick, Belart 2013).

Following the results and the expert recommendations of the Stiig-Um study a Strategic Action Plan has been defined by the Executive Council of the City of Basel.

17.4.4.4 Strategic Action Plan

In order to develop a prioritized Strategic Action Plan with traffic policy packages following general principles have been defined (Bau- und Verkehrsdepartement des Kantons Basel-Stadt 2015):

- effectiveness,
- cost minimization,
- regional alignment,
- monitoring and flexibility.

Furthermore, the defined policy objectives and strategic priorities for transport policies for Basel (as described in paragraph 17.4.3.2: Definition of Transport Policy Objectives and Strategic Priorities) have been the basis for developing the corresponding policy measures. The main idea behind that, is that only an integrated and balanced total policy package can bring about the synergies that for achieving the ambitious reduction goals. Hence, the following strategic action areas have been defined:

1) Road traffic: implementation of a system of urban and regional Transportation Demand Management.

2) Parking space: implementation of an urban and regional parking management.

3) Walking and cycling: further cycling promotion and development of attractive tri-national cycle route network.

4) Public transport: optimization of cross-border information and in the pricing system of the public transport.

5) Freight transport: city-friendly flow of goods with city logistics.

6) Public space: Further traffic calming measures and the appreciation of the public road space.

7) Mobility management: proactive mobility consulting and information.

In total, over 30 measures have been considered and included in the list of the Strategic Action Plan for Basel (Bau- und Verkehrsdepartement des Kantons Basel-Stadt 2015). Among the projects also interventions in the tri-national region have been considered. This is due to the recognition of the city administration that, even though the city can act independently in many areas, a sustainable and long-term transport policy should always be aligned regionally, that is, beyond the cantonal and national borders. Therefore, the Strategic Action Plan encompasses also the related projects from the Agglo Basel program. With this respect especially measures in the fields of traffic demand management, parking policy and mobility management have been included.

17.4.5 Monitoring, Controlling and Communication

Monitoring and Controlling of the Road Traffic Performance

In compliance with the Environmental Protection Act of the City of Basel the municipal administration is obliged to periodically collect data regarding traffic volumes by each road category. The purpose is to monitor and control the desired objectives. Hence, dedicated traffic volume and performance controlling is required. However, highly accurate measurement of the traffic performance is not possible without a great effort. The traffic load would need to be counted on all the city streets. The measurement of the absolute size of the transport volume is neither required nor relevant for monitoring. Rather, it is important to detect the relative annual change. The data is being collected by means of 35 selected and representative measurement stations spread throughout the city road network. According to the Environmental Protection Act the monitoring is done for high-performance streets (HLS) and streets in the urban network.

Figure 29 below shows the relative change in the total volume of private motor vehicle traffic measured by the methods described above. After a slight decrease between 2010 and 2012 the traffic volume rose again within the canton in 2013 and 2014. In 2014, the index was at 101,1 points. This development has been caused by a considerable increase on high-capacity roads (HLS) at the rate of 7% between 2010 and 2014 and only a slight decrease of 1,8% on the remaining urban road network (Bau- und Verkehrsdepartement des Kantons Basel-Stadt 2015, p. 45). However, it needs to be reminded that high-capacity roads have been excluded from the reduction goal. The objective aims chiefly at reducing the traffic volume on the urban and residential road network.

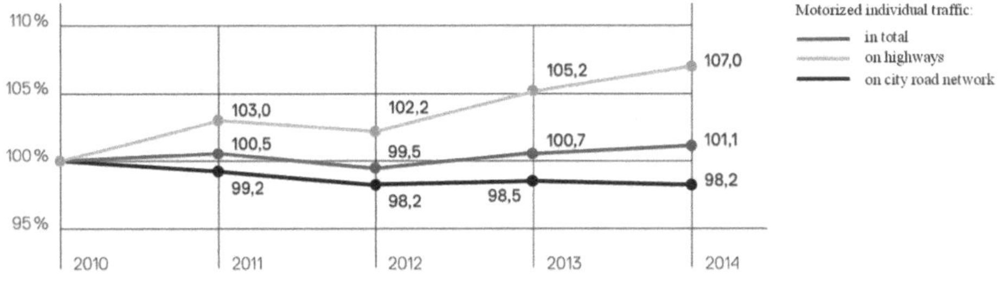

Figure 29: Development of the motorized individual traffic.
(Source: Bau- und Verkehrsdepartement des Kantons Basel-Stadt 2015, p. 45 based on author's own translation).[41]

[41] Reproduced with permission from the Canton of the City of Basel, Switzerland.

Communication, Coordination and Development

An active involvement of various target groups such as road users, business representatives or policy makers is required to achieve the intended effect of the Traffic Policy Model and the Strategic Action Plan. For that purpose regular consultation and professional coordination with involved parties is strictly mandatory. These efforts take place on two levels:

- political acceptance and
- functional alignment.

Project-specific decisions on the political level are required in order to implement the prioritized measures and policies. Hence, political acceptance needs to be strived at all levels: executive, parliament, external organizations and associations, public, and neighboring authorities in the tri-national region. The establishment of participatory planning processes at the project level is crucial. Especially the design of local interventions should be shaped using a joint and collaborative approach. Furthermore, early communication efforts are fundamental, particularly for politically sensitive projects such as parking management. In that way, the acceptance for funding and implementation can be fostered consistently.

Measures and policy interventions from the action plan need to be reviewed and revised periodically. This necessitates a functional and technical coordination between the specialized agencies of the city administration. For that purpose specific instruments have been created and implemented. However, in some areas also an agglomeration-wide alignment is compulsory. The latter is ensured by the cooperation within the existing bodies of the regional agglomeration program Agglo Basel.

17.5 Lighthouse Cases: Future of Mobility in Basel

In line with the mobility strategy and the principles of the integrated transport policy there are several measures and projects that have been defined to support the transition towards the paradigm of sustainable mobility, not only in the City of Basel but also in the entire tri-national region. Several cases will be briefly described and discussed below according to the strategic priorities as depicted in Figure 27. The list of projects is valid as of the end of 2015. Since 2016 there have been several new developments which could not be included due to the publication schedule of this dissertation.

17.5.1 Road Traffic: Case - Urban Traffic Management System

In the field of urban traffic the city administration has long ago understood that further extensions of the urban road network are neither desirable nor possible. Therefore, the main focus has been put on traffic management, the relocation of the urban traffic onto the motorway network and innovative mobility concepts.

Traffic Management

Traffic management encompasses effective control and dosing concepts for managing the overall traffic. However, such concepts need to be implemented without interfering with the public transportation system and without causing undesirable cut-through driving through residential areas, which is often the case today. As a foundation for that the city administration plans to implement a comprehensive regional intelligent transportation system (ITS) in the future. These advanced IT applications aim at providing innovative services relating to traffic management and different modes of transport. Moreover, they enable various road users to be better informed and make safer, more coordinated, and intelligent use of city road networks. Furthermore, by executing specific measures it regulates road capacity shortages, which are caused by various road events (accidents, constructions), and considerably reduces the resulting cut-through and rerouting traffic. It is expected that the traffic safety and the amenity values of the existing urban space can be increased. The development of the regional intelligent transportation system is led by the office of Agglo Basel and has been included in the third generation of the agglomeration program.

In the meantime, the municipal administration has been developing an overall concept for traffic management, which is the required foundation for intelligent services such as adaptive control of the road network or intelligent traffic signal control. In 2015, as a first important step, the 'Downtown Traffic Management Concept' was successfully implemented, however, not without any resistance. Today, the downtown consists only of pedestrian zones and shared spaces. There are several public transport corridors, restricted to a speed limit of 30 km/h. With that policy measure the main city center has effectively become car-free.

High-capacity Streets

Another approach to relieving the urban road network is the purposeful relocation of the city traffic onto the high-capacity streets (HLS). The City of Basel has two main suburban highways, the Northern and the Eastern Tangents. The former was opened in mid-2007, after almost 50 years of planning and construction history. It has been the missing link between the Swiss, German and French motorways (A2, A5 and A35). Despite some teething problems it has provided additional capacities and considerable relief to the residential areas of the city. The latter is one of the most important European main arteries, as it lies directly on the transit route between the north and the south of Europe. As of today, the highway cuts through the City of Basel and has been perceived as the symbol of the past automobility era in Basel. Both traffics, transit and urban, meet there every day. Hence, the eastern highway has been approaching its maximal capacity in recent years. The traffic flow is being disrupted on the daily basis, resulting in an immediate heavy overload of the urban road network. Hence, in summer 2014, the Swiss Federal Roads Office (ASTRA), which has the sovereignty over the national motorway network, introduced a proposal to completely bypass the overloaded Eastern Tangent. The idea is to construct a twin-tube tunnel which would connect the Northern City Tangent with the Swiss A2 highway outside of the city, and possibly also with the German A5 highway at the national boarder. From the perspective of the government and the administration of Basel this is a promising approach which can greatly contribute to the relief of the downstream transport network in the city and the region. However, the issue at point is the funding structure of the investment. The ASTRA estimates the total investment costs to amount 1,7 billion CHF (+/- 30%), which goes far beyond the previous, publicly not acceptable plans of an above-ground solution. Hence, it is expected that the cantons of Basel-City and Basel-Country will participate in the additional costs (Bundesamt für Strassen ASTRA 2014). A memorandum of understanding was signed off and the start of the construction project is being planned for approximately 2025 (Reinauer 2015).

Catch-a-Car

The administration of City of Basel has observed that around 50% of all urban car trips are shorter than 5 km. Furthermore, many city residents who still possess a car do not use it very often and tend rather to demand mobility services much more spontaneously (Bau- und Verkehrsdepartement des Kantons Basel-Stadt 2014a). Therefore, a free-floating carsharing scheme, labeled Catch-a-Car, was launched in 2014. With Catch-a-Car carsharing vehicles can be tracked via smartphone in real time. The trip can be made without the need to conduct the pre-reservation. The vehicles can be left at all parking places within the city zone. There are also exclusive parking lots at the main railway station in Basel and at the regional Euro-Airport (SBB.ch 2014). As of 2015, the service perimeter has been extended beyond the borders of the City of Basel and in this way this novel mobility service has expanded into the agglomeration area (Gohl 2015).

The two-year pilot program has been sponsored by Mobility Carsharing, Swiss Railway SBB, Allianz Suisse, AMAG and EnergieSchweiz. The project has been also accompanied by a research team from ETH Zürich in order to ensure that the effects of a free-floating carsharing scheme on the urban transportation system have been completely understood (SBB.ch 2014).

Catch-a-Car is seen as an innovative and promising form of urban mobility, particularly for the growing needs of the young population of Basel (Bau- und Verkehrsdepartement des Kantons Basel-Stadt 2014a).

17.5.2 Parking Space: Case - Parking Regime

In addition to the traffic management system, effective parking management is regarded to be a key measure in order to reduce and control car traffic in the city (Bau- und Verkehrsdepartement des Kantons Basel-Stadt 2015). This is an indirect instrument of the public authority that directly affects urban automobility by means of adjusting the price structure for and the supply of available on-street parking spaces.

Currently, there are approximately 100'000 parking lots in the city. Two thirds of those are privately owned and hence, cannot be managed by the public authority. Around 5% are publicly accessible parking garages and 30% are on-street spaces that are under administrative control. In general, until 2013 the concept of public parking in Basel encompassed White and Blue Zones, and chargeable parking spaces. The latter spaces are equipped with parking meter devices and must be paid for. Usually, the parking time is strictly limited on this kind of parking spots. The White Zone lots can be accessed without any limit and are, in most of the cases, free of charge, however they have been limited to approx. 12% of all parking spaces in the city. The lots in the Blue Zone can be used either for 1 hour only free of charge or unrestricted with an appropriate parking card (Bau- und Verkehrsdepartement des Kantons Basel-Stadt 2014b).

In 2011, the parliament of the City of Basel introduced a new and simplified parking management approach which is to be implemented gradually between 2013 and 2016 within the entire city area. All unmanaged white-labeled and other unmarked public parking spaces are to be converted into Blue Zone. In downtown all parking lots will be equipped with parking meters and the fees will be increased, depending on the location of the parking lot. The charges are expected to reach the level of other Swiss cities (Weibel 2015). Parking priority will be given to the city residents who will have the unrestricted right to use the parking lots, however, with an appropriate residential parking card. The priority is controlled by an appropriate cost structure (Regierungsrat des Kantons Basel-Stadt 2014):

- residents: 140 CHF for a year for one zip-code zone,
- visitors: 6 CHF for half-day or 10 CHF for a day,
- commuters: 740 CHF for a year for a specific zip-code.

Additional restrictions for commuters include following regulations:

- companies can purchase commuter parking cards for their employees, as long as the commute (door to door) takes more than 60 minutes by public transport,
- the number of commuter parking cards is limited to 20% of the company's staff,
- a single company can obtain maximum of 50 commuter parking cards.

This new parking concept is expected to bring about considerable improvements for local residents, retail and commercial facilities. Furthermore, the parking search traffic, i.e. looking for available parking spot, should be reduced in downtown as well as in the residential areas of the city. The priority is clearly to be given to the population of the metropolitan area. Whereas, the commuters should be encouraged to switch to public transport or to use privately owned parking lots.

Interestingly, in German language parking management is often referred to as the parking regime, which may give it a powerful meaning of a restricted field which is under strict administrative management and control.

17.5.3 Walking and Cycling: Case - Commuter Fund

The commuter fund is an exemplary form of cooperation practice in the tri-national region TEB. Its main objective is to reduce the usage of the commons, i.e. the city space. More specifically, it aims at shifting the commuting done by cars to the public transport system and at fostering the use of newly established multi-mobility concepts. Such concepts include: park-and-ride and bike-and-ride facilities, parking facilities for tenants of residential areas, and new public transport offers that support park-and-ride systems and relieve the overall inbound commuters traffic (Hammer 2015b).

The commuter fund receives 80% of the gross revenue that is raised by the parking management system from commuters and visitors to the City of Basel. The revenues come chiefly from the distribution of visitors' and commuters' parking cards which allow access to on-street parking lots in all zones of Basel. Occasional visitors are charged with 10 CHF per day for parking. The annual entitlement costs 740 CHF, whereas residents pay only 140 CHF per zone (Justiz- und Sicherheitsdepartment des Kantons Basel-Stadt 2015). The commuter fund currently amounts to 1 million CHF per year. In the long term it is expected that it will reach the annual level of 2 to 3 million CHF.

For example in 2015, the canton of the City of Basel awarded one million CHF for several regional projects (Hammer 2015c):

- park-and-ride parking system at the train station Saint-Louis,
- bike shelters at train stations in Steinen in Wiesental,
- park-and-pool facility in department Haut-Rhin near the highway A35.

Another prominent example for funding from the commuter fund, which is currently under eager public discussion, is the construction of an underground parking garage for 1'000 bikes. The investment is planned to be located at the Badischer Bahnhof, one of the main commuter railway hubs in the city. The costs are estimated at 8 million CHF. The project will be submitted to the cantonal parliament mid of 2017 and the construction is scheduled for 2019 (20 Minuten 2015).

The fact that the revenues from the parking tickets are redirected for initiatives to improve accessibility, availability and attractiveness of alternatives and to implement multi-modality concepts in the city is a strong communication instrument. If well-publicized, it can lead to public acceptability of push policies that aim at reducing the car traffic in the city, such as severe parking management.

17.5.4 Public Transport: Case - Herzstück

Herzstück is a new project that aims at establishing the connection between the three peripherally located train stations of Basel: the main railway station (SBB), the German station (Badischer Bahnhof) and the St. Johann station. It is located at the heart of the tri-national rapid transit system (Regio-S-Bahn) which connects the major cities of the entire region (France, Germany and Switzerland). The most important and at the same time challenging aspect of this is that the connection must be located underground due to lack of construction space, i.e. directly under the historic city of Basel. Hence, based on the geological conditions and the shape of the new line the appropriate tunnel system will need to be evaluated and selected. Also the location of additional stations must be taken into consideration. The primary goal of this project is threefold (Agglo Basel n.d.a):

- acceleration of the rapid transit lines by linking existing radial lines to diameter lines,
- separation of the rapid transit system from the delay-prone intercity railway transport which currently uses the same infrastructure,
- elimination of the disadvantages of the decentralized stations of the rapid transit system in Basel.

The implementation of the Herzstück will bring significant benefits to the users of the regional rapid transit system. Resulting travel time reductions compared to the situation today will amount to 13 minutes (Spillmann 2014). Detailed cost-benefit analyses have shown that the monetary benefits due to the travel time reductions and the improvement in the environmental and traffic safety amount up to 48 million CHF yearly. Beside these conventional user benefits there are additional economic profits for the city, the region and the nation. Due to the agglomeration effects the GDP of Switzerland is expected to increase by 0,17%, i.e. 111 million CHF. In total, the annual economic benefit of Herzstück is assumed to reach approx. 160 million CHF (B,S,S., RappTrans 2014). The costs of the project are assumed at 1,5 billion CHF for the first and 0,5 billion CHF for the second construction stage (Scheidegger 2013). The Herzstück project will apply for subsidies from the federal funds. Therefore, an application is being prepared for the federal fabi-program, which stands for financing and development of the rail infrastructure. In 2016, the Swiss Federal Council is expected to decide whether the project is included into the 2030 perspective (bz Basellandschaftliche Zeitung 2014).

In 2014, both cantonal parliaments of the City of Basel and Basel Country granted a credit line of 30 million CHF for the development of the preliminary project (Gschwind 2014). This project aims at providing a very detailed technical and operational examination in order to derive reliable cost estimates and time schedules for the implementation (Agglo Basel n.d.c). For the time being, it is difficult to make any statements about the completion date. According to Scheidegger (2013, p. 40) the planning and construction phases are expected to last 13 to 16 years. Additionally, one needs to include the time for political decisions and funding negotiations. Considering that the debate in the Swiss National Council will most likely have taken place in 2016, the kick-off of the Herzstück will not be possible before 2030 (Spillmann 2014, p. 4). Overall it can be said, that this 'generation project', once completed, will contribute considerably to the attractiveness , the economic strength, the relief of the roads and the promotion of the quality of living in the entire tri-national region.

17.5.5 Freight Transport: Case - Concept of Urban Freight Transport

The traffic volume of the freight transport amounts to 25% of the total traffic on the urban road network of Basel. The city administration has recognized that this traffic segment needs to be further optimized to achieve the objectives of reducing road congestion, pollution and noise levels in the residential areas. However, freight is a very complex sector due to heterogeneous start and destination points and the different technical requirements of various goods. Therefore, public authorities and private actors are required to take effective and coordinated actions.

One of the widely discussed interventions for optimizing freight transport in Basel is the implementation of the concept of city-logistics. In theory, the concept allows for a much higher efficiency of the urban freight transport. Inspired by positive experiences reported by some Swiss and other European cities, the administration of Basel considers solutions in the following areas (Bau- und Verkehrsdepartement des Kantons Basel-Stadt 2015):

- optimization of the first and last mile and increase in vehicle utilization (collection and distribution centers),
- courier services with sustainable transportation (e.g. bike courier services)
- restrictions on access and delivery outside of rush hours (spatio-temporal interventions),
- truck preferential network and guidance,
- optimization of the fleet regarding noise and air pollution (e.g. easier access rules for more preferable vehicle types).

Another considerable challenge for the city is the handling of the constantly increasing container traffic for import and export. It is assumed that the number of containers will double between 2012 to 2030 (finanzen.ch 2015). In order to cope with these rapidly growing volumes, the transport and logistics sector agreed to build new container terminals at the Rhine River. The container terminal Basel Nord, which is planned to be completed around 2022, will not only considerably expand the much-needed capacities but it will allow for a tri-modal container handling between the waterside, road and rail. Thus, ship-rail handling and vice versa will be possible at any time (SBB Cargo 2012). This is of highest importance for both national and international economies, as the Basel Nord container terminal lies directly at AlpTransit, also known as the New Railway Link through the Alps (NRLA), the main railway corridor on the route Rotterdam-Genoa (Bau- und Verkehrsdepartement des Kantons Basel-Stadt 2015).

17.5.6 Public Road Space: Case - Concept 30 km/h Zones

Basel supports the urban concept of the city of short distances. To support this urban design such mobility projects are implemented that aim at achieving attractive and pedestrian-friendly streets. With regard to organizing public road space the city administration promotes traffic calming in residential areas and the development of shared zones. In that respect, the attention of the long-term transport development is focused on the amenity values of the existing urban space. The needs of pedestrians are given the highest priority especially in residential centers. The revitalization of street spaces and squares is consistently coordinated with the ongoing urban maintenance and restoration measures. This coordination ensures cost effectiveness and minimizes the number of construction sites, which are usually not very well accepted by the public.

The traffic calming in residential areas has been implemented throughout the last 20 years. In Tempo 30 zones, there are usually no pedestrian crossings and the basic right of way is 'right before left'. Traffic signs with the reference Tempo 30 indicate the entrance to the calmed zone. So far, the Tempo 30 policy has contributed to the mitigation of negative effects (such as accidents, emission and noise), has resolved space use conflicts and has resulted in a more even flow of traffic (Löwengut 2015). In 2015, the length of all 30-zones has reached 150 km. In 2013, the parliament of the City of Basel passed a bill regarding the Tempo 30 concept, which aims at extending this policy gradually until 2018 by additional 25 km. Under certain conditions, traffic-oriented roads will also be converted in order to further promote traffic calming and public transport (Bau- und Verkehrsdepartement des Kantons Basel-Stadt 2015).

In 2000, there were only 1,5 kilometers of shared zones in Basel. The adjustment of the road traffic law in 2001 has brought about a strong growth in establishing more shared zones in the city (Bleile 2001). Since then, around seven streets of a total length of 1 km have been converted every year. The implementation of the Downtown Traffic Management Concept early 2015, raised the length of all shared zones in Basel to 17,7 km (Bau- und Verkehrsdepartement des Kantons Basel-Stadt 2015).

17.5.7 Mobility Management: Case - Basel on the Way

The planned projects for regional infrastructure development on the road and in favor of the public transportation systems are planned to be realized in the next 15 to 20 years. However, commuting flows and capacity constraints need to be addressed on the daily basis. Hence, besides the classical forms of transport planning, Basel has been implementing mobility management measures in order to influence desirable change in mobility patterns and behavior (Amt für Mobilität 2015a). Mobility management is a demand-driven approach to promoting urban and sustainable mobility. It aims at improving existing and establishing new mobility services for target groups such as companies based on their specific requirements. In general, the intervention measures encompass information provision, communication, organization and coordination (Handelskammer beider Basel 2015).

By implementing the action program 'Basel Unterwegs' (Basel on the Way), the city administration has significantly expanded the mobility management in the recent years. One of the most prominent campaigns is the 'Tri-nations Mobility Week Basel', which is conducted as part of the European Mobility Week. The actions aims at promoting sustainable mobility as a holistic concept. During seven days, several mobility events are conducted across Basel. The program includes more than 60 free offers to experience the sustainable City of Basel by innovative and environmentally friendly transport means (Dolleschel 2015). Another example is the Swiss-wide campaign, 'Bike to Work', which is a civic participatory action to promote cycling in companies. For example, 47 Basel companies took part in the action in 2015. The participating employees commuted a total of 390'865 km by bike and saved 62'538 kg of CO_2 equivalent (global warming potential) (Hammer 2015a).

Together with the Chamber of Commerce, the city administrations eagerly support Corporate Mobility Management, which aims at convincing employers to influence the travel behavior of their staff, particularly in the rush hour. The companies are given several instruments to motivate their employees not to use the car for commutes. For example, employees who do not occupy a company parking lot (which are usually very expensive in Basel) receive a recurring bonus for the annual ticket for public mobility services (Handelskammer beider Basel 2015). Other interesting measure were E-Bike Test Weeks conducted between 2012 and 2014. In total, 30 companies and 400 commuters were given the possibility to test e-bikes as an alternative to their daily car commutes (Bau- und Verkehrsdepartement des Kantons Basel-Stadt 2015).

It needs to be noted that the mobility management efforts for promoting sustainable mobility are intended to reach beyond the cantonal boundaries. This has been required by the Clean Air Act 2010 (Luftreinhalteplan beider Basel 2010). The act intends to promote a holistically sustainable transport culture, instead of unilaterally focusing on promoting only a single transport mode.

17.5.8 Mobility Pricing

Mobility Pricing is a usage-related charge for the use of the infrastructure and mobility services in private and in public transport. The aim is to effectively influence the demand for mobility. It can help to directly address the challenges related to the capacity constraints of the existing infrastructure and to directly react to the rising demand for mobility (Bundesamt für Strassen ASTRA 2015).

The Swiss Infrastructure Strategy (Bundesrat 2010) recommends to consider new financing models for road and rail. Pricing models should be implemented as appropriate mechanisms for demand management in terms of an efficient and sustainable use of the existing network capacity. In a market economy such as Switzerland it can only be reached through performance-, quality- and demand-related prices for the access to the transport infrastructure (Bundesrat 2010).

Also in Basel road pricing is an important aspect to consider. Experts have recognized that such restrictive push measures will be necessary at some point in time to effectively achieve the 10% reduction in car traffic in the long run. However, it has been also recognized that such restrictive solutions need to be aligned on the national level in the first place. An isolated application of such pricing models in Basel would be probably cost ineffective and most likely would bring competitive disadvantage for the location of Basel (Frick, Belart 2013).

Therefore, road pricing has been explicitly excluded as a policy measure in Basel for the time being. Preliminary political decisions have also indicated that the City of Basel is not suitable for any pilot projects because of its border location and economic importance for the regional and national economy of Switzerland. The administration is not completely averse to such pricing solutions; however, any implementation scenarios go beyond the horizon of 2020.

18 Transformative Literacy for the Transition towards the Paradigm of Sustainable Mobility

18.1 Preliminary Considerations

18.1.1 Introduction

In this chapter the author develops a comprehensive perspective on the transition processes towards the paradigm of sustainable mobility in the City of Basel. The author reveal specific challenges and barriers that the City of Basel has been facing on its transition path away from car dependence and towards a mobility system which aims at combining different transport modes in a consistent way. For that purpose he applies the conceptual framework of Transformative Literacy along the four domains: technology, economy, society and institutions (see chapter 1.3 for detailed description).

The acquired knowledge will serve two purposes:

1) To draw conclusions for the administration of Basel: what went well and what could be done better in the future to achieve the reduction goals of Stiig-Um with regard to car traffic in Basel. The researcher elaborates on barriers and enablers that have influenced the transition towards a sustainable mobility system.

2) To draw general recommendations for other cities that intend to transform their mobility system with an appropriate understanding and required tool set.

The author builds a holistic body of knowledge about important and critical aspects associated with transitioning towards a desirable state of sustainability in urban mobility. With that he aims at constituting the literacy for decision-makers and other parties interested in this topic.

18.1.2 Understanding Critical Influencing Factors

The output of the outlined case study of Basel enriches the body of knowledge by revealing the main influencing factors to support and promote the transition towards a paradigm of sustainable mobility in cities. The influencing factors can take two distinct forms: the critical success factors (CSF) and the critical barriers. CSFs are the essential areas of activity that must be considered and carried out well if the city is to achieve the desirable vision and objectives of urban mobility. Identifying success factors can help the administration, which is responsible for transition, to know which elements are the most crucial and how to navigate the process of policy development, alignment and implementation. Critical barriers are prominent obstacles which, if not considered or if overlooked, could significantly impact the city's ability to achieve its strategic objectives regarding the mobility system.

The literature shows that critical success factors and barriers have been often researched, identified and discussed to broach the issues of sustainable mobility projects in cities. Usually such studies highlight two main aspects of the implementation of sustainable mobility policies and concepts: the political and the social side. Assuming that a success or failure of sustainable mobility concepts is determined by political enforcement processes, then analysis of public actions is required (e.g. influence of stakeholders, objectives, interest groups as well as institutional patterns) (Bratzel 1999). If personal and behavioral aspects such as life stages or life and mobility styles are to be examined, then the emphasis is placed on approaches of social and behavioral science.

For political considerations the 'Policy Analysis' method prevails in political science research for systematic analysis of critical success factors and critical obstacles of political processes (Bratzel 1999; Rogge 1999; Flämig et al. 2001; Bohnet et al. 2005; Wilke 2005). The instrument deploys an ex-post and categorical analysis in order to detect and better understand the political conflicts and decision-making situations. They are investigated with respect to their consequences and reviewed and appraised from normative perspectives. The objective of the analysis is to derive typical structural relationships that can be transferred to similar future events (Bohnet et al. 2005). For example, Wilke (2005) has analyzed the importance of professional actors for an ecologically-oriented urban transport policy by examining both (i) upstream negotiation processes and (ii) downstream effects of implemented policy measures. Another study by Reh (2001) deploys the new institutional economics (NIE) for the analysis of organizational structures and incentive mechanisms to explain the successes or failures of environmentally oriented transport projects. The focus of political science studies lies in the interpretation of the municipal transport policy and in demonstrating the potential of implementing sustainable transport projects.

Other type of studies can be regarded as general social science studies. For example, Gertz (1998) assumes that the implementation of sustainable mobility is a social process that involves a change in awareness of issues associated with mobility, new and clear objectives, innovative measures and new procedures. In the study he interrelates the sociological aspects with the requirements of transport planning policy. Schlaffer et al. (2002) consider psychological and social factors for sustainable transport development. The authors have developed a generic scheme for behavioral change based on the mobility patterns of people. Other than that, Banister (2008) suggests two conditions which are necessary for the transition towards sustainable mobility: (i) high technical quality of implementation of innovative mobility systems and (ii) the acceptance from the public. The combination and compliance with core elements of these two conditions can lead to a sustainable mobility paradigm. Another good example is Browne et al. (2011) who perform a complex cross-sectional analysis. The extensive report covers critical economic, fiscal, behavioral- and preference-based, institutional and regulatory barriers for the transition towards sustainable mobility for the case of Ireland.

The author has selected ten papers and studies which investigated the past endeavors to implement sustainable mobility concepts in other European cities (e.g. Amsterdam, Zürich or Freiburg). The aim has been to analyze and synthetize a preliminary typology of relevant influencing factors in the field of transport policy. The result has set the required foundation for further investigation of the City of Basel and its transition towards sustainable mobility.

18.1.3 Summary of Previous Research Results

The analytical subject of selected studies are case studies of relative success in the arena of urban transport policy. Transport policies in the investigated cities have a clear direction for the development of transport policies. In their policy-making they distinguish clearly between (i) establishing sustainable mobility structures and (ii) implementing sustainable modes of transport (Rogge 1999, p. 20). Over time they have been implementing sustainability measures in individual fields of transport policy and could showcase absolute improvements in their mobility systems. In the general discussion about transport planning these cases are often regarded as representative and excellent examples of best-cases (Flämig et al. 2001, p. 39).

All ten studies sought to identify structures and critical factors that may significantly contribute to an environment-oriented change in these 'lighthouse' cities. For the research and analysis most authors applied the case study approach as a research method. In total, 30 case studies have been developed and analyzed. Samples were taken from four countries: Germany, Switzerland, France and the Netherlands. A separate case is the research initiative by Browne et al. (2011), who explicitly focused on the situation of Ireland and derived specific critical barriers which exist there.

It should be also noted that the generalization of critical factors may be limited by the fact that every case study is determined by a variety of individual variables (Bohnet et al. 2005, p. 12). Of course, this implies some difficulties for any generalization attempts. Nevertheless, findings of these analyses are regarded as general and holistic enough to be relevant for other cities. Therefore, certain patterns have been identified and systematized despite possible case- or country-specific considerations.

In summary, the researcher has identified a total of 306 influencing factors, both (i) critical success factors and (ii) critical barriers. By means of axial coding the influencing factors have been categorized into 28 general topics (see Table 26).

Table 26: Categories of critical factors' and their occurrence in the studies.

No.	Category	Number of identified factors
1	Communication	30
2	Political participation	27
3	Actors and stakeholders	27
4	Organizational structures	25
5	Participation	22
6	Financing	21
7	Regulations	17
8	Cooperation	16
9	Alternative and / or improved mobility offers	16
10	Integrated consideration	15
11	Marketing and policy mix	14
12	Evaluation	11
13	Increase of social pressure	9
14	Strategy of small steps	7
15	Well thought-out objectives	7
16	Incentives for behavioral change	7
17	Innovation	5
18	Knowledge / competence	5
19	Public relation	5
20	Showcasing benefits	5
21	Institutions	3
22	Political errors	2
23	Physical conditions	2
24	Professional project management	2
25	Restricted problem understanding	2
26	Adaptability	2
27	Complexity	1
28	Long planning cycles	1
	Factors determined in total	**306**

18.1.4 Conclusions for Further Investigation

The table above gives a preliminary frame of critical conditions to be taken into consideration by policy-makers and involved parties to ensure purposeful discussions and critical appraisal of sustainable mobility concepts. The frequency of occurrence of factors is not a proof that a specific category has a higher priority than others. Nonetheless, it gives a good first impression of which factors may play a significant role in the policy-making and implementation process. Based on that the author has drawn four general conclusions:

1) Political decision-making processes seem to play the most significant role as they constitute an indispensable element of every strategic urban planning activity. However, they are not a sufficient condition for introducing and successfully implementing innovative mobility concepts for sustainable transport.

2) Public acceptance is a factor as substantial as the previous one, yet often a neglected one. Addressing the right target groups, creating social pressure and awareness, influencing behavioral change by public demonstrations and implementing individual marketing measures can support the acceptance of innovative concepts.

3) The best possible usage of technology and high quality of the technical implementation of innovative mobility concepts are conditions *sine qua non*. On the one hand, the technology aspects encompass investments in transport infrastructure, traffic carriers, transport information systems and travel demand management. On the other hand, clear governmental directives are required (for example for industrial investment in new propulsion systems).

4) Eventually, mobility behavioral changes of citizens are essential. Altering unsustainable mobility patterns brings about a permanent modal shift towards sustainable mobility options. Not only does promoting ecological driving style or adherence to speed limits play a role, but establishing innovative and real mobility alternatives is essential.

Figure 30 depicts the main critical influencing factors that have been identified during the review of selected case studies. The four main themes are: politics, public acceptance, effective use of technology, and incentives for behavioral change of citizens.

Politics

- Actors
- Organizational structures
- Regional cooperation
- Participation and Communication
- Marketing for a sustainable transport policy
- Time and operational framework
- Financing
- Evaluation

Public Acceptance

- Ensuring participation and communication
- Actions for information dissemination
- Bundling of measures
- Explicit evidence of the benefits
- Gradual implementation of controversial measures
- Ensure consistency between the different policies
- Adaptability of policies

Best Use of Technology

- Promoting the readiness for innovation
- High quality of technical implementation of innovative and sustainable mobility concepts
- Investment in efficient transport vehicles, information systems and in the transport system itself
- Clear governmental directives for the industry, e.g.: investment in hybrid vehicles and alternative fuels
- Measures to increase the utilization rates of transport modes

Incentives for Action and Behavioral Changes

- Knowledge transfer and public relation management
- Managing attitudes and presenting new role models
- Demonstrating alternative behavior options
- Providing incentives for using alternative options
- Feedback on behavioral consequences
- Orientation on target groups
- Policy mix
- Effects evaluation

Figure 30: Critical success factors clustered by four main themes.
(Diagram by author based on author's analysis and assessment of the underlying papers).

18.2 Transformative Literacy: Analysis of the Case - City of Basel

18.2.1 Remarks regarding the analysis

Domains of Transformative Literacy

There are four relevant domains of the analysis framework at hand: Technology, Economy, Society and Politics. The author concisely describes each domain at the beginning of every paragraph. A more detailed explanation of Transformative Literacy can be found in chapter 1.3 of this book.

Themes

For every single domain of the Transformative Literacy several *themes* have been identified. These themes have emerged from the qualitative data analysis of interview transcripts and have been described in the following sections. An example of a theme is: *New business models*, in the section Economy. The themes have been previously derived by the applied coding procedure of the underlying transcripts (for the procedure see chapter 16.3).

Codes and Expert Statements

For the justification of a specific theme the author has used codes that support the theme. The reader may find footnote references at several spots within the text where the corresponding code applies. For each code the author has extracted real statements from expert interviews that correspond with the code. Every statement is titled and is marked bold in a footnote with the following reference: *"**Title:** the expert statement is listed in appx. 9, no. x"*. Following that, the statement can be found in Appendix 9 under the specified number.[42]

Anonymization

The statements have been anonymized with a specific coding taxonomy, which is only known to the author. Furthermore, the statements have been kept in German since all interviews were conducted in German language. To some extent the statements may appear as colloquial speech for German speaking readers. The interviewer aimed at creating an open environment and trusted atmosphere for the interviewees to gain most

[42] The complete list of expert statements is stored in Appendix 9 and can be accessed via OnlinePLUS.

valuable insights. Some grammatical shortcomings might have also resulted during the transcription process.

18.2.2 Technology

The first pillar of the Transformative Literacy is *Technology*. Technological innovations aim at challenging the existing socio-technical regimes. In addition to economic impacts the technological progress can also have cultural and social impacts that could implicate a structural change (Schneidewind 2013a).

Technology for Raising the Efficiency in Mobility

With respect to the case of Basel it can be assumed that the city has been assuming a strategy of a technology shift for better energy efficiency in the future, since about 35% of the energy consumption of the Swiss population is due to mobility (Bundesamt für Statistik BFS 2013b). There has been a general consensus among the experts that the urban mobility system based on fossil fuels is not environmentally friendly and therefore may be referred to as unsustainable.[43] Experts have been also aware that the existing car architectures, propulsion systems and manufacturing procedures were not established with sustainability in mind which has, in part, assisted in producing the significant social costs that are now associated with cars. Hence, a technological shift is being suggested.[44] In the first place electromobility has been seen as a most plausible solution for achieving energy efficiency in the context of automobility in urban areas. Other technological solutions such as the fuel cell have not been excluded, though.

However, energy efficiency is not regarded as the only main issue. In the urban context, major improvements can be achieved with regard to space consumption, traffic safety and quality of life. Autonomous driving has been an often discussed technology that could help addressing these issues. It is seen as a technological solution that could considerably contribute to higher efficiency of the transport infrastructure and increased traffic safety by the elimination of the 'human failure factor'.[45]

However, possible rebound effects associated with new technologies are considered and recognized as relevant challenges to introducing these technologies.[46] For example, there is a general awareness and agreement that any improvements in the area of energy efficiency, safety and quality of driving may also lead to an increased demand for such

[43] Unsustainable mobility system: the expert statement is listed in appx. 9, no. 1.
[44] Technological shift is required away from automobility: the statement is listed in appx. 9, no. 2.
[45] Traffic safety and quality of life: the expert statement is listed appx. 9, no. 3.
[46] Rebound Effects: expert statements are listed in appx. 9, no. 4 and 5.

autonomous cars and associated mobility services. In consequence, this could lead to a substantial increase in the total volume of traffic conducted by cars.

Information and Communication Technology (ICT)

It has been recognized that the digitalization through innovative ICT, that has been taking place in the society and in the economy in recent years, bear a significant potential for structural adjustments in the field of urban mobility. The opinion has been shared that technology, ICT in particular, should not be seen as a barrier anymore but rather it must be regarded as a critical success factor and an important prerequisite for further efficiency gains in mobility in the urban context in the future.[47] Technological developments and advancements are believed to address following issues associated with the car traffic in cities:

- to gain control over the car traffic in the city,
- to considerably raise the efficiency of the road infrastructure, and
- to offer as much mobility alternatives as possible.

The first and the second aim at reducing the overall traffic volume to regain the space. With respect to that it has been recognized that the central role might be played by the usage of most innovative ICT. For example, ICT enables the implementation of an intelligent transportation system (ITS), which is an advanced technological intervention for effective steering of urban traffic and transport infrastructure. The last one aims at introducing advanced technologies to public transportation systems, slow modes and mobility management. Especially, online information systems, which enable integrated journey booking, ticketing, payment and billing for public transport and national railway are regarded as contributors to the integration of mobility alternatives. Another example for implementing innovative mobility alternatives has been the introduction of a free-floating carsharing scheme in Basel and in its suburbs, labeled as 'Catch-a-Car'.

Nonetheless, there seems to be also skepticism with respect to the possibilities and potentials of new technologies, especially ICT. For example, it has been expressed that the role of ICT should not be overestimated. Despite its considerable impact in terms of holistic information provisioning and intelligent integration of several transportation modes, ICT does not provide transportation services on its own. It only enables an exact information flow. Eventually, there needs to be a physical vessel such as bus, tram, car or a bike that transports people or goods.[48]

Table 27 depicts the list of identified critical factors in the Technology dimension.

[47] Technology as a critical success factor: the expert statement is listed in appx. 9, no. 6.
[48] Skepticism towards the potential of ICT: the expert statement is listed in appx. 9, no. 7.

Table 27: Critical Factors in the Technology dimension.

- Monitor and understand the technological developments not only in the field of transportation but also in ICT or other digital services, - Provide mechanisms for better understanding of new technologies in the city administration, - Addressing the current spirit of the time: understand innovation, - Promote the willingness to develop and adopt innovation, - Ensure high quality of the technical implementation of innovative mobility concepts, - Investment in efficient modes of transport, information systems and in the transport system itself, - Establish clear directives for the industry, for example, investment in alternative vehicles or new fleet management schemes (corporate carsharing), - Implement measures that increase the utilization of transport modes, - Establish intelligent meta-integration of mobility alternatives with the help of ICT.

18.2.3 Economy

The second pillar of Transformative Literacy is *Economy*. This dimension aims at efficient organization of social and corporate-related processes and to mobilize efficiency reserves through new and innovative business concepts and approaches. At the micro level, i.e. the level of enterprises and individual economic actors, it is expressed in the form of more efficient organizational and production methods. Interestingly, in many industries innovative technological developments do not play a supporting role anymore, but rather they enable new business models or business networks, which were not feasible or conceivable before. This results in new business dynamics and possible economic growth and prosperity (Schneidewind 2013a).

Securing locational advantages

With respect to the case of Basel it can be assumed that the city has an extreme interest in securing and further developing its locational advantages, as Basel is unquestionably the economic center of the region, if not of Switzerland entirely. The authorities of the City (i.e. the Canton Parliament and the Canton Executive) are aware of this economic attraction power and of the need to sustain it.[49] The city aims at being recognized as a

[49] Securing locational advantages: the expert statement is listed in appx. 9, no. 8.

hub for passenger and freight transport in Europe. In order to sustain the economic prosperity Basel invests and develops excellent multimodal and cross-border transport infrastructure and connections to the main European and national economic centers. However, due to negative externalities and the resulting high marginal social costs the strategy from the automobile era - 'free streets for free citizens', is not feasible anymore. Therefore, mobility planning in Basel can be marked as urban-friendly, supply-side oriented and not demand driven.[50]

Accessibility, velocity and aligning the markets

A well-functioning city needs to consider mobility requirements from the surrounding regions as well. The commuter balance in the City of Basel amounts to over 50% (Bundesamt für Statistik BFS 2013c). Hence, the mobility needs of this group of people and the ease of accessibility to the city are important pillars of locational advantages of the city, too.[51] It seems that accessibility and the resulting workforce sourcing must be ensured in a sustainable way.

It is thought that further investments in transport infrastructure, i.e. increasing the accessibility, lead to changes in the price of land and also to increased productivity. The argument behind this is that better accessibility results in better balance and alignment of the markets: both in the goods market, as well as in the labor market. Hence, providing more accessibility to the urban area leads to gains in productivity of the city in all fields, regardless whether it is business or private. As such, accessibility can be regarded as one of the central components of urban economy. These two important aspects, i.e. accessibility and productivity, seem to be understood by all actors of the mobility domain, those in the City of Basel and in the entire city-surrounding region.[52]

Furthermore, when talking about the accessibility of a city one needs to take two further inherent components into account: the attainable velocity and the density, which in turn means the ease to reach urban destinations. On the one hand, the higher the velocities, the faster the destinations can be reached. However, the better the velocities get, the more space for transport is required and this will eventually lead to reduced densities. On the other hand, the denser the cities are, the easier a higher traffic occurs which can eventually lead to a possible system collapse. Therefore, for good accessibility of urban areas a compromise between the velocity and proper density is required.[53]

[50] Away from the strategy of 'free streets for free citizens': the statement is listed in appx. 9, no. 9.
[51] Considering needs of commuters as locational advantage: the statement is listed in appx. 9, no. 10.
[52] Importance of accessibility and productivity resp. balance and alignment of the markets: expert statements are listed in appx. 9, no. 11 and 12.
[53] Accessibility: the expert statement is listed in appx. 9, no. 13.

However, these dependencies between the economic factors and the transport system must be clearly articulated and accepted by all involved parties. Otherwise, a room for potential conflicts arises, which is being expressed by some emotional statements of the decision-makers. For example, outside of the city the opinion is shared that the car restricting measures of the City of Basel lead to the establishment of figurative 'city gates'. Partners perceive it as an attempt to relocate the urban traffic problems outside of the city to the neighboring cantons and communities. This might be considered by some parties as self-concerned and not partnership-oriented. Such perceptions and beliefs must be avoided at all costs.[54]

Moreover, it needs to be understood that radical changes in the mobility system are always perceived as experiments. 'Big bang' approaches entail certain disadvantages. For example, radical counter-movements are triggered and the conflicts are intensified. This holds especially true in case of adjustments in the car traffic. The attempt to reduce the car traffic volume in the city by a moderate 10% within 10 years has been seen as a radical intervention by some interest groups. The results of the Stiig-Um study indicate that a real reduction will be challenging, without decreasing the capacity on the city road network and without providing further alternatives to cars. In particular, it is required to convince the economy that the overall accessibility will remain secured and that no new congestion issues will arise. A step-by-step-approach is recommended.[55]

An additional topic which cannot be disregarded is velocity. There is a clear relation between the level of velocity and the level of feasible ranges. Every person has a constant time budget that they are prepared to invest for their daily journeys. With that in mind, the higher the velocity, the higher the possible range. Hence, the level of speed may play a significant role for designing an urban mobility system.[56] However, in Switzerland the time budget for mobility has remained relatively constant compared to the feasible ranges. This phenomenon has been labeled as 'consistency of mobility time budget'. Additionally, in urban areas one cannot allow for high speeds. Currently, the average car velocity in cities is at 25km/h. Instead of increasing the speed level to achieve higher ranges, it is rather more appropriate to reduce obstacles for an interference-free mobility in the city.[57] Hence, there seems to be an agreement that further increases of velocity, at least in urban areas, is not purposeful. For that reason the velocity plays a subordinate role in relation to accessibility.

---

[54] Avoiding emotions with regard to transport politics of the City of Basel: the expert statement is listed in appx. 9, no. 14.

[55] Promote a step-by-step Approach: expert statements are listed in appx. 9, no. 15 and 16.

[56] Velocity and time budgets: the expert statement is listed in appx. 9, no. 17.

[57] Interference-free mobility in the city: the expert statement is listed in appx. 9, no. 18.

New business models

There seems to be a general agreement amongst the experts that the automobility system is currently undergoing an adjustment process in its underlying business model. Especially, the observable paradigm shift from product ownership to mobility service provision (e.g. carsharing) is a prominent example of this adjustment. However, this process should not be considered in a dichotomous manner. A continuum of potential business models exists between owning a car and attaining flexible access to car-based mobility. With this point in mind, private sector companies, who are currently present in the market or are considering entering the system, may find it fruitful to experiment with different combinations of business models to tailor the services and products which they offer to meet the specific requirements of customers. In particular, the inclusion of more and more ICT components into the car can enable individualized services and products around mobility. In fact, this 'digitization process' of the car might represent the most drastic alteration to the prevailing mobility sector. The shift towards providing more and more individualized mobility services and products in and around the vehicle requires new forms of cooperation outside of the existing industry structures that were not conceivable before. For example, ICT companies such as Google and Apple are already entering the market. Further development and the convergence with the technology of autonomous driving and flexible mobility patterns, such as carsharing and ridesharing, may release a substantial proportion of the population from the burden of private car ownership. This might lead to the destruction of the existing business model of the automotive industry, which is constituted by selling as much cars as possible.[58]

Pursuing such a strategy could perhaps provide an option for facilitating a sustainability shift in cities, for example, in terms of more efficiency and accessibility. Although managing a transition of this nature would likely prove challenging. Several concerns arise when considering radical system adjustments such as integrating autonomous driving into the existing urban mobility system. One of the possible drawbacks is the generation of additional distance driven by autonomous vehicles because of more convenience and the supplementary empty car journeys. Such a system could also directly compete with the public transportation system.[59] Other aspects refer to regulatory and insurance issues that need to be clarified in the first place. For example, how to regulate and organize the mobility system in the first stage of the technology adoption. It is believed that in the first phase the urban mobility system will be based on mixed traffic of conventional and autonomous vehicles.[60]

[58] New business models (product-to-service shift): the expert statement is listed in appx. 9, no. 19.
[59] Concerns with regard to autonomous vehicles in the urban context: the expert statement is listed in appx. 9, no. 20.
[60] Insurance and responsibility: the expert statement is listed in appx. 9, no. 21.

There is also the aspect of organization and governance of such a system. For area-wide advanced mobility systems based on autonomous vehicles the discussion is still ongoing who will provide and who will operate them. Will it be a public provider and operator who will take the entire accountability for the system security? Or a private company which will provide the required technological platform and the vehicle infrastructure? Or will it be a public-private mix of private companies with various competencies and the state as a regulator? Then, who will take the responsibility for possible accidents in such a mobility system: will it be the car producer, the mobility ICT platform provider or the operator of the system?[61]

These challenges indicate that such radical innovations are still regarded to be far away from mass diffusion and adoption by the society. This will still require many political, regulatory, insurance and technical discussions.[62] The development of these technologies needs to be further supported. However, as of today they do not play a significant role in overcoming the burden of unsustainability related with automobility in the urban context of the City of Basel. It is advisable to establish and maintain a platform for public-private knowledge exchange for discussing and resolving the issues associated with radical innovations which might be implemented in the near future in urban areas.

More mature niche business models that occur on the market for flexible urban mobility services should be monitored and carefully investigated by city authorities. If they fit the mobility strategy of a city they should be implemented in the form of pilot projects. In the City of Basel these business models encompass the lighthouse free-floating car-sharing scheme Catch-a-Car or the online taxi dispatching system UBER. It needs to be kept in mind that implementing innovative technologies for sustainable mobility solutions must always be economically feasible for private companies who implement them.[63] Therefore, in the pilot and test phases of such niche mobility services appropriate support should be offered to the risk-taking actors. For example, additional start-up funding or access to appropriate promotion and marketing channels could be a valuable contribution to the success of such endeavors. Furthermore, during test phases monitoring and controlling actions are required to measure their impact on the long-term strategic goals of a city, such as reducing the total car traffic volume.[64]

Other than that, it seems that there is a need for technological and business solutions that would enable an overall integration of all mobility alternatives. Therefore, it is recommended to continuously seek for technology and business innovations that could bring about further efficiency gains in the usage of vehicles as well as the entire urban

---

[61] Organization and governance: expert statements are listed in appx. 9, no. 22 and 23.
[62] Adoption of technology: expert statements are listed in appx. 9, no. 24 and 25.
[63] Economic feasibility of new business models: the expert statement is listed in appx. 9, no. 26.
[64] Pilot phases, support and monitoring: expert statements are listed in appx. 9, no. 27 and 28.

transport infrastructure. For example, an area-wide dynamic ridesharing system, such as TwoGo by SAP, or a business concept for managing the private parking space in the city perimeter, such as ParkU, could be considered.[65]

Include powerful influencers and conduct appropriate stakeholder management

What needs to be borne in mind is that any changes to the existing structures of the mobility system can encounter resistance and counter movements from lobby groups. At the end, it is a kind of battle between different systems by promoting diverse mobility concepts and approaches. Like everywhere else, there are also powerful lobbying organizations involved.[66] The belief is shared among experts that measures addressing the inefficiencies associated with automobility are especially subject to strong criticism. The car-oriented interest groups employ many strategies to prevent changes to the competitive landscape, including lobbying of policy makers to water down proposed regulations. They consistently bring forward the argument of economic costs of any new policies in terms of sector output and jobs, whilst promoting structural inertias in the existing mobility system. Overcoming this conservative behavior on the part of incumbent business actors to improve the sustainability of the urban mobility is likely to prove a significant challenge. Additionally, the car-oriented lobby seems to possess strong instruments to communicate their position effectively.[67]

However, some opportunities are available to manage these powerful influencers. The strategies are for example: showcasing the value of sustainable mobility measures and balancing the interests. With that respect, cost-benefit considerations are a powerful instrument. Demonstrating that innovative solutions can bring about considerable cost savings, for example, in required parking space, is a good argument to convince big corporations which need to provide extensive parking capabilities to their employees.[68] What is also important in that regard, is the assurance that accessibility can be sustained regardless of the mode of transport. For that purpose, however, all partners, including the difficult ones, need to be included and policy coherence demonstrated.[69]

Table 28 depicts the list of identified critical factors with regards to the dimension of Economy.

[65] Integration of mobility solutions: the expert statement is listed in appx. 9, no. 29.
[66] Resistance and counter movements from lobby groups: the statement is listed in appx. 9, no. 30.
[67] Strong instruments and strategies from car-oriented interest groups: expert statements are listed in appx. 9, no. 31 and 32.
[68] Cost-benefit considerations: the expert statement is listed in appx. 9, no. 33.
[69] Demonstrate Value: the expert statement is listed in appx. 9, no. 34.

Table 28: Critical Factors in Economy dimension.

- Clear demonstration of the benefits for the economy, - Technology enables innovative business models. Allow small innovative niche actors entering the market and piloting innovative mobility concepts, - Manage the stakeholders by showing the benefits, - Promote a step-by-step approach; no radical changes, as radical changes are perceived as risky experiments, - Cost of parking (stationary traffic) as a catalyst and argument for convincing companies, - Promote mobility management measures for companies, - Execute effective marketing measures towards the economy and business, - Develop scientific understanding of the interdependencies between the economy and the transportation system.

18.2.4 Society

The third dimension of the Transformative Literacy is *Society*. This pillar aims at dealing with the dynamics and determinants of social change processes. Conducting research in this area helps to develop an understanding for cultural and value systems in the society. Especially, it helps to comprehend the dynamics of cultural change processes stimulated and catalyzed by developments such as technological innovations, e.g. the diffusion of the Internet or the growing importance of post-material values. The dimension encompasses also the recognition of different stakeholders and their roles in shaping cultural processes (Schneidewind 2013a).

Cultural shift and the reorganization of the value system

The dynamics of cultural change and the ongoing reorganization of the value system, at least in the Western societies, has had a considerable impact on urban mobility. The observable change of behavioral patterns in mobility is influenced not only by technological innovations. It is rather being recognized that social demands in the form of securing values such as autonomy, flexibility and freedom are the driving forces and have an impact on the societal attitudes towards well-functioning urban mobility.[70] Hence, it is expected that the mobility freedom is ensured and that mobility demands of the society are not reduced or limited.[71] However, there has been an observable raise of consciousness and willingness of individuals to take on social and environmental responsibility.

[70] Autonomy and flexibility: the expert statement is listed in appx. 9, no. 35.
[71] Ensuring mobility freedom: the expert statement is listed in appx. 9, no. 36.

These values and attitudes, which can be described as post-material, have been caused by the increased awareness about the marginal social costs of individual mobility and the associated environmental externalities. This has led to the development of the paradigm of sustainable mobility as a contradiction to the car-oriented paradigm which can be labeled by the term 'free streets for free citizens'. Sustainable mobility, however, does not necessarily equal the reduction of mobility needs, which would obviously cut back on the mobility freedom of the society. It rather denotes a holistic approach to balance the implicit societal need for the mobility freedom with the minimum of negative effects today and in the future.[72] Hence, the goal should not be the reduction of mobility per se but rather the provision of effective and more flexible alternatives to rigid car-mobility.[73] However, such changes do not happen radically; they occur rather gradually as value systems and associated behaviors seem to change generationally. Nonetheless, the observable shifts in behavioral patterns in the case of the City of Basel, e.g. in mobility or in lifestyles, suggest that a cultural shift has been taking place recently.[74]

For example, according to recent research the possibility of using smartphones is one of important factors determining the decline in attractiveness of cycling among children and young people in Basel (Sauter, Wyss 2014). Accessing electronic media is not possible while cycling and, to make matters worse, public transport companies have been offering free Wi-Fi access. At the center lies the social aspect that youngsters want to remain connected to their social networks. This finding argues rather against cycling in this age group since the connection of electronic media and bikes is not really possible and too dangerous. The future of cycling as a transportation mode among young people seems to be open (Sauter, Wyss 2014).

Responding to basic societal needs

The key cultural and societal aspects with regard to urban mobility have been clearly anchored in both strategic documents of Basel: (i) the cantonal legislative plan 2013-2017 (Regierungsrat Kanton Basel-Stadt 2013) and (ii) the strategic concept for urban transport policy development (Bau- und Verkehrsdepartement des Kantons Basel-Stadt 2015). Along with securing accessibility and ensuring cost-effectiveness it contains two important strategic objectives that aim at addressing the basic societal needs: (i) the increase in quality of life and (ii) the enhancement of traffic safety.[75] This can be regarded as a political response to public expectations with regards to the level of life standard and safety in the public space. It has been expressed by the statement in the legislative

[72] Sustainable mobility approach: the expert statement is listed in appx. 9, no. 37.
[73] Mobility freedom through flexible mobility services: the expert statement is listed in appx. 9, no. 38.
[74] Observable shifts in behavioral patterns: the expert statement is listed in appx. 9, no. 39.
[75] Quality of life and security: the expert statement is listed in appx. 9, no. 40.

plan: securing the health, providing social security, physical integrity and the protection of property are the overarching goals of the people of the City of Basel. Along with high-quality healthcare, the need for security in the public space and in transportation is a key prerequisite for high quality of life.

This clear definition of societal strategic needs has substantial implications for the design of the urban mobility system, as it requires to rethink the mobility concepts within the perimeter of the city and beyond it. The focus is to promote livable neighborhoods with short distances, thereby aiming at reducing the number of unnecessary trips within the city. With that, the focus on sustainability becomes an integral consideration of the land use and transport planning in the city.[76]

The belief has been shared among experts that the high quality of life and residential attractiveness along with affordable mobility and good accessibility are additional major locational factors to select Basel as a location for business and industry actors.[77] These factors are regarded as critical prerequisites for securing a long-term sourcing of skilled workforce by the companies located in Basel. 'Freedom for cars', that is, unrestricted automobility is not regarded as an indispensable advantage.

For the administration of Basel it has also an additional strategic advantage, since it seems that increasing residential attractiveness entices more people to move back to the city. Hence, the reurbanization of the city has been taking place in the recent years. Such development has two positive side effects: higher incomes from taxes and less car traffic, as the accessibility by public transport and bikes is exceptional within the perimeter of the city.

Managing behavioral changes

Experts have highlighted how behavior change of citizens will be required to allow for a more environmentally sustainable and socially just mobility system to be realized. Effectively managing behavioral changes of citizens has been outlined as a key factor for ensuring that the mobility system meets their strategic needs and desires. This needs to happen on several levels: demonstrating the financial benefits of certain behaviors, altering the patterns of car usage and ownership to allow for certain behaviors to take place and considering how social norms could be shifted to promote one set of behaviors whilst marginalizing others. Several mechanisms have been proposed through which the behavior change of citizens could be directed. Generally, the experts have agreed that appropriate pull measures (e.g. time and convenience losses on the road or implementing and promoting alternatives) are not enough to bring about relevant change in behavioral

[76] Consequence for the design of the urban mobility system: the statement is listed in appx. 9, no. 41.
[77] Sustainable urban mobility design as locational factor: the expert statement is listed in appx. 9, no. 42.

patterns that cause socially and environmentally negative externalities, such as the extensive automobility. This is based on the assumption that people always behave rationally and make decisions based on their subjective benefits. If no unexpected barrier occurs, they tend to behave as a matter of routine. For example, they always use cars instead of public transport. A rationalization process will begin only if obstacles to their routine will occur, i.e. if a conflict will arise between the routine behavior and experience. The first reaction is usually an attempt to remove barriers. However, if this attempt does not work, then a new rational behavior is developed.[78] With regards to urban mobility it means that additional restrictive (enforcing) push actions (e.g. parking regime or fiscal enforcement) are necessary to reach behavioral change.[79] [80]

An important aspect of managing the traffic behavior of citizens effectively is proper information provision about the trip purposes. This knowledge will enable to apply intervening measures selectively, i.e. more purposeful. ICT is anticipated to play a significant role in that matter as described previously.[81]

Ensuring Citizens' Participation

It has been recognized that considering citizens as only passive elements of the system would overlook the opportunity for citizens to interactively co-develop the mobility system. With the ways in which social practices evolve in response to changes in technical and institutional arrangements being difficult to predict, actively including citizens in the design process of the mobility system will likely lead to a higher level of flexibility in the potential pathways and an increased acceptance.[82] [83] Hence, it is essential that all possible actors, who are directly affected by complex interventions in the mobility system actively participate in planning and implementation processes. Participation processes that promote strong civic involvement encompass for example:

- participation in the decision-making processes on individual projects such as: reduction of parking spaces and the design of the new space,
- participation in the development of district development plans, e.g. in the form of neighborhood assemblies,
- participation in the design of general plans such as: transport development concept, zoning,
- participation in the strategic management of the entire municipality.

---

[78] Routine behavior and the need for rationalization: the expert statement is listed in appx. 9, no. 43.
[79] Mechanisms for managing behavioral change: expert statements are listed in appx. 9, no. 44 - 45.
[80] Enforce behavioral change: the expert statement is listed in appx. 9, no. 46.
[81] Individualized and flexible information provisioning: the expert statement is listed in appx. 9, no. 47.
[82] Considering citizens not as passive components: the expert statement is listed in appx. 9, no. 48.
[83] Right to participate: the expert statement is listed in appx. 9, no. 49.

In Basel a profound civic participation is being ensured by the possibility of conducting a civic voting and public consultations. In that way, the policy is being aligned with the citizens' needs. This in turn paves the way for enhanced public acceptance of the policies and measures. For example, the strategic concept for the urban traffic policy in Basel with the associated strategic action plan (Bau- und Verkehrsdepartement des Kantons Basel-Stadt 2014b) has been put under a sever pubic consultation process throughout the year 2014. The process involved citizens, trade associations, industry and interest groups, local authorities from neighboring cantons and communities and political parties. In total 43 organizations and institutions replied with statements regarding this strategic plan for mobility development in Basel (Frick, Belart 2014).

It has been also understood that citizens should be included throughout the policy planning and implementation process in the most effective way. The 'culture of participation', which has greatly gained in importance especially in Switzerland, has also shown some drawbacks. A difficulty that often occurs is that the involved consultative bodies assume the right, that they could actually make the decisions. For example, opinions are being expressed that are not substantiated on a professional expertise and depict only high-level ideas or suggestions. These opinions might then be weighted very heavily because they have been made by actors from powerful interest groups. The critical confrontation is then somehow diluted as one is not willing to interfere with the participation process.[84]

A complementary critical factor is an ongoing communication process to sustain and to moderate the social discourse. For that, the involvement of people and opinion makers who understand the mobility issues and who can multiply the communication to their respective groups would be of great value.[85] Finally, getting feedback and confirmation from the population repeatedly will ensure that the development is on the right track.[86]

10'000 KM Society (Social Road Pricing)

Currently, road pricing has been explicitly excluded from political discussions as an intervention (see Chapter 17.5.8). Nevertheless, experts have been convinced that Swiss municipal administrations will inevitably need to address this topic as a possible policy measure to counteract the externalities of citizens' mobility in a much more effective and determined way. It is also clear that mobility pricing would be strictly a push measure and as such very difficult to gain public acceptability for. Therefore, some ideas have been proposed to approach the topic in a delicate way. One idea is 'Social Mobility Pricing' or 'Social Mobility Bonus'. Such a policy would be based on a bonus-malus

[84] Drawbacks of participation processes: the expert statement is listed in appx. 9, no. 50.
[85] Involvement of strong opinion makers: expert statements are listed in appx. 9, no. 51 and 52.
[86] Moderate social discourse: the expert statement is listed in appx. 9, no. 53.

approach, which can be found, for example, in the energy sector. Such bonus models create financial incentives for implementing efficiency and/or saving measures. Businesses and households that achieve an efficiency or a saving target, benefit from a discount on tariffs.

For example, since 1999 an incentive tax on electricity has been levied in the City of Basel. This regulatory tax is added onto the kilowatt-hour price and is collected separately with every electricity bill. The cash-flows are incorporated into the 'saving fund Basel' (sfb) – a financing pool which is then uniformly refunded to every citizen and company in Basel once a year. At the end of the year every individual receives 72 CHF in return and each company gets back half a percent of its overall payroll (a so called 'employment bonus'). This tax has the purpose of steering the current energy consumption: people who save electricity, pay less incentive tax, but get the same bonus in return. On the other hand, the electricity prices are slightly raised. Consequently, investments in efficient equipment and innovative technologies should pay off more quickly.

It has been proposed that such a bonus concept could be transferred to the mobility sector instead of establishing a pure road pricing system which would be less feasible from the political standpoint. The rationale behind it could be as follows: 10000-15000 km are granted for each person per year. If citizens need less, then they get a bonus refunded and if they need more, a fee per additional kilometer is levied. Such a mobility bonus could be a new paradigm to effectively organize the pricing for mobility without creating the impression that an additional tax is imposed.[87] Most of all it would rationalize the mobility decisions and would demonstrate that the infrastructure cannot be extended in a limitless way, particularly in such a small country as Switzerland. Under specific conditions such an approach would be also socially just and politically acceptable, as the example from the energy sector exemplifies.

Table 29 depicts the list of identified critical factors with regards to the dimension of Society.

Table 29: Critical Factors in Society dimension.

- Knowledge transfer and public relations, - Addressing Attitudes and providing clear visions and guiding principles (concepts), - Behavior offers, - Incentives for desirable behavioral actions, - Ensuring participation: establish a clear process for public involvement, - Confirmation of behavioral consequences,

[87] Social Mobility Bonus (Social Road Pricing): the expert statement is listed in appx. 9, no. 54.

- Target group orientation,
- Evaluation of the effects.

18.2.5 Politics

The fourth dimension of Transformative Literacy is *Politics*. This pillar seeks to develop a comprehensive understanding and picture of the institutional background and structures. With that it aims at transferring this knowledge in political and social transition processes to make them more effective. Institutions are rules and mechanisms that organize human interactions. It needs to be distinguished between informal and formal institutions, however. An important expression of formal institutions are laws. Therefore, politics holds a key role in shaping the social functions such as mobility and in ensuring the stability of the system regimes (Schneidewind 2013a).

The strategic goals of Basel such as accessibility, economic competitiveness, locational advantages and the basic needs of the society such as high quality of life and safety are to be balanced by the appropriate political and institutional processes. For that purpose, the politics is expected to anticipate these partly contradictory expectations and match them up in a consistent and coherent manner.[88] However, the view has been shared among some experts that mistrust is being perceived within the executive institutions of Basel with regard to such radical requirements as the City Initiative has brought up.[89] If the perception is shared that sustainability brings about radical change in the lifestyles a strong collective resistance might result as people tend to perceive changes as a risk for their wealth and possibly for their quality of life. This is believed to be a critical factor for the acceptance of any systemic changes and therefore might be a severe obstacle for the transition process toward sustainability.[90]

With respect to the mobility system in Basel political decision-making processes play a significant role in discussing, developing and promoting the concepts of sustainable mobility and including them into long-term strategic policy planning. Basel has recognized to avoid promoting only one specific mode of transport, such as car or public transport only. The mobility policy needs to give attention to specific strengths of each mode to transition to the paradigm of sustainable mobility in the long run.[91] [92] Hence, it can be noted that the city strives to achieve a multi-modal, future-oriented and networked urban

[88] Politics as a referee for different mobility needs: the expert statement is listed in appx. 9, no. 55.
[89] Mistrust in the institutions towards radical requirements of the society: the expert statement is listed in appx. 9, no. 56.
[90] Fear of changes and of possible disadvantages: expert statements are listed in appx. 9, no. 57 and 58.
[91] Utilizing the strengths of every mode of transport: the expert statement is listed in appx. 9, no. 59.
[92] Urban-friendly mobility: the expert statement is listed in appx. 9, no. 60.

mobility system by implementing targeted and coherent policies and measures both at local and regional levels. Several factors have been identified that are regarded as critical to achieving this goal.

Leadership and Governance (for managing complexity and stakeholders)

It is expected that emerging technological innovations, the need for further economic growth and the evolving cultural trends will considerably add to the complexity of the mobility system in the future. Therefore, policies may need to be designed with the proper flexibility in mind to allow for fast adaptations. Experimentation with novel policies may uncover new and interesting opportunities for attaining the strategic goals of both the economy and the society. As a matter of fact, the changes in the urban mobility system are likely to get more radical if compared to current practices, through innovations such as shared ownership, autonomous driving or mobility pricing. Therefore, strong and clear leadership will be needed by policy makers to anticipate and to response to the needs of the economy and the citizens. For example, the Stiig-Um concept has been a clear signal for regional partners that the strategic direction for urban mobility in Basel has changed. Even though some experts have argued that such a unilateral approach might be perceived as self-concerned, not partnership-oriented or even counterproductive[93], the message has been sent that there is an expectation for policy interventions also outside of the perimeter of the city.[94] As a matter of fact, this signal can be also understood as an invitation to a closer cooperation towards a common mobility strategy for the entire region in the near future.[95]

Establishing and promoting platforms for cooperation based on cross-border partnerships, such as Agglo Basel, are appropriate instruments for finding strong compromises through negotiations between the various actors. Instead of a fight for one's own particular interests there is a mutual fight with a common purpose. Such an approach could also address the issue of short-termism, i.e. the conflict of inherent long-term nature of climate challenge (particularly in transport) and short term nature of transport policymaking.[96]

Finances

Indeed, the regional economic power of Basel is a major advantage for promoting projects that improve accessibility and raise the efficiency of the transportation network. Not many cities worldwide can afford such infrastructural mega projects as Herzstück

[93] Unilateral approach of the administration of Basel: expert statements are listed in appx. 9, no. 61-63.
[94] No decision by politics is the worst that can happen: the expert statement is listed in appx. 9, no. 64.
[95] Invitation for closer cooperation: expert statements are listed in appx. 9, no. 65 and 66.
[96] Strategic cooperation on regional level: expert statements are listed in appx. 9, no. 67 and 68.

or the twin-tube bypass tunnel under the river in parallel, albeit with the support of federal funds. Therefore, it can be assumed that financing, which is generally regarded as a very critical barrier, is a critical enabler for Basel to promote and support the strategic transition towards the new mobility paradigm in the city. Nonetheless, the budgets are limited and an appropriate prioritization must take place. Therefore, cost-benefit considerations are always included in the decision-making process in the administration of Basel. Hence, the rule has been that only transportation projects with a benefit factor of an investment greater than 1 are provided with funds.[97] Another general rule is that foreign infrastructure should not be financed from municipal funds.[98]

A critical specification of the City of Basel is, however, its geographic localization and the mutual symbiosis with the entire region. Therefore, many projects go beyond the city and national borders. Some good projects with low benefit ratio for the city, can be of value for the entire region. The experts generally agree that good policy interventions, even those with cross-border character, must never be simply canceled.[99] It is instead recommended that in such cases the strongest partner shows clear and strong leadership. For example, in case of some beneficial cross-border mobility projects where the funding has not yet been completely secured, the City of Basel should take the responsibility for the missing funds as the strongest actor in the region. It is postulated that such behavior shows clear leadership. Otherwise good projects can simply get lost and the perception is created that the city's commitment to the ambitious goals for sustainable mobility in the region is in fact not that strong.

The opinion has been also shared that along with financial resources from the cantonal Parliament other financing models or fundraising approaches should be considered.[100] A good practice is, for example, the Commuter Fund. Furthermore, the financial resources are to be strictly controlled and third-party funds exploit by employing appropriate resource planning and prioritization instruments.[101] This requirement applies in particular to projects with cross-border character.

Other critical factors in Financing encompass:

- always justify the investments with resulting benefits,
- financing should always be a multi-stage quality check process,
- correct investment prioritization: identify projects that are likely to be supported by the majority,

[97] Include cost-benefit considerations: expert statements are listed in appx. 9, no. 69 and 70.
[98] Financing foreign infrastructure: the expert statement is listed in appx. 9, no. 71.
[99] Support for good cross-border projects: expert statements are listed in appx. 9, no. 72 and 73.
[100] Other financing models, e.g. earmarked funds from the tax at source: the expert statement is listed in appx. 9, no. 74.
[101] Financing through a multi-stage quality check process: the statement is listed in appx. 9, no. 75.

- secure public installment loans (from the cantonal Parliament) for good projects and consider joint financing where possible,
- avoid bargaining about money with cooperation partners.

Value Perspective

Another important aspect is developing the perspective of securing the value for the society. As mentioned above it is necessary that the societal value outperforms the costs. A clear statement of the value proposition for the society is the prerequisite for effective political persuasion and public acceptance.

An understanding also needs to be fostered for the difference between the subjective and objective utility. For example, even though a car is objectively an inefficient mean of urban transportation if compared with others, it still possesses a high subjective and emotional utility. To achieve the cultural change, first of all, the new generation must be addressed. This needs to happen by highlighting the subjective and functional utility of other modes of transport and pointing out the objective inefficiency of cars. Generally, the experts have agreed that the car must be de-emotionalized, otherwise people will still depend on the most inefficient transportation mode that currently exists in the urban space. This can happen, for example, by raising the price awareness and showing the true costs of mobility for the people. In the future, it might lead to the introduction of mobility pricing measures.

Ensuring Consistency

The experts have been arguing that, in order to reduce impacts of automobility, the municipal administration does not need to breach libertarian economic principles, nor must restrictive push policies necessarily lead to a degradation of capitalism and the economic growth of the city. Admittedly, it has been stated that ensuring good accessibility levels is the key success factor for sustaining high productivity levels and any loses in accessibility can have negative impact on the economy (see chapter 18.2.3). On the other side, also the postulate has been shared that the local coherence of the transport policy needs to be ensured at all policy levels and with all other mobility-related policies to achieve objectives which initially might be perceived as contradictory. Additionally, also regional coherence beyond the city and national borders is to be pursued. Such harmony in policy-making requires, however, extensive efforts especially from the administration of the City of Basel. Firstly, from the perspective of urban transport planning it needs an integrated view of all transport modes. Secondly, an integration between transport planning, spatial planning and urban planning is required. Thirdly, close cooperation with regional partners in terms of strategic land use and transport planning is a final necessary condition.[102] Preferably, adopted strategies should be implemented coherently everywhere.

The administration itself is also required to pull in the same direction. An important prerequisite for that is the political will. It can foster the desirable level of cooperation between the departments for new and innovative projects. Helpful instruments include:[103]

- developing a holistic vision and thinking about the way of co-working among colleagues from different teams,
- defining common strategies,
- bringing about cultural change within the administration and eliminating silos.

What seems to be also advantageous is the possibility to work and cooperate in functional networks, within the administration and beyond it. It helps to overcome formalized administrative silos and to flexibly cross the managerial hierarchies. An interesting example from the Basel case is the internal business model for developing mobility and infrastructures projects. This administration process encompasses four main pillars: define, design, build and run. This process defines clear accountabilities and seeks to integrate transport and land use planning.[104] The responsibilities are distributed as follows:

- define: Office of Mobility Strategy and Management,
- design: Planning Office,
- build: Municipal Works Service Basel,
- run: operator, organization or respective institution.

It needs to be noted, however, that the sub-steps of this process are not separated from each other. They are rather interwoven. The entire process is coordinated by a professional Coordination Commission, which involves representatives from all involved administrative bodies and outside actors. The goal is to ensure that decisions are not taken solitary but rather collectively. This approach also ensures finding a strong compromise and developing the identification with the goals of the undertaken projects by all partners. There is also another important aspect to that, which is believed to democratize this collaborative approach, i.e. budgeting. Any measure that goes beyond the threshold of 300'000 CHF needs an agreement by the Parliament and by the Executive Council. This process provides the political assurance that the undertaken measures are correct

[102] Three main conditions for policy coherence: the expert statement is listed in appx. 9, no. 76.
[103] Ensuring cooperation within the administration: expert statements are listed in appx. 9, no. 77-79.
[104] End-to-end administration process ("Business Model Infrastructure"): the expert statement is listed in appx. 9, no. 80.

and in line with the overall strategy. In that sense, budgeting is a powerful controlling instrument that the decisions are made in democratic way.[105]

Furthermore, in terms of promoting and supporting regional partnerships, establishing functioning cross-border structures and functional spaces with decision-making and budgeting authority is regarded as fundamental. A good example is for instance one central institution for managing the regional land use and transport development beyond the national borders, such as the Agglo Basel with its mid-term action programs.[106]

Table 30 depicts the list of identified critical factors with regards to the transformative literacy dimension of Politics.

Table 30: Critical Factors in Politics dimension.

- Recognize and manage stakeholders, - Establish organizational structures for promoting innovation, - Foster local collaborations, - Information and communication, - Conduct effective marketing for a sustainable transport policy, - Clear time and operational framework, - Ensure proper financing, - Monitoring, controlling and evaluation, - Ensuring participation of various stakeholders, - Package the policies in a purposeful manner and ensure consistency between them, - Clear demonstration of the benefits, - Gradual (step-by-step) implementation of controversial measures.

18.3 Summary of the Case Study - City of Basel

18.3.1 Recommendations from the Case Study

The case of City of Basel has revealed some important patterns regarding the general approach to overcoming car dependence in urban areas and implementing the paradigm of sustainable mobility. The mobility system of a city is always in interaction with other municipal systems. Thus, an isolated view of a single responsibility area without considering other related aspects quickly reaches its limits. Based on the outcomes of the

[105] Details of the "Business Model Infrastructure" in the administration: the expert statement is listed in appx. 9, no. 81.

[106] Create functional spaces for regional cooperation: expert statements are listed in appx. 9, no. 82 - 83.

case study the author derived ten recommendations for approaching and implementing the paradigm of sustainable mobility in urban areas (see

Table 31). In chapter 19 the author then proposes a general and integrative framework for sustainable urban mobility.

Table 31: Ten specific recommendations derived from the case study City of Basel.

No.	Recommendation	Description
1.	Establishment of an office for Strategic Management in Mobility.	Main tasks of the office encompass: - vision and mission definition, - development and alignment of clear objectives, - monitoring and measurement.
2.	Definition of clear long-term objectives	Definition of superordinate and long-term objectives, that are valid for the entire urban area: - reduction of the overall traffic volume conducted by car by xx% by 2030, - GHG reduction by xx% by 2030, - increasing energy efficiency by xx% by 2030, - reduction of primary energy consumption per inhabitant to xx%, - increase the amount of green spaces in the cityscape to xx%.
3.	Establishment of implementation plans	Development of appropriate implementation plans in: - mid-term (3-5 years) and - long-term (10 years).
4.	Local consistency	- Conduct open discussions with individual districts to achieve binding consensus about the required policies and measures to reach the overall targets. - Develop individual plans by municipality departments for the entire city and then derive local plans for each urban district. - Break silos between the departments by enabling cross-departmental cooperation by involving departments beyond transportation, such as: spatial development and land use (public space, parks, playgrounds, sports facilities), economy and culture, waste management and recycling, urban logistics (e.g. for retail).
5.	Regional cooperation	Strive for political alignment with all local bodies and with regional partners beyond the city borders.
6.	Public acceptance	- Conduct critical reviews by citizens of defined objectives by the city council and the administration throughout the entire legislative period.

No.	Recommen-dation	Description
		- Pave the way for enhanced public acceptance of the policies and measures by organizing official public consultation days about current mobility concerns.
7.	Monitoring and controlling	- Implement and execute consistent monitoring, controlling and communication of measures carried out in terms of their effectiveness. - Publish reports every two years with assessments of each intervention in terms of its effectiveness.
8.	Altering decisions in case of failure	- Accept the need for implementing countermeasures if undesirable developments occur. - Foster the courage to undo decisions if they do not provide the expected results and do not contribute to the overall goals.
9.	Recurring review process	- Conduct discussions regarding the overall goals every 3-5 years at both levels (i) canton/city and (ii) district. - If required, execute of a reassessment process and realignment of objectives on both levels by, for example, voting.
10.	Citizen participation	Strengthen citizen participation by involving them to an appropriate extent into the decision and design processes.

18.3.2 Final Conclusions

There is an observable rethinking in the society with regard to sustainable development and mobility. It takes a form of a cultural change and shift in behavioral routines and lifestyles. Especially in Basel, the citizens seem to be aware of the current environmental and social challenges. A clear manifestation of this attitude in the field of urban mobility is the City Initiative. The initiative has had a major influence on the strategic orientation of the mobility paradigm. The society, acting as a demand side, has taken a proactive role in exerting societal pressure on the politics to fulfill its basic needs such as high quality of life, security, residential attractiveness along with affordable mobility. However, there has been a range of economic factors which cannot be ignored. These factors include: economic competitiveness, locational advantages, impact of mobility on the market and accessibility.

The author has shown that there are numerous enablers and barriers in all four investigated domains of Transformative Literacy: technology, economy, society and politics. They range from recognizing ICT as an enabler for more efficiency, to superiority of accessibility over higher velocity, to understanding and facilitating new business models, to resistance and counter movements from lobby groups, to considering basic societal needs and possible rebound-effects, to managing behavioral changes, to leadership and governance, to obtaining value perspective and to ensuring consistency and integration in policy implementation. Detailed elaboration on these critical factors has exposed the non-triviality of sustainable mobility.

However, the case of Basel has also indicated that it is not impossible. The main challenge is the achievement of an appropriate balance between (i) strategic locational advantages of a city, such as accessibility, economic competitiveness or efficient sourcing of the workforce, and (ii) the basic needs of the society, such as high quality of life, safety, maintaining residential attractiveness or affordable mobility. Hence, the paradigm of sustainable mobility needs to integrate two dynamics: sustain economic growth and secure societal prosperity (see Figure 31).

For that purpose, the politics must anticipate contradictory expectations and match them up by ensuring policy consistency, i.e. coherent political and institutional alignment over time. With that in mind:

- the transition needs to foster strategic locational advantages of a city, such as accessibility, economic competitiveness or efficient sourcing of the workforce. This can take place by promoting system innovation through technology and testing new efficiency strategies through new business models,
- on the other hand, the transformation dynamics should lead to greater wealth and affluence of the society. The basic needs of the society encompass: high quality of life, traffic safety, maintaining residential attractiveness or affordable mobility. This needs to take place by means of coherent and consistent policy development on all policy levels including local and regional policy alignment.

Furthermore, finding the balance and coherence between the needs of the society and the desires of the economy is not solely the responsibility of institutions. The case study indicates that the citizens are not 'customers', that is, demand side, but also partners in the process of designing an efficient and city-friendly mobility system. This removes any perceptions of manipulations by industrial lobby groups, reduces the system complexity and provides reliable information about societal expectations. The participation is necessary for an efficient and effective process of decision-development and decision-making. Finally, a modern and progressive city proactively seeks for new and innovative approaches to organizing the mobility function in its urban area. The case of Basel indicates a 'best of breed' approach, that is: integrating different transport modes and personalizing mobility services while utilizing the advantages of all mobility options.

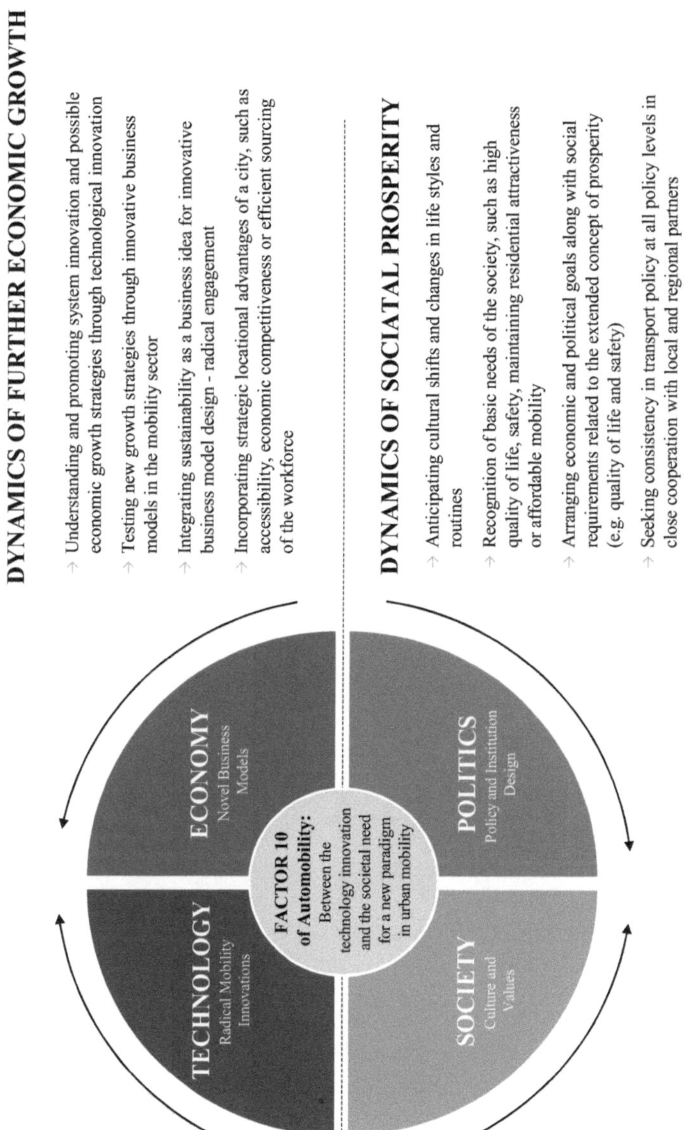

Figure 31: High-level results of the Transformative Literacy based on the case study City of Basel (Source: diagram by author).

The goal of this chapter has been to present the results of the qualitative analysis of the case study City of Basel. The framework of Transformative Literacy has assisted in clarifying how an innovative and sustainable urban mobility system is being considered and implemented by the stakeholders in Basel. The author has aimed at communicating the key aspects which were discussed during the expert interviews with those stakeholders. In particular, he has elaborated on the main enablers and obstacles that have influenced the sustainable mobility transformation in Basel. By doing so he has emphasized the aspects that might be of predominant relevance for the administration of City of Basel in the process of designing next steps on their way to achieving ambitious goals with regard to the reduction of the car traffic in the city.

19 Framework for Integrated Sustainable Urban Mobility

19.1 Towards an Integrated Framework of Sustainable Mobility

There seems to be little consensus in academia and practice about the precise nature of a more sustainable system of mobility in the urban context (Berger et al. 2014). Since sustainable mobility is a concept with interpretative flexibility a disagreement has arisen. It regards the fundamental question of whether the system of automobility can be transformed into a sustainable one or whether the reliance on cars needs to be reduced in the long run? The author of this work has been researching the strategies to reduce the overall number of cars on the roads in the urban context by the factor of ten to re-capture the invaluable city space. With this hypothesis, the author clearly opts for a radical shift in the prevailing dominance of cars in cities. On the other side, he understands that automobility is an important and indispensable element of every urban mobility system and economy, and hence, should be treated carefully and in a coherent way. Therefore, the author aims at developing an explanatory framework which will give an integrative understanding and guidance for policy-makers how to approach the car dependence in their cities without creating an attitude of declaring war against automobility. At this point, the author once again wants to firmly underline that dismantling car dependence does not mean banning the car completely from the cities, but rather raising the efficiency of available resources to gain both (i) more welfare for the residents and (ii) sustainable economic prosperity for the business.

The author proposes to transfer the well-established framework for corporate environmental management from environmental economics to propose a suitable framework for sustainable mobility in cities (Schaltegger et al. 2003; Fritz, Busch-Lüty 1995). In line with this concept, three distinct strategies for corporate sustainability management can be distinguished, i.e.: efficiency, sufficiency and consistency. The author has imported this framework in slightly modified form into the field of sustainable mobility. He assumes that there is a structural equivalence between the two areas of interest to allow the transferability of proven knowledge elements from a well-established research area into another one, which has been less well understood so far.

19.2 Framework Development

According to Berger et al. (2014) there are three well established approaches to achieving sustainable mobility: efficiency, alteration, and reduction. Following that logic, the automobility can become more sustainable along three lines:

- efficiency: people can travel more efficiently with their cars,

- alteration: they can travel differently than by car, and
- reduction: they can travel less by car.

With respect to that following considerations hold also true: the efficiency strategy assumes further car usage, whereas alteration and reduction strategies assume no car usage. For example, both (i) taking a bus instead of a car (modal shift, i.e. alteration of mobility) and (ii) videoconferencing (i.e. reduction of mobility), reduce the car usage.

Hence, the author proposes following two concepts for sustainable automobility:

1) Efficiency: people travel more efficiently with their cars.

2) Sufficiency: people travel less with their cars.

In the following two sections both concepts will be discussed in more detail. The third overarching element of the framework, the consistency in mobility, will be introduced afterwards.

19.2.1 The Concept of Efficiency in Mobility

The efficiency strategy refers to the considerations of input-output-relation. There are two efficiency principles to consider (Töpfer 2007):

1) Minimum principle: reach a given fixed target (output) with as few as possible resources (input), i.e. is it possible to cover the existing mobility needs by a decreased number of cars?

2) Maximum principle: achieve the maximum benefit (output) with given fixed resources (input), i.e. is it possible to cover more mobility needs with the same number of cars?

Applying these efficiency considerations to the case of automobility (remark: energy efficiency of cars is excluded and not considered here) the maximum principle would mean to achieve as much mobility as possible (for example in passenger-kilometers) with the available number of cars. However, the motivation for this study is to introduce interventions in automobility that would correspond with the minimum principle. Hence, the goal is to cover the existing mobility demand with as few cars as possible.

As discussed in previous chapters this can be achieved by implementing two main strategies for raising the productivity of automobiles:

- increasing the number of journeys per car by organizing time synchronized usage of cars, i.e. carsharing, and/or
- increasing the car occupancy level, i.e. ridesharing.

19.2.2 The Concept of Sufficiency in Mobility

The sufficiency approach assumes that more efficient technologies for raising the productivity of available cars will not be sufficient to meet the sustainability targets, such as a radical reduction of the number of cars. Therefore, additional efforts should be made to reduce unnecessary travel (e.g. through telecommuting) or to shift the indispensable mobility to other modes of transport (e.g. public transport or slow modes). The corresponding alteration of behavior and mobility patterns would aim at reducing the total number of journeys or the volume of traffic expressed in passenger-kilometers caused by private car usage. This would result in reduction of the overall travel demand, i.e. sufficiency in mobility, by two possible approaches: alteration and reduction.

Alteration (Modal Shift)

The alteration approach attempts to change existing transport patterns. Accordingly, the prevailing car transport patterns are to be shifted towards more collective forms of transport, such as a well-functioning public transportation system. This would lead to a substitution of cars with increased usage of buses, trains, and trams. Taking current occupancy rates into consideration all of these are more energy efficient than cars, at least in the urban context. An affordable and well-integrated public transport system would increase accessibility for low-mobility groups (Berger et al. 2014). The alteration approach also comprises the idea of increasing the share of slow modes, i.e. substituting individualized motorized travel with walking and cycling.

Reduction (Mobility Prevention)

Current policy patterns concentrate on improving the efficiencies of transport modes and the support of modal shift. However, the interventions lead rather to a relative alteration, instead of an absolute shift among modes (Berger et al. 2014). The reduction approach, i.e. the abstinence from mobility, seems to be of minor importance as it conflicts with the traditional logic of transport policy – an ever-increasing mobility demand.

This approach requires the adjustment of the mobility needs of the society. People would need to rethink their purposes for travel and decide whether some of their daily journeys are necessary. For example, office employees could stay and conduct their work at home by using the advantages of virtual connectivity at their homes. Obviously, it leads to the prevention of unnecessary car travel to the office, i.e. commuting. Many companies nowadays allow home-office work to their employees at least once a week. Such practices can be encouraged further by dedicated corporate mobility management policies. Another example is ordering groceries at local supermarkets and not at cash-and-carry supermarkets in the outskirt areas of cities which implies car usage. Another case is virtual ordering via Internet which eliminates an unnecessary car journey. A case in point is Coop, a Swiss retail and wholesale conglomerate, which offers an online shopping service - 'coop@home'. The delivery service is conducted on the same day after ordering (coop@home 2016). Coop offers also a delivery option for office employees who can place their orders until midday and collect their groceries at 5 p.m. before leaving the office.

However, this approach has gained little political traction since policy-makers are reluctant to direct interventions into people's lifestyles (Berger et al. 2014). The necessity of travel is established within the context of culturally embedded social practices, for example, social expectations about physical presence at the work place or for social occasions (Nijhuis 2013). Furthermore, it is also difficult to implement, as it requires a comprehensive tool box and rebound effects may occur (Maxwell et al. 2011; Sorrell 2007). The rebound effects are associated with the 'consistency of mobility time budget', i.e. if travelers save time from their daily mobility time budget they will spend it for other purposes, such as mobility to reach leisure activities.

Sufficient Accessibility (Mobility Security)

Over the past decade, there has been an increasing interest in the evaluation of transport policies and investments from the perspective of accessibility. The shift away from mobility towards accessibility as the prime performance indicator has been based on the argument that the goal of the transport network is ultimately to provide travelers with access to their desired destinations. Traditional mobility-centered performance indicators, such as the level-of-service, have described important qualities of the transport network, but have not provided sufficient insights into what is important for the users. Hence, the accessibility paradigm has gained in importance. The use of accessibility as a performance indicator captures both aspects: the performance of the underlying transport system and the land use pattern in a specific area. Low accessibility levels in a particular neighborhood may be as much the result of a poorly performing transport system, as of a low density of desirable destinations. Therefore, accessibility is now considered by many as performance criterion to assess the current state of the mobility system (Martens 2013).

If the accessibility is at an inappropriate level, residents belonging to such areas are likely to experience 'accessibility poverty'. As a result they face severe problems in accessing destinations and experience structural mobility-related social exclusion. According to Golub and Martens (2014) fairness of mobility requires sufficient but not necessarily equal accessibility levels. With that in mind, fairness would imply lower accessibility and less choice for people with low income and vice versa. In line with the accessibility-centered approach, the ultimate goal of transportation planning is and should be the provision of sufficient accessibility, so people can reach destinations and participate in out-of-home activities.

19.2.3 The Concept of Consistency in Mobility

For a real transition to sustainable mobility in the urban context all strategies need to be integrated and coordinated with each other. This integration must take place within the sociopolitical environment, as the case study of the City of Basel indicates. The interplay between politics and society has to ensure that efficiency and sufficiency policies lead to greater wealth of city residents, on the one hand, and do not neglect the important economic and locational factors of a city, on the other hand. For that purpose, the mobility system needs to be managed and coordinated in a coherent and harmonized manner. The author proposes a concept of 'consistency in mobility', however, not in the sense of 'eco-consistency'.

The author has developed an adequate working definition for the concept of consistency in mobility. For that he has used a transdisciplinary approach, that is, crossing the boundaries of different disciplines to provide multiple perspectives on the research issue. The researcher has utilized the notion of consistency from the area of 'gestalt psychology' and the related consistency theories. The author understands that this field refers to human psychology and explores the human mind as a perceptual system. However, this transdisciplinary attempt should be perceived strictly on a level of an analogy, which will help to shape and provide a proper definition of consistency and yet may give useful insight to the field of sustainable mobility.

19.2.3.1 Background

Gestalt Psychology and Holism

The research field, which is also referred to as 'gestaltism', aims at understanding the laws of people's ability to acquire and maintain meaningful perceptions in an apparently chaotic world. The gestalt effect is the capability of the brain to generate whole forms with self-organizing tendencies. This principle says that when the human mind (a perceptual system) forms a percept (or gestalt), the whole has a reality of its own, independent of its parts (Koffka 2013). A simple example is the visual recognition of global figures instead of just collections of simpler and unrelated elements such as points or lines. This view can be further extended by the idea of holism, which asserts that all systems (physical, biological, chemical, social, economic, mental, linguistic, etc.) and their properties should be viewed as wholes, and not as collections of parts (Oshry

2007). This often includes the view that systems function as wholes and that their functioning cannot be fully understood only in terms of their single components (Auyang 1999). With respect to that, the famous phrase of gestalt psychologist Kurt Koffka says: "The whole is other than the sum of the parts" (Hothersall 2004).

Consistency Theories

Within the field of gestalt psychology several consistency theories have been developed. These theories deal with aspects of compatibility and harmony which are sought for the development of a coherent, cohesive and self-contained whole. In the particular case of Gestalt psychology the theories refer to humans' mental activities and to the claim that the organism strives for compliance between concurrent neuronal and mental processes. The ultimate goal of the organism is the target state of consistency, that is, a harmonious and coherent state without contradictions (Grawe 2007). According to the Consistency Theory by Grawe (2007) the following assumptions regarding consistency can be made:

- during interactions with the environment motivational schemas are formed with the aim of meeting basic needs,
- if the activated motivational objectives are not met, a mismatch occurs, i.e. incongruence,
- if motivational schemas are activated simultaneously and they hinder each other a motivational conflict occurs, i.e. discordance,
- consistency is achieved if the basic needs are balanced, and the motivational goals are achieved,
- the higher the level of consistency is, the healthier the organism becomes.

According to Grawe (2007) consistency is a concept that expresses the compatibility between motivational goals and actual perceptions of reality. In other words, the way we perceive our interaction with the environment will have a certain correlation with our motivational goals (what we want so as to satisfy our basic needs), and the degree of agreement is the degree of compatibility. Incongruence signals come from the feedback mechanism that contrasts our perceptions with our goals. The diagram below shows this feedback mechanism where the loop between 'Experiences and Behavior' connects to 'Motivational Schemas' (Dahlitz 2013). These feedback loops depict also the self-regulatory processes of the organism.

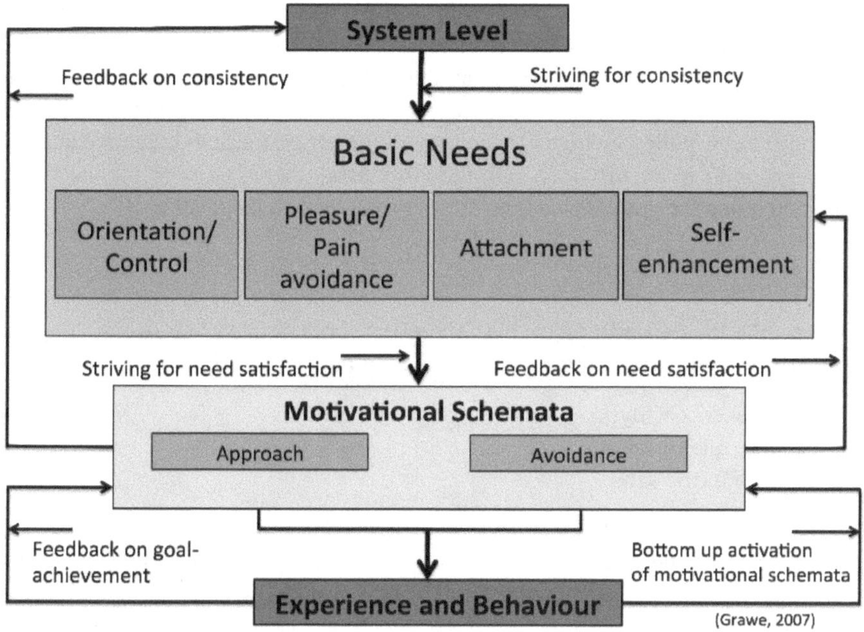

Figure 32: Consistency-theoretical Model.
(Source: Dahlitz 2015; adapted from Grawe 2007, p. 171).[107]

19.2.3.2 Developing of Consistency in Mobility

The author proposes the usage of the 'consistency-theoretical model', described above, as a mental model for developing the concept of consistency in urban mobility. The author will refer to the findings of the case study of the City of Basel, presented in chapter 17, to operationalize it with regard to sustainable mobility. The following guiding principles are proposed to describe the concept of consistency:

Urban System Level

The urban system is a whole that strives to avoid inconsistency and develops various mechanisms to move from a dissonant and inconsistent state to a more harmonious state.

[107] Courtesy of Taylor and Francis Group LLC Books.

The urban and regional mobility is one part of this system which needs to be brought in coherence with other sectors of the urban organism (land use planning, social services, health, energy, education, enforcement and policing etc.). For that purpose horizontal and vertical policy alignment and cooperation are needed. On the one hand, this alignment requires new policy linkages and joint working across local and regional authority departments and service providers. On the other hand, there is a need for the vertical cooperation along the governance lines from the national to the local level.

Basic Urban Needs

With respect to the transport sector the City of Basel has defined four overarching strategic goals for the forward-looking urban transport policy:

- secure accessibility,
- increase quality of life,
- enhance traffic safety,
- ensure cost-effectiveness.

Numerous conflicts between these basic needs arise. They occur because urban space and the municipal budget are limited. There are differentiating demands and objectives of the road users, on the one side, and the residents, employees or recreational visitors on the other side. In addition, there are different implications of various modes of transport on aspects such as: space demand, emissions or speeds. Following main trade-offs between the four transport policy objectives arise:

- accessibility versus quality of life,
- traffic safety versus quality of life and accessibility,
- cost-effectiveness versus accessibility and quality of life.

By drawing an analogy to Grawe (2007, p. 170), consistency in mobility can be described as the compatibility of many simultaneously transpiring goals. When the relationship between these objectives is harmonious, there is a state of consistency. The urban system strives to avoid inconsistency and develops various mechanisms to move from a dissonant, inconsistent state to a more harmonious state.

Motivational Mobility Schemas

In the consistency-theoretical model motivational schemas are the interventions or actions to satisfy and protect basic needs (Dahlitz 2013; Grawe 2007). The case of Basel showcases, how the motivational schemas can be established in the context of sustainable mobility.

In order to achieve the basic needs, as discussed above, the Office of Mobility of the City of Basel has established a vision and mission statements for the future development of the urban mobility system. The vision states the trade-off between the main urban needs in the context of mobility and defines the motivational objective, i.e. (Stalder 2011, p. 3): "bring urban and regional mobility in coherence with the urban residential quality and the locational advantage of the economy". The mission statement, on the other hand, states how to satisfy and protect these basic needs, i.e. (Stalder 2011, p. 2): "optimize the entire transport system, promote urban and environmentally sound mobility, ensure the locational accessibility of Basel, and support an efficient and reliable operations of the cantonal transport infrastructure".

To address and ensure the achievement of the motivational objective (i.e. the vision), motivational schemas have been defined. They have been expressed in the form of strategic priorities and the strategic action plan. Strategic priorities encompass: road traffic, parking space, walking and cycling, public transport, freight transport, public space, and mobility management. The strategic action plan includes over 30 specific transport policies and measures.

Furthermore, an additional motivational schema is the requirement for ensuring territorial coordination and integration on the level of neighborhoods, metropolitan area (i.e. agglomeration), regional (i.e. neighboring cantons) and national level (i.e. including Germany and France). This form of coordination and integration takes place through political alignment, spatial and transportation policy alignment, and regional alignment. In the case of Basel this is being achieved through the Agglomeration Program Basel (Agglo Basel).

It is important to note that the motivational schemas must be quantifiable and also measurable. This is an essential prerequisite for the establishment of the feedback mechanism. Such an example of a quantifiable motivational schema in Basel is the formal statement that the total volume of the individual motorized traffic must decrease by at least 10% until 2020 (compared to 2010) within the entire city area.

Experience and Feedback Loops

Experience is a construct that expresses the perception process of congruence (compatibility) between the motivational goals and the actual achievement in reality. The degree of agreement, is the degree of congruence. The degree of congruence is derived from the feedback mechanism which is established between Experience and Motivational Schemas (Grawe 2007; Dahlitz 2013).

In the case of Basel, the experience processes and feedback loops have been established through appropriate monitoring and controlling mechanisms. The assessments are carried out for the following key performance indicators (KPI): volume of motorized individual road traffic (expressed in relative change as compared to 2010), accessibility (expressed in accessibility index), quality of life (expressed in grade point average from the population survey), and traffic safety (expressed in annual development of traffic accidents). These KPIs activate different feedback loops:

- the KPI 'volume of motorized individual road traffic' activates the 'feedback on strategic goal achievement', whereas
- remaining KPIs activate the 'feedback on basic need achievement'. However, global indicators for cost effectiveness have not yet been available.

The 'feedback on consistency' is activated through the congruence, which expresses the compatibility between motivational goals and actual experience of the reality, i.e. whether the basic urban needs are satisfied and protected in a sustainable way.

19.2.3.3 The Concept of Consistency in Sustainable Mobility

So how can congruence and consistency be achieved in the context of sustainable urban mobility? The motivational schemas are activated in the form of policy interventions to satisfy and protect the basic urban needs. The key is to understand how motivational schemas influence the mobility behavior of urban residents.

If a specific urban area has become car dominant over the years (e.g. through suburban development), then car-oriented schemas for the mobility system are likely to develop and societal behavior is generally car-orientated. In contrast, a city which is aware of the negative externalities of cars and has a basic need for high quality of life is more likely to develop such motivational schemas that promote sustainable mobility alternatives. Essentially, the basic urban needs may depend on both:

- the expectations of the society and the economy with regards to the organization of urban environment and
- the politics' perception of these societal and economic expectations.

Depending on the basic urban needs, appropriate policy schemas can be activated by the politics. The consistency is reached if a certain degree of congruence is achieved, that is, there is compatibility between many objectives that are pursued simultaneously.

For example, in the case of Basel the city administration strives for sustainable mobility by radically reducing the volume of motorized individual traffic on the urban road network. This has been forced by the society through the civic initiative, the City Initiative. The congruence condition is achieved only if the reduction of the road traffic volume will happen, while simultaneously the basic urban needs are secured, i.e.: quality of life, traffic safety and cost-effectiveness. This ambitious strategic goal, however, can have a negative impact on the basic need of securing accessibility, which in turn might have a severe negative impact on the economy. In this case incongruence is experienced which leads to inconsistency in the system. Hence, appropriate intervening policies need to be activated which support the avoidance of the inconsistency.

Another aspect of inconsistency is discordance. Discordance occurs when two or more motivational schemas (intervening policies) are activated at the same time and are incompatible with each another. Taking the example of the City of Basel, discordance would occur if for achieving the intended reduction in road traffic two incompatible motivational schemas would be implemented simultaneously, for example: limiting supply of public parking space, on the one hand, and expanding the urban road network, on the other. This would lead to inconsistency in transport policy as limiting the parking space usually reduces the traffic volume, while expanding the road capacity is likely to lead to more traffic.

Incongruence and discordance, and the impact that transpires along with them, can happen implicitly or explicitly and cause inconsistency in the system. Taken to extremes, such inconsistency can impair the achievement of basic urban needs and lead to increasingly negative tendencies, such as economic downturn or urban sprawl.

Figure 33 depicts the author's concept of Consistency in Sustainable Mobility which is based on the consistency-theoretical model of Grawe (2007) and the findings of the case study of the City of Basel.

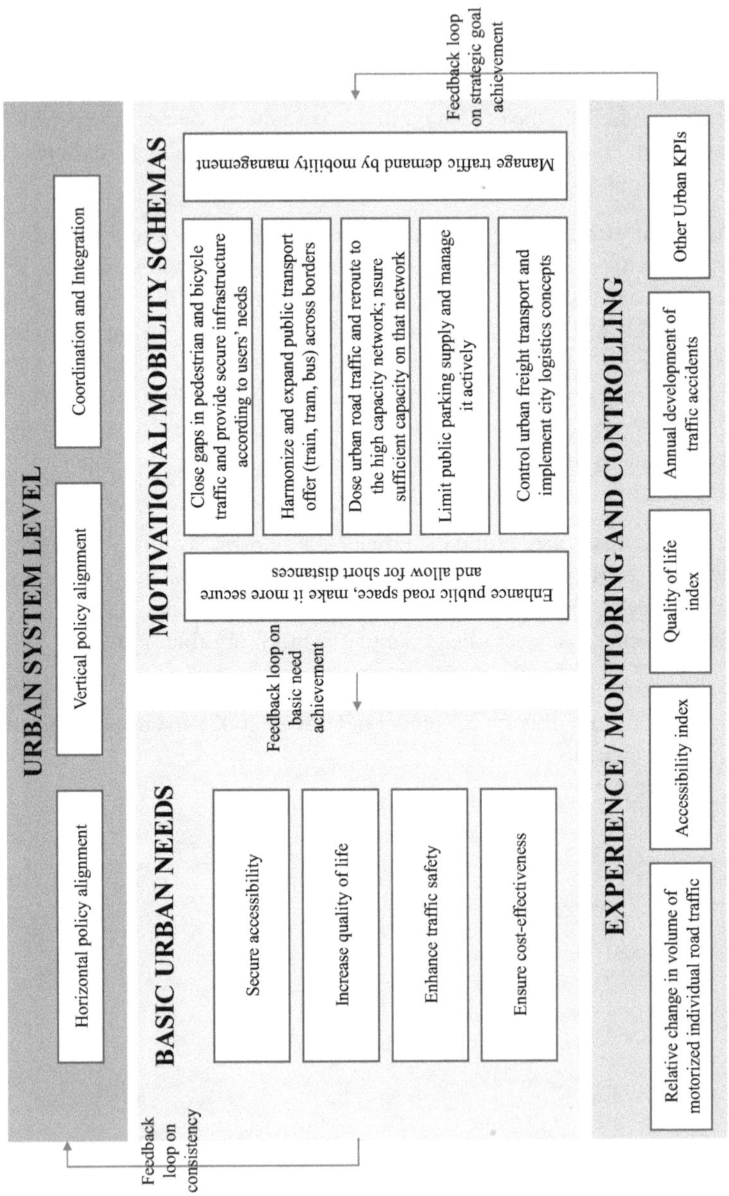

Figure 33: The concept of Consistency in Sustainable Mobility. (Source: diagram by author).

19.3 Framework for Integrated Sustainable Urban Mobility

In this chapter the author has described three concepts for understanding and establishing sustainable mobility: efficiency, sufficiency and consistency. He proposes an overarching framework by integrating these three pillars. The framework aims at giving clear guidance for policy-makers who need to deal with the diversity of approaches for overcoming the auto-dependence in their urban context. Figure 34 depicts following elements of the framework:

Efficiency

In the context of automobility the efficiency strategy means to radically increase the productivity of cars. In other words, it implicates that people travel more efficiently with their cars. Two distinct approaches apply: the cars are used more frequently and the available space in the cars is used more rationally. The following tactics are possible to operationalize the concept of efficiency:

- increase the number of rides per car, i.e. carsharing,
- increase the occupancy rate, i.e. ridesharing,
- combine carsharing with ridesharing.

Sufficiency

Sufficiency in the context of automobility aims at achieving an absolute (not only relative) reduction of the overall travel made by cars. Sufficiency can manifest itself in three approaches. The alteration approach attempts to change existing transport patterns to more collective forms of transport, namely an affordable and well-functioning public transport system (modal shift). The prevention of automobility assumes a reduction of unnecessary travel in favor of other mobility options, such as virtual mobility. In a more radical way it can take the form of the abstinence from automobility, which would imply a change in personal lifestyles (e.g. car-freedom). Overcoming accessibility poverty by ensuring sufficient accessibility is the last approach to sufficiency. The following tactics are possible to operationalize the concept of sufficiency:

- increase the relative modal shift, i.e. away from car to public transport and slow modes,
- reduce the overall car traffic volume, i.e. the passenger-kilometers conducted by cars,
- provide sufficient, not necessary equal, accessibility levels.

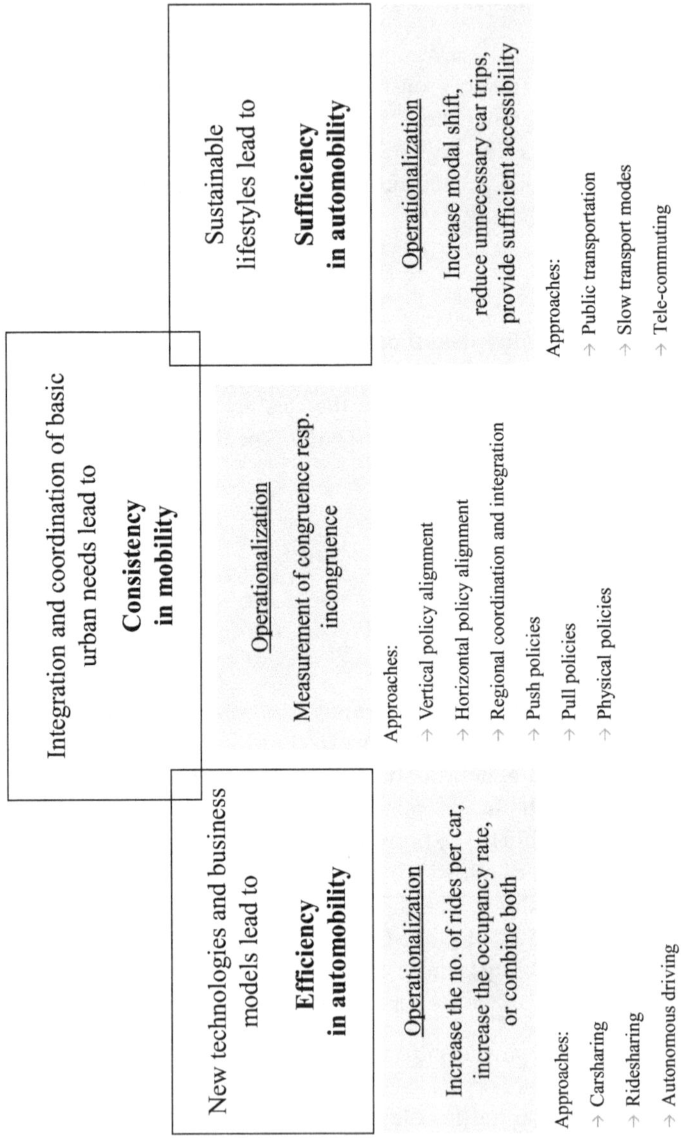

Figure 34: An integrative Framework of Sustainable Urban Mobility. (Source: diagram by author).

Another approach to achieving sufficiency in mobility would be the reduction of the drive ranges by:

- reduction of traffic speeds,
- conscious choice of destinations, e.g. choosing local shopping centers, which might be slightly more expensive, rather than cheaper ones which are far more distant,
- compact development, by establishing more destinations in the immediate proximity of residential areas.

Consistency

The term consistency in mobility means to achieve compatibility and congruence between the basic urban needs, e.g. between local quality of life and economic locational advantages, and to maintain it over a longer period of time in a consistent and sustainable way. Fundamental to consistency is a clear definition of basic urban needs and establishing specific and measurable KPIs. The performance indicators aim at monitoring and controlling the congruence or incongruence of the needs in the context of the entire urban system as a whole. There are several approaches to achieve consistency in mobility:

- defining coherent push, pull and physical interventions,
- ensuring vertical and horizontal policy alignment,
- pursuing regional coordination and integration of policies.

19.4 Summary

Based on the acquired pool of knowledge the researcher has proposed the framework of Integrated Sustainable Urban Mobility which incorporates three main concepts: mobility efficiency, mobility sufficiency and mobility consistency. The framework offers a holistic understanding of the main pillars of sustainable mobility and a tool set for developing practical strategies for overcoming auto dependence in urban areas. The author has provided guiding principles for policy-makers who need to deal with both (i) the diversity of approaches to sustainable mobility, and (ii) with a coherent integration of these approaches into the long-term policy planning in their urban contexts.

The author has contributed to the existing body of knowledge predominantly by developing the concept of 'consistency in mobility'. Admittedly, coordinated policy packaging has been recognized as an important prerequisite for shifting towards sustainable mobility paradigm, however, it has not been yet conceptualized in such an integrated way. The author has defined the following systemic elements of mobility consistency:

the urban system level, basic urban mobility needs, motivational mobility schemas, and experience and feedback loops.

Consistency is reached, if no major contradictions exist between the many objectives that are simultaneously pursued by a city and if compatibility of policy interventions can be ensured. As indicators for the consistency in mobility the researcher has proposed to apply incongruence and discordance.

The developed body of knowledge contributes to a holistic understanding of the idea of sustainable mobility in modern cities and how the transition can be tackled. It shall assist and support mobility specialists and policy-makers in setting up own strategies for their transformation path towards the paradigm of sustainable mobility in their urban context. The City of Basel describes a real case how such a transition can be designed and executed in a consistent way.

PART V
Conclusions and Further Research

20 Summary of the Dissertation

The main goal of this dissertation has been to uncover the efficiency potentials with regard to automobility in the urban context. To establish a solid foundation for his further investigations along his research interests the author has shown in Part 1 that, given the available technology and innovative mobility concepts, the *factor 10 of automobility* is definitely possible. Motivated by this result the author has undertaken the challenge to develop a deep understanding about current inefficiencies in urban mobility in terms of car usage and possible scenarios for transitioning towards a paradigm that could effectively eliminate them. He has applied the framework of Transformative Literacy in order to structure his research and to acquire the knowledge about the business-techno-institutional co-evolution as well as transformative dynamics in the currently dominant mobility system. The framework encompasses following dimensions: technology, business models, politics and the socio-political interplay.

In Part II he has focused on developing the required body of knowledge about the current state of research and developments in mobility technologies, innovative mobility concepts, and diffusion strategies in the form of possible business models. The main research interest encompassed digital technologies and technological platforms for shared automobility services as well as organizational and managerial concepts that make it possible to commercialize and offer these services to end users. Furthermore, in Part II the researcher has also developed a general theoretical approach for evaluating, assessing and developing business models – the P4C Business Model Framework. By means of this approach he has analyzed two case studies of commercial endeavors that provide innovative mobility services to the society. He has also given further insights by analyzing potential innovations for future mobility services based on autonomous cars.

Following that in Part III the author has concentrated on the aspect of the required institutional shift. For that purpose, he synthetized the current state of knowledge about the range of possible policies for overcoming the car dependence in urban areas. Moreover, he has pointed out the necessity for policy integration and combination, and he has introduced the concept of policy consistency. Finally, in Part IV the researcher has presented the case study of the City of Basel. The author has illustrated a possible transition path towards the paradigm of sustainable mobility based on a careful investigation of the past approach and the most recent innovations in the agglomeration's transport policy. Based on a numerous expert interviews he has developed and elaborated on a mental map of possible technological, institutional, cultural and economic critical success factors and barriers to overcoming auto dependence in urban areas. The author has concluded with the framework of Integrated Sustainable Urban Mobility which features three main concepts: (technological) efficiency, (behavioral) sufficiency and (political) consistency. With that the author has developed a holistic and integrative body of knowledge for experts who seek to facilitate a transition towards a sustainable mobility paradigm in the future.

Applying the concept of Factor 10 to the context of automobility has offered a new perspective on the current shortcomings of urban mobility systems which still tend to operate in the increasingly outdated paradigm of car orientation. Most of all, it has helped to precisely diagnose the inefficiencies associated with privately owned cars and their ineffective usage patterns today. Furthermore, structuring the research along the main dimensions of the Transformative Literacy has proven valuable as it regards understanding complex transformation dynamics which are currently observable in the mobility sector. As such it has constituted a useful heuristic analysis instrument that has covered important aspects from the domains of: technology, economy, society and institutions. With that it has aimed at eliminating the disparity of the technology-bias, which has been often experienced in other discussions about important paradigm shifts. It has helped to derive recommendations and actions to support and promote desirable transition processes towards the paradigm of sustainable mobility in modern cities.

In the following section the author will critically review his work and will summarize the most important findings of his research efforts. To conclude the work, he will indicate areas for further research.

21 Conclusions

Applying the concept of Factor 10 to the context of automobility offers a new perspective on the current shortcomings of urban mobility systems which still tend to operate in the increasingly outdated paradigm of car dependence. Most of all, it helps to precisely diagnose the inefficiencies associated with privately owned cars and their ineffective usage. It sheds light on their underutilization in terms of (i) the service provision as an average car remains parked for 90-95% every day, and (ii) the occupancy rate as it often carries only one passenger. It becomes clear that under these circumstances such a high-valued investment good, as a privately owned car is, is for all rational purposes a complete waste of available resources. Moreover, further negative impacts occur such as the irrational use of available space in cities for infrastructure extensions and extensive parking supply, which leads to increasingly unattractive land-use patterns in cities. Thus, investigating thought-provoking opportunities for a radical reduction of the number of cars in cities has been justified.

The mobility concepts of carsharing and ridesharing, which have been revitalized in recent years by means of adopting innovative digital and platform technologies, bear a potential for overcoming this inefficiency clinch. By applying a simplified calculation scheme the author has illustrated how the efficiency mechanisms behind these concepts work. Using real data from Switzerland he has shown considerable efficiency reservoirs for two traffic sectors: leisure and work travel. The findings have indicated that for the leisure sector a hypothetical *factor 10 of automobility* would be indeed attainable, whereas for work traffic a factor of 4,5 would be realistic. For that to happen, however, a fulfillment of two conditions is required: (i) the cars will need to be shared in a timely synchronized way to allow more parties to use them much more frequently than today, and (ii) the freely available seats in the cars will need to be utilized at higher occupancy rates, meaning that travelers have to accept shared rides. By doing so the author has shown that under certain circumstances the reduction of the total number of cars would be possible without the need to cut back on the mobility needs of people.

A plethora of limitations have been raised, however, which clearly restrict the achievement of such efficiency goals as factor 10. Most of all, a mobility system based on patterns of carsharing and ridesharing would need to be fully flexible and highly convenient. Hence, it would require that a car can be easily relocated between the users to provide mobility services on-demand, that is, without previous preparations, reservations or the need to pick it up. Today's solutions, such as advanced free-floating carsharing schemes, do not offer these advantages in the required scale. These considerations have led the researcher to the conclusion that the required flexibility and convenience could be only attained by a mobility system which works in a fully autonomous way, i.e. without a human driver and manual interactions.

Therefore, the technology of autonomous vehicles has gained the researcher's attention with regard to the factor 10 investigation. The prospect of applying autonomous driving for future mobility systems has been appearing increasingly in the most recent academic and applied-research discussions as well as in the conducted expert interviews. Mobility systems that are partially or solely based on autonomous vehicles could considerably reorganize the current mobility paradigm. The literature indicates that the convergence of shared mobility patterns with the autonomous technology could lead to fundamentally different forms of urban mobility based on highly intelligent mobility services. In other words, a fleet of shared autonomous vehicles (SAV) can enable an efficient and convenient carsharing scheme along with dynamic ridesharing. In such a setting a single SAV is expected to serve many trips for many travelers during a day. The high transformative capacity of such a transport solution is justified by its impact on car utilization and the consumption of space for parking purposes. The efficiency implications are radical. The simulations studied by the author have shown a clear tendency that over 90% of privately owned cars can be successfully removed from streets of urban areas. The actual size of the fleet of SAV, however, would depend on the trip demand, the system configuration, the assignment scheme of cars and the quality of the service provided to customers. All studies have also implied that self-driving fleets would contribute to the significant elimination of the need for on-street and off-street parking and hence would free up substantial amounts of space in a city. Under such circumstances and conditions the paradigm of car ownership would become almost obsolete. Combined with an appropriate powertrain technology and energy supply this would be a quantum leap in shifting the system towards the paradigm of sustainable mobility. With these findings at hand author's calculation efforts for Switzerland have become credible and the underlying radical hypothesis of *factor 10 of automobility* even more realistic.

Even though the autonomous technology and mobility concepts for sharing cars are promising new approaches to relevant challenges in urban mobility such as overcoming car dependence, it is pretty obvious that a reorganization of such a scale will require time, especially for the further development, adoption and diffusion of the technology. Advancements will be required on all levels of the mobility system, which in the author's understanding encompass the areas of: Automobile Innovation, Mobility Services, Mobility Infrastructure and Mobility Information. Innovative activities and applications can be observed in all these fields. One of the most prominent examples are the Intelligent Transportation Systems (ITS). Such systems encompass services for traffic management to enable various users to be better informed and make safer, more coordinated, and smarter (i.e. more efficient) use of transport networks. Hence, ITS aims at optimizing the usage of existing infrastructure.

However, in the context of this work the most important innovations are localized in the cluster of Mobility Services. They include the new wave of carsharing and ridesharing which is based on the introduction and wide adoption of digital technologies. Digital technologies are clusters of interrelated information and communication technology systems and applications. They extend far beyond the boundaries of the digital industry they have established. Such surges of change eventually transform the rest of the economy, elevate the expected level of productivity across the board and open new innovation trajectories also in mature industries. As such digital technologies merit the term of technological revolution.

In fact, ubiquitous digitalization in recent years has stimulated innovation processes which have touched upon almost every single sphere of human life. Recently, one further domain has been affected – the system of automobility. This can be justified by the emergence of niche players who aim at disrupting the existing market by providing digital services in mobility. A case in point is smexx (innovation in smart car access and keyless carsharing), Car2Go (innovation in free-floating on-demand carsharing), TwoGo by SAP (innovation in dynamic ridesharing) or UBER (a total market disruption in the taxi sector). These cases demonstrate that important adjustments are currently happening in the prevailing automobility paradigm. The author has referred to them as digitally enabled Shared Automobility Services.

This is in line with the theory of system innovation which states that at times when new technologies are emerging one can often observe new Schumpeterian companies trying to explore and commercialize them. They join the market which performs as a system of rewards and punishments, thus checking and selecting amongst different technological alternatives. What is important, however, is that these early adopters do not develop the technology themselves, but they generate added value for the consumers by means of creative applications. The notion of value is important as it denotes that an offering must satisfy customers' needs, that is, generate value. It is thought that pairing innovative technology offerings with a corresponding commercialization approaches is a prerequisite for the scaling of groundbreaking technology. Therefore, innovative companies are expected to create, deliver and capture value for the end-users. The recent management literature refers to value adding processes as business models. In order to build purposeful and economically feasible applications another research field has been coined, that of business model innovation.

During the research special attention has been paid to these phenomena in the urban mobility sector. The understanding about business models in carsharing and ridesharing has been developed by synthetizing the literature review and analyzing case studies. The literature review has revealed that there are numerous approaches to carsharing and ridesharing which seem to be dependent on the kind of value they provide to customers. Therefore, the investigation of case studies has been conducted in the context of the value which is generated by incorporating digital technologies into these concepts. For that purpose two innovative niche actors, who have emerged in these novel mobility market in recent years, have been thoroughly investigated: smexx and TwoGo by SAP.

Both case studies have indicated that the know-how about and the application of digital technologies have been crucial assets to setting up their businesses. More specifically, both business endeavors have developed dedicated digital platforms, web pages, mobile apps and innovative services. In this vein, they aim at directly linking multiple buyers and sellers. Hence, they act as intermediaries who bring together the demand and the supply side of the market. Moreover, even though they do facilitate urban mobility, by no means they can be regarded as classic mobility service providers. As a matter of fact, the business approaches can be classified as Mobility Platform Providers. This business model pattern describes a provider of a single point of access, not only to the mobility service but also to other cross services which facilitate the obtaining of this mobility service. Such cross services encompass: identification, information and planning, booking, payment and billing. It seems, however, that offering such one-stop-shop mobility requires also the involvement of many additional actors such as: policymakers, public transport operators, banks and payment firms, telecommunication companies, and ICT suppliers. Such collaboration networks are necessary in order to further extend the service portfolio and to overcome the niche character of these mobility services. For that reason smexx has established a rather unexpected strategic cooperation with an independent leasing bank for car dealers and with T-Systems, whereas TwoGo is an innovative initiative of SAP. With that approach they aim to scale, break through and reach the required critical mass of users. If such innovative concepts and business models succeed, the perception of the car in general will be further changing leading to less dependence on car ownership over time.

It is claimed that autonomous vehicle technology is a ground-breaking technological advancement that has the capacity to considerably alter current mobility system structures and personal mobility patterns. Similarly to aforementioned digital technologies it can merit the term of technological revolution. As such it will lead to the emergence of Schumpeterian companies. They, in turn, will undertake the attempt to pair this innovative technology offering with corresponding commercialization approaches to create, deliver and capture value for the end-users. This will happen by means of innovative applications and creative business models. Both will eventually undergo the selection process of the market. The author has made an attempt to design new mobility services and possible business models which incorporate and commercialize the technology of autonomous vehicles.

The author has approached this part of research in an exploratory manner. This approach has been based chiefly on subjective points of view extracted from the expert interviews. Several innovative ideas for mobility services, which are not yet available or are being prepared for the realization, have been qualitatively described. Furthermore, possible business models have been developed based on the previously acquired knowledge. This research effort for envisioning future mobility concepts has resulted in a list of six distinct technology-enabled business models which can be used as blueprints for area-wide marketability and scalability in urban areas in the near future. All proposed business models aim at commercializing current inefficiencies by means of digital technologies and/or autonomous vehicle technology and as such contribute to the achievement of the factor 10 scenario.

Summing up, business model creation and innovation is crucial for the high diffusion of any new technology. The necessary prerequisite for the industry to provide specific innovative applications of the new technology is to gain profits out of it. Commercial companies will contribute and commit to the development and implementation of system-level innovations in urban mobility only if a fair return on investment is assured, commensurate with the financial risks taken. Hence, technology innovation and business model innovation are strongly linked to each other.

Commercializing technology-enabled innovative mobility services and bringing them to the market via sophisticated business models, even if promising with regard to efficiency gains of car usage, will not be sufficient to overcome the underlying challenge of auto dependence in urban areas. Additional directive measures from municipalities will be required to overcome this challenge. Such commercially shared automobility services will be only effective if linked to a wider idea of shifting towards the paradigm of sustainable mobility in cities. This requires a very clear and structured approach to all possible methods of delivering significant reductions in car dependence, urban congestion, pollution and community disruption. In that respect, local policy design and coherent policy implementation hold a fundamental role in shaping the future of urban mobility in accordance with societal needs. The author has identified and synthetized three main areas that constitute rules and mechanisms for organizing mobility in the urban context: push policies, pull policies and physical measures. However, choosing policy measures for sustainable mobility requires weighing a set of conflicting concerns, such as environmental effects, safety, tax revenue, local economic competitiveness of domestic firms, accessibility or social equity. If applied in isolation the policies are ulikely to achieve their stated goals of increasing transport sector efficiency and ovecoming car dependence. In some unfavorable cases they may even lead to severe discrepancies and contradictions. The lack of coordination can cause unsustainable lock-ins such as car-oriented urban developments. Such locked-in developments cannot be served other than by a car and have proven to have a long-life lasting.

The researcher has shown that policy consistency across different and seemingly unrelated sectors is a vital element in making sustainable mobility politically feasible and publicly acceptable. Successful transport policy must not only be internally consistent, i.e. integrating advantages of different modes of transport through regulation, pricing, appraisal criteria and appropriate budgeting. But it also needs to be consistent with government objectives in policy areas other than transport by acknowledging the interdependencies between land-use, local economy, environmental and social objectives (such as health, education, affordability and inclusion). On the one hand, this requires *vertical integration*, i.e. cooperation and alignment of relevant legislation, guidelines and supporting policies on national, regional and local levels. On the other hand, *horizontal integration* needs to be ensured through sectoral integration (cooperation of departments in various policy areas) and territorial integration (coordination of policies and activities between neighboring local authority areas).

Therefore, breaking down the complexity of local policy practice and developing an understanding of how policies are selectively packaged and applied is vital. The ladder of integration has been introduced to illustrate how the conceptualization of horizontal and vertical integration can be differentiated into several (eight) stages of achievement. With that the author has created an important foundation for the development of the concept of 'Policy Consistency' which has been included in the final framework of 'Integrated Sustainable Urban Mobility'.

Irrespective of how advanced the innovative technologies are and how effective the available policies appear to be, the reality of the policy practice at local levels is an extremely complex field and is not trivial to steer. Implementation deficits might result from the lack of integration, divergent agendas and the lack of fit between different disciplinary and administrative policy areas. Unexpected dynamics may also result from changes of basic needs of local societies as well as from cultural shifts which occur on the global scale. Additionally, there are many involved parties and actors which might pursue contradictory goals. Hence, overcoming car dependence and transitioning towards sustainable mobility paradigm can be a very difficult and painful process which might become diluted if not correctly understood, well thought out and consistently executed over time. The author has investigated the sociopolitical environment when overcoming structural car dependence by analyzing the case study of the City of Basel. Basel is a Swiss progressive canton-city which has been on the path of reducing its car dependence since the 1970s. A clear manifestation has been the City Initiative, which has taken a major influence on the strategic reorientation of the mobility paradigm. The society has agreed to reduce the motorized road traffic volume by 10% until 2020. The acceptance of this goal has revealed that there has been a considerable rethinking in the society of Basel with regard to the urban mobility function. It has been understood as a civic request for facilitating the shift towards the paradigm of sustainable mobility. This has also revealed that there are considerable challenges to consider on several sociopolitical layers when overcoming structural urban car dependence.

The author has shown that there are numerous critical factors in all four investigated domains of Transformative Literacy: technology, economy, society and politics. They range from recognizing ICT as an enabler for more efficiency, to superiority of accessibility over velocity, to understanding and facilitating new business models, to resistance and counter movements from lobby groups, to considering basic societal needs and possible rebound-effects, to managing behavioral changes, to leadership and governance, to obtaining value perspective and to ensuring consistency and integration in policy implementation. Detailed elaboration of these critical factors has exposed the non-triviality of managing transition processes towards sustainable mobility. However, the case of Basel has also indicated that it is not impossible. The main challenge is the achievement of an appropriate balance between (i) strategic locational advantages of a city, such as accessibility, economic competitiveness or efficient sourcing of the workforce, and (ii) the basic needs of the society, such as high quality of life, safety, residential attractiveness and affordable mobility. For that purpose, the politics is expected to anticipate contradictory expectations and match them up by ensuring policy consistency, i.e. coherent political and institutional alignment over time. Furthermore, finding the balance and coherence between the needs of the society and the desires of the industry is not solely the responsibility of institutions. The case study indicates that the citizens should not be seen as customers, i.e. the demand side, but as partners in the process of designing an efficient and city-friendly mobility system. Finally, a modern and progressive city proactively seeks for new and innovative approaches to organizing the mobility function in its urban area. The case study clearly indicates a best of breed approach, which means: integrating transport modes and personalizing mobility services while utilizing the advantages of all mobility options.

The case of City of Basel has also revealed some general patterns of sustainable mobility. Based on the acquired pool of knowledge the researcher has developed the framework of 'Integrated Sustainable Urban Mobility' which incorporates three main concepts of: efficiency, sufficiency and consistency. The framework offers a holistic understanding of possible strategies for overcoming auto dependence and establishing the path towards the paradigm of sustainable mobility for modern cities. The framework aims at giving a clear guidance for policy-makers who need to integrate the ideas of sustainable mobility into the long-term policy planning in a coherent way. With that the author contributes to the holistic understanding of the transition towards sustainable mobility in cities.

22 Further Research

The topics of digitization and automation of cars, shared mobility patterns as well as business model innovation constitute a novel research territory. These fields have gained paramount importance from the perspective of sustainable urban mobility. The work at hand does not claim to offer a final explanation for these phenomena, but should be seen as a firm foundation for further research in this arena. During this dissertation project many fascinating research fields have been revealed with many open questions. Obviously, starting points for further work arise along the investigated areas. However, the author has recognized two possible further research paths (i) implementing practically observable innovations in urban context, and (ii) extending knowledge about managing the transition for sustainable mobility from urban to non-urban environment. To provide guidance for possible future research projects, some interesting questions are hereinafter stated and briefly discussed.

Experimenting in Urban Context

Shared mobility services such as carsharing and ridesharing are already available in the mobility sector and are projected to further expand. Two distinct case studies of smexx and TwoGo by SAP have illustrated how current concepts contribute to the reduction of the number of cars in cities and what business model options are available. As highlighted in this dissertation real efficiency boosts are expected with the introduction of autonomous vehicles. Numerous simulations have shown these potentials. However, the research has also indicated that there is a range of challenges that need to be further investigated. Simulations constitute a good starting point for discussions, however, only field research can help acquiring important knowledge about possible implications of the new technology. Therefore, the author suggests that real-life experiments with fleets of SAV should be conducted, initially in closed environments (e.g. airports, university campuses) and later in urban areas. This could lead to assessing the *transformative capacity* and *system adaptability* of mobility concepts based on autonomous vehicles.

Transformative capacity can only be determined based on the possibilities to use and further develop a new technology in a specific sectoral context and on the institutional and structural conditions in this specific sector. The author has attempted to answer some crucial aspects with regard to the sector of urban mobility. However, field experiments will help to indicate the actual degree of required changes in socio-economic institutional structures. Evaluating transformative capacity will deliver detailed answers to following aspects:

(1) Technological profile:

- How will the autonomous technology interact with the prevailing socio-technical system?
- What are possible transition paths to alter the prevailing urban mobility systems?
- How to integrate autonomous technology into an integrated mobility system (mobility platforms, access to information, communication protocols etc.)?

(2) Patterns of interaction:

- How should mobility service based on autonomous vehicles exactly look like?
- How to technologically integrate carsharing and ridesharing options into autonomous vehicles?
- How to best design the user experience?
- Which business models would take hold for providing such service offerings?

(3) (In)Formal institutions:

- Would such mobility systems decrease or increase the traffic volume in cities under real conditions (e.g. empty miles traveled)?
- How many autonomous vehicles would be really needed to achieve a certain quality of service? What would be the real impact on the space and energy consumption? Would it be environmentally sustainable?
- What are the regulatory, liability and insurance requirements? Who would regulate the service level standards to guarantee maximum safety?
- Who would operate such mobility systems? Would such solutions be socially and politically acceptable?

System adaptability, on the other hand, describes how established sectoral structures, institutions and actors react to such a new technology. It needs to be determined by assessing the possible tensions within the prevailing system with regard to patterns of resource allocation and distribution of economic and political power. This can be related, for example, to a specific city which would aim at implementing such a revolutionary mobility solution. One would need to investigate the required changes in infrastructures, regulations, land-use patterns, business models and user practices.

The author wants also to highlight the necessity to undertake substantial research effort within the automotive sector. Entire economies of several highly industrialized countries have been dependent on this sector as one of the most important industrial branches. Therefore, it is of paramount importance to understand how such a radical shift as *factor 10 of automobility* would impact power constellations and resource allocation in this and other related industries. The system adaptability assessment requires to investigate organizational, institutional and structural aspects.

Evaluating both transformative capacity and system adaptability for the technology of autonomous vehicles would provide an answer whether a system innovation, which would require only the tenth of currently available vehicles, is possible.

Extending Knowledge about Sustainable Mobility in Rural Areas

The author has focused on the challenges of urban mobility and possible strategies to overcome the structural car dependence. Urban mobility systems face the most challenging problems today due to undesirable externalities, energy inefficiency and undesirable space consumption and land-use patterns. Admittedly, the underlying patterns and causal connections in urban areas are pretty well understood. Therefore, it is somehow easier to make predictions with respect to technological shifts. The aspect of mobility in rural areas seems to be much more challenging to grasp and, in the opinion of author, might be even more crucial in the context of optimizing the transportation system in a holistic way. For example, the car is a much more efficient transport mode in rural areas as compared to an underutilized bus or light rail.

As the case of City of Basel indicates it is not a trivial exercise to couple a rural mobility system with an urban one. Against the backdrop of the tendency towards urbanization, the need for more freedom and autonomy, awareness of environmental impacts and resource reallocation, the following questions remain open for further investigation:

- What are the determinants for achieving policy consistency on the local and regional level for providing sufficient accessibility for rural areas?
- Which innovative technologies will ensure the same mobility level for people from outside the city without the need to possess a car?
- How to improve physical interfaces such as train stations or park and ride systems to allow for new highly flexible on-demand and multimodal mobility concepts for the urban agglomeration and farther rural regions?

Suggestions Regarding Possible Research Approaches

The author would also like to suggest possible research approaches for further studies. The case study approach which was applied for this dissertation has shown some drawbacks with regard to generalization attempts. Especially, investigating the Case of Basel has revealed that mobility systems are strongly dependent on local or regional factors and some findings need to be evaluated before transferring to own context of sustainability in urban mobility. For example, for some cases assuming a strategy to overcome car dependence might not be necessary an optimal one. Important aspects need to be deliberately considered such as for example: urban density, previous land-use patterns, economic situation, political power constellations or current societal attitudes. In that respect developing sophisticated and advanced simulation models would be advantageous. Especially, mathematical modelling of variables such as age structures, individual mobility patterns, important economic factors or accessibility and incorporating them in global models to explain a specific urban mobility system would considerably contribute to understanding of the interplay between different factors and possible impacts on the city as a whole. However, the prerequisite for such models is the availability of accurate data about mobility demand, modal splits, urban structures and other important variables.

Furthermore, the author suggests to start implementing small niche experiments in order to enable researchers to make practical observations and to draw real-life conclusions from technological innovations such as autonomous driving and new mobility concepts. This would definitely contribute to the small body of knowledge in these fields. More important, experimenting with the technology facilitates the processes of social learning and in this way stimulates transformative processes – especially in the case of technology with a high potential for system innovation and where prevailing system actors play a significant role. Linking such experiments with innovative research designs such as Transformative Literacy would help understand transition dynamics towards sustainable futures in a much more holistic way.

Publication Bibliography

20 Minuten (2015): Kein automatisches Hochregal für Velos. Edited by Tamedia AG. Available online at http://www.20min.ch/schweiz/basel/story/26432955, checked on 12/14/2015.

Abdelkafi, N.; Makhotin, S.; Posselt, T. (2013): Business model innovations for electric mobility-what can be learned from existing business model patterns? In *International Journal of Innovation Management* 17 (1). DOI: 10.1142/S1363919613400033.

Abdelkafi, Nizar (2012): Open business models for the greater good–a case study from the higher education context. In *Die Unternehmung* 66 (3), pp. 297–316.

Abrate, Graziano; Piacenza, Massimiliano; Vannoni, Davide (2009): The impact of Integrated Tariff Systems on public transport demand: Evidence from Italy. In *Regional Science and Urban Economics* 39 (2), pp. 120–127.

Adler, Oliver; Carnazzi Weber, Sara; Botteron, Maxime; Eberhardt, Björn; Gehrig, Lukas; Horlacher, Jonathan et al. (2014): Monitor Schweiz mit «Spezial Inflation». Die Schweiz steht im Stau. Edited by Giles Keating. Credit Suisse. Available online at http://publications.credit-suisse.com/tasks/render/file/index.cfm?fileid=22F2CB39-0DE5-26C7-84AC0AEB06E4D09C, checked on 11/4/2015.

Agglo Basel (n.d.a): Definition - Herzstück Basel. Available online at http://www.herzstueck-basel.ch/definition.html, updated on 12/11/2015, checked on 12/11/2015.

Agglo Basel (n.d.b): Projektliste. Available online at http://www.agglobasel.org/projektliste.html, updated on 12/12/2015, checked on 12/12/2015.

Agglo Basel (n.d.c): Vorprojekt. Available online at http://www.herzstueck-basel.ch/vorprojekt.html, checked on 12/12/2015.

Agglo Basel (2015): Ausgangslage und Auftrag. Available online at http://www.agglobasel.org/ausgangslage-und-auftrag.html, checked on 12/10/2015.

Agrawal, Divyakant; Das, Sudipto; El Abbadi, Amr (2011): Big data and cloud computing. Current State and Future Opportunities. In Anastasia Ailamaki, Sihem Amer-Yahia, Jignesh Pate, Tore Risch, Pierre Senellart, Julia Stoyanovich (Eds.): Proceedings of the 14th International Conference on Extending Database Technology. Uppsala, Sweden, p. 530.

Alexander, Christopher; Ishikawa, Sara; Silverstein, Murray (1977): A pattern language: towns, buildings, construction: Oxford University Press.

Allen, Tammy D.; Golden, Timothy D.; Shockley, Kristen M. (2015): How Effective Is Telecommuting? Assessing the Status of Our Scientific Findings. In *Psychological Science in the Public Interest* 16 (2), pp. 40–68.

Al-Roomi, May; Al-Ebrahim, Shaikha; Buqrais, Sabika; Ahmad, Imtiaz (2013): Cloud computing pricing models: a survey. In *International Journal of Grid & Distributed Computing* 6 (5), pp. 93–106.

Amshoff, Benjamin; Dülme, Christian; Echterfeld, Julian; Gausemeier, Jürgen (2015): Business Model Patterns for Disruptive Technologies. In *International Journal of Innovation Management* 19 (03), p. 1540002. DOI: 10.1142/S1363919615400022.

Amt für Mobilität (2015a): Mobilitätsmanagement. Edited by Bau- und Verkehrsdepartement des Kantons Basel-Stadt. Available online at http://www.mobilitaet.bs.ch/ueber-uns/verkehrs strategie/mobilit%C3%A4tsmanagement.html, checked on 12/16/2015.

Amt für Mobilität (2015b): Parkleitsystem. Edited by Bau- und Verkehrsdepartement des Kantons Basel-Stadt. Available online at http://www.mobilitaet.bs.ch/motorfahrzeuge/parkieren-in-basel/parkleitsystem.
html, updated on 12/28/2015, checked on 12/28/2015.

Anable, Jillian (2005): 'Complacent car addicts' or 'aspiring environmentalists'? Identifying travel behaviour segments using attitude theory. In *Transport Policy* 12 (1), pp. 65–78.

Anable, Jillian; Lane, Ben; Kelay, Tanika (2006): An evidence base review of public attitudes to climate change and transport behaviour. In *Department for Transport, London*. Available online at http://www.pdfwww.china-up.com:8080/international/case/case/1457.pdf, checked on 11/27/2015.

André, Michel; Hammarström, Ulf (2000): Driving speeds in Europe for pollutant emissions estimation. In *Transportation Research Part D: Transport and Environment* 5 (5), pp. 321–335.

Andrew, James P.; Sirkin, Harold L.; Butman, John (2013): Payback: reaping the rewards of innovation: Harvard Business Press.

Arnott, Richard; Small, Kenneth (1994): The economics of traffic congestion. In *American Scientist*, pp. 446–455.

Arnould, G.a; Khadraoui, D.a; Armendáriz, M.b; Burguillo, J.C.b; Peleteiro, A.b (2011): A transport based clearing system for dynamic carpooling business services. In *2011 11th International Conference on ITS Telecommunications, ITST 2011. DOI:* 10.1109/ITST.2011.6060114.

Atzori, Luigi; Iera, Antonio; Morabito, Giacomo (2010): The internet of things: A survey. In *Computer networks* 54 (15), pp. 2787–2805.

Augenstein, Karoline (2014): E-Mobility as a Sustainable System Innovation. Insights from a Captured Niche. 1. Aufl. Herzogenrath: Shaker (Schriftenreihe der Reiner Lemoine-Stiftung).

Augenstein, Karoline (2015): Analysing the potential for sustainable e-mobility–the case of Germany. In *Environmental Innovation and Societal Transitions* 14, pp. 101–115.

Austin, Jon (2016): REVEALED: Why Google is so desperate to stop YOU from driving. Edited by Daily Express. Available online at http://www.express.co.uk/news/science/631819/REVEALED-Why-Google-is-desperate-to-stop-YOU-from-driving, checked on 2/6/2016.

Automobilwoche (2015): Carsharing: Santander startet Pilotprojekt. Automobilwoche. Available online at http://www.automobilwoche.de/article/20150311/NACHRICHTEN/150319986/carsharing-santander-startet-pilotprojekt#.VgLlnMvtlBc, updated on 3/11/2015, checked on 9/23/2015.

Auyang, Sunny Y. (1999): Foundations of complex-system theories: in economics, evolutionary biology, and statistical physics: Cambridge University Press.

B,S,S.; RappTrans (2014): Entwicklungsszenarien trinationaleAgglomeration Basel mit und ohne Herzstück der Regio-S-Bahn. Quantitative und qualitative Abschätzung des volkswirtschaftlichen Nutzens von Durchmesserlinien. Available online at http://www.herzstueck-basel.ch/nutzenstudie.html?file=files/theme/herzstueck/content/downloads/berichte/studie_volkswirtschaftlicher_nutzen_durchmesserlinien_fuer_region_basel.pdf, checked on 12/12/2015.

Baber, Jonathan; Kolodko, Julian; Noel, Tony; Parent, Michael; Vlacic, Ljubo (2005): Cooperative autonomous driving: intelligent vehicles sharing city roads. In *Robotics & Automation Magazine, IEEE* 12 (1), pp. 44–49.

Bacco, Claudia (2015): What do banking and connected cars have in common? Available online at http://www.rcrwireless.com/20150605/connected-cars-2/emea-what-do-banking-and-connected-cars-have-in-common-tag11, checked on 9/21/2015.

Banister, David (2005): Unsustainable transport. The transport crisis / David Banister. London: Spon (Transport, development and sustainability).

Banister, David (2008): The sustainable mobility paradigm. In *New Developments in Urban Transportation Planning* 15 (2), pp. 73–80. DOI: 10.1016/j.tranpol.2007.10.005.

Banister, David; Hickman, Robin (Eds.) (2006): How to design a more sustainable and fairer built environment: transport and communications. Intelligent Transport Systems, IEE Proceedings: IET (4).

Barter, Paul (2013): Cars are parked 95% of the time. Let's check! Available online at http://www.reinvent
ingparking.org/2013/02/cars-are-parked-95-of-time-lets-check.html, updated on 11/17/2015, checked on 11/18/2015.

Basler Verkehrs-Betriebe (2010): Alles im Blick. Basler Verkehrs-Betriebe Zahlen 2010. Available online at http://www.bvb.ch/docs/geschaeftsberichte/2011/05/19/BVB%202010%20in%20Zahle n.pdf?Status=Master, checked on 12/28/2015.

Bassett Jr, David R.; Pucher, John; Buehler, Ralph; Thompson, Dixie L.; Crouter, Scott E. (2008): Walking, cycling, and obesity rates in Europe, North America, and Australia. In *Journal of Physical Activity and Health* 5 (6), pp. 795–814.

Bau- und Verkehrsdepartement des Kantons Basel-Stadt (2014a): Catch a Car. Edited by Amt für Mobilität. Available online at http://www.mobilitaet.bs.ch/motorfahrzeuge/catch-a-car.html, checked on 12/15/2015.

Bau- und Verkehrsdepartement des Kantons Basel-Stadt (2014b): Verkehrspolitisches Leitbild und Massnahmenplan. Available online at http://www.umverkehr.ch/sites/default/files/verkehrs politischesleitbild_vernehmlassungsbericht.pdf, checked on 12/13/2015.

Bau- und Verkehrsdepartement des Kantons Basel-Stadt (2015): Verkehrspolitisches Leitbild und Massnahmenplan. Available online at http://www.medienmitteilungen.bs.ch/verkehrspolitisches _leitbild_juni_2015.pdf, checked on 12/13/2015.

Baudepartement des Kantons Basel-Stadt (2005): Basel fährt anders – Basel fährt Velo! Mit dem Velo unterwegs bringt Schwung in den Alltag und in die Freizeit. Available online at http://www.mobilitaet.bs.ch/dms/mobilitaet/download/6_Velo/34_Basel_faehrt_anders_Basel_faehrt_Velo.pdf, checked on 12/28/2015.

Baumol, William J.; Oates, Wallace E. (1988): The theory of environmental policy: Cambridge University Press.

BBC (2015): Uber banned in Germany as police swoop in other countries. BBC. Available online at http://www.bbc.com/news/technology-31942997, checked on 9/23/2015.

bcs (2015a): Carsharing City Ranking 2015. Pressemitteilung vom 10.06.2015. Bundesverband CarSharing e.V. Available online at http://www.carsharing.de/pressemitteilung-vom-10062015, updated on 9/22/2015, checked on 9/22/2015.

bcs (2015b): Pressemitteilung vom 16.03.2015. CarSharing wächst in der Fläche - mehr als ein Viertel neuer CarSharing-Orte gegenüber dem Vorjahr. Bundesverband CarSharing e.V. Available online at http://www.carsharing.de/presse/pressemitteilungen/carsharing-waechst-flaeche-mehr-viertel-neuer-carsharing-orte-gegenueber-0, checked on 9/22/2015.

Bélanger, France; Collins, Rosann Webb (1998): Distributed work arrangements: A research framework. In *The Information Society* 14 (2), pp. 137–152.

Berger, Gerald; Feindt, Peter H.; Holden, Erling; Rubik, Frieder (2014a): Sustainable Mobility—Challenges for a Complex Transition. In *Journal of Environmental Policy & Planning* 16 (3), pp. 303–320. DOI: 10.1080/1523908X.2014.954077.

Berger, Gerald; Feindt, Peter H.; Holden, Erling; Rubik, Frieder (2014b): Sustainable Mobility—Challenges for a Complex Transition. In *Journal of Environmental Policy & Planning* 16 (3), pp. 303–320. DOI: 10.1080/1523908X.2014.954077.

Beutel, M.C.a; Samsel, C.a; Mensing, M.b; Krempels, K.-H.a; Holzinger A., van Sinderen M., Dolog P., Obaidat M.S. (2014): Business model framework to provide heterogeneous mobility services on virtual markets. In *ICE-B 2014 - Proceedings of the 11th International Conference on e-Business, Part of ICETE 2014 - 11th International Joint Conference on e-Business and Telecommunications*. Available online at http://www.scopus.com/inward/record.url?eid=2-s2.0-84910053939&partnerID=40&md5=c6 bfd0258492b09e5c43de503eba07df.

Beyer, Paul: Mixed-use zoning. Available online at http://www.aging.ny.gov/livableny/resource manual/planningzoninganddevelopment/ii2g.pdf, checked on 12/1/2015.

Bialystok Science and Technology Park: About us. Municipality of Bialystok. Available online at http://bpnt.inet.bpnt.bialystok.pl/en/, checked on 3/22/2016.

Bieger, Thomas; Reinhold, Stephan (2011): Das wertbasierte Geschäftsmodell–Ein aktualisierter Strukturierungsansatz. In Thomas Bieger, Dodo zu Knyphausen-Aufseß, Christian Krys (Eds.): Innovative Geschäftsmodelle: Springer, pp. 13–70.

Binswanger, Hans Christoph (2009): Vorwärts zur Mässigung. Perspektiven einer nachhaltigen Wirtschaft. 1. Aufl. Hamburg: Murmann.

Bischoff, Joschka; Maciejewski, Michal (Eds.) (2016): Autonomous taxicabs in Berlin–a spatiotemporal analysis of service performance. International Scientific Conference on Mobility and Transport Transforming Urban Mobility. Munich, Germany, 6-7 June 2016.

Bleile, Urs (2001): Wichtige Änderungen im Strassenverkehrsrecht. Edited by Kanton Basel-Stadt. Available online at http://www.bs.ch/news/2001-04-17-mm-35151.html, checked on 12/16/2015.

Boehm, M.; Flechl, B.; Froetscher, A. (2013): ICT concepts for optimization of mobility in Smart Cities.

Boesch, Patrick M.; Ciari, Francesco; Axhausen, Kay W. (Eds.) (2016): Required Autonomous Vehicle Fleet Sizes to Serve Different Levels of Demand. Transportation Research Board 95th Annual Meeting (16-2682).

Bohnet, Max; Frehn, Michael; Holz-Rau, Christian (2005): Umsetzung und Akzeptanz einer nachhaltigen Verkehrspolitik - NAPOLI. Forschungs- und Entwicklungsvorhaben im Auftrag des Bundesministeriums für Verkehr, Bau- und Wohnungswesen, FOPS-Projekt-Nr. 70.695/2002. Abschlussbericht. With assistance of Andreas Iland, Sabrina Pflaum, Kerstin Suhl, Tim Völlmer. Edited by Das Institut für Landes- und Stadtentwicklungsforschung und Bauwesen Landes Nordrhein-Westfalen (ILS NRW), Fachbereich Mobilität und Siedlungsentwicklung. Bundesministerium für Verkehr, Bau- und Wohnungswesen. Dortmund. Available online at https://www.deutsche-digitale-bibliothek.de/binary/RXOUT7A2ITZAPXCK4KNNFQUUX63 GAJ3M/full/1.pdf, checked on 4/25/2016.

Bonakdar, Amir (2015): Business Model Innovation. Studies on business model design, protection, and anchoring. University of St. Gallen.

Bonaventure, Lionel (2014): France Says It Will Ban Uber's Low-Cost Service in New Year. Edited by The New York Times. Available online at http://www.nytimes.com/2014/12/16/business/inter national/france-says-it-will-ban-ubers-low-cost-service-in-new-year.html, checked on 10/9/2015.

Bratzel, Stefan (1999): Erfolgsbedingungen umweltorientierter Verkehrspolitik in Städten. Analysen zum Policy-Wandel in den "relativen Erfolgsfällen" Amsterdam, Groningen, Zürich und Freiburg (i. Brg.). Basel [u.a.]: Birkhäuser (Stadtforschung aktuell, 78).

Bringezu, S.; Schütz, H.; Arnold, K.; Merten, F.; Kabasci, S.; Borelbach, P. et al. (2009): Global implications of biomass and biofuel use in Germany – Recent trends and future scenarios for domestic and foreign agricultural land use and resulting GHG emissions. In *Journal of cleaner production* 17, pp. S57-S68. DOI: 10.1016/j.jclepro.2009.03.007.

Bringezu, Stefan; Schütz, Helmut; Pengue, Walter; O'Brien, Meghan; Garcia, Fernando; Sims, Ralph et al. (2014): Assessing global land use. Balancing consumption with sustainable supply. Nairobi, Kenya: United Nations Environment Programme.

Browne, David; Caulfield, Brian; O'Mahony, Margaret (2011): Barriers to Sustainable Transport in Ireland. Climate Change Research Programme - CCRP Report 7.

Browne, John; Nuttall, Robin; Stadlen, Tommy (2015): Connect. How companies succeed by engaging radically with society. London: WH Allen.

Browne, John; Nuttall, Robin; Stadlen, Tommy (2016): How companies succeed through radical engagement. Edited by McKinsey Insights. McKinsey & Company. Available online at http://www.mckinsey.com/business-functions/strategy-and-corporate-finance/our-insights/how-companies-succeed-through-radical-engagement, updated on 02.2016, checked on 3/3/2016.

Bundesamt für Raumentwicklung ARE (2015): Agglomerationsprogramme Verkehr und Siedlung. Bundesamt für Raumentwicklung ARE. Available online at http://www.are.admin.ch/themen/agglomeration/00626/01680/index.html?lang=de, updated on 12/10/2015, checked on 12/10/2015.

Bundesamt für Statistik (2007): Mobilität in der Schweiz. Wichtigste Ergebnisse des Mikrozensus 2005 zum Verkehrsverhalten. Neuchâtel.

Bundesamt für Statistik BFS (2012a): Ergebnisse des Mikrozensus Mobilität und Verkehr 2010. Anzahl Wege pro Person und Tag. Neuchâtel. Available online at http://www.bfs.admin.ch/bfs/portal/de/index/news/01.Document.156819.xls, updated on 2012, checked on 8/18/2015.

Bundesamt für Statistik BFS (2012b): Ergebnisse des Mikrozensus Mobilität und Verkehr 2010. Durchschnittlicher Besetzungsgrad von Personenwagen (in Personen pro Auto, distanzgewichtet). Neuchâtel. Available online at http://www.bfs.admin.ch/bfs/portal/de/index/news/01.Document.156515.xls, updated on 2012, checked on 8/18/2015.

Bundesamt für Statistik BFS (2012c): Ergebnisse des Mikrozensus Mobilität und Verkehr 2010. Freizeitwege: Länge, Zeit, Anzahl Etappen pro Weg. Neuchâtel. Available online at http://www.bfs.admin.ch/bfs/portal/de/index/news/01.Document.156879.xls, updated on 2012, checked on 8/18/2015.

Bundesamt für Statistik BFS (2012d): Mobilität in der Schweiz. Ergebnisse des Mikrozensus Mobilität und Verkehr 2010. Neuchâtel (Statistik der Schweiz. 11, Mobilität und Verkehr). Available online at http://www.portal-stat.admin.ch/mz10/docs/840-1000.pdf, checked on 4/25/2016.

Bundesamt für Statistik BFS (2013a): Bestand und Struktur der Haushalte 2010. Available online at http://www.bfs.admin.ch/bfs/portal/de/index/news/medienmitteilungen.html?pressID=8678, updated on 1/11/2012, checked on 11/7/2015.

Bundesamt für Statistik BFS (2013b): Energieverbrauch - Kennzahlen. Endenergieverbrauch nach Verbrauchergruppen. Available online at http://www.bfs.admin.ch/bfs/portal/de/index/themen/08/02/blank/key/verbrauch/verbrauchgruppen.html, updated on 1/27/2016, checked on 1/27/2016.

Bundesamt für Statistik BFS (2013c): Pendlermobilität in der Schweiz 2011. Available online at http://www.bfs.admin.ch/bfs/portal/de/index/themen/11/04/blank/04.html, checked on 11/5/2015.

Bundesamt für Statistik BFS (2013d): Pendlermobilität in der Schweiz 2011. Neuchâtel. Available online at http://www.bfs.admin.ch/bfs/portal/de/index/themen/11/22/publ.Document.171257.pdf, checked on 12/10/2015.

Bundesamt für Statistik BFS (2015): Verkehrsinfrastruktur und Fahrzeuge – Fahrzeuge. Strassenfahrzeuge - Bestand, Motorisierungsgrad. Available online at http://www.bfs.admin.ch/bfs/portal/de/index/themen/11/03/blank/02/01/01.html, updated on 11/6/2015, checked on 11/7/2015.

Bundesamt für Strassen ASTRA (2014): Engpassbeseitigung Osttangente Basel: ASTRA legt neue Variante vor. Edited by Bundesamt für Strassen ASTRA. Available online at https://www.news.admin.ch/message/index.html?lang=de&msg-id=53707, checked on 12/15/2015.

Bundesamt für Strassen ASTRA (2015): Mobility Pricing. Bundesamt für Strassen ASTRA. Available online at http://www.astra.admin.ch/themen/00901/index.html?lang=de, checked on 2/27/2016.

Bundeskanzlei (3/23/2005): SR 131.222.1 Verfassung des Kantons Basel-Stadt, vom 23. März 2005. Available online at https://www.admin.ch/opc/de/classified-compilation/20060954/index.html#a40, checked on 12/20/2015.

Bundesrat (2010): Die Zukunft der nationalen Infrastrukturnetze in der Schweiz. Bericht des Bundesrates. Edited by Eidgenössisches Departement für Umwelt, Verkehr, Energie und Kommunikation UVEK. Available online at https://www.admin.ch/opc/de/federal-gazette/2010/8665.pdf, updated on 9/17/2010, checked on 2/27/2016.

Bureau of Planning and Sustainability (2012): Cost Comparison: Parking Prototype Impacts on Form and Affordability. The City of Portland. Available online at https://www.portlandoregon.gov/bps/article/420062, checked on 3/7/2016.

Burns, Lawrence D.; Jordan, William C.; Scarborough, Bonnie A. (2013): Transforming personal mobility. In *The Earth Institute*.

Buschmann, Frank; Henney, Kelvin; Schimdt, Douglas (2007): Pattern-oriented Software Architecture: On Patterns and Pattern Language: John Wiley & Sons.

Buyya, Rajkumar; Yeo, Chee Shin; Venugopal, Srikumar; Broberg, James; Brandic, Ivona (2009): Cloud computing and emerging IT platforms. Vision, hype, and reality for delivering computing as the 5th utility. In *Future Generation Computer Systems* 25 (6), pp. 599–616. DOI: 10.1016/j.future.2008.12.001.

bz Basellandschaftliche Zeitung (Ed.) (2014): Dank FABI: Bund soll Herzstück für die neue Regio-S-Bahn bezahlen. Available online at http://www.basellandschaftlichezeitung.ch/basel/basel-stadt/dank-fabi-bund-soll-herzstueck-fuer-die-neue-regio-s-bahn-bezahlen-128066261, checked on 12/12/2015.

Cairns, Sally; Sloman, Lynn; Newson, Carey; Anable, Jillian; Kirkbride, Alistair; Goodwin, Phil (2004): Smarter choices-changing the way we travel. Available online at http://discovery.ucl.ac.uk/1224/1/1224.pdf, checked on 11/27/2015.

Cardrops (2016): Cardrops. Available online at http://www.cardrops.com/, updated on 10/30/2012, checked on 1/23/2016.

CarJump (2015): Das sind wir. Was ist CarJump? Available online at http://carjump.me/de/DE/about, checked on 10/7/2015.

Carzapp (2015): carzapp startet als Carsharing-Komplettanbieter durch. carzapp GmbH. Available online at https://www.carzapp.net/de/press/release, checked on 9/21/2015.

Chakravarty, Debalina; Dasgupta, Shyamasree; Roy, Joyashree (2013): Rebound effect: how much to worry? In *Current opinion in environmental sustainability* 5 (2), pp. 216–228.

Chan, Nelson D.; Shaheen, Susan A. (2012): Ridesharing in North America: Past, present, and future. In *Transport Reviews* 32 (1), pp. 93–112. Available online at http://www.tandfonline.com/doi/full/10.1080/01441647.2011.621557, checked on 10/7/2015.

Chapron, Romain (2015): Big Data and Smart Mobility the 2015 goals for Auto Manufacturers. L'Atelier: Accelerating Business. Available online at http://www.atelier.net/en/trends/articles/big-data-and-smart-mobility-2015-goals-auto-manufacturers_433248, checked on 9/10/2015.

Chen, Hsinchun; Chiang, Roger H. L.; Storey, Veda C. (2012a): Business Intelligence and Analytics: From Big Data to Big Impact. In *MIS quarterly* 36 (4), pp. 1165–1188.

Chen, Min; Wan, Jiafu; Li, Fang (2012b): Machine-to-Machine Communications. In *KSII Transactions on Internet and Information Systems (TIIS)* 6 (2), pp. 480–497.

Chesbrough, Henry (2010): Business model innovation: opportunities and barriers. In *Long range planning* 43 (2), pp. 354–363.

Christensen, Clayton M. (1997): The innovator's dilemma. When new technologies cause great firms to fail. Boston, Mass.: Harvard Business School Press (The management of innovation and change series).

Christensen, Clayton M.; Grossman, Jerome H.; Hwang, Jason (2009): The innovator's prescription. In *A disruptive solution for health care. New York: McGraw-Hill.*

Cindy Costain; Carolyn Ardron; Khandker Nurul Habib (2012): Synopsis of users' behaviour of a carsharing program: A case study in Toronto. In *Transportation Research Part A: Policy and Practice* 46 (3), pp. 421–434. DOI: 10.1016/j.tra.2011.11.005.

CIVITAS (2013): Personalised travel plans. Available online at http://civitas.eu/content/personalised-travel-plans-1, checked on 11/27/2015.

civity Management (2014): Urbane Mobilität im Umbruch? Available online at http://matters.civity.de/, updated on 8/26/2014, checked on 9/22/2015.

Climate-KIC (2011): Climate-KIC yearly review 2011. Driving climate innovation in Europe and beyond. Progress Towards our Strategic Objectives | 2011/12. Available online at http://www.climate-kic.org/wp-content/uploads/2013/02/Climate-KIC_yearly_review_2011.pdf, checked on 9/23/2015.

Cohen, B.a; Kietzmann, J.b (2014): Ride On! Mobility Business Models for the Sharing Economy. In *Organization and Environment* 27 (3), pp. 279–296. DOI: 10.1177/1086026614546199.

Coldefy, Jean; Lyon, Grand (Eds.) (2014): OptiCities, a Project for an Efficient Urban Mobility, Through the Development of Innovative ITS and Public/Private Cooperation.

Columbia Law Review (1942): Rationing of consumer goods. In *Columbia Law Review*.

coop@home (2016): Liefergebühren, Bestellschlusszeiten und Bestellmengen. Coop. Available online at http://www.coopathome.ch/images/layout/BestellschlussDE.pdf, checked on 3/18/2016.

Correia, G.; Viegas, J. M. (2009): A conceptual model for carpooling systems simulation. In *Journal of Simulation* 3 (1), pp. 61–68.

Crane, Randall (2000): The influence of urban form on travel: an interpretive review. In *Journal of Planning Literature* 15 (1), pp. 3–23.

Cusumano, Michael (2010): Cloud computing and SaaS as new computing platforms. In *Communications of the ACM* 53 (4), pp. 27–29.

Dahlgren, Joy (2002): High-occupancy/toll lanes: where should they be implemented? In *Transportation Research Part A: Policy and Practice* 36 (3), pp. 239–255. DOI: 10.1016/S0965-8564(00)00047-1.

Dahlitz, Matthew (2013): Consistency Theory. Available online at http://www.neuropsychotherapist.com/consistency-theory/, checked on 1/6/2016.

Dahlitz, Matthew (2015): Neuropsychotherapy: Defining the Emerging Paradigm of Neurobiologically Informed Psychotherapy. In *International Journal of Neuropsychotherapy* 3 (1), pp. 47–69. DOI: 10.12744/ijnpt.2015.0047-0069.

Daimler AG (2016): Der Mercedes-Benz F 015 Luxury in Motion. Available online at http://www.mercedes-benz.de/content/germany/mpc/mpc_germany_website/de/home_mpc/pass engercars/home/world/innovation/news/f_015_luxury_in_motion.html, checked on 3/1/2016.

Dalkmann, Holger; Brannigan, Charlotte (2007): Transport and climate change. In *Module 5e. Sustainable Transport: A Sourcebook for Policy-makers in Developing Cities. Deutsche Gesellschaft fuer Technische Zusammenarbeit (GTZ)*. Available online at http://www.gtkp.com/assets/uploads/20091123-095443-1692-5e_TCC.pdf.

Dargay, Joyce (2008): Personal transport choice. In *OECD Journal: General Papers* 2008 (2), pp. 59–93. Available online at http://www.keepeek.com/Digital-Asset-Management/oecd/economics/personal-transport-choice_gen_papers-v2008-art11-en#page1, checked on 11/27/2015.

Dimitrakopoulos, G.; Demestichas, P.; Koutra, V. (2012): Intelligent management functionality for improving transportation efficiency by means of the car pooling concept. IEEE Transactions on Intelligent Transportation Systems 13 (2), pp. 424–436. DOI: 10.1109/TITS.2011.2169669.

Dolleschel, Martin (2015): Mobilitätswoche Basel Dreiland. Edited by Amt für Mobilität. Bau- und Verkehrsdepartement des Kantons Basel-Stadt. Available online at http://www.mobilitaet.bs.ch/basel-unterwegs/kampagnen-aktionen/mobilitaetswoche.html, checked on 12/16/2015.

Dosi, Giovanni (1982): Technological paradigms and technological trajectories: A suggested interpretation of the determinants and directions of technical change. In *Research policy* 11 (3), pp. 147–162. DOI: 10.1016/0048-7333(82)90016-6.

El-Gendy, M. A.; Bose, A.; Shin, K. G. (2003): Evolution of the Internet QoS and support for soft real-time applications. In *Proceedings of the IEEE* 91 (7), pp. 1086–1104. DOI: 10.1109/JPROC.2003.814615.

Elsevier (2015): What content is included in Scopus? Available online at http://www.elsevier.com/solutions/scopus/content, updated on 8/28/2015, checked on 8/31/2015.

Eltis (2015a): Integration. European Commission. Available online at http://www.eltis.org/glossary/integration, checked on 12/3/2015.

Eltis (2015b): Sustainable Urban Mobility Plan. European Commission. Available online at http://www.eltis.org/glossary/sustainable-urban-mobility-plan, checked on 12/2/2015.

Eltis (2015c): The SUMP concept. European Commission. Available online at http://www.eltis.org/mobility-plans/sump-concept, checked on 12/2/2015.

Enoch, Marcus (2012): Sustainable transport, mobility management and travel plans. Farnham: Ashgate (Transport and mobility series).

ISO 14040:2006, October 2006: Environmental management – Life cycle assessment. Principles and framework. Available online at http://www.bifne.de/fileadmin/bifne/userdata/Bilder_und_Grafik /DIN-EN-ISO_14040_-_2006.pdf, checked on 3/7/2016.

Epple, Ruedi; Fridrich, Anna C.; Hagmann, Daniel; Kurmann, Fridolin; Leuenberger, Martin; Schnyder, Albert (2010a): Geschichte des Kantons Basel-Landschaft. Ausbau und Reform im Verkehrswesen. Verlag des Kantons Basel-Landschaft. Available online at http://www.geschichte.bl.ch/wirtschaft/wachstumsbewaeltigung/ausbau-und-reform-im-verkehrswesen.html, updated on 8/21/2009, checked on 12/28/2015.

Epple, Ruedi; Fridrich, Anna C.; Hagmann, Daniel; Kurmann, Fridolin; Leuenberger, Martin; Schnyder, Albert (2010b): Geschichte des Kantons Basel-Landschaft. Neues Umweltbewusstsein. Edited by Verlag des Kantons Basel-Landschaft. Available online at http://www.geschichte.bl.ch/no_cacche/wirtschaft/wachstumsbewaeltigung/wachstumsbewaeltigung-nebentext/nebentext/231/neues-umweltbewusstsein.html, updated on 8/21/2009, checked on 12/28/2015.

Epple, Ruedi; Fridrich, Anna C.; Hagmann, Daniel; Kurmann, Fridolin; Leuenberger, Martin; Schnyder, Albert (2010c): Geschichte des Kantons Basel-Landschaft. Wohlstandssymbol Auto. Available online at http://www.geschichte.bl.ch/no_cache/wirtschaft/wachstumsbewaeltigung/wachstums bewaeltigung-nebentext/nebentext/231/wohlstandssymbol-auto.html, updated on 8/21/2009, checked on 12/28/2015.

Eriksson, Louise; Garvill, Jörgen; Nordlund, Annika M. (2008): Acceptability of single and combined transport policy measures: The importance of environmental and policy specific beliefs. In *Transportation Research Part A: Policy and Practice* 42 (8), pp. 1117–1128.

European Parliament (2010): Directive 2010/40/EU of the European Parliament and of the Council on the framework for the deployment of Intelligent Transport Systems in the field of road transport and for interfaces with other modes of transport. Directive 2010/40/EU. Available online at http://eur-lex.europa.eu/LexUriServ/LexUriServ.do?uri=OJ:L:2010:207:0001:0013:EN:PDF, checked on 8/31/2015.

Eurostat (2015): Durchschnittliche Haushaltsgröße. Available online at http://appsso.eurostat.ec.europ a.eu/nui/show.do?dataset=ilc_lvph01&lang=de, checked on 8/18/2015.

Evans, Jennell (2010): Vision and Mission - What's the difference and why does it matter? Psychology Today. Available online at https://www.psychologytoday.com/blog/smartwork/201004/vision-and-mission-whats-the-difference-and-why-does-it-matter, updated on 12/17/2015, checked on 12/17/2015.

Ewing, Reid H.; Hodder, Robert (1998): Best development practices: a primer for smart growth: Smart Growth Network Washington, DC.

Fagnant, Daniel J.; Kockelman, Kara (2015a): Preparing a nation for autonomous vehicles. Opportunities, barriers and policy recommendations. In *Transportation Research Part A: Policy and Practice* 77, pp. 167–181. DOI: 10.1016/j.tra.2015.04.003.

Fagnant, Daniel J.; Kockelman, Kara M. (2014): The travel and environmental implications of shared autonomous vehicles, using agent-based model scenarios. In *Transportation Research Part C: Emerging Technologies* 40, pp. 1–13. DOI: 10.1016/j.trc.2013.12.001.

Fagnant, Daniel J.; Kockelman, Kara M. (Eds.) (2015b): Dynamic ride-sharing and optimal fleet sizing for a system of shared autonomous vehicles. Transportation Research Board 94th Annual Meeting (15-1962).

Favaro, Ken (2015): Vertical Integration 2.0: An Old Strategy Makes a Comeback. Edited by strategy+business. PwC. Available online at http://www.strategy-business.com/blog/Vertical-Integration-2-0-An-Old-Strategy-Makes-a-Comeback?gko=41fe1, updated on 5/6/2015, checked on 3/2/2016.

Feibel, Charles Edward (1987): Paratransit and urban public transport policy in low-and medium-income countries: a case study of Istanbul, Turkey. North Carolina Univ., Chapel Hill (USA).

Ferguson, Erik (1997): The rise and fall of the American carpool: 1970–1990. In *Transportation* 24 (4), pp. 349–376.

Ferreira, João; Trigo, Paulo; Filipe, Porfírio (2009): Collaborative car pooling system. In *World Academy of Science, Engineering and Technology* 54, pp. 721–725.

Fichter, Klaus (2002): E-Commerce: Sorting Out the Environmental Consequences. In *Journal of Industrial Ecology* 6 (2), pp. 25–41.

finanzen.ch (2015): Neues Containerterminal Basel Nord soll bis 2022 trimodal sein. finanzen.net GmbH. Available online at http://www.finanzen.ch/nachrichten/Aktien/Neues-Containerterminal-Basel-Nord-soll-bis-2022-trimodal-sein-1000942469, checked on 12/15/2015.

Firnkorn, Jörg; Müller, Martin (2015): Free-floating electric carsharing-fleets in smart cities. The dawning of a post-private car era in urban environments? In *Environmental Science & Policy* 45, pp. 30–40. DOI: 10.1016/j.envsci.2014.09.005.

Flämig, Heike; Bratzel, Stefan; Wulf-Holger, Arndt; Hesse, Markus (2001): Politikstrategien im Handlungsfeld Mobilität. Politikanalyse von lokalen, regionalen und betrieblichen Fallbeispielen und Beurteilung der Praxis im Handlungsfeld Mobilität. Berlin: IÖW (Schriftenreihe des IÖW / Institut für Ökologische Wirtschaftsforschung gGmbH, 156).

Fleiter, Judy J.; Lennon, Alexia; Watson, Barry (2010): How do other people influence your driving speed? Exploring the 'who' and the 'how' of social influences on speeding from a qualitative perspective. In *Transportation Research Part F: Traffic Psychology and Behaviour* 13 (1), pp. 49–62. DOI: 10.1016/j.trf.2009.10.002.

Ford Media Center (2015): Mobility Experiment: Big Data Drive. Dearborn. Available online at https://media.ford.com/content/fordmedia/fna/us/en/news/2015/01/06/mobility-experiment-big-data-drive-dearborn.html, checked on 9/10/2015.

Ford Motor Company (2013): Ford Embracing Analytics and Big Data to Inform Eco-Conscious Decisions, Stay Green. Edited by Ford Media Center. Available online at https://media.ford.com/content/fordmedia-mobile/fna/us/en/news/2013/10/25/ford-embracing-analytics-and-big-data-to-inform-eco-conscious-de.html, updated on 10/25/2013, checked on 4/12/2016.

Ford Motor Company (2015): SYNC AppLink Overview. Ford Motor Company. Available online at https://owner.ford.com/how-tos/sync-technology/sync/sync-applink/sync-applink-overview.html, updated on 9/10/2015, checked on 9/10/2015.

Franchi, Federica; Malpezzi, Silvia (2013): Infomobility: an Integrated Framework. In *Global Journal on Technology* 3.

Frank, Lawrence D.; Pivo, Gary (1994): Impacts of mixed use and density on utilization of three modes of travel: single-occupant vehicle, transit, and walking. In *Transportation Research Record*, p. 44.

Frankfurter Allgemeine Zeitung (2015): Prognose: Wirtschaftsforscher sagen Pendlerrekord vorher. Frankfurter Allgemeine Zeitung GmbH. Available online at http://www.faz.net/aktuell/beruf-chance/arbeitswelt/prognose-wirtschaftsforscher-sagen-pendlerrekord-vorher-13713682.html, checked on 10/10/2015.

Frick, Roman; Belart, Benjamin (2013): Studienauftrag "Stiig-Um". Synthesebericht. Fachliche Basis für Umsetzungskonzept § 13 Umweltschutzgesetz. Edited by Beurteilungsgremium Stigg-um. Available online at http://www.umverkehr.ch/sites/default/files/stiig-um_synthese_studienauftrag_final.pdf, checked on 12/21/2015.

Frick, Roman; Belart, Benjamin (2014): Verkehrspolitisches Leitbild und Massnahmenplan §13 USG. Vernehmlassungsbericht. Edited by Bau- und Verkehrsdepartement Basel-Stadt. Available online at http://www.mobilitaet.bs.ch/dms/mobilitaet/download/3_Gesamtverkehr/2014-11-19_Vernehmlassungsbericht.pdf, checked on 1/15/2016.

Fritz, Peter; Busch-Lüty, Christiane (1995): Nachhaltigkeit in naturwissenschaftlicher und sozialwissenschaftlicher Perspektive. Eine Publikation der Karl-Heinz-Beckurts-Stiftung. Stuttgart: Hirzel [u.a.] (Edition Universitas).

Fujii, Satoshi; Garling, Tommy (2007): Role and Acquisition of Car-Use Habit. In Tommy Gärling, Linda Steg (Eds.): Threats from car traffic to the quality of urban life. Problems, causes, and solutions. Amsterdam, Oxford: Elsevier, pp. 235–250.

Future Internet Architecture Group (2012): Future Internet Design Principles. Edited by European Commission. Available online at http://www.future-internet.eu/uploads/media/FIArch_Design_Principles_V1.0.pdf, checked on 2/5/2016.

Gassmann, Oliver; Frankenberger, Karolin; Csik, Michaela (2013): Geschäftsmodelle entwickeln: 55 innovative Konzepte mit dem St. Galler Business Model Navigator: Carl Hanser Verlag GmbH Co KG.

Gerla, Mario; Lee, Eun-Kyu; Pau, Giovanni; Lee, Uichin (Eds.) (2014): Internet of vehicles: From intelligent grid to autonomous cars and vehicular clouds: IEEE. Available online at http://ieeexplore.ieee.org/xpl/login.jsp?tp=&arnumber=6803166&url=http%3A%2F%2Fieeexplore.ieee.org%2Fxpls%2Fabs_all.jsp%3Farnumber%3D6803166, checked on 4/25/2016.

Gertz, Carsten (1998): Umsetzungsprozesse in der Stadt- und Verkehrsplanung. Die Strategie der kurzen Wege. Berlin: TU, Univ.-Bibliothek, Abt. Publ. (Schriftenreihe ... des Instituts für Strassen- und Schienenverkehr / Technische Universität Berlin, 30).

Geschäftsstelle Agglomerationsprogramm Basel (2012): Agglomerationsprogramm Basel 2. Generation. Teil 1 - Hauptbericht.

GetMobility (2015): Spotcar Carsharing schließt die Pforten. GetMobility - News und Infos zu On-demand und same day delivery Entwicklungen. Available online at http://getmobility.de/20150512-spotcar-carsharing/, checked on 9/23/2015.

Geurs, Karst T.; van Wee, Bert (2004): Accessibility evaluation of land-use and transport strategies: review and research directions. In *Journal of Transport Geography* 12 (2), pp. 127–140.

Ghezzi, Antonio; Dramitinos, Manos (2016): Towards a Future Internet infrastructure. Analyzing the multidimensional impacts of assured quality Internet interconnection. In *Telematics and Informatics* 33 (2), pp. 613–630. DOI: 10.1016/j.tele.2015.10.003.

Gidoin, Daniel; van Schoonhoven, Bas; Bodea, Gabriella; Dubus, Nathalie; van Oort, Sander (2013): Multimodal services in a city: security and privacy challenges. Final report. Available online at http://cordis.europa.eu/fp7/ict/netinnovation/deliverables/instant-mobility/instant-mobility-d79.pdf, checked on 9/13/2015.

Gohl, Julia (2015): «Catch a Car» erobert die Agglomeration. Edited by bz Basellandschaftliche Zeitung. Available online at http://www.basellandschaftlichezeitung.ch/basel/baselbiet/catch-a-car-erobert-die-agglomeration-129433617, checked on 12/15/2015.

Golub, Aaron; Martens, Karel (2014): Using principles of justice to assess the modal equity of regional transportation plans. In *Journal of Transport Geography* 41, pp. 10–20.

Goodchild, Michael F. (2001): Specialist Meeting on Location Based Services. Final Report. Santa Barbara (Specialist Research Meetings—Papers and Reports).

Goodwin, Antuan (2009): Ford unveils open-source Sync developer platform. CNET. Available online at http://www.cnet.com/news/ford-unveils-open-source-sync-developer-platform/, checked on 9/9/2015.

Goodwin, Phil (2008): Policy incentives to change behaviour in passenger transport. In *May-2008.[Online]. Available: http://www. internationaltransportforum. org.[Accessed: 14-Dec-2012]*.

Google (2014): Just press go: designing a self-driving vehicle. Edited by Google Inc. Available online at https://googleblog.blogspot.ch/2014/05/just-press-go-designing-self-driving.html, updated on 5/27/2014, checked on 2/8/1016.

Google (2016): Google Self-Driving Car Project. Available online at https://www.google.com/selfdrivingcar/, updated on 2/5/2016, checked on 2/8/2016.

Gorringe, Carl (2009): OpenTrip: an open protocol for the interchange of travel information among rideshare providers. Presented at the MIT/CMU Real-Time Rides Workshop, Cambridge, MA. Available online at http://ridesharechoices.scripts.mit.edu/home/wp-content/papers/RTRWorkshop-OpenTrip.pdf, checked on 10/7/2015.

Government of the Canton Basel-Stadt (2007): Politikplan 2008-2011. Das Planungs- und Steuerungsinstrument des Regierungsrates mit Bilanz 2006/2007. Edited by Staatskanzlei des Kantons Basel-Stadt. Available online at http://www.bs.ch/news/2007-09-26-mm-31668.html, checked on 12/10/2015.

Grant, Jill (2002): Mixed use in theory and practice: Canadian experience with implementing a planning principle. In *Journal of the American Planning Association* 68 (1), pp. 71–84.

Grawe, Klaus (2007): Neuropsychotherapy: How the neurosciences inform effective psychotherapy: Lawrence Erlbaum Associates Publishers.

Gruel, Wolfgang; Piller, Frank (2016): A New Vision for Personal Transportation. In *MIT Sloan Management Review* 57 (2). Available online at http://sloanreview.mit.edu/article/a-new-vision-for-personal-transportation/, checked on 2/8/2016.

Grupp, Laura M.; Davis, John D.; Swanson, Steven (Eds.) (2012): The bleak future of NAND flash memory: USENIX Association.

Gruyter, Chris de; Rose, Geoffrey; Currie, Graham (2015): Enhancing the impact of travel plans for new residential developments. Insights from implementation theory. In *Transport Policy* 40, pp. 24–35. DOI: 10.1016/j.tranpol.2015.02.008.

Gschwind, Eva (2014): Vorschau auf die Grossratssitzung vom 10. und 17. September 2014. Available online at http://www.grosserrat.bs.ch/de/service/news-archiv/361-vorschau-auf-die-grossratssitzung-vom-10-und-17-september-2014, checked on 12/12/2015.

Gu, Guan-Qun; Luo, Jun-Zhou: Some Issues on Computer Networks: Architecture and Key Technologies. In *Journal of Computer Science and Technology* 21 (5), pp. 708–722. DOI: 10.1007/s11390-006-0708-2.

Gubbi, Jayavardhana; Buyya, Rajkumar; Marusic, Slaven; Palaniswami, Marimuthu (2013): Internet of Things (IoT): A vision, architectural elements, and future directions. In *Future Generation Computer Systems* 29 (7), pp. 1645–1660.

Hammer, Antje (2015a): Bike to work. Edited by Amt für Mobilität. Bau- und Verkehrsdepartement des Kantons Basel-Stadt. Available online at http://www.mobilitaet.bs.ch/basel-unterwegs/kampagnen-aktionen/bike-to-work.html, checked on 12/16/2015.

Hammer, Antje (2015b): Pendlerfonds. Edited by Bau- und Verkehrsdepartement des Kantons Basel-Stadt. Available online at http://www.mobilitaet.bs.ch/gesamtverkehr/verkehrsstrategie/pendler/fonds.html, updated on 12/13/2015, checked on 12/13/2015.

Hammer, Antje (2015c): Pendlerfonds Basel-Stadt unterstützt drei weitere Infrastrukturprojekte in der Agglomeration Basel, die dem umweltfreundlichen Pendlerverkehr dienen. Edited by Bau- und

Verkehrsdepartement des Kantons Basel-Stadt. Available online at http://www.bs.ch/news/2015-03-05-mm-62683.html, checked on 12/13/2015.

Handelskammer beider Basel (2015): Witschaftsfreundliches Mobilitätsmanagement Basel. Available online at http://www.hkbb.ch/Standortpolitik/Engagements%20und%20Mandate/Mobilit%C3%A4tsmanagement, checked on 12/16/2015.

Handy, Susan; Cao, Xinyu; Mokhtarian, Patricia L. (2005): Correlation or causality between the built environment and travel behavior? Evidence from Northern California. In *Transportation Research Part D: Transport and Environment*, pp. 427–444. Available online at http://escholarship.org/uc/item/5b76c5kg, checked on 4/25/2016.

Hanley, M.; Henning, J.; Valsan, A.; Tremblay, J-F.; Scholz, R.; Byron, R. (2013): Urban mobility blueprint. Business strategies in an emerging ecosystem. Edited by EYGM Limited. Available online at http://www.ey.com/Publication/vwLUAssets/Urban_mobility_blueprint_-_executive_summary/$FILE/Urban_mobility_blueprint-executive_summary.pdf, checked on 9/6/2015.

Harder, Sören (2014): ÖPNV-nahe Studie: Carsharing soll Stadtverkehr verschlimmern. Edited by Spiegel Online. Available online at http://www.spiegel.de/auto/aktuell/car2go-und-drivenow-studie-kritisiert-carsharing-von-bmw-und-mercedes-a-987998.html, updated on 9/3/2014, checked on 9/22/2015.

Harvey, Francis (2008): Primer of GIS: Fundamental geographic and cartographic concepts: Guilford Press.

Hasselbring, W.; Reussner, R. (2006): Toward trustworthy software systems. Computer. In *Computer* 39 (4), pp. 91–92. DOI: 10.1109/MC.2006.142.

Hayashi, T.; Hidaka, K.; Teshima, S. (2014): Carsharing and IT enabled services. Available online at https://www.scopus.com/record/display.uri?eid=2-s2.0-84906752977&origin=inward&txGid=0, checked on 4/25/2016.

Heckley, Steve; Cre, Ivo; Da Cunha Ferreira, Antonio; Guehnemann, Astrid; Marsden, Greg; May, Tony; Mullen, Caroline (2014): Why is Cooperation a challenge in sustainable urban mobility planning? Available online at http://www.eltis.org/sites/eltis/files/trainingmaterials/challenge_cooperation_final.pdf, checked on 4/25/2016.

Hegarty, Christopher J.; Chatre, Eric (2008): Evolution of the global navigation satellitesystem (GNSS). In *Proceedings of the IEEE* 96 (12), pp. 1902–1917.

Heikkilä, Sonja (2014): Mobility as a Service - A Proposal for Action for the Public Administration. Case Helsinki.

Heim, Michael (2011): Wer finanziert wem die Fahrt mit Bus und Tram? Edited by bz Basellandschaftliche Zeitung. Available online at http://www.basellandschaftlichezeitung.ch/basel/basel-stadt/wer-finanziert-wem-die-fahrt-mit-bus-und-tram-116134839, checked on 12/28/2015.

Helfrich, Silke (2012): Commons. Für eine Neue Politik Jenseits von Markt und Staat: Heinrich-Böll-Stiftung.

Henderson, Jason (2006): Secessionist automobility: racism, anti-urbanism, and the politics of automobility in Atlanta, Georgia. In *International Journal of Urban and Regional Research* 30 (2), pp. 293–307.

Hepburn, Cameron (2006): Regulation by prices, quantities, or both: a review of instrument choice. In *Oxford review of economic policy* 22 (2), pp. 226–247.

Hertel, Martina; Bührmann, Sebastian (2014): Ruhender Verkehr. Push and Pull. Edited by Deutsches Institut für Urbanistik. Available online at http://www.difu.de/projekte/2014/push-pull.html, checked on 11/23/2015.

Heylighen, Francis (2002): Complexity and Information Overload in Society: why increasing efficiency leads to decreasing control. Draft paper, version: April 12, 2002, to be submitted to: The Information Society. Available online at http://web.archive.org/web/20070103090951/http://pespmc1.vub.ac.be/Papers/Info-overload.pdf, checked on 8/11/2015.

Hine, Julian; Scott, J. (2000): Seamless, accessible travel: users' views of the public transport journey and interchange. In *Transport Policy* 7 (3), pp. 217–226.

Hinterberger, Fritz (2009): Der Ressourcen-Rucksack. STANDARD Verlagsgesellschaft m. b. H. Available online at http://derstandard.at/1241622478584/Der-Ressourcen-Rucksack, checked on 8/11/2015.

Hothersall, David (2004): History of psychology. 4th ed. New York, London: McGraw-Hill.

Hu, Tian-Yi; Xie, Xiaofei; Han, Xiao-Yan; Ma, Xiao-Qin (2012): How do passengers influence drivers' propensities for angry driving? Different effects of supervisors versus friends. In *Accident Analysis & Prevention* 49, pp. 429–438. DOI: 10.1016/j.aap.2012.03.015.

Huff, Anne S.; Floyd, Steven W.; Sherman, Hugh D.; Terjesen, Siri (2009): Strategic management. Logic & action. Hoboken, NJ: John Wiley & Sons. Available online at http://www.loc.gov/catdir/enhancements/fy0814/2008009618-d.html.

Hull, Angela (2005): Integrated transport planning in the UK: From concept to reality. In *Journal of Transport Geography* 13 (4), pp. 318–328.

Induct Technology (2014): Induct Launches Navia, The First 100 Percent Electric, Self-Driving Shuttle In The U.S. Navia launches as the World's first and only commercially available driverless vehicle. Edited by Newswire Association LLC. PR Newswire. Available online at http://www.prnewswire.com/news-releases/induct-launches-navia-the-first-100-percent-electric-self-driving-shuttle-in-the-us-238980311.html, updated on 1/1/2014, checked on 2/8/2016.

Institut der deutschen Wirtschaft (2015): Eine halbe Stunde reicht. Institut der deutschen Wirtschaft Köln. Available online at http://www.iwkoeln.de/infodienste/iwd/archiv/beitrag/pendler-eine-halbe-stunde-reicht-233555?highlight=pendler, checked on 10/10/2015.

International Council on Clean Transportation (2014): EU CO2 standards for passenger cars and light-commercial vehicles. International Council on Clean Transportation. Available online at http://www.theicct.org/eu-co2-standards-passenger-cars-and-lcvs, checked on 3/9/2016.

International Transport Forum (2015): Urban Mobility System Upgrade. How shared self-driving cars could change city traffic. Edited by International Transport Forum. OECD. Available online at http://www.internationaltransportforum.org/Pub/pdf/15CPB_Self-drivingcars.pdf, checked on 7/31/2015.

Investopedia (2015): Subprime Loan Definition. Investopedia, LLC. Available online at http://www.investopedia.com/terms/s/subprimeloan.asp, checked on 9/23/2015.

Jacobs, Adam (2009): The pathologies of big data. In *Communications of the ACM* 52 (8), p. 36. DOI: 10.1145/1536616.1536632.

Jacobsen, Peter L. (2003): Safety in numbers: more walkers and bicyclists, safer walking and bicycling. In *Injury prevention* 9 (3), pp. 205–209.

James, Peter (2007): Conferencing at BT. Results of a Survey on its Economic, Environmental and Social Impacts. UK Centre for Economic and Environmental Development.

Janasz, Tomasz (2015): Brave New World - The Future of Automobility. In *Getty Science* 06, pp. 18–19. Available online at http://gettyscience.org/2015/10/brave-new-world-the-future-of-automobility/, checked on 4/24/2016.

Janasz, Tomasz; Janasz, Dominika (2013a): Smart Ways. Intermodal Urban Mobility. Innovative Mobility for Innovative Society. Available online at http://www.emobility-award.ch/fileadmin/BilderF%C3%B6rderpreis/20131208_Smart_Ways_One_Pager_en.pdf, checked on 3/22/2016.

Janasz, Tomasz; Janasz, Dominika (2013b): Smart Ways. Biznesplan. Innowacyjna mobilność dla innowacyjnego społeczeństwa. Białystok.

Janasz, Tomasz; Schneidewind, Uwe (2017): The Future of Automobility. In Michael Kleinemeier, Gerhard Oswald (Eds.): Shaping the Digital Enterprise. Trends and Use Cases in Innovation and Transformation: Springer Verlag.

Johnson, Mark W. (2010): Seizing the white space. Business Model Innovation for Growth and Renewal: Harvard Business Press.

Jones, Peter (2012): Developing sustainable transport for the next generation: The need for a multi-sector approach. In *5IATSS6 Research* 35 (2), pp. 41–47. DOI: 10.1016/j.iatssr.2011.11.001.

Justiz- und Sicherheitsdepartment des Kantons Basel-Stadt (2015): Pendlerparkkarte. Available online at http://www.polizei.bs.ch/verkehr/strassenverkehr/parkieren/pendlerparkkarte.html, checked on 12/14/2015.

Kaisler, S.; Armour, F.; Espinosa, J. A.; Money, W. (Eds.) (2013): Big Data: Issues and Challenges Moving Forward. System Sciences (HICSS), 2013 46th Hawaii International Conference on. System Sciences (HICSS), 2013 46th Hawaii International Conference on.

Kanton Basel-Stadt (4/20/1986): Verordnung über unbeschränktes Parkieren in Blauen Zonen. Parkkartenverordnung, revised 3/29/2015. Available online at http://www.lex-find.ch/dta/3972/2/952.560.pdf, checked on 12/28/2015.

Kanton Basel-Stadt (3/13/1991): Umweltschutzgesetz Basel-Stadt - 780.100. USG BS, revised 12/28/2014. Source: http://www.gesetzessammlung.bs.ch/frontend/versions/3258?locale=de.

Kanton Basel-Stadt (2010a): Kantonale Abstimmungsvorlagen vom 28. November 2010: Schlussresultat. Edited by Kanton Basel-Stadt. Available online at http://www.umverkehr.ch/sites/default/files/w-a-10-11-28-schlussresultat-kantonal.pdf, checked on 12/17/2015.

Kanton Basel-Stadt (2010b): Stellungnahme und Gegenvorschlag des Regierungsrates zur kantonalen Volksinitiative zur Förderung des ÖV, Fuß- und Veloverkehrs im Kanton Basel-Stadt (Städte-Initiative). Abstimmung vom 28. November 2010. Available online at http://www.grosser-rat.bs.ch/dokumente/100353/000000353763.pdf, checked on 12/17/2015.

Kanton Basel-Stadt (2015): Richtplan des Kantons Basel-Stadt. Strategie. Bau- und Verkehrsdepartement des Kantons Basel-Stadt. Available online at http://www.richtplan.bs.ch/richtplantext/strategie.html, checked on 12/20/2015.

Kanton Basel-Stadt (2016): Branchenprogramme. Edited by Amt für Wirtschaft und Arbeit des Kantons Basel-Stadt. Available online at http://www.awa.bs.ch/standortfoerderung/wirtschaftspolitik/branchenprogramme.html, checked on 3/17/2016.

Kaufmann, Alfred (2011): Das Institute for Mobile Communications (IMC) setzt die Segel. Available online at https://www.hitech.bfh.ch/fileadmin/data/2011_3/dt_pdf/Deutsch_Ganz.pdf, checked on 2/5/2016.

Kejariwal, Arun; Kulkarni, Sanjeev; Ramasamy, Karthik (2015): Real Time Analytics: Algorithms and Systems. In *Proceedings of the VLDB Endowment* 8 (12).

Kelly, Kalon L. (2007): Casual carpooling-enhanced. In *Journal of Public Transportation* 10 (4), p. 6.

Kenworthy, Jeffrey R.; Laube, Felix B. (1996): Automobile dependence in cities: an international comparison of urban transport and land use patterns with implications for sustainability. In *Environmental impact assessment review* 16 (4), pp. 279–308.

Kenyon, Susan; Lyons, Glenn (2003): The value of integrated multimodal traveller information and its potential contribution to modal change. In *Transportation Research Part F: Traffic Psychology and Behaviour* 6 (1), pp. 1–21.

Kietzmann, Jan H.; Hermkens, Kristopher; McCarthy, Ian P.; Silvestre, Bruno S. (2011): Social media? Get serious! Understanding the functional building blocks of social media. In *Business horizons* 54 (3), pp. 241–251.

Kircher, David; Wapensky, Lawrence (1978): Vanpooling: An Overview (EPA/908/1-78/001).

Kitamura, Ryuichi; Mokhtarian, Patricia L.; Laidet, Laura (1997): A micro-analysis of land use and travel in five neighborhoods in the San Francisco Bay Area. In *Transportation* 24 (2), pp. 125–158.

Knoflacher, Hermann (2006): A new way to organize parking: the key to a successful sustainable transport system for the future. In *Environment and Urbanization* 18 (2), pp. 387–400.

Koffka, Kurt (2013): Principles of Gestalt psychology: Routledge.

Kornhauser, Alain (2011): Personal Rapid Transit. A Transportation Plan for New Jersey. Princeton University. Available online at http://www.mist-er.com/PrincetonPRTReport2011.pdf, checked on 8/20/2015.

Kornhauser, Alain L. (2013): Uncongested Mobility for All: NJ's Area-wide aTaxi System. Princeton Autonomous Vehicle Engineering (PAVE), Princeton University. Available online at http://smartdrivingcar.com/ataxis-for-nj-08.11.13.html, checked on 11/9/2015.

Koscher, K.; Czeskis, A.; Roesner, F.; Patel, S.; Kohno, T. (2010): Experimental security analysis of a modern automobile. In *2010 IEEE Symposium on Security and Privacy*, pp. 447–462.

Köster, Oliver (2014): Systematik zur Entwicklung von Geschäftsmodellen in der Produktentstehung. Paderborn, Universität Paderborn, Diss., 2013.

Kratz, Sven; Hemmert, Fabian; Rohs, Michael (2011): Natural User Interfaces in Mobile Phone Interaction.

Krisher, Tom (2013): GM to offer nearly self-driving car by 2020. Edited by USA TODAY. Available online at http://www.usatoday.com/story/money/cars/2013/08/30/gm-general-motors-self-driving-autonomous-car/2725091/, checked on 11/9/2015.

Kryder, Mark H.; Kim, Chang Soo (2009): After hard drives—what comes next? In *Magnetics, IEEE Transactions on* 45 (10), pp. 3406–3413.

Kühn, Peter (2014): TwoGo or not TwoGo. Available online at http://www.dynamic-ridesharing.de/TwoGoOrNotTwoGo, updated on 10/12/2015, checked on 10/12/2015.

Kwon, Jaimyoung; Varaiya, Pravin (2008): Effectiveness of California's high occupancy vehicle (HOV) system. In *Transportation Research Part C: Emerging Technologies* 16 (1), pp. 98–115.

Lah, Oliver (2015): The barriers to low-carbon land-transport and policies to overcome them. In *Eur. Transp. Res. Rev.* 7 (1). DOI: 10.1007/s12544-014-0151-3.

Lanctot, Roger (2015): Carzapp, Santander Will Change Auto Lending. Available online at https://www.strategyanalytics.com/strategy-analytics/blogs/automotive/infotainment-telematics/infotainment-telematics/2015/07/07/carzapp-santander-will-change-auto-lending#.VgJ14svtlBc, checked on 9/23/2015.

Le Vine, Scott (2014): A Pareto–efficient market–clearing mechanism for shared–mobility systems. In *International Journal of Automotive Technology and Management* 14 (3-4), p. pp 271-285.

Le Vine, Scott; Zolfaghari, Alireza; Polak, John (2014): Carsharing: Evolution, Challenges and Opportunities. Association des Constructeurs Européens d'Automobiles. Available online at https://www.acea.be/uploads/publications/SAG_Report_-_Car_Sharing.pdf, checked on 11/26/2015.

Lencer (2007): Topographische Karte vom Großraum Basel. Available online at https://de.wikipedia.org/wiki/Datei:Grossraum_Basel.png?previous=yes, checked on 1/4/2016.

Lerner, W.; Koob, Daniel; Korniichuk, Oleksii (2012a): How business can help solve urban mobility. In *Traffic Engineering and Control* 53 (1), pp. 6–7.

Lerner, Wilhelm; Ali, Salman; Baron, Ralf; Doyon, Antoine; Herzog, Boris; Koob, Daniel et al. (2012b): The Future of Urban Mobility: Towards Networked, Multimodal Cities in 2050. With assistance of Global Future of Urban Mobility LabTeam. Arthur D. Little. Available online at http://www.adlittle.com/downloads/tx_adlreports/ADL_Future_of_urban_mobility.pdf, checked on 4/28/2016.

Levin, Irwin P. (1982): Measuring tradeoffs in carpool driving arrangement preferences. In *Transportation* 11 (1), pp. 71–85.

Lexikon der Nachhaltigkeit (2014): Ökologischer Rucksack (MIPS-Konzept). Edited by Aachener Stiftung Kathy Beys. Aachener Stiftung Kathy Beys. Available online at https://www.nachhaltigkeit.info/artikel/schmidt_bleek_mips_konzept_971.htm, checked on 8/11/2015.

Leypoldt, Patrick (2012): Strategie 2030. Trinationale Agglomeration Basel. Available online at http://www.agglobasel.org/id-2-generation.html?file=files/theme/agglobasel/content/dokumente/g2/AP2_Basel_Strategiebericht_2012_06_30_de.pdf, checked on 12/11/2015.

Li, Jianling (2001): Explaining high-occupancy-toll lane use. In *Transportation Research Part D: Transport and Environment* 6 (1), pp. 61–74. DOI: 10.1016/S1361-9209(00)00013-4.

Li, Xu; Lu, Rongxing; Liang, Xiaohui; Shen, Xuemin; Chen, Jiming; Lin, Xiaodong (2011): Smart community: an internet of things application. In *Communications Magazine, IEEE* 49 (11), pp. 68–75.

Lin, Dong; Allan, Andrew; Cui, Jianqiang; McLaughlin, Ralph (2012): The Effects of Polycentric Development on Commuting Patterns in Metropolitan Areas. In *Regional Studies Association.*

Litman, Todd (2000): Evaluating Carsharing Benefits. In *Transportation Research Record: Journal of the Transportation Research Board* 1702, pp. 31–35. DOI: 10.3141/1702-04.

Litman, Todd (2006): Parking management: strategies, evaluation and planning: Victoria Transport Policy Institute. Available online at www.vtpi.org/park_man_comp.pdf, checked on 4/25/2016.

Litman, Todd (2014): Autonomous Vehicle Implementation Predictions. Victoria Transport Policy Institute. Available online at www.vtpi.org/avip.pdf, checked on 4/25/2016.

Litman, Todd; Doherty, Eric (2009): Parking Costs. In Todd Litman, Eric Doherty (Eds.): Transportation Cost and Benefit Analysis II. Techniques, Estimates and Implications. Available online at http://www.vtpi.org/tca/tca0504.pdf, checked on 3/7/2016.

Liu, Ang; Wuest, Thorsten; Wei, Wei; Lu, Stephen (2014): Application of Prospect Theory on Car Sharing Product Service System. In *Procedia CIRP* 16, pp. 350–355. DOI: 10.1016/j.procir.2014.02.022.

Lohr, Steve (2012): The Age of Big Data. The New York Times. Available online at http://www.nytimes.com/2012/02/12/sunday-review/big-datas-impact-in-the-world.html?_r=2&scp=1&sq=Big%20Data&st=cse, checked on 4/25/2016.

Loshin, David (2014): Adressing Five Emerging Challenges of Big Data. Progress Software Corporation. Available online at https://www.progress.com/docs/default-source/default-document-library/Progress/Documents/Papers/Addressing-Five-Emerging-Challenges-of-Big-Data.pdf, checked on 9/11/2015.

Löwengut, Stephan (2015): Tempo 30. Edited by Bau- und Verkehrsdepartement des Kantons Basel-Stadt. Available online at http://www.mobilitaet.bs.ch/gesamtverkehr/verkehrskonzepte/tempo-30.html, updated on 12/16/2015, checked on 12/16/2015.

Lubbes, Sara (2006): Babcock developer wants to add units. Available online at http://www.herald-tribune.com/apps/pbcs.dll/article?AID=/20060614/NEWS/606140576/-1/RSS01, checked on 11/11/2015.

Lyndon, Henry (2014): How rail public transportation has been a leader in the Analytics and Big Data revolution | Light Rail Now on WordPress.com. Available online at http://lightrailnow.wordpress.com/2013/09/03/how-rail-public-transportation-has-been-a-leader-in-the-analytics-and-big-data-revolution/, updated on 4/13/2014, checked on 4/14/2014.

Maitrey, Seema; Jha, C. K. (2015): MapReduce: Simplified Data Analysis of Big Data. In *Procedia Computer Science* 57, pp. 563–571.

Manjrasoft Pty Ltd.: Manjrasoft - Aneka Architecture. Manjrasoft Pty Ltd. Available online at http://www.manjrasoft.com/aneka_architecture.html, checked on 9/12/2015.

Manns, Jonathan (2010): Beyond Brundtland's Compromise. In *Town & Country Planning*, pp. 337–340.

Markoff, John (2014): Google's Next Phase in Driverless Cars. No Steering Wheel or Brake Pedals. Edited by The New York Times. Available online at http://www.nytimes.com/2014/05/28/technology/googles-next-phase-in-driverless-cars-no-brakes-or-steering-wheel.html?_r=0, checked on 11/9/2015.

Marks, Paul (2012): Hands off the wheel. In *New Scientist* 213 (2858), pp. 19–20.

Marletto, Gerardo (2011): Structure, Agency And Change In The Car Regime. A Review Of The Literature (Working Papers, 0610). Available online at http://host.uniroma3.it/centri/crei/pubblicazioni/workingpapers2010/CREI_06_2010.pdf, checked on 4/29/2016.

Martens, Karel (2013): Accessibility and potential mobility as a guide for policy action. Paper presented at the CVS Conference 21-22 November 2013 Rotterdam, the Netherlands.

Martin, Elliot; Shaheen, Susan; Lidicker, Jeffrey (2010): Impact of carsharing on household vehicle holdings: Results from North American shared-use vehicle survey. In *Transportation Research Record: Journal of the Transportation Research Board* (2143), pp. 150–158.

Martinez, Luis M.; Correia, Gonçalo H. A.; Viegas, José M. (2015): An agent-based simulation model to assess the impacts of introducing a shared-taxi system. An application to Lisbon (Portugal). In *J. Adv. Transp.* 49 (3), pp. 475–495. DOI: 10.1002/atr.1283.

Matas, Anna (2004): Demand and revenue implications of an integrated public transport policy: the case of Madrid. In *Transport Reviews* 24 (2), pp. 195–217.

Maxwell, D.; Owen, P.; McAndrew, L.; Muehmel, K.; Neubauer, A. (2011): Addressing the rebound effect. A report for the European Commission DG Environment. Available online at http://ec.europa.eu/environment/archives/eussd/pdf/rebound_effect_report.pdf, checked on 1/6/2016.

May, Anthony D.; Kelly, Charlotte; Shepherd, Simon (2006): The principles of integration in urban transport strategies. In *Transport Policy* 13 (4), pp. 319–327.

McAfee, Andrew; Brynjolfsson, Erik; Davenport, Thomas H.; Patil, D. J.; Barton, Dominic (2012): Big data. In *The management revolution. Harvard Bus Rev* 90 (10), pp. 61–67. Available online at https://hbr.org/2012/10/big-data-the-management-revolution/ar, checked on 9/11/2015.

McDonald, Mark P.; Rowsell-Jones, Andy (2012): Digital Business: How Technology Will Support Growth - Forbes. Gartner Inc. Available online at http://www.forbes.com/sites/gartnergroup

/2012/11/28/digital-business-how-technology-will-support-growth/#60422b0f2972, checked on 2/4/2016.

Meadows, Donella H. (1972): The limits to growth. A report for the Club of Rome's project on the predicament of mankind. New York: Universe Books.

Mechnich, Markus (2014): Teilen und schützen. Mobilitätsprojekt "Carzapp". Der Tagesspiegel. Available online at http://www.tagesspiegel.de/mobil/mobilitaetsprojekt-carzapp-teilen-und-schuetzen/9346520.html, checked on 4/23/2016.

medGadget (2012): Google's Self-Driving Car for Blind People. Edited by The Atlantic. Available online at http://www.theatlantic.com/health/archive/2012/04/googles-self-driving-car-for-blind-people/255594/, checked on 2/6/2016.

Meena, Jagan Singh; Sze, Simon Min; Chand, Umesh; Tseng, Tseung-Yuen (2014): Overview of emerging nonvolatile memory technologies. In *Nanoscale research letters* 9 (1), p. 526. DOI: 10.1186/1556-276X-9-526.

Mell, Peter; Grance, Tim (2011): The NIST definition of cloud computing. Special Publication 800-145. National Institute of Standards and Technology. Gaithersburg.

Metz, David (2012): The Limits to Travel: How Far Will You Go? London: Routledge.

Michaels, Ed; Handfield-Jones, Helen; Axelrod, Beth (2001): The war for talent. Boston, Mass., Great Britain: Harvard Business School Press.

Mindali, Orit; Raveh, Adi; Salomon, Ilan (2004): Urban density and energy consumption: a new look at old statistics. In *Transportation Research Part A: Policy and Practice* 38 (2), pp. 143–162.

Minsch, Jürg; Feindt, Peter Henning; Meister, Hans-Peter; Schneidewind, Uwe; Schulz, Tobias; Tscheulin, Jochen (1998): Institutionelle Reformen für eine Politik der Nachhaltigkeit. Studie im Auftrag der Enquete-Kommission" Schutz des Menschen und der Umwelt" des Deutschen Bundestages: Heidelberg/New York/Berlin: Springer.

Miorandi, Daniele; Sicari, Sabrina; Pellegrini, Francesco de; Chlamtac, Imrich (2012): Internet of things: Vision, applications and research challenges. In *Ad Hoc Networks* 10 (7), pp. 1497–1516.

MIT "Real-Time" Rideshare Research (2009): Selective History of Ridesharing. MIT "Real-Time" Rideshare Research. Available online at http://ridesharechoices.scripts.mit.edu/home/2009/02/history-of-ridesharing/, checked on 10/7/2015.

MIT Mobile Experience Lab; Smart Cities Group (2014): Green Wheel - Smart Mobility and Ubiquitous Computing. Available online at http://mobile.mit.edu/greenwheel/, updated on 8/5/2014, checked on 9/7/2015.

Mitchell, W. J.; Borroni-Bird, C. E.; Burns, L. D. (2010): Re-Inventing the Automobile: Urban Mobility for the 21st Century: MIT Press, Cambridge, MA. Available online at http://www.amazon.de/Reinventing-Automobile-Personal-Mobility-Century/dp/0262013827.

Mollman, Steve (2009): From cars to TVs, apps are spreading to the real world. CNN.com. Available online at http://edition.cnn.com/2009/TECH/10/08/apps.realworld/, checked on 9/9/2015.

Mont, Oksana K. (2002): Clarifying the concept of product–service system. In *Journal of cleaner production* 10 (3), pp. 237–245.

Morelli, John (2013): Environmental sustainability: A definition for environmental professionals. In *Journal of Environmental Sustainability* 1 (1), p. 2.

Mori, Tomoya (2006): Monocentric versus polycentric models in urban economics. Kyoto University, Institute of Economic Research.

Mossberg, Walt (2016): Apple and Google should win the war for the dashboard. Edited by The Verge. Available online at http://www.theverge.com/2016/1/13/10754966/walt-mossberg-apple-car play-android-auto-car-infotainment?xing_share=news, checked on 2/5/2016.

Motavalli, Jim (2010): G.M. EN-V: Sharpening the Focus of Future Urban Mobility. Edited by The New York Times. Available online at http://wheels.blogs.nytimes.com/2010/03/24/g-m-en-v-sharpen ing-the-focus-of-future-urban-mobility/, checked on 2/8/2016.

Müller, Thierry (2012): Attraktive Mobilitätsangebote. In Mostviertel Tourismus (Ed.): Nachhaltigkeit auf den Weg gebracht. Dokumentation zur 5. Mostviertler Nachhaltigkeitskonferenz. 5. Mostviertler Nachhaltigkeitskonferenz. Steinschaler Dörfl, Pielachtal, 3. und 4. September 2012, pp. 20–21. Available online at http://brochures.austria.info/pdfs/0000/5235/12_NHKDok_Inter net1s.pdf, checked on 8/18/2015.

Naess, Petter; Sandberg, Synneve Lyssand (1996): Workplace location, modal split and energy use for commuting trips. In *Urban Studies* 33 (3), pp. 557–580.

Nash, Chris; Whitelegg, John (2016): Key research themes on regulation, pricing, and sustainable urban mobility. In *International Journal of Sustainable Transportation* 10 (1), pp. 33–39.

Neuenschwander, René; Walter, Felix; Bertschy, Kathrin; Büchler, Simon (2012): Urbane Herausforderungen aus Bundessicht. Ein Diskussionsbeitrag zur Weiterentwicklung der Agglomerationspolitik. Edited by Ecoplan AG. Available online at http://www.are.admin.ch/themen/agglomeration/?lang=de&download=NHzLpZeg7t,lnp6I0NTU042l2Z6ln1acy4Zn4Z2qZpnO2Yuq2Z6gpJCEeHx6fGym162ep-Ybg2c_JjKbNoKSn6A--, checked on 12/10/2015.

Newman, Peter (2007): Beyond peak oil: will our cities collapse? In *Journal of urban technology* 14 (2), pp. 15–30.

Newman, Peter G.; Kenworthy, Jeffrey R. (1989): Cities and automobile dependence: An international sourcebook.

Newman, Peter W. G.; Kenworthy, Jeffrey R. (1996): The land use—transport connection: An overview. In *Land use policy* 13 (1), pp. 1–22.

Nickel, Werner (Ed.) (2013): Recycling-Handbuch. Strategien - Technologien - Produkte. Berlin: Springer Berlin (VDI-Buch).

Nijhuis, Jorrit O. (2013): Consuming mobility: a practice approach to sustainable mobility transitions. Wageningen: Wageningen Academic Publishers.

Nissan Motor Company (2013): Nissan Announces Unprecedented Autonomous Drive Benchmarks. Edited by NissanNews.com. Available online at http://nissannews.com/en-US/nissan/usa/releases /nissan-announces-unprecedented-autonomous-drive-benchmarks, checked on 11/9/2015.

NIST (2015): Draft NIST Big Data Interoperability Framework. Volume 1, Definitions. Special Publication 1500-1. National Institute of Standards and Technology. Gaithersburg.

NSW Government (2015): Point to Point Transport Taskforce. Discussion Paper. Available online at https://p2p-prod-assets.s3.amazonaws.com/p2p/s3fs-public/discussion-paper.pdf, checked on 10/9/2015.

NZZ (2009): Rund eine Million Einwohner lebt ohne eigenen Wagen: Lust und Last der Autofreiheit. Neue Zürcher Zeitung AG, Schweiz. Available online at http://www.nzz.ch/lust-und-last-der-autofreiheit-1.1639721, updated on 1/5/2009, checked on 12/16/2015.

OECD (2004): Communicating environmentally sustainable transport. The role of soft measures. Report of the Workshop held in Berlin, December 2002. OECD. Paris. Available online at http://www.oecd-ilibrary.org/environment/communicating-environmentally-sustainable-transport_9789264106642-en, checked on 4/25/2016.

OECD (2013): Government at a Glance 2013. Paris: OECD Publishing. Available online at http://www.oecd.org/gov/govataglance.htm, checked on 2/9/2016.

Ohnmacht, Timo; Götz, Konrad; Haefeli, Ueli; Deffner, Jutta; Matti, Daniel; Stettler, Jürg; Grotrian, Jobst (2008): Freizeitverkehr innerhalb von Agglomerationen: Eidgenössisches Departement für Umwelt, Verkehr, Energie und Kommunikation UVEK, Bundesamt für Strassen.

Oshry, Barry (2007): Seeing systems. Unlocking the mysteries of organizational life. 2nd ed., Rev. and expanded. San Francisco: Berrett-Koehler Publishers.

Osterwalder, Alexander (2004): The business model ontology: A proposition in a design science approach. Available online at http://www.hec.unil.ch/aosterwa/PhD/Osterwalder_PhD_BM_Ontology.pdf, checked on 4/25/2016.

Osterwalder, Alexander; Pigneur, Yves (2010): Business model generation: a handbook for visionaries, game changers, and challengers: John Wiley & Sons.

Paech, Niko (2012): Vom grünen Wachstumsmythos zur Postwachstumsökonomie. Warum weiteres wirtschaftliches Wachstum keine zukunftsfähige Option ist. In Woynowski, B., Becker, P., Bertram, A., Bhandari, S., Burger, J., Haver, M., Janssen, A., Lange, J., Miyazaki, J., Peters, G., Ruf, F., Schneider, J., Sempach, J., Wang, C. (Ed.): Wirtschaft ohne Wachstum?! Notwendigkeit und Ansätze einer Wachstumswende. Reihe Arbeitsberichte des Instituts für Forstökonomie 59-2012. Freiburg, p. 131.

Parikh, Aashna; Deshmukh, Sanjay (2013): Search Engine Optimization. In *International Journal of Engineering Research and Technology* 2 (11).

Parry, Ian W. H.; Small, Kenneth A. (2007): Should urban transit subsidies be reduced? In *Available at SSRN 1001430*.

Paskaleva, Krassimira Antonova (2011): The smart city: A nexus for open innovation? In *Intelligent Buildings International* 3 (3), pp. 153–171.

Patterson, David A. (2008): The data center is the computer. In *Communications of the ACM* 51 (1), p. 105.

Pavone, Marco (2015): Autonomous mobility-on-demand systems for future urban mobility. In M. Maurer, J. C. Gerdes, B. Lenz, H. Winner (Eds.): Autonomes Fahren: Technische, rechtliche undgesellschaftliche Aspekte: Springer, pp. 399–416.

Peppard, Joe; Rylander, Anna (2006): From value chain to value network:: Insights for mobile operators. In *European Management Journal* 24 (2), pp. 128–141.

Peter Wells; Paul Nieuwenhuis (2012): Transition failure: Understanding continuity in the automotive industry. In *Technological Forecasting and Social Change* 79 (9), pp. 1681–1692. DOI: 10.1016/j.techfore.2012.06.008.

Petrunoff, Nicholas; Rissel, Chris; Wen, Li Ming; Bindon, Jeni (2015): We need more active travel intervention research–why not travel plans? In *Health Promotion Journal of Australia* 25 (3), pp. 209–210.

Pieper, N.; Heußler, T.; Woisetschläger, D.; Backhaus, C. (2013): Relevanz der Intermodalität für Car-Sharing-Konzepte. In Heike Proff (Ed.): Schritte in die künftige Mobilität. Technische und betriebswirtschaftliche Aspekte. Wiesbaden: Springer Gabler, pp. 379–399.

Popken, Ben; NBC News (2015): Amazon Tests Delivery To Your Car Trunk. Available online at http://www.nbcnews.com/business/autos/amazon-testing-delivery-your-car-trunk-n346886, checked on 1/23/2016.

Porter, Michael E. (1998): Competitive advantage. Creating and sustaining superior performance. With a new introduction. New York, London: Free Press.

Pucher, John; Komanoff, Charles; Schimek, Paul (1999): Bicycling renaissance in North America?: Recent trends and alternative policies to promote bicycling. In *Transportation Research Part A: Policy and Practice* 33 (7), pp. 625–654.

Randelhoff, Martin (2014): Vergleich unterschiedlicher Flächeninanspruchnahmen nach Verkehrsarten (pro Person). Available online at http://www.zukunft-mobilitaet.net/78246/analyse/flaechenbedarf-pkw-fahrrad-bus-strassenbahn-stadtbahn-fussgaenger-metro-bremsverzoegerung-vergleich/, updated on 1/1/1970, checked on 11/2/2015.

Rapp, Peter; Tempier, Rémi (2011): Study regarding a European Multi-Modal Journey Planner. European Commission Directorate-General Energy and Transport. Available online at http://ec.europa.eu/transport/themes/its/consultations/doc/2011_05_27-multimodal-journey-planner-results.pdf, checked on 2/8/2016.

Regierungsrat des Kantons Basel-Stadt (12/22/1992): Verordnung über die Erstellung von Parkplätzen für Personenwagen. Parkplatzverordnung, PPV, revised 1/20/2013. Available online at http://www.gesetzessammlung.bs.ch/frontend/versions/2454, checked on 12/28/2015.

Regierungsrat des Kantons Basel-Stadt (2014): Verordnung über die Parkraumbewirtschaftung. Edited by Regierungsrat des Kantons Basel-Stadt. Available online at http://www.polizei.bs.ch/dms/polizei/download/verkehr/mfk/Verordnung--ber-die-Parkraumbewirtschaftung-29.03.2015/Verordnung%20PRBV%20.pdf, checked on 12/14/2015.

Regierungsrat Kanton Basel-Stadt (2013): Legislaturplan 2013 –2017. Edited by Kanton Basel-Stadt. Available online at http://www.bs.ch/publikationen/entwicklung/legislaturplan_2013_2017.html, updated on 2013, checked on 12/17/2015.

Reh, Werner (2001): Strategien zur Umsetzung des 4-Säulen-Konzeptes zur Sicherung einer nachhaltigen Verkehrsentwicklung. Erfolgsfaktoren für Projekte einer dauerhaften umweltverträglichen Mobilität in Deutschland: eine politikwissenschaftliche Analyse im Auftrag des Umweltbundesamtes. (Forschungsvorhaben Nr. 20096132/01, März 2001), updated on 2001.

Reid, Axel (2012): Big data and decision-making. Available online at http://alex-reid.net/2012/02/big-data-and-the-coffee-cup.html, checked on 9/11/2015.

Reinauer, Roger (2015): Rheintunnel – erste Schritte zur Realisierung eingeleitet. Edited by Bau- und Verkehrsdepartement des Kantons Basel-Stadt. Available online at http://www.bs.ch/news/2015-01-28-mm-62465.html, checked on 12/15/2015.

Rigole, Pierre-Jean (2014): Study of a Shared Autonomous Vehicles Based Mobility Solution in Stockholm.

Riofrio, Melissa (2014): Car apps: Ford's Sync AppLink marries car to phone, but the relationship's complicated. Available online at http://www.techhive.com/article/2449816/car-apps-fords-sync-applink-marries-car-to-phone-but-the-relationships-complicated.html, updated on 9/10/2015, checked on 9/10/2015.

Ritthoff, Michael; Rohn, Holger; Liedtke, Christa (2002): Calculating MIPS. Resource productivity of products and services. Wuppertal: Wuppertal Inst. for Climate, Environment and Energy (Wuppertal spezial, 27e).

Robèrt, K.-H.; Schmidt-Bleek, B.; Aloisi de Larderel, J.; Basile, G.; Jansen, J. L.; Kuehr, R. et al. (2002): Strategic sustainable development – selection, design and synergies of applied tools. In *Journal of cleaner production* (10), pp. 197–214. Available online at http://www.sciencedirect.com/science/article/pii/S0959652601000610#.

Roberts, Marion; Turner, Chris; Greenfield, Steve; Osborn, Guy (2006): A continental ambience? Lessons in managing alcohol-related evening and night-time entertainment from four European capitals. In *Urban Studies* 43 (7), pp. 1105–1125.

Rogge, Ludger (1999): Erfolgsbedingungen und Handlungsblockaden umweltorientierter kommunaler Verkehrspolitik. In *Schriftenreihe des IÖW* 140.

Roland Berger (2014): Shared Mobility. How new businesses are rewriting the rules of the private transportation game. Roland Berger. Available online at https://www.rolandberger.com/media/pdf/Roland_Berger_TAB_Shared_Mobility_20140716.pdf, checked on 8/29/2015.

Romph, Erik de (2013): Using BIG data in transport modelling. In *Data & Modelling Magazine* (10).

Rückriem, Georg (2009): Digital technology and mediation: A challenge to activity theory. In *Learning and expanding with activity theory*, pp. 88–111.

Rye, Tom; Ison, Stephen (2005): Overcoming barriers to the implementation of car parking charges at UK workplaces. In *Transport Policy* 12 (1), pp. 57–64.

Saleh, Wafaa; Sammer, Gerd (2009): Travel demand management and road user pricing. Success, failure and feasibility. Burlington, VT: Ashgate (Transport and society).

Sanchez, Thomas W. (1999): The connection between public transit and employment: the cases of Portland and Atlanta. In *Journal of the American Planning Association* 65 (3), pp. 284–296.

Santi, Paolo; Resta, Giovanni; Szell, Michael; Sobolevsky, Stanislav; Strogatz, Steven H.; Ratti, Carlo (2014): Quantifying the benefits of vehicle pooling with shareability networks. In *Proceedings of the National Academy of Sciences* 111 (37), pp. 13290–13294.

Santos, Georgina; Behrendt, Hannah; Maconi, Laura; Shirvani, Tara; Teytelboym, Alexander (2010a): Part I: Externalities and economic policies in road transport. In *Road Transport Externalities, Economic Policies And Other Instruments For Sustainable Road Transport* 28 (1), pp. 2–45. DOI: 10.1016/j.retrec.2009.11.002.

Santos, Georgina; Behrendt, Hannah; Teytelboym, Alexander (2010b): Part II: Policy instruments for sustainable road transport. In *Road Transport Externalities, Economic Policies And Other Instruments For Sustainable Road Transport* 28 (1), pp. 46–91. DOI: 10.1016/j.retrec.2010.03.002.

SAP Global Corporate Affairs (2015): Corporate Fact Sheet. SAP: Run Simple - The World's Largest Provider of Enterprise Application Software. SAP SE. Available online at http://www.sap.com/bin/sapcom/en_us/downloadasset.2015-07-jul-22-01.SAP-Corporate-Fact-Sheet-en-2015-07-22-pdf.html, checked on 10/11/2015.

SAP News (2013): New Ride-Sharing App from SAP Helps Organizations Reduce Costs, Save Resources and Better Engage Employees. SAP SE. Available online at http://news.sap.com/new-ride-sharing-app-from-sap-helps-organizations-reduce-costs-save-resources-and-better-engage-employees/, checked on 10/11/2015.

SAP SE (2014): Integrated Report 2014. Environmental Performance. Energy and Emissions. Available online at http://sapintegratedreport.com/2014/en/performance/environmental-performance/energy-and-emissions.html, checked on 10/12/2015.

Sauter, Daniel; Wyss, Kurt (2014): Pilotstudie: Velonutzung von Jugendlichen im Kanton Basel-Stadt. Schlussbericht. Bau- und Verkehrsdepartement des Kantons Basel-Stadt. Available online at http://www.mobilitaet.bs.ch/dms/mobilitaet/download/Basel-bewegt/velonutzung_jugendl_kt_bs_schlussbericht.pdf, checked on 1/15/2016.

SBB Cargo (2012): Ein grosser Bahnhof für Container. Available online at http://www.sbbcargo.com/content/sbbcargo/de/desktop/medien/publikationen/cargomagazin/cargomagazin-212/212-basel nord/_jcr_content/relatedPar/contextmenu/downloadList/cargo_magazin_2_2011.spooler.download.pdf, checked on 12/15/2015.

SBB.ch (2014): Catch a Car – das erste Free Floating Carsharing in der Schweiz. Edited by SBB AG. Available online at http://www.sbb.ch/bahnhof-services/auto-velo/mieten-und-ausleihen/catch-a-car.html, checked on 12/15/2015.

Schade, W.; Krail, M.; Kühn, A. (2014): New mobility concepts: myth or emerging reality? Transport Research Arena 2014. Paris.

Schafer, Elizabeth D. (2003): Digital Technology. Cengage Learning. Available online at http://www.encyclopedia.com/doc/1G2-3401801216.html, checked on 9/8/2015.

Schäfer, Andreas (2009): Transportation in a climate-constrained world. London, England: MIT press.

Schaltegger, S.; Burritt, Roger; Petersen, Holger (2003): An introduction to corporate environmental management. Striving for sustainability. Sheffield: Greenleaf.

Scheidegger, Peter (2013): Durchmesserlinien dank Herzstück. Technischer Schlussbericht der Vorstudien 2008-2012. Edited by Planungsgemeinschaft Herzstück (Kantone BL und BS, SBB). Available online at http://www.herzstueck-basel.ch/vorstudien.html?file=files/theme/herzstueck/content/downloads/berichte/schlussbericht_vorstudien_2012.pdf, checked on 12/12/2015.

Schellnhuber, Hans Joachim; Messner, Dirk; Leggewie, Claus; Leinfelder, Reinhold; Nakicenovic, Nebojsa; Rahmstorf, Stefan et al. (2011): World in transition: a social contract for sustainability. Flagship Report 2011. In *Berlin: German Advisory Council on Global Change (WBGU)(Flagship Report)*. Available online at http://www.wbgu.de/en/flagship-reports/fr-2011-a-social-contract/, checked on 3/3/2016.

Schlaffer, Alexandra; Hunecke, Marcel; Dittrich-Wesbuer, Andrea; Freudenau, Henrik (2002): Bedeutung psychologischer und sozialer Einflussfaktoren für eine nachhaltige Verkehrsentwicklung 2002.

Schmid, Daniel (2013): Wer alleine ins Büro fährt, ist selber schuld. Focus Online. Available online at http://www.focus.de/finanzen/experten/schmid/nachhaltigkeit-macht-freude-wirtschaftliche-fort entwicklung-wer-alleine-ins-buero-faehrt-ist-selber-schuld_id_3477918.html, updated on 12/12/2013, checked on 10/10/2015.

Schmidt-Bleek, F. (1994): Wieviel Umwelt braucht der Mensch? MIPS, das Mass für ökologisches Wirtschaften. With assistance of Rainer Klüting. Berlin: Birkhäuser.

Schmidt-Bleek, Friedrich (2014): Grüne Lügen. Nichts für die Umwelt, alles fürs Geschäft - wie Politik und Wirtschaft die Welt zugrunde richten. München: Ludwig Verlag.

Schneider-Sliwa, Rita; Kampschulte, Andrea; Nommel, Jens-Ulrich; Sandtner, Martin; Strassmann, Renato; Waffenschmidt, Christian (1999): Bevölkerungsstruktur und Bevölkerungsdynamik beider Basel. Available online at https://web.archive.org/web/20070928151534/http://wwww.statistik-bs.ch/publikationen/stadt_region/heft1/sr_bevoelkerung.pdf, checked on 12/10/2015.

Schneidewind, Uwe (2013a): Transformative Literacy. Gesellschaftliche Veranderungsprozesse verstehen und gestaltenTransformative Literacy. Understanding and Shaping Societal Transformations. In *GAIA-Ecological Perspectives for Science and Society* 22 (2), pp. 82–86.

Schneidewind, Uwe (2013b): Wandel verstehen: auf dem Weg zu einer" Transformative Literacy". In Harald Welzer, Klaus Wiegandt (Eds.): Wege aus der Wachstumsgesellschaft: S. Fischer Verlag, pp. 115–140.

Schneidewind, Uwe; Feindt, Peter Henning; Meister, Hans-Peter; Minsch, Jürg; Schulz, Tobias; Tscheulin, Jochen (1997): Institutionelle Reformen für eine Politik der Nachhaltigkeit: Vom Was zum

Wie in der Nachhaltigkeitsdebatte. In *GAIA-Ecological Perspectives for Science and Society* 6 (3), p. 182.

Schonberger, Ben; Gutmann, Steve (2013): A Self-Driving Future: At The Intersection Of Driverless Cars And Car Sharing. Available online at http://www.sightline.org/2013/06/04/a-self-driving-future/, checked on 2/6/2016.

Scientific Applications international Corporation (2006): Life Cycle Assessment: Principles and Practice. US EPA. Available online at http://nepis.epa.gov/Exe/ZyPURL.cgi?Dockey=P1000L86.txt, checked on 3/7/2016.

Sessa, C. (2007): Achieving sustainable cities with integrated land use andtransport strategies. In Stephen Marshall, David Banister (Eds.): Land use and transport. European research towards integrated policies / edited by Stephen Marshall, David Banister. 1st ed. Amsterdam, London: Elsevier, pp. 37–70.

Shaheen, Susan; Cohen, Adam; Roberts, J. (2006): Carsharing in North America: Market growth, current developments, and future potential. In *Transportation Research Record: Journal of the Transportation Research Board* (1986), pp. 116–124.

Shankland, Stephen (2013): Self-driving cars will bristle with sensors. Available online at http://www.cnet.com/news/self-driving-cars-will-bristle-with-sensors/, updated on 9/3/2013, checked on 2/10/2016.

Shoup, Donald C. (2006): Cruising for parking. In *Transport Policy* 13 (6), pp. 479–486.

Small, Kenneth A.; Verhoef, Erik T. (2007): The economics of urban transportation. Milton Park, Abingdon: Routledge.

Solar Roadways (2015): Solar Roadways. Introduction. Available online at http://www.solarroadways.com/intro.shtml, checked on 9/7/2015.

Sorrell, Steve (2007): The Rebound Effect: an assessment of the evidence for economy-wide energy savings from improved energy efficiency: UK Energy Research Centre London. Available online at http://aida.econ.yale.edu/~nordhaus/homepage/documents/UK_ReboundEffectReport.pdf, checked on 1/6/2016.

Spector, Dina (2015): Uber will deliver free ice cream across the UK today. Edited by Business Insider Inc. Available online at http://uk.businessinsider.com/uber-ice-cream-promotion-2015-7, updated on 7/24/2015, checked on 2/8/2016.

Spickermann, Alexander; Grienitz, Volker; von der Gracht, Heiko A. (2014): Heading towards a multimodal city of the future? In *Technological Forecasting and Social Change* 89, pp. 201–221. DOI: 10.1016/j.techfore.2013.08.036.

Spiegel Online (2015): Umstrittener Fahrdienst: Gericht stoppt Uber in ganz Deutschland - SPIEGEL ONLINE. Spiegel Online. Available online at http://www.spiegel.de/wirtschaft/unternehmen/uber-gericht-stoppt-taxidienst-in-ganz-deutschland-a-989332.html, updated on 9/2/2014, checked on 9/23/2015.

Spieser, Kevin; Treleaven, Kyle; Zhang, Rick; Frazzoli, Emilio; Morton, Daniel; Pavone, Marco (2014): Toward a systematic approach to the design and evaluation of automated mobility-on-demand systems: A case study in Singapore. In Gereon Meyer, Sven Beiker (Eds.): Road Vehicle Automation: Springer, pp. 229–245.

Spillmann, Hans-Jürg (2014): Argumentarium. Herzstück - Durchmesserlinie für die Regio S-Bahn Basel. Available online at http://www.herzstueck-basel.ch/files/theme/herzstueck/content/downloads/berichte/argumentarium_herzstueck_regio_def_version_140828.pdf, checked on 12/12/2015.

Stadt Walldorf: Mitfahren. Mitfahrlösung TwoGo by SAP. Available online at http://www.walldorf.de/2010/index.php?seite=2833, checked on 10/12/2015.

Stadt Walldorf (2010): Daten und Fakten die für Walldorf sprechen. Stadt Walldorf. Available online at http://www.walldorf.de/2010/uploads/dokumente/Daten_und_Fakten_die_fuer_Walldorf_sprechen.pdf, checked on 10/12/2015.

Städtekonferenz Mobilität (2012): Städtevergleich Mobilität. Vergleichende Betrachtung der Städte Basel, Bern, Luzern, St.Gallen, Winterthur und Zürich. Edited by Basel-Stadt Mobilität, Stadt Bern Verkehrsplanung, Stadt Luzern Tiefbauamt, Stadt St.Gallen Tiefbauamt, Stadt Winterthur Amt für Städtebau, Stadt Zürich Tiefbauamt. Available online at http://skm-cvm.ch/cmsfiles/130124_stadtevergleich_mobilitat.pdf, checked on 12/10/2015.

Stähler, Patrick (2002): Geschäftsmodelle in der digitalen Ökonomie: Merkmale, Strategien und Auswirkungen. Köln: JOSEF EUL VERLAG.

Stalder, Beatrice (2011): Einführung strategisches Management im Amt für Mobilität BVD Basel-Stadt. Presentation. Amt für Mobilität.

Statistical Office of the Canton of Basel-Stadt (2009): Motorisierungsgrad. nach Wohnviertel, 2009. Basel. Available online at http://centos.4teamwork.ch/Daten_Stata/Export-Stata/karten/themen/verkehr/D17_Motorisierungsgrad.pdf, checked on 12/10/2015.

Statistical Office of the Canton of Basel-Stadt (2015a): Bevölkerung. Bestand und Struktur. Available online at http://www.statistik.bs.ch/zahlen/tabellen/1-bevoelkerung/bestand-struktur.html, checked on 12/10/2015.

Statistical Office of the Canton of Basel-Stadt (2015b): Bevölkerungsszenarien 2015. Available online at http://www.statistik.bs.ch/zahlen/analysen/bevoelkerungsszenarien.html, checked on 12/10/2015.

Stubbs, Michael (2002): Car parking and residential development: sustainability, design and planning policy, and public perceptions of parking provision. In *Journal of Urban Design* 7 (2), pp. 213–237.

Studnia, I.; Nicomette, Nicomette,.; Alata, E.; Deswarte, Y.; Kaaniche, M.; Laarouchi, Y. (Eds.) (2013): Security of embedded automotive networks: state of the art and a research proposal. 32nd International Conference on Computer Safety. Toulouse, France, September 2013.

Suo, H.; Wan, J.; Zou, C.; Liu, J. (2012): Security in the Internet of Things: A Review. International Conference on Computer Science and Electronics Engineering (ICCSEE), 2012.

Sweeting, Walter J.; Winfield, Patricia H. (2012): Future transportation: Lifetime considerations and framework for sustainability assessment. In *Energy Policy* 51, pp. 927–938.

Tapscott, Don; Lowy, Alex; Ticoll, David (2000): Digital capital: Harnessing the power of business webs: Harvard Business Press.

Teal, Roger F.; Fielding, G. J.; Giuliano, G.; Marks, J. V.; Goodhue, R. E. (1980): Shared Ride Taxi Services as Community Public Transit.

The Associated Press (2011): Officials in car-centric LA approve bike lane plan. Available online at http://www.scpr.org/news/2011/03/01/24568/officials-car-centric-la-approve-bike-lane-plan/, checked on 1/4/2016.

The Economist (2014): In the self-driving seat. Available online at http://www.economist.com/news/business/21603029-google-miles-ahead-its-rivals-race-autonomous-motoring-self-driving-seat, checked on 2/10/2016.

The Levin Institute (2012): Rio 20+, a Failed Effort to Build a New Worldwide Sustainability Agreement. Edited by Globalization101. The State University of New York. Available online at http://www.globalization101.org/rio-20-a-failed-effort-to-build-a-new-worldwide-sustainability-agreement/, checked on 3/4/2016.

The Ministry of Education of New Zealand (2006): Enabling the 21 st Learner. An e-Learning Action Plan for Schools 2006–2010. Available online at http://www.nzceta.co.nz/pages/digital_technologies.htm, updated on 5/22/2014, checked on 2/4/2016.

Thrun, Sebastian (2010): Toward robotic cars. In *Communications of the ACM* 53 (4), pp. 99–106. Available online at http://cacm.acm.org/magazines/2010/4/81485-toward-robotic-cars/fulltext, checked on 11/9/2015.

Tietenberg, Thomas H. (2007): Environmental economics and policy. 5th ed. Boston, Mass., Harlow: Pearson/Addison-Wesley (The Addison-Wesley series in economics).

Tils, Gabriele; Rehaag, Regine; Glatz, Andreas (2015): Carsharing – ein Beitrag zu nachhaltiger Mobilität. Working Papers des KVF NRW, Nr. 2 Juni. Verbraucherzentrale NRW/Kompetenzzentrum Verbraucherforschung NRW. Düsseldorf.

Timmers, Paul (1998): Business models for electronic markets. In *Electronic markets* 8 (2), pp. 3–8.

TNW Tarifverbund Nordwestschweiz (2015a): TNW Jahresrückblick 2014 und Ausblick. Available online at http://www.tnw.ch/fileadmin/redacteur/pdf/Allgemein/MM_TNW_R%C3%BCck-__Ausblick_2014_Final.pdf, checked on 3/17/2016.

TNW Tarifverbund Nordwestschweiz (2015b): Unternehmen TNW. Available online at http://www.tnw.ch/unternehmen-tnw/, updated on 6/26/2014, checked on 12/28/2015.

Töpfer, Armin (2007): Betriebswirtschaftslehre. Anwendungs- und prozessorientierte Grundlagen. 2., überarb. Aufl. Berlin [u.a.]: Springer.

Transport Research & Innovation Portal (2015): Transport Technology. Edited by TRIP consortium. European Commission. Available online at http://www.transport-research.info/web/themes/technology.cfm, updated on 7/9/2015, checked on 9/7/2015.

Transportation Research Board (2015): About TRID. Transportation Research Board. Available online at http://www.trb.org/InformationServices/AboutTRID.aspx, checked on 8/31/2015.

Trinationaler Eurodistrict Basel TEB (2016): Bevölkerung TEB. Eine Agglomeration von fast 1 Mio. Einwohnern. Available online at http://www.eurodistrictbasel.eu/de/agglomeration/bevoelkerung.html, checked on 1/4/2016.

Tschoegl, Adrian; Guillén, Mauro F. (2008): Building a Global Bank. The Transformation of Banco Santander. Princeton, N.J.: Princeton University Press.

Tschopp, Jürg (1997): Integration of bicycles and public transport in Basel, Switzerland. In Rodney Tolley (Ed.): The greening of urban transport. Planning for walking and cycling in Western cities / edited by Rodney Tolley. 2nd ed. Chichester: Wiley.

Tschudin, Patrik; Beck, Renato (2013): Wir werden in den Abgrund regiert. Ein Interview mit Peter Sloterdijk. Available online at http://www.tageswoche.ch/de/2013_10/kultur/517701/, checked on 3/4/2016.

Tukker, Arnold; Tischner, Ursula (2006): Product-services as a research field: past, present and future. Reflections from a decade of research. In *Journal of cleaner production* 14 (17), pp. 1552–1556. Available online at http://www.sciencedirect.com/science/article/pii/S0959652606000862, checked on 9/23/2015.

U.S. General Services Administration (2016): Life Cycle Assessment (LCA) Overview. GSA Sustainable Facilites Tool. U.S. General Services Administration. Available online at https://sftool.gov/plan/400/life-cycle-assessment-lca-overview, checked on 3/7/2016.

Uber Technologies Inc. (2016): The Uber story. Available online at https://www.uber.com/our-story, checked on 2/9/2016.

Uhl, Axel; Born, Matthias; Koschmider, Agnes; Janasz, Tomasz (2014a): Digital Capability Framework. A toolset to become a digital enterprise. In Axel Uhl, Lars A. Gollenia (Eds.): Digital Enterprise Transformation. A Business-Driven Approach to Leveraging Innovative IT. Farnham: Gower, pp. 27–60.

Uhl, Axel; Born, Matthias; Koschmider, Agnes; Janasz, Tomasz (2014b): The importance of technological trends and how to exploit them for business excellence. In Axel Uhl, Lars A. Gollenia (Eds.): Digital Enterprise Transformation. A Business-Driven Approach to Leveraging Innovative IT. Farnham: Gower, pp. 1–25.

UK Commission for Integrated Transport (2009): Physical integration. Non-physical measures to encourage integration. UK Commission for Integrated Transport. Available online at http://webarchive.nationalarchives.gov.uk/20110304132839/http://cfit.independent.gov.uk/pubs/2000/physical/physical/02.htm, updated on 8/17/2009, checked on 11/23/2015.

UK Department for Transport (2008): A sustainable future for cycling.

UK DETR (1998): A new deal for transport: better for everyone. White Paper: Department of the Environment, Transport and the Regions. Available online at http://www.persona.uk.com/a5dunstable/deposit-docs/DD001-DD025/DD-020.pdf, checked on 11/23/2015.

umverkehR Schweiz (2008): Kantonale Volksinitiative zur Förderung des ÖV, Fuss- und Veloverkehrs im Kanton Basel-Stadt (Städte-Initiative). umverkehR Schweiz. Available online at http://www.umverkehr.ch/sites/default/files/initiativtext_s-i_basel.pdf, checked on 12/17/2015.

umverkehR Schweiz (2015a): Die Städte-Initiativen. umverkehR Schweiz. Available online at http://www.umverkehr.ch/staedte-initiativen, checked on 12/16/2015.

umverkehR Schweiz (2015b): Organisation. umverkehR Schweiz. Available online at http://www.umverkehr.ch/organisation, checked on 12/16/2015.

United Nations General Assembly (2005): 2005 World Summit Outcome. United Nations (Resolution A/60/1). Available online at http://data.unaids.org/Topics/UniversalAccess/worldsummitoutcome_resolution_24oct2005_en.pdf, checked on 3/4/2016.

Urban ITS Expert Group (2013): Guidelines for ITS deployment in urban areas: multimodal information. Edited by Dorota Szeligowska, Christian Egeler. Urban ITS Expert Group.

Urry, John (2008): Governance, flows, and the end of the car system? In *Global Environmental Change* 18 (3), pp. 343–349. DOI: 10.1016/j.gloenvcha.2008.04.007.

Vaidyanathan, Shruti (2014): Energy Savings from Information and Communications Technologies in Personal Travel.

van Audenhove, François-Joseph; Dauby, Laurent; Korniichuk, Oleksii; Pourbaix, Jérôme (2014): The Future of Urban Mobility. Imperatives to shape extended mobility ecosystems of tomorrow. Arthur D. Little. Available online at http://www.uitp.org/sites/default/files/members/140124%20Arthur%20D.%20Little%20%26%20UITP_Future%20of%20Urban%20Mobility%202%200_Full%20study.pdf, checked on 4/25/2016.

van Goeverden, Cees; Rietveld, Piet; Koelemeijer, Jorine; Peeters, Paul (2006): Subsidies in public transport. In *European Transport* 32, pp. 5–25.

van Ierland, E.; van der Straaten, J.; Vollebergh, H.R.J. (2001): Economic Growth and Valuation of the Environment: A Debate: Edward Elgar Publishing, Incorporated. Available online at https://books.google.ch/books?id=nzBmAwAAQBAJ.

VCS Verkehrs-Club der Schweiz (2010): Städte-Initiative Basel-Stadt. Edited by Verkehrs-Club der Schweiz. Available online at http://www.vcs-blbs.ch/in-der-region/staedteinitiative/, checked on 12/16/2015.

Verband Deutscher Verkehrsunternehmen VDV (2013): Der ÖPNV: Rückgrat und Motor eines zukunftsorientierten Mobilitätsverbundes. Available online at https://www.vdv.de/vdv-positionspapier-mmm.pdfx?forced=true, checked on 2/8/2016.

Vlacic, Ljubo; Parent, Michel; Harashima, Fumio (2001): Intelligent Vehicle Technologies: Theory and Applications. Oxford: Butterworth-Heinemann.

Wagner, Jana (2013): Gebühr kostet mitfahrgelegenheit.de Kunden. Focus Online. Available online at http://www.focus.de/reisen/service/tid-30661/gebuehr-kostet-mitfahrgelegenheit-de-kunden-wo-sie-ohne-provision-mitfahren-koennen_aid_962641.html, checked on 10/12/2015.

Walters, Alan A. (1961): The theory and measurement of private and social cost of highway congestion. In *Econometrica: Journal of the Econometric Society*, pp. 676–699.

Walther, Grit; Wansart, Jörg; Kieckhäfer, Karsten; Schnieder, Eckehard; Spengler, Thomas S. (2010): Impact assessment in the automotive industry. Mandatory market introduction of alternative powertrain technologies. In *Syst. Dyn. Rev.* 26 (3), pp. 239–261. DOI: 10.1002/sdr.453.

Watson, David S.; Piette, Mary Ann; Sezgen, Osman; Motegi, Naoya; Hope, Laurie ten (2004): Machine to machine (M2M) technology in demand responsive commercial buildings. Published in the Proceedings from the ACEEE 2004 Summer Study on Energy Efficiency in Buildings: Breaking out of the Box, August 22-27, 2004, Asilomar, Pacific Grove, CA. Washington D.C.: American Council for an Energy-Efficient Economy. Available online at http://escholarship.org/uc/item/3286r367, checked on 4/25/2016.

Weber, Jutta; Berscheid, Anna-Lena; Müller, Samuel (2014): Self-driving cars and the transformation of public and private transportation. Department of Media Studies, University of Paderborn. Available online at https://www2.hu-berlin.de/dests/?p=1334, checked on 2/6/2016.

Wegener, Michael (1996): Reduction of CO2 emissions of transport by reorganisation of urban activities. In *Transport, land-use and the environnement, Kluwer Academic Publishers, Netherlands*, pp. 103–124.

Weibel, Martin (2015): Parkraumbewirtschaftung. Edited by Bau- und Verkehrsdepartement des Kantons Basel-Stadt. Available online at http://www.mobilitaet.bs.ch/motorfahrzeuge/parkieren-in-basel/parkraumbewirtschaftung.html, updated on 12/14/2015, checked on 12/14/2015.

Weill, Peter; Malone, Thomas W.; D'Urso, Victoria T.; Herman, George; Woerner, Stephanie (2005): Do some business models perform better than others? A study of the 1000 largest US firms. MIT Center for Coordination Science Working Paper No. 226.

Weill, Peter; Vitale, Michael (2013): Place to space: Migrating to eBusiness Models. Boston, Mass.: Harvard Business Press.

Weizsäcker, Ernst Ulrich von; Desha, Cheryl (2010): Faktor Fünf. Die Formel für nachhaltiges Wachstum. München: Droemer.

Wesołowski, Jacek (2008): miasto w ruchu. Przewodnik po dobrych praktykach w organizowaniu transportu miejskiego. Łódź: Instytut Spraw Obywatelskich. Available online at http://www.miastowruchu.pl/doc/miasto_w_ruchu_ebook.pdf, checked on 12/28/2015.

Whitelegg, John; Haq, Gary; Cambridge, H.; Vallack, H. (2010): Towards a zero carbon vision for UK transport. Project Report - 2010. Stockholm Environment Institute. Stockholm.

Wilke, Georg (Ed.) (2005): Die Bedeutung der professionellen Akteure für eine ökologisch orientierte kommunale Verkehrspolitik. Ergebnisse eines ExpertInnen-Workshops am 13./14. März 1997 in

Wuppertal ; Projektbereich C, Regulation / hrsg. vom Forschungsverbund "Ökologisch Verträgliche Mobilität". Projektleitung: Georg Wilke. Wuppertal: Wuppertal-Inst. für Klima, Umwelt, Energie.

Williams, Andrew (2007): Product service systems in the automobile industry: contribution to system innovation? In *Journal of cleaner production* 15 (11), pp. 1093–1103.

Wilson, Matthew W. (2012): Location-based services, conspicuous mobility, and the location-aware future. In *Geoforum* 43 (6), pp. 1266–1275. DOI: 10.1016/j.geoforum.2012.03.014.

Wittig, Rüdiger; Niekisch, Manfred (2014): Biodiversität. Grundlagen, Gefährdung, Schutz. Berlin: Springer Spektrum.

World Commission on Environment and Development (1987): Our common future. Oxford: Oxford University Press.

Yelton, Andromeda (2012): Who are smartphone users? Available online at https://journals.ala.org/ltr/article/view/4653/5507, checked on 9/14/2015.

Zuppo, Colrain M. (2012): Defining ICT in a boundaryless world: The development of a working hierarchy. In *International Journal of Managing Information Technology* 4 (3), p. 13.

Kolibri 360 GmbH
Ferdinand-Jühlke-Straße 7
99095 Erfurt, Deutschland
produktsicherheit@kolibri360.de